S0-AHD-551

Africanizing Anthropology

THE AIMS
OF THE INSTITUTE

TO ANALYSE SCIENTIFICALLY THE
SOCIA LIFE F ODERN MAN
WHITE AND B A K IN C TR L
AF ICA

TO PROVIDE ACCURATE SCIENTIC
INFORMATION ON OCIAL LIFE
OF MEN FOR GOVE NMEN S AND
OT ER PERSO S WORKING WITH
HUM N BEING IN THIS AR A

TO DISSEMINATE TH A C PA E
INFORMATION AS W DEL C .
SI TO THE P LIC

Lyn Schumaker

AFRICANIZING ANTHROPOLOGY

Fieldwork, Networks, and the

Making of Cultural Knowledge

in Central Africa

Duke University Press   Durham & London   2001

© 2001 Duke University Press

All rights reserved

Printed in the United States of America on acid-free paper ∞

Designed by C. H. Westmoreland

Typeset in Sabon by Keystone Typesetting, Inc.

Library of Congress Cataloging-in-Publication
Data appear on the last printed page of this
book.

Frontispiece art: The Rhodes-Livingstone
Institute aims, engraved on a stone placque at
the Lusaka headquarters. The Africans in the
RLI's urban survey team sometimes carried a
copy to explain their work to their
research subjects. (Photo by author.)

To Theresa Valentine Hughes,

Nellie Schumacher, and Edwin Darwin Hughes,

who taught me oral history.

CONTENTS

Acknowledgments   ix

1 "The Water Follows the Stream"   1

2 Contexts and Chronologies   22

3 Archetypal Experiences   39

4 The Laboratory in the Field   75

5 "A Lady and an American"   117

6 Atop the Central African Volcano   152

7 Africanizing Anthropology   190

8 The Culture of Fieldwork   227

Epilogue   260

Notes   263

Bibliography   339

Index   363

ACKNOWLEDGMENTS

This book is based on oral history and archival work conducted in Zambia, Britain, the United States, South Africa, Zimbabwe, Tanzania, the Netherlands, and Malaŵi. This included twenty-two months of fieldwork in Zambia in 1991–92, six months of work in South Africa and Britain in 1993, subsequent visits to Zambia in 1995 and 1996, and follow-up interviews and archival work in Britain from 1995 to 1999. Several foundations provided financial support for this project: Fulbright (IIE), the Social Science Research Council, the National Science Foundation, Mellon, the University of Pennsylvania, Sigma Xi, and the University of Cape Town African Studies Centre. In addition, the Wellcome Trust provided me with travel funds for research into the links between Manchester School anthropology and the origins of medical sociology in Zambia. I am also grateful to the editors of Duke University Press, especially Ken Wissoker and Pam Morrison, for their support and encouragement during the transformation of this work from manuscript to finished text.

I cannot possibly name all of those who deserve thanks for the support and intellectual stimulation that have made this book possible. My greatest debt of gratitude is to the former Rhodes-Livingstone Institute people and their associates, family, and friends, African and European, who contributed interviews, insights, and criticism to the writing of this book. To those in later generations of the Manchester School who have been neglected in this history, my sole excuse is that the Manchester School's far-flung network became too large for me to encompass in one book. I hope to write another based on the interviews I have not yet used and on private papers as yet unavailable to scholars. For the names of people in a few of the photographs, I have relied on the sometimes conflicting memories of informants and my own rather haphazard detective skills. I apologize in advance for any mistakes and welcome corrections.

Thanks are due the staffs of the archives and libraries that contributed to this project: Special Collections at the UCT African Studies Centre; Special Collections at the University of Zambia; Special Collections at the University of the Witwatersrand; the National Archives of Zambia; the National Museum in Livingstone, Zambia; the Public Record Office in Kew Gardens, London; and Rhodes House Library, Oxford. Chris Wright and Hermione Cornwall-Jones at the Royal Anthropological Institute in London provided invaluable help during my study of the Gluckman photographic collection. Alan Macfarlane of the Cambridge University Social Anthropology Department must be thanked for preserving the papers of J. A. Barnes. I also thank the Curator of Ethnography, George Mudenda, at the Moto Moto Museum, Mbala, Zambia, and the museum staff there who facilitated my fieldwork in Northern Province. Moreover, I could not have written the history of the RLI's urban research without the support of the Zambia Consolidated Copper Mines (ZCCM) and the excellent staff at the ZCCM Archives in Ndola, Zambia. Max Mukwakwa, at the ZCCM Head Office in Lusaka, and Joseph Phiri, Group Archivist in Ndola, deserve the highest recognition for their respect for Zambia's history and their efforts to preserve the history of the mines.

I am grateful to the staff of the Institute for African Studies, now the Institute of Social and Economic Research (INESOR). I especially thank its former director, Professor Oliver Saasa, who encouraged my work on the Institute's history and whose father facilitated my research in Western Province. Stephen Mwale, head librarian of the Institute, deserves thanks for his assistance in finding and preserving the Institute's remaining records, as well as for his careful maintenance of its collection of books and reports. The Institute's current intellectual network also sustained me during my fieldwork and subsequent visits—a network that includes Virginia Bond, Mubanga Kashoki, Chileshe Mulenga (now acting director), Neo Simutanyi, Lisa Cliggett, Thayer Scudder, Elizabeth Colson, Karen Hansen,

Brad Strickland, Achim van Oppen, and many other local and ex-patriate researchers. To Ilse Mwanza, the former affiliation officer who still provides the central link that brings us all together, I owe the greatest thanks.

I thank those at the University of Cape Town who facilitated my research in South Africa: Pamela Reynolds, Christopher Saunders, Howard Phillips, Allie Dubb, and Francis Wilson. I also thank Samuel Chipungu, Mwelwa Musambachime, Hugh Macmillan, and other former staff in the University of Zambia History Department who responded to early versions of my work.

In Oxford, Terence Ranger generously encouraged my work and made me welcome in the dynamic group of researchers gathered around him at St. Antony's College. Richard Brown was unstintingly helpful with his knowledge of the RLI and its history, having already set a high standard with his own work. I am grateful to William Beinart, Megan Vaughan, Jonathan Harwood, Roger Cooter, and Tim Ingold, for fostering my research and writing in Britain. I also owe a debt of gratitude for moral and intellectual support to the network of Africanists in Oxford, and most especially to Marieke Faber Clarke, JoAnn McGregor, Mark Leopold, Jocelyn Alexander, David Maxwell, Diana Jeater, Fiona Armitage, and Helen Tilley. I have benefited from the advice of numerous researchers in the history of anthropology and sociology in Africa who have responded to my work over the years, especially Frank Füredi, Robert Gordon, Matthew Engelke, and Peter Pels.

I am especially grateful to Charles Rosenberg, Lee Cassanelli, and Sandra Barnes for their help during my doctoral studies at the University of Pennsylvania. And my approach to anthropology as a field science owes its origins to Henrika Kuklick and Robert Kohler, whose 1988 "Science in the Field" seminar at Penn's History and Sociology of Science department stimulated many path-breaking dissertations. I want to thank my fellow students there, especially Jennifer Gunn, Marta Hansen, and Maneesha Lal.

I owe a great debt to Steven Feierman for his many insightful comments on the dissertation and book manuscript, as well as for his support in moving the book toward publication.

Finally, I thank Henrika Kuklick, not only for her intelligent supervision of my doctoral dissertation and support during its transformation into a book, but also for food, shelter, and inspiration (and the attentions of a certain cat) during periods of recuperation from fieldwork and job hunting.

1

"The Water Follows the Stream"

Historical Ethnography, History of Anthropology,

and Indigenous Anthropologists

Matshakaza Blackson Lukhero grew up in Feni, the Ngoni paramount chief's village in eastern Northern Rhodesia (now Zambia). While still a child in 1935, he saw the British anthropologist Margaret Read, while she was doing a short period of fieldwork in Northern Rhodesia to supplement her main work on the Ngoni of Nyasaland (now Malaŵi). She wore leather riding breeches, he recalled, and, because she did not speak the local language and stayed such a short time in Feni, she was "not close to the people." Read was his first anthropologist.[1]

Recruited for war service in 1941 when only fifteen, Lukhero served in Kenya in the Seventh Northern Rhodesia Field Ambulance Corps, trained in first aid by Desmond Clark, archeologist and first curator of the Rhodes-Livingstone Museum. Clark couldn't pronounce "Matshakaza" and so he nicknamed the young African "Matchbox," a name that didn't survive Lukhero's war service. Back in Feni in 1946, Lukhero became an interpreter for a newly arrived anthropologist, Max Marwick, a Colonial Social Science Research (CSSRC) fellow attached to the Rhodes-Livingstone Institute (RLI). Marwick soon left the Ngoni to do fieldwork on the Cheŵa people. J. A. Barnes, an RLI research officer, then arrived in the Ngoni area and hired Lukhero as interpreter and research assistant for the duration of his fieldwork. With only a few breaks after that, Lukhero continued to work for the RLI and its anthropologists or former anthropologists in rural and urban fieldwork until 1966, a career as research assistant that spanned twenty years and included research in three countries.

From the later 1960s through the 1970s Lukhero worked for the copper mines on aptitude testing in the newly independent Zambia, taking up anthropology again in the 1980s when he became involved with the revival of the Ngoni Nc'wala traditional ceremony and wrote a book on it. When I met him in 1991, he was doing fieldwork for a second book on Ngoni chiefly succession. He answered my questions about the RLI fieldwork in which he had participated, as well as assisting my own interviews with people who had been Barnes's informants and attempting to train me in what he called "the RLI way" of fieldwork. It was during my second interview with him that I asked about the names local people gave to anthropologists and their assistants. According to Lukhero, people usually referred to Barnes as "one who learned (or studied) people's traditions." Lukhero himself they gave the nickname "Manzi okhonkha mkolo — the water follows the stream." "I am following Barnes's footsteps," he explained.[2]

Lukhero did not say what he thought of this nickname. It suggests a dependency and loyalty — of African assistant to white anthropologist — that we are not comfortable acknowledging today. At the same time it describes, as well as contradicts, Lukhero's account of his work for Barnes and later research for his own books. In his description, "following" amounted to his leading Barnes to the people, introducing him, interpreting for him, teaching him the language, discussing local traditions, and afterward talking to people about their reactions to the anthropologist and assuring them Barnes was not a spy.

On the other hand, Lukhero also sometimes followed Barnes as they worked in the field together, learning (and helping to develop) "the RLI way" of doing research. Later, he continued asking questions and collecting material for the anthropologist after Barnes had left the field. And in subsequent years Lukhero followed the RLI way after his own fashion, using its style of titling for one of his books, claiming professional anthropological skills as a way of legitimating his part in the revival of the Nc'wala ceremony, and, especially, using the word "fieldwork" for his activities, something indigenous anthropologists do not generally do.

M. B. Lukhero with
John and Frances
Barnes's child, Rory,
during fieldwork in
the Ngoni area in
Eastern Province in
1946. (Reproduced
by permission of
John and Frances
Barnes.)

In the following chapters I treat Lukhero's nickname as suggestive in ways that its original speakers may not have intended, working with its different possibilities as a kind of thought experiment: how does the water follow the stream, or the research assistant the anthropologist? Indeed, *does* the water follow the stream—isn't it the water that makes the stream, or the assistant who shapes the anthropologist's knowledge? And how much does Africa itself—the land that the water flows through—determine the course of the stream, the anthropology that results? Here is a research agenda for telling the history of the RLI as a story of the coproduction of cultural knowledge. In other words, how did Africans and the African context shape the work of anthropologists there?

From History of Anthropology to Historical Ethnography

The Rhodes-Livingstone Institute, founded in 1937 in Northern Rhodesia, was the first social science research institute in Africa. Until that country gained its independence as Zambia in 1964, the RLI carried out a coordinated research program involving several teams of anthropologists and their African assistants. The Institute also coordinated research in Nyasaland and Southern Rhodesia — the other two countries of what was to become, between 1953 and 1963, the British Central African Federation. From 1949 when its second director, Max Gluckman, became chair of the University of Manchester's new department of sociology and social anthropology, the RLI acted as the locus of fieldwork for an evolving school of anthropology, later known as the Manchester School. The Manchester School became a major force in British social anthropology in the 1950s and 1960s and exerted a strong influence outside the British scene, as well.[3]

This book is not a history of anthropology in the usual sense. Such a history of the Manchester School would focus on its place in the story of British functionalism, as in Kuper's *Anthropology and Anthropologists* (1983), or on its innovations in theory and method, as in Werbner's article, "The Manchester School in South-Central Africa" (1984). This book does not focus on the intellectual genealogy of theories or the intellectual connections of famous anthropologists that such a history would entail. Instead, this history focuses on the cultural and social factors in the particular historical situation of the Manchester School that were as important as the intellectual factors. It attempts to discover people, ideas, and practices that, though important at the time, have left no recognized disciplinary descendants.[4] And it reveals the influences on anthropology that came from nonscientific activities that shared a location with it, whether in the fieldwork site, at the institute headquarters, or in the daily domestic life of the anthropologists in Northern Rhodesia. Thus, this history explores in detail the often acknowledged but rarely analyzed role played by colonial settler culture and mission and administrative practices in shaping the work of anthropologists.[5]

This book places anthropology and anthropologists in multiple contexts—social, cultural, political, historical, and material—and discusses the forces that have mutually shaped both anthropology and the world around it. Social histories of this kind can provide a richer understanding of the processes involved in *doing* anthropology, useful to anthropologists as well as historians.[6] The social context dealt with in this kind of history can be construed very broadly, as in Stocking's *Victorian Anthropology* (1987) and Kuklick's *The Savage Within* (1991), or more narrowly and with greater focus on the discipline's more immediate academic context and social and intellectual networks, as in Stocking's *After Tylor* (1995) and Vincent's *Anthropology and Politics* (1990).[7] Here I deal with the multiple contexts of anthropology, but center these on Africa, where the fieldwork of the Manchester School began.

The field often appears as an important context in social histories of anthropology. Rarely, however, have scholars taken the fieldsite as the *central* context for a social history of anthropology, as this book will do. Such an approach requires a different type of chronology of events relevant to the evolution of the Manchester School as an anthropological research school and, indeed, requires an altogether different construction of its identity. Use of the name "Manchester School" focuses attention on the British metropolitan character of a group of anthropologists famous for specific advances in theory and method.

Instead, this study takes the RLI as its focus—a very different and more Africa-centered phenomenon. Although it has resonances of institutional and colonial history, the name "Rhodes-Livingstone Institute" captures many of the *local* social and cultural factors and the nonanthropological personnel and perspectives that would be neglected in a metropolitan-centered history. The comments of Zambians on this name today reveal a rich local history quite different from the Manchester School's better-known metropolitan and disciplinary history. The name resulted from early fund-raising activities aimed at local white benefactors interested in the upcoming Rhodes Jubilee and Livingstone Centenary in 1940.[8] Although the fundraisers did not consult African opinion, Africans may have seen the name as neutral, balancing the imperialist reputation of

Rhodes with the more positive reputation Livingstone enjoyed at the time.[9]

To tell the history of anthropology with the field as the central context, I have used approaches from the history and sociology of science and technology.[10] First, I have examined anthropology from the perspective of the history of the field sciences — those sciences that use fieldwork instead of, or in addition to, laboratory work.[11] This approach draws attention to the field itself; to the material side of fieldwork; and to the infrastructure, equipment, and work organization necessary to conduct scientific work in a particular fieldsite. It also allows one to relate scientific activities to nonscientific activities occurring in the same fieldsite, such as the sharing of practices between colonial administrators and anthropologists, one of the subjects to be considered in this study. Ideally a field science perspective allows one to examine the relationship between the material culture and technology of a science and the view of the field that informs its daily practice and that makes the field what it is for a particular science. What this perspective brings to the history of a colonial science in Africa such as anthropology is the ability to ground that science in its African context and thus to understand what is African about anthropology in Africa.

The history of colonial science in Africa has often suffered from too sharp a dichotomy between what is seen as the external metropolitan and the local indigenous, with science being viewed as a European import more or less successfully transferred into a hostile environment. Looked at from the perspective of the field sciences, however, colonial science in some respects looks more like science in other, noncolonial, contexts — adapting to its environment, as well as changing it, surviving through local connections as much as through external impetus. This study shows how this process occurred in the case of anthropology — a science in which fieldwork plays a central role in both practice and disciplinary ethos. A field science perspective on anthropology will show that it is not simply a product of Western thought brought to bear upon African societies but is itself a product of Africa. The anthropology of the RLI was in many respects an anthropology that had become Africanized —

through the influence of research assistants, African informants, white settlers, administrators, missionaries, and others who played a role in shaping its fieldwork, and through its adaptation to the landscape of Africa itself and to the material constraints and opportunities it found there.[12]

Despite the fact that RLI anthropology developed in a colonial setting, I will not treat it simply as an example of colonial anthropology. As terrible in its consequences as colonialism was, colonial actors never exercised complete domination and colonial subjects never behaved solely as passive victims. Analyses of anthropology as a "handmaiden of colonialism" often portray colonialism as a hegemonic system, more or less uniform in its discourse, motives, and practice. In these accounts, anthropologists are implicated by their position in the system, and little scope is given for their own agency or the agency of the people they study.

Recently, however, a number of scholars have begun to look in detail at particular anthropologists in particular colonial situations or at anthropology's changing relationship with colonialism over the course of its history.[13] These studies have captured the changing character of colonialism across time and place and point to the need to look at particular contexts in order to understand how anthropologists and the people they studied negotiated issues of power and understandings of racial and cultural difference.

Colonialism is a historically situated and diverse process, as well as a global phenomenon, and looking at anthropologists' relationships with particular colonial projects rather than evoking the dominant influence of a hegemonic and homogeneous colonialism promises a more productive approach to the history of anthropology in colonial settings. The "anthropology of colonialism" can also take this approach, providing a kind of historicized reflexivity or "anthropology of anthropology" in its analysis of both anthropology's origins in colonial contexts and its continuing struggles to critique and reinvent itself as a discipline.[14]

Second, in writing this history I have focused more on the practices of anthropologists than on the theories of anthropology. As a result, RLI anthropology can be seen not only as a science but as a practical activity engaged in by various kinds of people in various kinds of location. Moreover, the practices of anthropological fieldwork can become a window on the politics and society of the time, as well as a means of tracing the impact of social and political forces on anthropology. "Practices" here will be defined as the practical daily activities of scientists pursuing their work and will include the more or less routinized ways of dealing with the basic problems of fieldwork, such as getting into the field, living there, and doing the research. I draw no sharp distinction between practices and methods, for I see methodology as growing out of practices, even very mundane ones like choosing a tent site or hiring a cook. When practices become standardized and mythologized, scientists call them methods, but this should not obscure the fact that a variety of often contingent daily activities is what gets the work done and shapes the theory, as well. Nonetheless, the distinctions that some anthropologists draw between practices and methods will not be ignored but will be considered in the light of what they say about the disciplinary concerns and professional politics of anthropology at the time.[15]

An approach that focuses on the practices of science also avoids the problems inherent in one of the dominant approaches to the history of anthropology: the analysis of anthropological texts using the methods of literary criticism, part of the larger enterprise of colonial discourse theory. My desire to avoid a narrow focus on Western anthropologists' discourses, metanarratives, and other textual phenomena does not derive from a naive positivist position. I am motivated by a need to find ways to check and criticize the products of a textual approach and to escape the dominance of a Eurocentric textual metaphor for making sense of culture.

This is not to say that practices are in some way closer to reality, that practices do not have text-like features, or that a focus on practices frees one from the need for interpretation. I am, however, using practices comparatively with textual evidence as a means of getting at the variety of ways that people relate to the physical and social world and the senses in which practices involve technical skills that cannot be subsumed in language. Practices can also be treated as constituted by discourses. In doing this, however, colonial discourse theory captures only a more limited aspect of experience and—especially in its recent application to non-Western peoples and their histories—takes on a totalizing character, neglectful of agency and intention. The effect produced is such that "the subjects and objects of colonial discourse theory seem sometimes to be captured in a closely-woven web of the language of theory. It makes little difference that this theoretical language is one of indeterminancy, contingency, fragmentation."[16]

For a science like anthropology, the rhetoric found in its classic monographs was but one of a number of strategies for disciplinary definition and survival, and one that is particularly amenable to discourse analysis. But an approach that focuses on practices and material conditions, as well as discourses and representations, can evaluate the usefulness of different strategies in a particular historical context and trace their origins and subsequent influence on other activities. For the history of anthropology, a focus on practices can lead to a re-evaluation of the meaning of fieldwork for the discipline and the relevance of that activity for other field-based endeavors, such as development work in Africa. It can also address the neglect of the experiential side of anthropology that has, as yet, found little place in published monographs.[17] This aspect of anthropology can also be explored through an examination of other texts besides the classic monographs, texts that grow out of the daily experiences of anthropologists and assistants, such as their correspondence, informal newsletters, collections of field photographs, field reports, and fieldnotes, all of which are analyzed in this study.

Third, I have used an analytical concept adapted from the history and sociology of technology—the idea of a "work culture." For the purposes of this book, work culture comprises the sum of the technologies, work organization, work processes, uses of space and material artifacts, and ways of representing and thinking about these that are unique to a particular small group or institution.[18] In the case of the RLI, a unique work culture developed out of anthropologists' and assistants' shared experiences of fieldwork and then further evolved into an institutional culture that characterized the RLI headquarters (located in Lusaka after 1951), where many of the

researchers and assistants lived, spent breaks from the field, or attended conferences during the course of their research. The political
and social background of these researchers, the technologies available to them in postwar Central Africa, the work relationships and
methods of communication developed by them, and the RLI ethos of
rural and *urban* fieldwork constitute the chief elements of a work
culture unusual in the history of anthropology.

This book will also contribute to recent work that joins anthropology and history together for studies of Africa.[19] It is a serious attempt
to do a historical ethnography of anthropology itself — to evoke the
nature of life in the field and the processes of fieldwork, and to gain
an understanding of the relations and rituals of a diverse group of
people drawn together for the production of cultural knowledge. I
have pursued this goal through a number of field strategies and
archival and secondary sources. I did fieldwork in many of the RLI
anthropologists' research sites, where I sought out people who had
acted as informants, domestic employees, interpreters, and assistants
and interviewed them about their perceptions of anthropology. I also
observed over time their reactions to my own fieldwork and any
comparisons they made between what I was doing and what RLI
anthropologists had done. This included observations, in a number
of communities, of how local people managed and shaped my own
experience of the field and used my presence for local purposes.
In addition, many of the former RLI assistants provided me with
lengthy accounts of their work for the RLI and their subsequent
careers. During the two years that I lived in Zambia I followed two
of the former assistants in their rural and urban cultural activities,
becoming a participant-observer in the promotion of a traditional
ceremony and the planning for an ethnic museum, in the case of one,
and the fieldwork for a book on local social organization, in the case
of the other.

This study also is based on interviews with the researchers and
extensive work with archival sources, including researchers' personal papers, RLI personnel files, research assistants' field reports,
British and Zambian government records, the records of the mining
companies, and collections of the anthropologists' field photographs

and home movies. In the process of looking at this material, as well as at research assistants' and informants' accounts, I have discovered many RLI and Manchester School "legends" and field anecdotes, and have compared and analyzed these for what they say not only about the RLI's history, but also the numerous interpretations by participants of the meaning of that history and its place in their construction of their identity. Finally, in writing up this material, I have blended anthropological and historical secondary sources, including the Manchester School monographs, trying to situate the latter in their historical context and relate them to the anthropologists' own accounts of their fieldwork and theoretical insights. Because of the great number of monographs produced by the RLI researchers, I have only made a start in this endeavor, but I hope that I have provided the basis for future work. Although this book cannot be considered a thorough restudy[20] of the classic topics of the Manchester School, I hope that it will cast some light on the making of this corpus of anthropological knowledge and provide a history of fieldwork that anthropologists and historians will find useful.[21]

Indigenous Anthropologists, or Why All the Fuss about Muchona?

One of the problems involved in writing a history of anthropology that deals with a group of anthropologists, their research assistants, and informants is to find concepts appropriate for analyzing a diverse group of people with often very different notions of what they are doing. The literature on anthropology, as well as on other activities in a colonial setting, provides a number of possibilities. Scholars have conceptualized assistants and informants as colonized by anthropologists or, alternatively, as indigenous anthropologists themselves. Or they have put them in categories that include anthropologists as so-called marginal men or culture brokers. All these choices have drawbacks.

In "Anthropology's Hidden Colonialism," Roger Sanjek discusses the ways that anthropologists and their texts have made the work of research assistants invisible (though he sees the RLI anthropologists as something of an exception to the rule).[22] This approach has much to recommend it; research assistants generally *are* invisible in the finished texts of anthropologists both today and in the past and, like wives, often receive only a token measure of gratitude in the preface. A field-centered history of anthropology can make research assistants' work visible again. Nevertheless, seeing research assistants solely as an exploited group of local actors misses two other important aspects of their position. Research assistants differ as individuals, and, for some, their work as assistants is more like that of the discipline's own students in the metropolitan universities, subject to an internal colonialism that they tolerate in order to rise in the profession. Some of the RLI's educated, urban assistants viewed their careers this way, though it is essential to explore what effect the colonial color bar, differential access to education, and the coming of Zambian independence had on their aspirations.

A simple model of exploitation is especially inappropriate for the Munali Secondary School students in Lusaka who, in the late 1950s and early 1960s, worked for the RLI during their school vacations. Some saw this work as a step in a possible future career, while others did the work simply because it was an interesting way to earn money during breaks from school. Nevertheless, even for rural assistants and less well-educated members of the the urban survey teams, the model of exploitation fails to capture the assistants' own motives and goals in taking on anthropological work.

A more significant problem with this approach, however, is that a focus on the anthropologists' exploitation of assistants may cause one to play down assistants' agency in fieldwork and exploitation of anthropologists for *their* own ends. Some scholars have attempted to capture this aspect of the situation by stressing the potential equality between anthropologist and assistant in field and text. Some, like James Clifford, have pointed out that assistants and informants can be "indigenous ethnographers" with their own independent interest in cultural matters already existing or stimulated by the anthropologist's presence.[23] Others have focused on the "decentering" of anthropology's texts when the anthropologist portrays assistants or informants in the text as "indigenous anthropologists" with voices of their own. This is the case in Bennetta Jules-Rosette's analysis of Victor Turner's relationship with his informant, Muchona, the subject of his famous essay "Muchona the Hornet."[24]

I do not believe this view of the anthropologist as a conduit for local voices actually solves the problem of the inegalitarian relationship between anthropologist and informant; moreover, the concept of the indigenous anthropologist is inadequate for dealing with the range of people who worked as assistants for the RLI. This is because it privileges the rural assistant or informant like Muchona, supposedly rooted in indigenous society (even if in some ways marginal to the community Turner studied) and in touch with traditional knowledge. Most of the RLI assistants — including Turner's main formally employed assistant, who rarely appears in his texts — were nothing like Muchona, at least as Turner portrays him. Most had a mixed background of urban and rural experience and some had traveled extensively in Africa and elsewhere for education, work, or military service. Most had an intrinsic interest in culture but at the same time saw racial politics as a far more important issue. Many sought employment with the RLI for other reasons than the study of culture, and they used their expertise in culture as a means to other ends.

A concept that captures the use of culture as both intrinsically of interest and as a means to other ends is the concept of "culture broker." This concept also does honor to Turner's sense of a common ground between himself and Muchona, without accepting his notion that he and Muchona shared a kind of professional objectivity, or equality.[25] Culture brokers use their cultural knowledge to broker relationships between different ethnic or racial groups involved in struggles for power and resources. Chiefs, mission-educated Africans, traders, missionaries, and anthropologists have all acted as culture brokers at various times[26] and institutions can perform a similar role, as well.[27] Both RLI researchers and assistants acted as culture brokers, with the assistants most frequently acting as brokers between the anthropologists and the people they studied.

In addition, the RLI itself acted as an institutional culture broker in its role as an interpreter of cultural and social knowledge, situated between Africans and government administrators in the often difficult terrain of colonial development policy. Through its association with the Rhodes-Livingstone Museum, the RLI also played a role in the collection and display of African material culture to both white and black publics at a time when culture often provided the ammunition for political debate. Individual anthropologists and research assistants also acted as culture brokers, claiming a special professional expertise in debates about African political and social development. This book focuses on the process of the professionalization of this kind of brokerage, placing both the researchers and their African assistants in a wider context of technical experts in Africa at a time when many sciences — anthropology among them — sought to play a role in postwar colonial development planning. Former RLI assistants have continued to act as culture brokers in the postcolonial period, writing tribal histories and reviving or "inventing" traditional ceremonies in an atmosphere of ethnic rivalry for development resources and recognition from the state.[28]

Even this concept, however, must be used with caution, because it focuses too much attention on culture as the key difference to be negotiated by anthropologists and assistants. The racial politics of central Africa also played an important role in the daily activities of anthropologists and assistants in the field and informed the thinking and writing of many of them. Assistants facilitated the research, particularly in urban areas, by negotiating the color bar that separated whites from blacks in most work and social situations — a negotiation that dealt directly with historically situated ideas of racial difference rather than cultural difference.

Similarly, like "indigenous anthropologist," the term "culture broker" suggests a central identification with a local culture, and this may not always be appropriate. Use of the term "intellectuals" can get around these problems, because it allows for different degrees and types of attachment to the local on the part of both assistants and anthropologists. "Intellectuals," in its broadest sense, refers to people who take an active and conscious role in shaping and elucidating various kinds of knowledge, whether or not their audiences recognize them as professionals. Used in the context of fieldwork, it allows for study of a spectrum of people employed by, and otherwise assisting, anthropologists in their work, rather than implying a simplistic distinction between informant and assistant. Like Muchona, informants, friends, or others who volunteer their views in the field can be as influential as paid assistants.

Neither does this concept exclude apprenticeship in a profession as part of the research assistants' perspective on their work. Moreover, it is a term that can be applied equally to the anthropologists themselves.[29] The term is not unproblematic, however. Not all those who volunteer their views in the field can be classified as intellectuals, but their views can nevertheless substantially inform the researcher's work.

Anthropologizing Africa and Africanizing Anthropology

"The problem with doing statistical surveys in African towns is that Africans aren't used to sociological methods," remarked an anthropology student in the middle of fieldwork in one of the urban centers previously studied by the RLI. "They don't know how to respond like Americans do, when an interviewer comes round asking questions."

When I heard this comment in 1991 — when I was beginning my own fieldwork on the RLI — I felt something was not quite right in this assumption that Africans are naive about sociological methods — especially in Zambia, with a history that included the RLI in the colonial period, as well as extensive development research and intervention in the postcolonial period. This comment stimulated me to consider how extensive the African experience with anthropology — or research of any kind — *was* and where this experience fit in the larger context of Africans' understanding and use of cultural knowledge in central Africa.

To explore this issue, this study examines two processes in the history of anthropology in the region. The first I call "anthropologization." Anthropologists at RLI spoke of African societies as having been "anthropologized" when these societies had been studied by a researcher and put on the ethnographic map. Anthropologizing, however, was not merely a process of gathering data and making it known in Western academic circles. Africans observed the researchers' interest in African society and culture, compared it with the sometimes similar interests of missionaries and administrators, controlled the research to a considerable extent, and used the resulting data or the process of fieldwork itself for their own purposes — in conflicts with the colonial government over administration or development, as well as in rivalries with other African groups. Thus, anthropologists' activities became part of a larger process of increasing awareness by Africans and Europeans of cultural differences in southern Africa and the propensity to emphasize and use these differences in political debates. Africans still find anthropologists — and historians — useful in this process, as evidenced by the role researchers have played in ethnic politics in recent Zambian history.

Anthropologization was more than that, however. The work of the RLI covered all the major ethnic groups and multiethnic urban areas of Zambia and many in Malaŵi and Zimbabwe, as well. The RLI was a presence in Northern Rhodesia from 1937 to 1964, known to most educated Africans and familiar even to the uneducated in the ethnic areas and towns where the researchers had done fieldwork, sometimes repeatedly, for over two decades. During this time, Africans in these areas developed their own understanding of what anthropology was and their own ways of accommodating or resisting research. These historical experiences have had a lasting effect on Zambians' attitudes toward research and researchers, even into the postcolonial period.

The second process I examine is "Africanization." This concept is adapted from what Patrick Chabal calls "political Africanisation": "[T]he process by which colonial politics was re-appropriated by Africans (rulers and ruled) in the context of a (historically) modern world of nation-states . . . the process by which post-colonial Africans 'digested' the political legacy left by their European conquerors."[30] An important difference between anthropology and politics in this process is that the replacement of whites by local

Africans has not taken place in professional anthropology, which is still carried on primarily by expatriates. In spite of this, some of the RLI assistants have developed an anthropological activity that modifies the ideas and practices of professional anthropology for use in local African contexts. What these assistants have reappropriated, digested, and transformed are fieldwork practices, as well as ways of talking and writing about culture and society.

As with political Africanization, the transformation has occurred mainly after independence, but it is based on precedents in their work for the RLI in the late colonial period when they actively took part in the coproduction of cultural knowledge. This book examines the fieldwork activities, the writing of local history, and the cultural promotion of ethnic museums and traditional ceremonies that these former assistants have accomplished since leaving the RLI. It also makes a beginning toward placing them in the context of the larger political arena of Zambia today, including the current process of democratization and the renewed debate about tribalism, nationalism, and indigenous identity that has accompanied it. It particularly engages with questions of the production of locality and anthropology's role in this process in the colonial and postcolonial periods.[31]

Anthropology became Africanized in the course of fieldwork and the interactions that make up the processes of fieldwork. Thus, the title of this book, *Africanizing Anthropology: Fieldwork, Networks, and the Making of Cultural Knowledge in Central Africa*, is intended to emphasize the understanding of the process of Africanization that can come from a study of fieldwork. It is a study of the anthropologists' and assistants' own overlapping social and cultural fields, a unit of analysis with no sharp geographical or chronological boundaries and with links extending into a number of larger contexts.

The title emphasizes Africanization over anthropologization. This emphasis is a product of the methods of the history of the field sciences; if one looked solely at texts one would be more likely to see the anthropologization of Africa, that is, the anthropologists' work of transforming descriptions of daily life into theories about human culture and social organization. The history of fieldwork, however, tells a different story, with emphasis on Africanization — the shaping of anthropology's methods and theories by Africa, by Africans, and by others living and working in Africa. Returning from looking at fieldwork to looking at texts, we can read the texts in a new way and see how much the RLI theories and methods owe to the anthropologists' fieldwork and social networks in the field, balancing that with what the anthropologists brought to the field with them from their background and training.

Thus, for example, Lukhero's image of Margaret Read and her riding breeches could tell a story about anthropology and Africa that is as significant for the shaping of theory as any of the formal methods this anthropologist used or the theories she learned in her training. With sufficient contextualization, one could answer several fascinating questions about her understanding of gender, nature, class, and culture in Africa during her fieldwork, using clues from this image. Africa as frontier, fieldwork as sport—did Read have such expectations of Africa? Similarly, how does her choice of dress reflect her class background or her need to project a certain image as a woman in the field? Indeed, are anthropology's practices gendered? Of interest also is the larger story of Read's negotiations with the local community of white settlers, with the hierarchy of colonial administrators, and with the Ngoni royalty and villagers, implied in Lukhero's image of the anthropologist in the field.

In the following chapters I use images such as these to build a picture of the RLI anthropologists and assistants to show how cultural and social factors shaped their theories. Chapter 2, "Contexts and Chronologies," outlines briefly the numerous contexts in which the RLI can be placed, focusing particularly on the southern African context and the influence of South Africa's intellectual, political, social, and economic presence on the Institute's development. This will include the idea of the "field generation" as a way of conceptualizing stages in the development of the RLI's work culture. The RLI's character at each point reflected a particular grouping at the headquarters and extending into the field, reflecting the social network the researchers could establish with the help (or constraint) of administrators, settlers, and assistants.

Chapter 3, "Archetypal Experiences," examines the early field experiences and directorships of Godfrey Wilson and Max Gluckman, showing how the colonial administration, white settlers, and mining companies placed limits on the political range of their research, how the anthropologists circumvented some of these limits, and how the strategies they used affected their perspective on African societies. Here I focus on the politics of identity revealed in the clothing, talk, and technologies of the researchers — strategies that were effective in defining and making a place for anthropology in the field.

Out of these experiences, the second director, Max Gluckman developed a research plan for the RLI that was put in motion after the Second World War. He drew on ideas from the development planning movement and from the South African political situation to explore the social field of Northern Rhodesia and Central Africa as if it were an ethnic and racial laboratory — the subject of chapter 4, "The Laboratory in the Field." He trained a team of talented young anthropologists to carry out the plan, using technologies for fieldwork newly available in the postwar environment to evolve a coordinated, comparative style of research that had the potential to challenge the dominant functionalist categories that supposedly shaped the anthropology of the time.

The fifth chapter, "A Lady and an American," discusses the directorship of Elizabeth Colson, 1947–1950. The experiences of Colson, and of other women associated with the RLI as wives, mothers, doctors, assistants, and fieldworkers in their own right, is discussed in relation to current ideas about the effect of gender on method and the experiences of women anthropologists. This discussion engages with recent work on husbands and wives in the field, on masculinities, on gender and colonialism, and on the social and cultural construction of biological sex and gendered bodies.[32]

Also during this time the RLI's intellectual network extended to Manchester where Gluckman had taken up the first chair in social anthropology. The chapter examines this link and places it in the context of the RLI's earlier links with the universities of Cape Town, Witwatersrand (Wits), and Oxford. The decision to move the Institute's headquarters from Livingstone to Lusaka, moreover, signaled an important confirmation of the RLI's institutional focus,

moving from the cultural capital of the country to its political capital, where the RLI positioned itself for its future political and social
studies of the nearby Copperbelt. Meanwhile RLI institutional culture benefited from the proximity of the first African secondary
school in Northern Rhodesia, Munali Secondary, where many postindependence leaders got their education in the 1950s.

Chapter 6, "Atop the Central African Volcano," deals with the
pathbreaking research program in urban anthropology begun by the
RLI in 1950. The adaptation of rural practices for urban quantitative and qualitative research took place during this period, along
with technological innovation in the use of early computers for
statistical analysis. Chapter 7, "Africanizing Anthropology," discusses the transition from rural to urban research from the perspective of the RLI research assistants, examining both their rural and
urban practices, experiences, and conceptualization of anthropological research. These chapters engage with recent debates about the
nature of Copperbelt ethnography and historiography, showing in
what ways the ethnography reflected African research assistants'
perspectives and concerns.[33]

Both of these chapters analyze the politicization of fieldwork and
African informants' views of urban and rural research during a period of escalating political struggle. Another theme is the shaping of
theory by the urban research assistants' political and social activities,
as well as by their and the anthropologists' experiences of daily life in
the Copperbelt towns at a time when the nature of the African city
itself was being defined by competing groups. Assistants enabled the
urban survey to go on despite the difficulties of the political situation, doing work in areas anthropologists sometimes could not enter
either because of the European-imposed color bar or because of
African hostility to Europeans gathering information. The assistants
themselves experienced some difficulty in carrying out the survey but
succeeded when they represented their work to urban Africans as
part of the production of an urban African history. This strategy
worked because it helped urban Africans to define and control their
urban experience at a time when Africans' permanent settlement in
colonial towns was still contested.

With the imposition of the Central African Federation on Northern Rhodesia's dissenting African majority in 1953 and the Colonial Office's support for the founding of other social science research institutes in Africa, important changes in the Institute's status began to shape its research. The final chapter, "The Culture of Fieldwork," considers the historical impact of the RLI, its subsequent history, and the conclusions that can be drawn from its history about the nature of fieldwork in anthropology. This chapter follows the legacy of the RLI, beginning with the fourth director J. Clyde Mitchell's move to the Federation's first university in Southern Rhodesia in 1956. The diaspora of researchers and research assistants that began in 1956 with these changes is described, as RLI people, practices, and ideas moved into academic, government, and development contexts, both in central Africa and elsewhere. Meanwhile, from 1960 to 1970 the experience of political decolonization, rapid economic development, and escalating liberation struggles in Central Africa led to a complete change of identity and purpose for the RLI at its headquarters in Lusaka.

2

Contexts and Chronologies

This chapter treats the appropriate contexts and periodization of RLI history as a question, rather than as an obvious aspect of its story. First, three larger political, cultural, and economic contexts are considered—the British, the American, and the southern African. Reasons will be given for placing greatest emphasis on the southern African context, while not neglecting the importance of the other two. In addition to broad political and scientific movements and economic conditions, this chapter considers cultural events in these three contexts because of their effect on the RLI's work as a producer of cultural knowledge. Similarly, the chapter develops, rather than takes for granted, a chronology for RLI history in terms of the timing of important influences—the dates that emerge from stories told by the actors themselves and from archival records of their reactions at the time to important events.

At the end of this chapter, I discuss useful ways to think about the chronology of changes in practice at the RLI, taking a "generational" rather than genealogical approach to understanding the cohorts of researchers who moved through Central Africa in the course of its history. During the most productive ten years of the RLI's history, its anthropologists and assistants developed methods and theories largely through their activity in teams that received field training together, supervised by directors or, in the case of the research assistants, senior assistants who had been members of earlier teams. Partly because of this unusual pattern of training and teamwork, the RLI became the center of a research school whose members based their cohesiveness on fieldwork experiences as much as on their later academic experiences at Manchester or their intellectual lineage before coming to the RLI. Thus, I refer to these successive teams as "field generations," to distinguish what they had in common through their association within a shared field from what they and others had in common through their intellectual lineage or academic experience.

The British Context

A story of the RLI told from the perspective of British social anthropology from the 1930s to the 1960s would be the story of those RLI anthropologists who figured prominently in the history of functionalist anthropology.[1] This would be a story of disciplinary rivalries among groups of anthropologists based at British universities, focusing on the territorial aspects of the process of their development of fieldwork areas, methods, and theories, and the fostering of careers of academic disciples. Within the larger context of twentieth-century British history, the story would describe the movement of professional anthropologists into the African field for the first time, just before and after the Second World War, to do research stimulated by the changing nature of the British Empire. Few untouched societies remained to be studied in Britain's colonial territories, and anthropology had to justify its growth as a profession by demonstrating the need for research in areas where European penetration and resulting social change were far advanced, as they had become in some of Britain's African colonies. Moreover, new funding became available for African research beginning after World War One, because of the need to obtain knowledge useful for the governing of other territories more recently acquired, such as the former German colonies like Tanganyika, where British knowledge of traditional African political organization was scant.[2]

Colonial social research also received support from the so-called development science movement that emerged after World War One and gained in strength with World War Two. The development science movement was part of the planning movement that had arisen during the drive for national efficiency following World War One.

Indeed, part of the inspiraton for the early functionalists' approach to research derived from the increased emphasis on government planning and economic regulation after the First World War. These movements received further impetus from the highly planned and researched war effort on the home front in World War Two and the continuing need to deal with shortages of commodities during the period of reconstruction in Britain after the war, all of which furthered the cause of social research.[3]

The Utility Scheme, which affected building and furnishing styles and the manufacture and distribution of goods in Britain from 1941 to 1951, also focused attention on efficient functioning and the careful rationing of resources in daily life.[4] The vision of society and the planning necessary to carry out the scheme owed much to functionalist ideas in the social sciences. The resulting building and furnishing styles affected colonial architecture in central Africa, which experienced a building boom in the postwar period due to the large numbers of demobilized British servicemen attracted to the colonies, plus government and mining company programs to improve African housing in the towns. Postwar scarcity also fueled a push for development in British Africa, which was intended to become the source of the products and revenues necessary for British reconstruction. Because of the loss of the Asian colonies after the war, British hopes had turned to Africa: "The colonies were an important source of the dollars desperately needed to buy American goods. Because of restrictions on the free exchange of sterling, surpluses that the colonies acquired from the sale of raw materials to the United States were used by Britain to offset its vast trading deficit with the U.S."[5]

British cultural events echoed postwar revival of identity themes (and the need for spectacle, according to Arthur Marwick), as, for example, in the 1951 Festival of Britain and the coronation of Elizabeth II.[6] Worries about national identity resulted equally from political and economic problems — from political crises like the Suez, which challenged Britain's international image, as well as from the loss of international economic power with respect to the United States. Government and opposition campaigns to shape public opinion and bring about social change developed out of models used for war propaganda and the management of civilian morale. These became a part of everyday life, not only in the transfer of McCarthy-style anticommunist rhetoric from the United States but also in more subtle ways—for example, the popular BBC Radio series *The Archers* developed out of a propaganda show aimed at mobilizing rural society for the war effort.

Along with the wartime emphasis on food self-sufficiency, the postwar campaign for more amenities in villages and small towns, and an enormous increase in agricultural subsidies under the Labour government, a "renewed cult of the countryside" emerged after 1945.[7] This had ramifications for African development policy, which strongly emphasized reform of agricultural practices and which in some respects echoed a romantic vision of English village life, transferred to Africa. In chapters 3 and 4 I expand on the ways that RLI researchers who did rural fieldwork often found themselves interacting with technical officers who had come out to Africa to assist in colonial agricultural interventions and who, in a few cases, shared with the anthropologists a deep interest in African practices and understandings of the land.

The political success of the British labor movement after the Second World War, signaled by the Labour Party's election victory in 1945 and the resulting growth of the welfare state, also influenced policy in Africa. For the first time, the Labour Party and left-wing groups in Britain expressed sympathy for the aspirations of Africans instead of seeing the colonies as a burden that should be either dispensed with or more efficiently exploited for the benefit of the metropolitan working class. The increasing importance of sociology, social work, and social research in the postwar period paralleled the growth of social welfare programs in Britain. To a small extent, social welfare programs were extended to the colonies especially where urbanization was taking place—though never implemented as fully as in Britain. Thus, researchers in Africa began to carry out surveys of urban poverty, which had a long history in Britain beginning with Booth's survey of London in the nineteenth century. In the colonies, however, the continuing strength of white settler and business interests usually compromised social welfare programs, for whites as well as for Africans.

The shift in colonial policy toward aggressive development plan-

ning for Africa came as a response both to a similar British development campaign at home spurred by Labour and to international
pressure on the imperial nations to divest themselves of their colonies. The Labour government devised a development and decolonization policy intended to lead to the eventual independence of most
of its colonial possessions in Africa, though not without considerable struggle on the part of colonized peoples, who demanded much
faster change than the colonial authorities envisioned. Colonial Secretary Arthur Creech Jones led this development and decolonization
policy, called by some, "Fabianising the Empire,"[8] because of its im-
plementation of some social welfare ideas. Andrew Cohen, known
as the "King of Africa," acted as undersecretary in charge of African
affairs from 1947 and joined in promoting devolution and development.[9] (He also supported the funding of social science at the RLI at
several crucial turning points, as will be discussed in chapters 4 and
5.) The amount of spending toward development and, especially,
toward social welfare of Africans, was limited by budgetary concerns, and the pace envisioned for devolution shifted with each political shift in the ruling party in Britain.[10]

Overall British postwar policy led to increased paternalism toward
black colonies and disastrous concessions to white settler-dominated
colonies.[11] The amalgamation of smaller territories to create economically more viable "federations" — an empire-wide policy — also
had disastrous political results. At the Victoria Falls Conference in
1949, Creech Jones, Cohen, and others urged the federation of the
Rhodesias and Nyasaland. Underlying motives included stopping
South African expansion northward and preserving good relations
with Southern Rhodesian settlers who controlled the mining of strategic minerals.[12] African leaders unanimously opposed the Federation, and the process of its imposition and eventual dissolution
caused much bitterness in Northern Rhodesia and Nyasaland, as
well as a bloody African independence struggle in Southern Rhodesia. Many of the development programs initiated in the British
African colonies also failed, including the notorious Groundnuts
Scheme in Tanganyika. Creech Jones's political career foundered in
1950, and he became a forgotten figure.[13] The prominent woman

social anthropologist Audrey Richards — who did research in Northern Rhodesia between the wars and became the representative of anthropology on the Colonial Social Science Research Council in 1944 — named a cat after him, probably not for flattering reasons.[14]

The international movement for decolonization, which had put pressure on the British, was exemplified by United Nations' policies. The UN pressured colonial powers to prove the benefits of colonialism to subject peoples and also developed international standards in the area of human rights — the UNESCO statement on race being one of the most influential of these on public and scientific opinion.[15] At the same time a movement for decolonization developed in Britain itself, crystalizing around older groups such as the Aborigines Protection Society that had been associated with the antislavery movement, but gaining momentum with the emergence of new groups such as the Movement for Colonial Freedom founded in 1954.[16] Gluckman and several other RLI anthropologists joined this movement while in Manchester.

The United States and the Soviet Union spearheaded the movement to enforce international standards of human rights, using this movement to further their own rival foreign policy objectives.[17] As the Cold War developed, ideological concerns partly motivated British interventions into the development of African institutions in the colonies, as, for example, in the African trade union movement. American Cold War interests in this area had already been channeled through British unions, by way of delegations from American trade unions that had purged themselves of radical, left-wing members and who urged British trades unions to do the same.[18]

The delegations which the British unions then sent to the African colonies encouraged African labor leaders to model their organizations on America's and Britain's newly depoliticized type of union organization. The RLI researcher A. L. Epstein would study the development of the African miners' union (see chapter 6). Although the British Colonial Office had earlier expressed concerns about the possible influence of communism or fascism on colonized peoples, Cold War McCarthyism in the United States played a powerful, though indirect, part in intensifying security fears in the British African colonies, which would also lead to the suspicion that anthropologists might play a subversive role if they studied African political organization or mentioned politics while doing fieldwork. The impact of this on RLI fieldwork is taken up particularly in chapters 3, 6, and 7. In other areas American involvement was more direct.

The American Context

The history of the RLI could also be told as an American story, both in terms of the discipline of anthropology and in terms of the history of Africa. For Anglo-American anthropologists, finding work to do in the postwar world led to an interest in doing research for development, as well as an interest in urbanizing, industrializing societies with multiracial dimensions. Thus, central and southern Africa held interest for anthropologists whatever their nationality, and particularly for American anthropologists, who themselves lived in a racially divided society. American anthropological theory also had particular relevance for this area. Rural development policy in the late colonial period focused on making changes in African agricultural practices and moving Africans toward types of economic behavior that would further the British goal of increasing colonial production for the world market. Thus, the "cattle complex" theory, developed by American anthropologist Melville Herskovits, may have influenced some anthropologists who advised the colonial government after the war.[19] This theory purported to explain the cultural aspects of African cattle-keeping societies that made it difficult to persuade Africans to produce cattle for the market.

Another more general influence on colonial agricultural development policy derived from the American Dust Bowl experience. Particularly in southern Africa from the 1930s onward, agriculturists and ecologists used this model to make recommendations for changes in African pastoral and farming systems in semiarid regions.[20]

The model for the interest in urban Africa, however, lay not so much in anthropology, with its rural precedents, as in sociology. The

American sociology of the Chicago School provided a model of urban research focused on ethnic and racial differences.[21] Some of the RLI anthropologists drew on the Chicago School studies for their early conceptions of urban anthropology, especially J. Clyde Mitchell, who played a role in developing the RLI's method of network analysis.

American cultural influences also permeated Britain's central African colonies. "Cowboy music" and "cowboy movies" dominated popular entertainment, including the film shows taken to Africans in the countryside and shown in the urban recreational centers provided by the mining companies. American folk music influenced African township bands and helped to inspire the African nationalist protest songs of the 1950s. Latin American styles also reached British central African colonies by way of West Africa and the Belgian Congo, and these included the Cha Cha Cha, a 1950s dance craze that provided an apt metaphor for the African independence movement in Northern Rhodesia and its desire to make the colonial government dance to its nationalist tune, just as a man dancing Cha Cha Cha controls his female partner.[22]

The importance of the race question in the United States led American foundations to fund social research in Africa. In their view, southern Africa's multiracial societies could be used as a human laboratory for testing future policies on black education, race relations, and other areas before putting them into practice at home. The reverse was also true, with American models such as the Tuskegee Institute being used by colonial educationists for developing programs in Africa.

Both the Rockefeller Foundation and the Carnegie Corporation began funding British anthropology between the wars. Although Rockefeller did not fund the RLI studies, its funding channeled through the International African Institute supported many of the students of the prominent functionalist anthropologist Bronislaw Malinowski, who promoted social anthropology in the interwar period at the London School of Economics, where he was professor of anthropology. Some of his students worked in Northern Rhodesia, as in the case of Audrey Richards, or nearby, as in the case of Godfrey and Monica (Hunter) Wilson, who worked together in Tanganyika.[23] Godfrey would later become the first director of the RLI and Monica already had an established career as a South African social anthropologist before the Tanganyika work. These scholars had an impact on the development of the RLI and its research goals, which is discussed at greater length in chapter 3. The Carnegie Commission in South Africa in 1928 was the forerunner of American funding initiatives in Africa, though local white South African scholars in this case managed to divert the foundation's original intention to fund research on black South Africans toward funding a "multidisciplinary social science investigation" of *white* poverty.[24]

In the 1920s the Rockefeller Foundation also began to fund anthropological research in Africa, urged on by the missionary J. H. Oldham, a prominent critic of colonial policy. Oldham used the argument that "a nation with so many of the 'African race' within its own borders could not afford to remain indifferent" to the changes occurring in Africa itself, an argument that apparently worked since Rockefeller began funding the British-based International Institute of African Languages and Cultures a year later.[25] American money provided the main support for anthropology in Africa until the late 1930s.[26] After World War Two, the Fulbright Act also began to finance American scholars' research in British colonies. The Colonial Office listed the RLI as an institution that should benefit from this program, and by the late 1950s American Fulbright researchers began to arrive in small numbers.[27]

In the international context, America pressured the British to decolonize in order to open an African market for U.S. goods, while the start of the Cold War in the late 1940s fueled American interest in Africa's strategic importance, and especially its mineral production. This led to the establishment of African area studies programs in the American universities, which, along with the Fulbright program, added to a growing number of American researchers finding their way into British Africa.

The history of copper mining in Northern Rhodesia, which is discussed in greater detail in chapter 6 as the context for the RLI's urban industrial studies, is also partly an American story. Capital for the early development of the mines in the 1920s came from the American A. Chester Beatty, whose Selection Trust, Ltd., was based in London, as well as from Anglo-American, a South African company.[28] Beatty's Rhodesian Selection Trust, which was heavily backed by the American Metal Company, brought numerous American managers to the Copperbelt and established management policies on the American "company town" model — emphasizing greater stabilization of labor and provision of services to workers than the South African company. Although American and British capital also provided part of the backing for Rhodesian Anglo-American — later Rhokana Corporation Ltd. — the two mining companies always competed for labor in Northern Rhodesia. Rhokana attempted as much as possible to continue its dependence on migrant labor backed by the compound system of housing developed in South Africa. Both companies, however, reduced the cost of labor by sending the old, disabled, and unemployed back to their villages rather than caring for them in town.[29] This pattern of labor management derived from the established model of labor management on the South African Rand. Indeed, the influence of South Africa on developments in Northern Rhodesia and all of southern Africa was a crucial element in the context of the RLI's research.

The African Context

The most neglected context of the history of the RLI and its research is Africa itself. An institutional history, such as Brown's work on the founding and early years of the RLI, captures some of the local African context but more from the perspective of the metropolitan British institutions instrumental to the birth of the Institute.[30] An Africa-centered perspective would start with the movements in southern Africa that provided both a context and a motivation for establishing the RLI there. The RLI's birth resulted from local initiatives long before the Colonial Office began its postwar program of founding African research institutes.[31] Moreover, until the Colonial Development and Welfare Fund began providing support, the Institute was funded primarily from local sources.[32] Indeed, the growth of the RLI out of local needs shaped it in ways that sometimes jeopardized its support from its metropolitan funders. For example, when the newly formed Colonial Social Science Research Council attempted to interpret in the strictest sense its policy that research institutes should be based near colonial universities, the establishment of a university in Northern Rhodesia was not felt to be possible in the foreseeable future. Some members of the Council used this as a reason to argue against funding any expansion of the Institute's program, though they were overridden by others.[33]

The local initiatives that led to the RLI's founding also derived from South Africa and its developing scientific community, particularly the natural science disciplines, because the country's unusual flora and fauna drew worldwide interest, and some branches of the human sciences, especially archeology and physical anthropology. The 1920s brought the "South Africanization" of these sciences, as studies of the Bushmen and archeological discoveries of early humans made this country, and Africa more generally, appear to be the most promising arena for the study of human prehistory. At the time, this had inescapably eugenic overtones, with the leading American physical anthropologist, Ales Hrdlicka, viewing the country as a racial laboratory.[34] Partly because of South Africa's reputation for archeology, the white settler population of Northern Rhodesia and its governor in the 1930s, Hubert Young, felt positively disposed toward archeological investigations being done in *their* country, and this motive figured in the governor's plans for the RLI. Archeology did, indeed, benefit from the founding of the RLI. Its associated museum and the important discoveries of its first curator and later director Desmond Clark led to a thriving tradition of archeological research. For the African population, as well, the prominence of the Museum at Livingstone and its association with cultural performances and sale of curios for tourists visiting Victoria Falls would have long-term effects on their use of cultural resources to argue for greater attention from the colonial and postcolonial states.

The so-called native question, however, would be the single most important feature of the RLI's larger southern African context. This issue spawned movements both to the left and to the right on the political spectrum, and these would influence the Institute's work. The emergence of experts and the establishment of university departments of Bantu studies and social anthropology in South Africa was a direct response to the importance there of the native question in the 1920s and 1930s.[35]

The increasingly segregationist thrust of South African politics in the postwar years, and the liberal and radical dissent from it, continued to keep this issue on the agenda.[36] South African social scientists figured prominently in liberal and radical dissent and formed the primary political network supporting the RLI's particular research program as it was delineated by South African or South African-connected directors such as Godfrey Wilson (who was married to the South African anthropologist Monica Hunter), Max Gluckman, and J. Clyde Mitchell. Max Gluckman, the second director, ensured that the influence of the South African anthropologist Isaac Schapera and the historian W. M. Macmillan contributed to the shaping of RLI theory. (This influence is discussed in greater detail in chapters 3 and 4.) Moreover, institutions that grew out of the South African social welfare movement — the South African Institute of Race Relations and the National Institute for Personnel Research, for example — along with the more liberal South African universities, provided an institutional network for the RLI throughout its existence that was just as important for its work as its Oxford and Manchester connections. Until 1948, Lovedale Press in South Africa produced the RLI's publications.[37] Prominent South African scholars served on the RLI's selection committees, and RLI or RLI-associated researchers followed career paths that sometimes included posts in South African universities.

Placing the RLI in the context of South African liberal and radical social science casts in a different light some of the assumptions that its researchers brought to their work. Social science has been criticized for its so-called universalizing gaze. In the context of South African racial politics and the justification of segregation through claims of essential racial difference, however, the refusal of RLI researchers to define the problems of African societies simply in terms of cultural differences was not a failure to recognize important cultural differences but part of a political stance against segregationist policies.[38]

Other aspects of the RLI's approach derived from South African social science, including Gluckman's interest in learning how systems with major racial conflicts and cleavages, as in South Africa, managed to function. Gluckman also used the term "sociology" more often than "anthropology" to describe the kind of social research he had in mind, and this was also partly a product of the South African context. The influential British anthropologist A. R. Radcliffe Brown had introduced the term to South Africa during his stay as professor of anthropology at the University of Cape Town from 1921 to 1925, using it "as a synonym for social science or as a general term to describe the scientific study of society."[39] In South Africa the term may have also carried the message that Africans should be studied in the same way that whites were studied—sociologically as *similar*, rather than anthropologically as *different*—and Schapera and Gluckman always emphasized that white and black societies must be studied together as a single social system.

In addition, certain types of research, such as in-depth urban research, could rarely be done in South Africa, especially after the imposition of apartheid. This and other similarly politically dangerous kinds of research could be deflected north, particularly to Northern Rhodesia, with its similar problems but somewhat more tolerant political and racial atmosphere. The move north was also natural for South African anthropologists, for central Africa had long been an economic and political hinterland of South Africa. It was seen as a frontier useful for experimentation—as in the case of Anglo American's experiments with labor stabilization on the Copperbelt—and a place to send excess population—as in the case of the numerous white South African emigrants who settled in Northern Rhodesia as farmers, miners, or traders. Use of the "Human Laboratory across the Zambesi," at least in Gluckman's view, however, could produce *political* lessons as relevant to South Africa's future development as to its own.[40]

Historically, Northern Rhodesia lay in the path of major influences from the Belgian Congo and East Africa, as well as from southern Africa. Most of the peoples of Zambia migrated from the Congo/ Angola region prior to the nineteenth century, with some immigration continuing into the nineteenth and twentieth centuries. Important migrations in the nineteenth century also came from the Nguni and Tswana peoples from the south, the Swahili from the northeast, and the Portuguese-influenced Mang'anja from the east. War service in East Africa in first and second world wars increased the East African contacts and experiences of Northern Rhodesian Africans. Labor migration to the Congo/Katanga region became extremely important between the wars. Belgian colonial social welfare policies that stressed settlement of workers and their families and the encouragement of a high birthrate often figured as models for those planners who wished to promote the idea of a settled African working class in British Central Africa. Direct competition with the Belgian Union Miniere company for African mine labor, in particular, made the Congo an important influence on mines' and government thinking in the post–World War Two period.

The RLI was not only Africa-centered in the sense of being primarily shaped by Africa-centered colonial policies, but also in terms of its own personnel, the majority of whom were Africans when all job categories are counted as relevant. Collectors, clerks, cleaners, and gardeners outnumbered the researchers but may have only minimally influenced the RLI's character. African research assistants, however, had enormous influence — outnumbering the anthropologists and being employed in greater numbers than was usually the case in anthropology because of the Institute's need for urban survey teams. Like the anthropologists, the assistants functioned self-consciously in a regional African context. Sometimes educated in secondary schools in Southern Rhodesia, in South Africa's Lovedale Mission School, or Nyasaland's Livingstonia Mission School — with some going for further education to Fort Hare in South Africa[41] — the assistants understood from personal experience the broader issues of segregation and early African struggles for self-determination in a regional context. Even assistants with little education often had war experience or labor migration histories that gave them a knowledge of regional African or worldwide black movements. Their previous work for government or the mines in clerical positions also fostered their regional connections and experience, a good example being the mines' preference for employing educated Nyasaland Africans as clerks on the Copperbelt and the significant presence of Africans of this background in the RLI survey teams. These issues are discussed in chapter 7, on the RLI research assistants' teams.

Genealogies and Generations

One of the goals of this book is to produce a field history of the RLI anthropologists. To do this, I have found it necessary to depart from a theory-focused discussion of their work, centered on their articles and monographs and their relation to previous and subsequent work within the discipline. Several fine articles have been written about the Manchester School and its characteristic theories, placing them more generally in the history of anthropological work and relating each anthropologist's ideas to the theories of their teachers, disciples, and rivals. These accounts of theory development and genealogies of scholarly descent, though they are often called "histories," are not actually historical accounts. They function, rather, as programmatic interpretations of anthropology's history, pointing the discipline in a particular direction of development by emphasizing some historical connections over other connections that may have been equally important to the actors at the time.

What is ahistorical about this genre of anthropological writing is not only this differential emphasis, but the fact that theories do not simply spring from other theories. Theories grow out of practices and interactions within intellectual, social, and cultural networks that contain many nonanthropological actors. A genealogical approach puts the field in an incorrect relationship with theory, producing a picture of fieldwork in which the field only provides raw material to be fit into existing theory or from which to fashion new theories. This type of explanation fails to capture the way theory is shaped by the practices of a particular group of people living their daily lives in a particular setting—how the *culture* of a working group of scientists produces its science. Although the field is not prior to theory—for anthropologists do come to the field with some theories already in mind—neither does the field simply provide the raw material from which theory is developed.

For most of the RLI anthropologists, fieldwork was a group experience, and this, perhaps more than any other factor, shaped their work. In order to tease out the influence of this particular style of anthropological research, this book employs a field-based mode of analysis that analyzes researchers and their experiences in terms of their field training and interactions in the field rather than in terms of the theories in which they were trained and the theories which they produced. To do this, I focus on "field generations"—those groups of RLI researchers who entered the field at approximately the same time, who often received an introduction to fieldwork from the same previous researcher, and who shared a larger social network and common experience of historical events during their time in the field.

In the case of the RLI, one finds a clear generational aspect to the development of the researchers' and assistants' social contacts and research experiences. This came about because specific directors, senior researchers, or senior assistants consciously recruited and trained most of the researchers and assistants as teams. Each team got field training at a specific time and place and from particular supervisors, thus developing a group character and approach. This generational aspect of the RLI experience also shaped the professional hierarchy within the group of people who worked at the RLI and in the research school as it continued to evolve at Manchester.

Seen by way of this generational approach, RLI history does not emerge simply as a chronology of successive directorships, though each director left a mark on the Institute's style of anthropology that must not be neglected. Field generations sometimes overlapped more than one directorship, while at other times more than one field generation developed within a single directorship. Moreover, the evolution of the Manchester School as a research school can be directly related to the common experiences of these field generations, and the movement of its center from the RLI to Manchester and other universities can be partly explained by the loss of common field training and contacts that increasingly characterized the researchers who worked at the Institute after 1956. In addition, one can use field generations and their varying levels of commonality of experience and coordination from the RLI as a meaningful way to periodize the RLI's history. Thus, I begin each of the following chapters with a brief discussion of where it fits in this periodization.

3

Archetypal Experiences

The first field generation at the RLI spanned the first directorship and most of the second, covering the years 1938 to 1945. Included in this generation were Godfrey Wilson, the first director from 1938 to 1941; Monica (Hunter) Wilson, who had already published work on Pondoland in South Africa; Max Gluckman, the senior sociologist from September 1939 and second director from 1941; Mary Gluckman; J. Desmond Clark, the archaeologist and curator of the Rhodes-Livingstone Museum, who would continue as curator until 1961; Betty Clark, who temporarily served as curator while Desmond Clark was away for war service; Gluckman's research assistants and close associates in his Lozi research, Davidson Sianga, Francis Suu, and Mwendaweli Lewanika, the second being the administrative secretary of the Barotse native authority and the third a core member of the Lozi royal family; a number of African clerks, interpreters, and collectors; and, finally, a number of loosely associated administrators and technical officers, including Thomas Fox-Pitt, Hugh Cary-Jones, Colin Trapnell, D. U. Peters, and William Allan. By befriending the Gluckmans, Roy Welensky, then a trade unionist and later prime minister of the Central African Federation, became the most prominent white settler to participate in the RLI's social network.

This generation did not share intellectual or fieldwork experiences to as great a degree as some of the later ones, though Godfrey Wilson's conceptualization of the RLI's research goals had a major impact on Gluckman's later research plan. Most of the people associated with the RLI, however, shared a social network at the headquarters in Livingstone or in Broken Hill where Wilson did his fieldwork or in Mongu, the administrative capital of Barotseland where Gluckman did his work. When the Wilsons, Clarks, and Gluckmans lived in Livingstone, three anthropologists and an archeologist shared this setting, but for much of the time Gluckman was away doing fieldwork in Barotseland and Wilson was away doing fieldwork in Broken Hill north of Lusaka, both a considerable distance from Livingstone. During the war, after Wilson's resignation, Gluckman was the only anthropologist at the headquarters in Livingstone, working among administrators and settlers but maintaining a lively connection to his assistants and informants in Barotseland. In 1944 he took part in the reconnaissance survey of land tenure and land usage among the Tonga of Mazabuka District, in conjunction with the technical officers, Allan, Trapnell, and Peters—a shared field experience that had a major impact on his subsequent work and on Allan's work, as well as on the approach that Gluckman used in training the next generation of RLI researchers.

The politics and patronage involved in the founding of the RLI and Wilson's and Gluckman's early work there have been masterfully analyzed by Richard Brown, and portions of his argument will be referred to throughout this and the following chapters.[1] I also draw on Hugh Macmillan's insightful analysis of Gluckman's Zululand fieldwork in relation to his earliest published work.[2] Where I go further than their work is to cast light on the cultural and material factors that characterized the Institute's birthplace, Livingstone, and that shaped the research that the first two directors attempted to carry out. I also further flesh out some incidents in that fieldwork and in earlier fieldwork conducted by Gluckman in South Africa, based on new sources of information—Godfrey Wilson's papers, as well as interviews with a number of people familiar with Wilson's and Gluckman's early work. Unfortunately, my access to Wilson's papers was limited, and I was unable to see Gluckman's papers, which are under closed file.[3] Therefore the arguments in this chapter are necessarily speculative and subject to future correction.

The oral material, however, carries significance that goes beyond questions of accuracy. The informants' stories I have used in this chapter reflect the meaning of Wilson's and Gluckman's experiences for later anthropologists, who would tackle similar problems in their fieldwork. Incidents in the first two directors' fieldwork became archetypal experiences that shaped the attitudes of researchers, mining companies, white settlers, and colonial administrators.[4] Told and retold, reinterpreted and misinterpreted, stories of these incidents have passed into a folklore of fieldwork in southern Africa. The painful silence surrounding certain aspects of these incidents points to the continuing vulnerability of anthropologists to political and commercial powers that can damage the lives and careers of young researchers.

The Dancing Anthropologist

In the course of my research many people told me stories of Max Gluckman dancing Zulu dances at faculty parties while he was a professor of social anthropology at Manchester.[5] It is well known that anthropologists engage in demonstrations of identification with the people they have studied. At their universities or at conferences, whether dancing Zulu dances or wearing ethnic clothing and jewelry, anthropologists make reference to the experience of fieldwork to legitimize their status as cultural experts, in everyday life doing what Malinowski did in his texts with his famous photograph of "the ethnographer's tent" — authenticating his knowledge of the Trobriand people by showing that he had been there.[6]

While referring to the field, these demonstrations may also mimic experiences that actually took place in the field and, along with anecdotes about the field, teach novice anthropologists about proper field behavior while proving the actor's own proficiency in that behavior. As the professor of anthropology at the London School of Economics, Raymond Firth, observed of Gluckman's stories: "He found Malinowski's account of myth, in which narration of the story was linked with boasting about status, both vivid and cogent, and turned it to account in talking of his own field experiences."[7]

The meaning of these experiences *in* the field, however, is different from their meaning in the university setting. In the field these experiences play a role in a process of legitimation performed for a very different audience — for those who already occupy that field, for the administrators, settlers, Africans, and others with whom the anthropologist must struggle for status and earn credibility in order to be allowed into the field. Thus, another story lies behind the tale of Zulu dances in Manchester.

While Gluckman did research in Zululand in 1936–1938 after receiving his D.Phil. at Oxford, another young anthropologist, J. F. Holleman, took a brief trip to Zululand with his mentor at the time, P. J. Schoeman, from the University of Stellenbosch in South Africa. There he saw (but did not meet) Gluckman in Nongoma, the administrative center, a small town containing government offices, a hotel for whites, and a number of shops run by white traders. According to Holleman, Gluckman had come in from the village where he did fieldwork in order to buy supplies, while wearing traditional Zulu dress. This aroused the disapproval of the local shopkeepers who complained to the authorities. Later this incident caused feelings of antagonism when Holleman and Gluckman met at the RLI in 1946, because (according to Holleman) Gluckman believed it had been Holleman or Schoeman who reported him to the authorities. Holleman stayed at Gluckman's home while in Livingstone, and he felt that they ironed out their differences during his visit. As he summed up the relationship: "We were good friends, but our style is different."[8]

This story invites comparison with the event Gluckman described in his "Analysis of a Social Situation in Modern Zululand," the article that resulted from the sixteen months he spent in Zululand and that first employed what would become the characteristic Manchester School method of situational analysis.[9] In this article he described the official opening of a bridge in the district of Mahlabatini in 1938 and a magistrate's district meeting in Nongoma on the same day. He described the various white and African groups involved in the ceremony at the bridge and in the later meeting. He analyzed the groups' relationships with each other in the context of South Africa as a single society containing antagonistic but interrelated white and black groups. Ultimately he situated the different groups within the context of Zulu history, South African racial politics, and the larger world economy.

In his descriptive sections he used distinctions in dress and be-havior to clarify the affiliations and oppositions that existed within and between the groups involved in the ceremony, particularly be-tween Christian and pagan Zulus and the white and black groups as a whole. He argued that the main distinction between Christian and pagan Zulus' dress lay in the *amount* of European clothing worn—Christians wore "full European dress," while pagans wore shirts and perhaps jackets over skin girdles called *bheshu*, a term also used to indicate that the wearer was pagan.[10] It was this kind of dress—*bheshu*—that Holleman claimed he saw Gluckman wearing.

Gluckman built reflexivity into his text by using his own move-ments and behavior during the course of the day to explore the racial politics of the larger context. This is significantly different from Malinowski's use of a photograph of his tent to authenticate his presence as a participant-observer in Trobriand society. Although Gluckman's description of his own movements also textually au-thenticates his presence, while in the field itself he used this device as a self-conscious method to achieve an understanding of the political and racial situation. Moreover, in the resulting text he directly ad-dressed the question of how far the anthropologist or any other European could enter into Zulu society, a question that, rather than simply supporting the efficacy of participant-observation, high-lighted its limitations in a racially charged situation.[11]

Holleman's story about Gluckman, like Gluckman's story of the opening of the bridge, could be analyzed in terms of relationships among various groups acting in the context of South African racial politics. But in his story the important groups are the three different types of *anthropologist* to be found in South Africa, and the differ-ences among the anthropologists are what drives Holleman's story.

Gluckman was a young South African Jew from a well-off family, whose lawyer father sometimes defended African clients. He had attended a liberal South African English-speaking university (Wit-watersrand) and went to Oxford on a Rhodes Scholarship. Holle-man was Dutch, born in colonial Java where his father worked as a judge and magistrate and developed a reputation as a pioneer in the study of indigenous *adat* law. Because Holleman's grandfather had lived in South Africa and left for Holland after the Anglo-Boer War in which he had supported the Afrikaner cause, the family had long wanted to resettle in South Africa. Young Holleman returned first, to do his university degree, and he strongly identified with the rising Afrikaner self-consciousness of the interwar period. While studying anthropology and law at the Afrikaans-speaking University of Stellenbosch he quickly became fluent in Afrikaans and wrote a novel that was nominated for a prize. (The book failed to win because its characters used curses, which were considered "unAfrikaans" in the strict Dutch Reformed Church atmosphere of the time).[12] Despite their substantial differences in background, however, Gluckman and Holleman shared an interest in indigenous legal systems derived from their fathers' law careers.

The third anthropologist in Holleman's story is his mentor, Schoeman. An Afrikaner anthropologist, he played a role in developing the discipline of South African *volkekunde*, a type of anthropology that brought together German ethnology and German missionary views.[13] In the South African context the German elements became melded with the elements of Dutch Reformed Church religious ideology that justified Afrikaner claims to self-determination. Volkekunde posited the unique creation by god of each ethnic group — or *ethnos* — and its god-given right to separate development. Volkekunde evolved as a discipline in conjunction with interwar Afrikaner intellectuals' concerns about the effects of English-speaking whites' political dominance and the growing poverty and urbanization of Afrikaners, who, like Africans, were leaving the farms and congregating in mixed race urban slumyards. It blossomed with the triumph of apartheid politics after the Nationalist Party victory in 1948, and key volkekundiges, like Schoeman, played a central role in the development of apartheid policies.[14]

Schoeman, however, had also attended Malinowski's famous seminars in London and understood the basic tenets of functionalism, as had Gluckman. Thus, both had been exposed to a type of anthropology that had emerged with interwar British colonial concerns. Malinowski echoed these concerns in his promotion of the "culture contact" approach — an anthropological approach that examined the changes in African societies that came about due to exposure to Western influences and that stressed African maladjustment. (Gluckman's later challenge to that idea is discussed in greater detail in chapter 4.)

Schoeman and Gluckman, however, took very different lessons from Malinowski's seminars. Malinowski had become the great promoter of both functionalism and the participant-observation method, claiming credit for its development. Gluckman embraced participant-observation with fervor, but his particular interpretation of functionalism had already been shaped by his teachers in South Africa, who had been strongly influenced by A. R. Radcliffe-Brown during his years at the University of Cape Town from 1921 to 1925. (Gluckman also participated in Radcliffe-Brown's seminars at Oxford in 1938–39[15] and, through them, had been influenced by a mature form of the latter's structural-functionalist approach, which encouraged the comparative study of social structure.) Furthermore, he would become a critic of Malinowski's culture contact approach. Schoeman, it seems, did not take up participant-observation or many elements of functionalist analysis, but, like many volkekundiges, he may have found the culture contact theory useful as "ideological groundwork" for apartheid policy making.[16] Both Gluckman and Schoeman, however, imbibed the idea of anthropology as public service, which was strongly promoted by interwar functionalists, as well as by volkekundiges (who interpreted it as service to the Afrikaner people, who had long suffered under British domination in South Africa).[17]

As in Gluckman's text, dress plays a crucial role in Holleman's story of clashing anthropological styles at Nongoma. Gluckman wore Zulu traditional dress while Schoeman and Holleman wore European clothing suitable for the bush, perhaps very similar to that worn by administrators.[18] Moreover, when telling me the story, Holleman stressed that Christian Zulu would have looked down on Gluckman for wearing *bheshu*. He further claimed that the complaints of shopkeepers led to Gluckman being asked to leave Zululand. Whether or not the latter was true, his claim says a great deal about the larger context of South African racial politics. Like his description of himself in "Analysis," Gluckman in Nongoma moved among different groups, white and black, in a culturally complex field where no simple identification with Africans was possible — where neither the Africans nor the Europeans constituted a homogeneous group. It is not unlikely that his sensitivity to the importance of identification, evidenced later in his writing, may indeed have been heightened by differences with the authorities or white settlers over the proper behavior of researchers in the Zululand Reserve, whether or not he had to leave because of such differences.[19] In any case, the South African authorities subsequently prevented him from returning to Zululand.[20]

Most important, however, is the fact that differences over dress style in this story are a shorthand for differences over fieldwork style — as Holleman summed it up, "Our style is different." His story about Gluckman speaks of their larger differences over the proper way to conduct research, and the story itself may have been Holleman's retrospective defense (for my benefit) of his own field practices which were criticized at the RLI when he later worked under its auspices. His fieldwork style owed some of its elements to his mentor, Schoeman, who may have picked up some tenets of functionalist theory but had not taken up Malinowski's challenge to anthropologists to do intensive fieldwork. Volkekundiges based their writing on many brief visits to their fieldsites, where they stayed with local whites or lived in tents outside the villages and spent most of their time interviewing elderly informants selected as experts on various topics by the Zulu authorities. Staying with other whites or living in tents outside the villages was also the rule among English-speaking anthropologists in South Africa, though some took advantage of the greater freedom of the interwar period to participate in African daily life (relative to research conditions under apartheid after 1948).[21] Heavy teaching loads in recently established departments also kept both English and Afrikaans-speaking anthropologists from spending large amounts of time on fieldwork, though Afrikaner anthropologists may have used this as an excuse to mask their distaste for close relations with Africans.

Nevertheless, the political difficulty of living with one's informants in South Africa remained a constant feature of doing anthropology there regardless of the individual anthropologist's methodological or political commitments. And despite his short visits to the field, Schoeman had a reputation at Stellenbosch as an avid fieldworker; he had become fluent in the Zulu language as a child; and he flavored his teaching with vivid descriptions of Zulu and Swazi life that students found compelling. He compensated for his brief fieldtrips by keeping an uneducated Zulu "from a good family" at his home in Stellenbosch, finding the man useful for practicing his language skills and asking questions about customs.[22] For Schoeman, as for the volkekundiges more generally, good fieldwork meant understanding the language and its deeper nuances, as well as talking to the "right" people — those whom one could expect to be experts on tribal customs because of their position in indigenous society.

The emphasis on language fit with volkekunde's roots in the highly philological German school of ethnology, as well as with the dominance of ethnolinguistics (and its evolutionary assumptions about the links between languages and races) that dominated South African anthropology at both the English and Afrikaans universities well into the interwar period.[23] Through his education at Stellenbosch Holleman picked up this respect for language-learning and concern with speaking to the Africans most knowledgeable about local customs.

Although Holleman learned to distance himself socially from Africans in a way similar to that practiced by Schoeman, later he would cultivate a style of fieldwork based on the practices of administrators in British colonial Africa, influenced also by his memories of his father's willingness to visit people in their homes in Java while learning *adat* law. Although still maintaining some distance from their subjects, British administrators toured villages, lived in tents on the outskirts (though they justified this for health, rather than racial, reasons), mimicked indigenous styles of authority, and prided themselves on having an empathy with their subjects based on frequent and lengthy tours among them, as well as on language skills. When he did his later fieldwork in Southern Rhodesia, Holleman built a separate compound for his family in which he interviewed Africans brought to him by his assistant. This was very similar to the way a visiting administrator would call the people to himself, collect taxes, and hear local cases — as well as being similar to Schoeman's interviewing of elderly expert informants. At times in his eventual career in government and municipal service in Southern Rhodesia, Holleman adopted other administrative behaviors, holding informal courts and settling disputes among his African informants — proudly describing to me the time a group of his informants traveled hundreds of miles to ask his support against a local district officer's land tenure decision.[24] Unlike most administrators, however, he carefully observed local African etiquette and shook hands with Africans, a behavior frowned upon by both Northern and Southern Rhodesian whites.

Finally, Gluckman clearly admired and promoted the Malinowskian participant-observation style of fieldwork (despite his differences with Malinowski over theoretical approach; see chapter 4). Nevertheless, he was also fascinated by administrators' behavior, both as a subject for research and as a strategy for the anthropologist's survival in the field. Although he may have dressed in Zulu traditional clothing at some point during his first fieldwork, most of the time he dressed appropriately for interacting with the administrators he met there. Later in Northern Rhodesia he wore khaki shirts, shorts and/or trousers that mimicked administrators' dress, and he keenly observed and styled his own behavior on that of technical officers from the colonial agricultural service. Paternalism marked his field style, as well as Holleman's, though Gluckman expressed it by making lavish gifts and payments to his assistants and informants. Holleman, in contrast, expressed it through a fatherly authoritarianism and intervention into their daily lives, tempered, at least in his accounts, by stories of his own cultural mistakes — usually pointed out by his research assistant, whom he gave the kind of fatherly admiration administrators reserved for their loyal African messengers.

A sense of romanticism permeated Holleman's descriptions of his fieldwork and paternalistic relations with Africans. Neither were Gluckman's descriptions entirely free of romanticism, particularly

"*Cool Solution*"

The tailoring of Tropical Clothing for the Colonial Services calls for exacting care and long experience. Here at Alkit the art of the cutter, the fine needlework of the tailor, the keen eye of the fitter and the knowledge of Dress Regulations combine towards your complete satisfaction and correct dress for every tropical occasion

Estimate and full details on request

TROPICAL KIT

by

alkit LTD.

CAMBRIDGE CIRCUS, LONDON, W.C.2

Telephone : Temple Bar 1814 [7 lines]
Cables & Telegrams: "Alclothes," Westcent, London

Branches at :
ALDERSHOT, AMESBURY, CAMBERLEY, CHESTER, CAMBRIDGE, FOLKESTONE, NEWARK, OXFORD.

Advertisement for colonial administrators' clothing. See photo of Gluckman in chapter 8 for the similarity of his choice of clothing for fieldwork. (From the Colonial Office List, 1949 [Rhodes House Library shelfmark .010.r.92.1949; opposite p. i]. Reproduced by permission of the Bodleian Library, University of Oxford.)

when he described his reactions to the landscape of Barotseland, which he loved and avidly photographed. A sense of irony, however, and the same reflexivity that stands out in his "Analysis" marked his explicit and implicit observations of both the Malinowskian and administrative elements in his field style. In his collection of photographs at the Royal Anthropological Institute there is a photo of his tent in Barotseland—an allusion to Malinowski's famous photo and possibly also an allusion to a photo used by the first social anthropologist who worked in Northern Rhodesia, Audrey Richards, who had a picture of her tent at the beginning of her book, *Land, Labour and Diet*.[25]

In another picture, either Gluckman or an administrator is captured in the act of photographing a Lozi scene—the face of the photographer is hidden and it is impossible to tell from the clothing whether the man is an administrator or anthropologist. And again and again one finds photos Gluckman took of the Lozi mimicking the administrators and the administrators mimicking the Lozi, processes he discussed in his scholarly and popular writing. He took a particular interest in the roots of administrative authority and African reactions to it, strikingly illustrated in photographs of the admixture of symbols of authority fostered by indirect rule in Barotseland — as, for example, in the provincial and district administrators' participation in the Lozi Kuomboka ceremony.[26]

Clashes in fieldwork style reflected the racial politics of southern Africa, but fieldwork as a practice could also affect the political situation, at least according to the settlers and administrators who sometimes saw the anthropologist's work as useful, but who more often saw it as a threat to the racial order. South Africa was a difficult field site for an anthropologist such as Gluckman, attempting to develop egalitarian relations with his informants but subject to surveillance by local whites and the administration. Northern Rhodesia would prove to be a similarly complex field but with a somewhat different mix of local powers and possibilities that would play a significant role in shaping RLI field practices. Wilson, Gluckman, and the later RLI researchers had to create for their discipline a legitimate place in that Northern Rhodesian field, and to do this they had to prove their credibility to a wide array of people who lived and worked in that field — to African chiefs, educated Africans, and Africans working for government, pagan, Christian, and Muslim, as well as to colonial administrators and technical officers of various kinds, to mining companies and their officials, and to missionaries, settler farmers, traders, and local newspaper editors. The latter frequently published letters and editorials warning of the dangers that could result from anthropologists' behavior.[27]

One of the few certainties in the anthropology of the last twenty-five years has been that social facts are constructed out of fragile human observations and that truth is always contested and contestable. Usually the so-called functionalist anthropology of the interwar and postwar periods is used as the foil against which this new awareness stands out. Nevertheless, because of the contests that took place within the field and the battles that they had to fight to carry on their work, many anthropologists of that time keenly appreciated the precarious nature of the production of knowledge and

District Commissioner H. Vaux, on his barge at the Lozi Kuomboka
Ceremony. This photo by Gluckman illustrates his interest in the roles
of colonial administrators in African societies and their mimicking of
indigenous symbols of authority. Vaux's official barge with Union Jack
flying deliberately imitated the official barges of the Lozi authorities.
(Photo no. 30970 in the Gluckman Collection, Royal Anthropological
Institute. Reproduced by permission of the Royal Anthropological
Institute.)

the political and social constraints placed on their understanding of
the subjects of their research. They employed a number of strategies
to get around these limitations, as many of which failed as succeeded. They saw social knowledge as a hard-won and precious
commodity, and, whether or not they questioned its truth they were
aware of the role that power and politics played in its making.

But before discussing the early battles fought by Wilson and
Gluckman at the RLI, it is necessary to look at the processes of
cultural mixing and conflict that shaped the first setting for the RLI
as an institution — the town of Livingstone, formerly the capital of
Northern Rhodesia.

Saints, Sinners, and Tourist Attractions

The British anthropologist (and one of Gluckman's mentors at Oxford) E. E. Evans-Pritchard called the Rhodes-Livingstone Institute "the Saint and the Sinner Institute."[28] Zambians today generally agree with the meaning behind this joke and describe the position of the colonial Institute as "neutral" because of the balancing of the associations of the two names that make up its title.[29] The reference is to the reputations of the missionary, David Livingstone, and the colonizing entrepreneur, Cecil Rhodes. Colonial Northern Rhodesia itself can be understood as a product of their partly conflicting, partly overlapping enterprises to open central Africa to Christianity, civilization, and capitalism. This section shows how these contradictory forces set the stage for the RLI's work.

The town of Livingstone, the site of the first RLI headquarters, had been a mecca for tourists visiting Victoria Falls since the late nineteenth century. When founded there in 1938, the Institute would absorb the influences of earlier traditions of anthropology and archeology, museum-style collecting and tourist trading in African curios, as well as styles of exploration and prospecting, labor recruiting and frontier administration that figured in local white and black attitudes to cultural knowledge. For Africans, the Old Drift—the shallow crossing place on the Zambezi River where the first town was situated—was a feature of the landscape far more important than the Falls that had captured the imaginations of the earliest European explorers. Central and southern African societies tell their histories in terms of migrations marked by river crossings, and the groups that migrated into present-day Zambia from the Congo/Kola region to the northwest brought with them a riverine mapping of space rooted in that humid and heavily forested landscape.[30]

The Drift and other shallow crossings on the Zambezi in the area between today's towns of Katima Mulilo and Livingstone represented an important trade, migration, and warfare route, because of their position between the rapids north of Katima Mulilo and the Falls below Livingstone. This was especially the case during the

nineteenth-century conquest of the Lozi kingdom (known as Barotseland to Europeans) to the north on the Upper Zambezi, by the
Makololo, a Sotho people who came from the south and crossed the
river to attack the Lozi. Ndebele raiders from western Southern Rhodesia also followed this route for their raids on the Lozi. When the
Lozi regained their ascendancy in the late nineteenth century, white
traders, cattle buyers, missionaries, and hunters followed the same
route north across the Zambezi into the kingdom. Prospectors and
representatives of the British South Africa Company also used this
route and exploited the struggles for hegemony between the Ndebele
and Lozi, as well as the dissatisfaction of the many groups that lived
within their spheres of influence, in order to gain control of mineral
rights in western Northern Rhodesia.

In the years just before the turn of the century, as the British South
Africa Company made treaties with the Lozi and established their
own control of Northern Rhodesia, Southern Rhodesia, and the
Barotseland Protectorate, labor recruiters visited both the Lozi kingdom and Tonga areas east of the Falls (claimed as Lozi territory),
enticing young men with promises of wealth in the South African
Rand mines or rounding them up for the enforced labor of the *chibaro* system that supported the Southern Rhodesian mines. Missionaries with Sotho-speaking assistants followed the linguistic pathway
into Barotseland hacked out for them by the Sotho-speaking Makololo invaders.

The name "Livingstone," given to the town when it moved to a
higher and healthier site in 1906, honored the first missionary to
travel to Barotseland, David Livingstone, who had visited in 1851
during the Makololo ascendancy. The Northern Rhodesian territory
was also a projection of Cecil Rhodes's speculative mining ventures.
The railway that opened up these northern territories partly fulfilled
Rhodes's Cape to Cairo vision, extending from Johannesburg to
Livingstone in Northern Rhodesia in 1905 and from there to the
Copperbelt and Belgian Congo Katanga mines in 1910.

Despite the campaign by anthropologists, including Malinowski
and Audrey Richards in the interwar period, to advertise the usefulness of their work for African administration, the RLI's origin owed

as much to an older anthropological tradition as it did to the efforts of Richards and her association with the Northern Rhodesian government and its governor, as discussed by Brown.[31] Governor Hubert Young's interest in anthropology included the then new social anthropology with its focus on social change, but it also included archeology and the goal of building a museum that would display archeological collections and the rapidly vanishing material culture of contemporary Africans.

Local settlers supported the latter aim, and this support brought about the construction of a museum much earlier than a social science institute. The idea of collecting and preserving African material culture on a colony-wide scale was first suggested in 1930, and district commissioners began buying local craft items shortly after the Legislative Council allocated money for the purpose in the 1930–31 budget.[32] The David Livingstone Memorial Museum was founded in Livingstone in 1934, later to incorporate the Institute in 1938.[33] Local support grew out of the needs of Livingstone as a town, which would lose its status as Northern Rhodesia's administrative headquarters because of the move of government to the more central position of Lusaka in 1935.[34] Livingstone had long been developing into a center for culture and tourism because of its location near Victoria Falls, so making it the cultural capital in compensation for the shifting of government offices to Lusaka seemed a natural move.[35]

Thus, the RLI's local roots derived to a large degree from its site in Livingstone, its potential use for tourism, and the idea of the local white settlers that anthropology was practically synonymous with archeology.[36] During the early years of the RLI, its museum acted as an institutional culture broker, supervising the collection and marketing of African culture to the white settler public.[37] The first researchers in the postwar period wrote pamphlets about the material culture of the societies they studied, playing an educational role with respect to local whites that had political overtones in that setting because it stressed respect for African culture. Battle lines in this war over the uses of cultural knowledge had been drawn even before the Institute's official founding. Brown quotes Leopold Moore, owner of the *Livingstone Mail* in 1937, who feared that the Institute would become "a means of disseminating religious propaganda as witness the BBC."[38] The religious propaganda he no doubt meant was the "Negrophilia" that local whites felt was practiced by the colonial government and missionaries at their expense.[39] They deeply resented Colonial Office policies that limited their exploitation of African land and labor and limited settler political power, in contrast to the devolution of government to white settlers that was taking place in neighboring Southern Rhodesia in the interwar period.

And, as settlers feared, the RLI's work did highlight the conflict between the commercial interests of settler society and the welfare of Africans.

Benevolent Empires and Mining Empires

Godfrey Wilson became the first RLI director in 1938 and conducted research in the mining town of Broken Hill (now Kabwe). Wilson directed his work toward solving the problems of Africans experiencing rapid social change due to the effects of the mining industry in Northern Rhodesia. Wilson interpreted social anthropology's goal of public service as a personal moral commitment. Both he and the senior sociologist, Gluckman, raised moral and political issues in their early fieldwork, which led to controversy over the purposes of social anthropology in a colonial setting.

In his Christian commitment to ameliorating the African condition, Wilson had the support of his wife, Monica (Hunter) Wilson, the daughter of a missionary family at the famous Lovedale Mission in South Africa.[40] Educated partly at Fort Hare in South Africa, she went on to Cambridge, returning to South Africa to do her doctoral fieldwork on the Pondo people. That study, *Reaction to Conquest*, had focused on the Pondo's responses to changes brought about by colonialism and included brief sections on their life in urban areas and on European farms, instead of confining itself to the more conventional focus on rural traditions.[41] While writing up at Cambridge she attended Malinowski's seminars at the London School of Economics. She also met and married Godfrey Wilson, son of the

British Shakespearean scholar John Dover Wilson. Through her, he became interested in anthropology. They both worked in Tanganyika from 1935 to 1938, doing fieldwork on Nyakuysa society under the auspices of the Rockefeller-funded International African Institute scheme, which actualized Malinowski's plans for the study of culture contact by supporting the fieldwork of a large number of young scholars.

In 1939 Godfrey Wilson began his study of the African miners of Broken Hill, a town halfway between Lusaka and the Copperbelt. Also, until his death in 1941, he and Monica worked together on a book, *The Analysis of Social Change*, which set out their approach to research in Africa.[42] The argument of the book focused on African responses to the increases of scale (in the social, political, and economic realms) brought about by colonialism. The Wilsons emphasized the loss of equilibrium and the conflict experienced by African societies affected by large-scale Western systems, revealing a Malinowskian concern with the maladjustments caused by culture contact, though they did not uncritically accept Malinowski's scheme.[43] A South African scholar attending the LSE seminars, Jack Simons (whose work is discussed in chapter 4), observed the arguments that took place between Malinowski's radical students and the "more establishment ones" on the role of anthropology. "Godfrey Wilson would argue that the anthropologist should be more than an observer and recorder of practices—he or she must also evaluate the trend of policies and should speak up, if they are harmful, in the role of consultant."[44]

Max Gluckman and the African scholar Z. K. Matthews also attended Malinowski's seminar at this time.[45] As Hugh Macmillan has argued, Gluckman's "Analysis" constituted "a systematic assault on the concept of the 'bounded tribe'" through its attack on the idea that any society could be made up of a homogeneous group.[46] Taking a different approach, the Wilsons' ideas about African adaptation to increases in scale also represented an early effort to find methods for dealing with social change that would allow researchers to go beyond the tribe as the primary unit of analysis.[47] Moreover, Godfrey Wilson's study of African miners at Broken Hill would be the "most direct confrontation with the tribal model of Africa" cherished by the mines and the colonial government.[48] (Whatever differences Godfrey Wilson may have had with Malinowski then or later with respect to the role of anthropologists or the nature of change in Africa, Malinowski prized him as a student and was delighted when he got the RLI job.[49])

In his career at the RLI, Wilson found himself caught between the very forces he would describe as causing the uneven development that he blamed for African maladjustment in the mining towns and rural labor reserves of Northern Rhodesia. In the work he published based on his research at the RLI, "The Economics of Detribalization in Northern Rhodesia," he noted the ways that industry's demand for cheap labor depended on both the underdevelopment of African agriculture in the reserves and Africans' temporary residence in towns, both allowing the colony's young industries to avoid the cost of supporting its African workers at the same level demanded by European workers.[50] He was also sensitive to the ways that European miners used race prejudice to maintain an impermeable hierarchy of skilled European and unskilled African labor—like a rigid caste system, but one that would inevitably break down, in Wilson's view, as a new social and economic equilibrium emerged with inevitable changes in the world economic system. Most importantly, he did not see maladjustment as a condition limited to those African societies struggling to deal with the Western systems imposed on them. Maladjustment characterized the world system as a whole, particularly while in a state of war—a factor he was well aware of, for World War Two broke out while he was in the midst of his fieldwork.

The Hegelian Marxism of many of Cambridge's young left-wing Christian students influenced Wilson's interpretation of Malinowskian functionalism, and in particular, the idea of societies as harmonious interdependent organisms: in Wilson's view, equilibrium emerged only after Marxist-style contradictions worked themselves out. And, as Brown has noted, disequilibrium did not simply lead to maladjustment but became the "motor of permanent change" in the Wilsons' work.[51] Much of Godfrey and Monica Wilson's argument about uneven development and the uneasy coexistence of subsistence agriculture with a tiny but rapidly industrializing sector could be recast in the "articulation of modes of production" language of later Marxist anthropology, as well as in the language of later critiques of imperialism and its fostering of underdevelopment.[52]

The forces that pressed upon Wilson's fieldwork included the world capitalist system, represented locally by the mining companies — American, British, and South African — which had followed the path laid out by Rhodes's vision of southern Africa's development and the British South Africa Company's style of colonialism. The Anglo-American Corporation (a South African based company) descended directly from Rhodes's ventures, and its mining empire had become one of the most powerful economic forces in the world by the interwar period, through its production of a large portion of the world's gold supply, as well as control of many of the copper mines that would become so important during the war.

But another empire existed in an uneasy relationship with the mining companies, an empire which in many parts of southern Africa predated them — the so-called benevolent empire of the missions.[53] A wide variety of missions had already carved out their territories in Northern Rhodesia before the mines got a foothold, and their influence on anthropological research was profound. Mission-ethnographers, along with administrator-ethnographers, did the first ethnographic mapping of the territory; they provided some of the first experiences from which Africans drew their expectations of European behavior; and they provided the English education that shaped the outlook of the research assistants who worked for anthropologists.[54]

Not only did the missions often oppose capitalist forces and, in a paternalistic way, attempt to protect Africans from their degenerative influence, with few exceptions they also promoted agriculture and skilled trades as the appropriate arena for transforming African culture and morality. Thus, the descendants of mission families often joined the new agricultural professions that began to flourish in Africa in the interwar period, seeing in the nascent work of agricultural development a natural extension of the ameliorative goals of the missions. This was not surprising, considering that many of those who sought careers in the agricultural sciences saw themselves as "missionaries of science."[55] Mission influences on the agricultural services in central Africa were strong. Descendants of the Moffat mission family, into which David Livingstone had married after his arrival in South Africa, worked in both the agricultural and administrative services in Northern Rhodesia, and a former missionary headed the agricultural services in Southern Rhodesia for many years.

The narrow rural focus of the mission view, however, would begin to change in the interwar period, with profound implications for anthropological research. Thus, Godfrey Wilson's sensitivity to the relationship between the urban industrial sphere and the underdevelopment of rural agriculture would arise from his links with a missionary tradition that was changing in response to industrial forces.

Social anthropology, like the agricultural development professions, had roots in a morally informed vision that characterized the late nineteenth- and early twentieth-century social sciences. Professionalization of the social sciences in that period did not demand the renunciation of social activism. Rather, a shared organic view of society gave these professions an agenda for shaping human evolution in a healthy direction.[56] Although not evolutionists, many interwar social anthropologists argued that they deserved a role in colonial policy making, and they made these arguments from a similarly principled stance about the usefulness of their field for development. R. H. Tawney, whose vision of a functional society called for an end to the wastefulness of the slumps and booms of uncontrolled capitalism, represented the larger currents of functionalist thought in the professions in the interwar period. In 1928 his call for a "Christian sociology" inspired professionals, as well as missionaries, toward activism.[57] Godfrey Wilson's "Anthropology as a Public Service" set out this activist agenda for the RLI at the outset, though he carefully stood back from claiming a decision-making role for the anthropologist.[58]

Although Africans never mistook anthropologists for missionaries, settlers and government officials often put the two in the same category as so-called Negrophiles. In their relationships with settlers and administrators, both anthropologists and missionaries often played the role of advocates for African interests. Godfrey and Monica Wilson fell into this pattern of interaction with government officials on their arrival in Northern Rhodesia when they became part of the social scene in Livingstone. According to their son, Francis, his parents' relationship with the administrators was intellectually "ambivalent and creative," as they played chess and attended dinner parties hosted by colonial officials.[59] They carried on the mission tradition by acting as "congenial gadflies," reminding officials of African interests and becoming a thorn in the side of government over its policies.[60]

The mission tradition of social critique had customarily focused on the condition of rural Africans and the degenerative influence of Africans' exposure to the money economy, but at the same time restricted mission activity to the villages. This began to change in the 1930s, resulting in an important 1933 publication sponsored by the International Missionary Council — *Modern Industry and the African* — based on research on Northern Rhodesia's Copperbelt.[61] Governor Young used this book in his arguments with the Colonial Office about the need to establish an institute to study social change. Later the British missionary J. H. Oldham suggested Wilson for the directorship of the RLI. Oldham's support of anthropological research reflected an interwar shift in mission attitudes to African cultures — viewing them more positively and taking care not to dissolve the bonds that held African societies together. Oldham had taken a particular interest in the effects of industrialization and since the 1920s had seen Northern Rhodesia's nascent copper industry as an example of the need for greater control of modernizing processes.[62]

The mission critique of industrialization emphasized the pathology of urban conditions for Africans,[63] which would have reinforced Wilson's Malinowskian focus on maladjustment. Ultimately, the findings of his research on Africans at the Broken Hill mines would be taken up by local missionaries and used in a further exposé of conditions in the mining industry on the Copperbelt. The missionary author of this later study had some anthropological training and cited Wilson's research in support of his argument for improved conditions for African workers and their families.[64]

Before it was finished, however, Wilson's research in Broken Hill suffered because of tensions surrounding the outbreak of World War Two — an event that caused the mining companies to see fieldwork as likely to stir up African discontent while being superfluous to the war effort. Before war broke out Wilson had permission to conduct his research on mine property, had completed a portion of the study, and had planned to extend his work to the Copperbelt, but after the war began, the Broken Hill Development Company first temporarily, and later permanently, revoked his permission. African and European workers' strikes and riots on the Copperbelt, as well as the possibly disturbing nature of anthropologists' questions, were the explicit reasons given by mine officials, but the political implications of anthropologists' patterns of interaction with Africans were the underlying, and more important, reason. Wilson's behavior had undermined the color bar and the image of the European that whites used to safeguard their dominant political position.

Ironically, the LSE-trained American anthropologist Hortense Powdermaker, later living in Luanshya during the RLI Copperbelt surveys in the 1950s, was favorably impressed by the local white attitude toward anthropologists, in comparison with that of whites in the southern United States where she had previously done research: "The upper levels of the white hierarchy were more sophisticated as well as less fearful than the Mississippi whites, and, even more important, an anthroplogist was not a new phenomenon to them. The head of a department on the mine rebuked an unusually liberal employee sitting on a bench and smoking a cigarette with an African during the lunch hour, by saying, 'You looked like an anthropologist!' "[65]

Powdermaker, however, was not aware of the real threat to anthropologists that lay behind this rebuke, for both Mitchell and Epstein working there at the time had been criticized for such too-familiar behavior, and, like Wilson earlier, Epstein lost his permission to conduct research on mine property. Wilson had been told by a compound manager that it was all right "to *give* cigarettes to workers, but *not* right to smoke with them — that was letting down the prestige of the white man."[66] As the mining compound manager, Young, complained in a meeting at which Wilson attempted to persuade him to allow him to continue his research, "the white man, in a chair and the natives on the floor, that is what we are accustomed to . . . It is said you have been seen sitting on a box with a Native on a chair."

This meeting took place in the office of the company's general manager, T. R. Pickard, who claimed neutrality on the issue but abided by the views of his compound managers. In a subsequent letter to Wilson, he added, perhaps sarcastically, that the importance of the mines' established traditions for managing African life in the compounds was something that Wilson, as an anthropologist, would surely appreciate.[67] Wilson's threat to fight the case publicly may have angered Pickard, for Wilson had appealed to Governor John Maybin, Hubert Young's successor, at several points during his negotiations with the mines.[68] The government, however, customarily allowed the mines to exercise complete control over their own domain, and Maybin's intervention had little effect.

Wilson also fell afoul of the gender aspect of Northern Rhodesia's racial politics, for local whites criticized him for giving lifts to African women, and the mining compound managers in the African housing areas objected to his entering the houses of Africans in the course of his research. Local settlers criticized him and his wife for visiting Chirupula Stephenson, a retired colonial administrator whose values dated from a much earlier ethos of administration and who was notorious for having several African wives.[69] Other issues raised against anthropological fieldwork also focused on the domestic realm, which, given the poverty of Africans' lives in towns, the authorities had good reasons for wanting to keep private. When the mines revoked Wilson's permission to work on mine property, the municipal authorities also barred him from doing work in the municipal location he had been surveying, ostensibly because Africans had "protested against Europeans making enquiries about their domestic life and habits." In his answer Wilson implied that these charges had been trumped up by the compound managers.[70]

The banning from the municipal location, as well as the mining compounds, made it impossible for Wilson to continue his research. As he observed: "The effect of my absence from the Location, even for a few days, is to create a most serious gap in my observations. It is as if a chemist, in the middle of a delicate experiment, needing continuous watching, were to find the door of his laboratory shut and locked in his face."[71]

Wilson's pacifism in the context of the early months of World War Two and the applications for conscientious objector status by him and Desmond Clark, the curator of the Rhodes-Livingstone Museum (both on religious grounds), however, may have been a more important factor than the social conventions that Wilson broke. As Brown argues, pacifism was considered a bad example to be set by a European whose work required him to deal with Africans.[72]

At the time, the author of a local newspaper article about Wilson's application for exemption as a conscientious objector expressed outrage at Wilson's claim in the hearings that his work at the RLI was "of the greatest importance from which he should not be removed."[73] Frank Ayer, the general manager of Roan Antelope Mine in Luanshya on the Copperbelt — and one of the most influential members of the mining community — sent a cutting of the article to the Rhodesia Selection Trust secretary in London, complaining about Wilson's testimony: "For your information Mr. Wilson kept insisting on coming here to study our native conditions and I repeatedly turned him down telling him that we did not want anyone going about the Compound questioning natives during the War as it might be misunderstood. In view of the above you may wish to postpone your contribution [to funding the RLI] until some future date when these two gentlemen [Wilson and Clark] are not connected with the Rhodes-Livingstone Institute."[74]

Although mining company officials, such as Pickard, repeatedly assured Wilson that his banning from mine property was "a question of principle" caused by the possible disquiet among Africans that might result from any sort of anthropological enquiry and that

"[Wilson] personally had not caused anxiety or embarassment to them,"[75] behind the scenes the mining companies did indeed see Wilson and the staff of the RLI as an embarassment. The elected members of the Northern Rhodesia Legislative Council (representing white settler interests) agreed with this assessment and made known their opposition to the government's renewal of the Institute's £1000 grant if Wilson and Clark remained on the staff. Wilson resigned, partly because he could not guarantee that his pacifist views could be kept from the Africans he studied.[76] He stayed on long enough to finish his report on Broken Hill. In the case of the Museum curator, Clark, the RLI Trustees decided to keep his post open for him after he joined an ambulance unit in east Africa.[77]

During his negotiations to continue his work, Wilson also fought to keep Gluckman from being ousted from his fieldsite in Barotseland.[78] Gluckman had offended local administrators with remarks they construed as "anti-British" and brought to the Governor's attention. In a confidential letter to Wilson, the Chief Secretary reported the Governor's conclusion that Gluckman had merely criticized "pre-war lethargy and post-war complacency," but "on the other hand he had been ill-advised and indiscreet"—the latter remark possibly meant to chide Wilson for not ensuring that Gluckman behaved properly.[79] Gluckman's favorable references to the Soviet *kolkhoz* had also led some whites in Northern Rhodesia to regard him as a communist.[80] This, along with the anti-Semitism cited by Brown, would make his later transition to the directorship difficult.

Wilson finished his report on the Broken Hill fieldwork before leaving Northern Rhodesia and volunteering for noncombatant military service, some of it in the ambulance corps in North Africa. J. Clyde Mitchell, a South African who would work at the RLI after the war, met Wilson briefly by chance while himself serving in the South African air force. He recalled Wilson as being torn between his principles and his war work. The educational work he had been assigned to do with recently recruited troops in South Africa required him to propagandize them against communism and fascism, as well as motivate them for their military duties. When Mitchell returned to South Africa some weeks later, he found that Wilson had committed suicide.[81]

Gluckman did not explicitly use Wilson's experiences as a warning to the researchers he would later introduce to fieldwork in Northern Rhodesia. Nevertheless the story of the first director's banning was well known to those who eventually contributed to the RLI's urban research program.[82] As Brown has astutely observed, this incident motivated Gluckman's attempt to get concrete assurance from government that any future urban researchers would be free to carry on their work, and his failure to get this assurance may have led both to his not taking up the urban study himself and to his insistence on the theoretical soundness of studying urban and rural areas separately.[83] This, and Gluckman's own near loss of permission to conduct fieldwork in a rural site, may have inspired the caution that he and later directors practiced when dealing with the mines, though it did not stop them from making strong recommendations for change based on their research once it was accomplished.

Despite the seriousness of these conflicts, a third, more positive, experience would also significantly shape the RLI's future research practices, as well as their relations with another important group, the agriculturists.

Culture and Agriculture

When Gluckman became acting director after Wilson's resignation, he assiduously developed links with government and settlers in Northern Rhodesia despite his earlier problems with the provincial administration in Barotseland. His interactions with individuals in the administration continued to be ambivalent, as they no doubt had been in Zululand. But Holleman's story notwithstanding, Gluckman's application for a job at the RLI had received a glowing recommendation from a Zululand administrator in Nongoma.[84] Two things are important to understand about the nature of RLI researchers' interactions with the colonial government. Anthropologists and administrators were united by some shared elements in their ethos of fieldwork and public service, and the people who worked for the colonial government were diverse in their training and attitudes toward Africans. Thus, anthropologists could develop productive relationships based on a variety of partially shared interests. Gluckman became a master of this project (as did Mitchell when he took on the task of cajoling mines and government to facilitate the Copperbelt studies). Because this project aimed at acquiring legitimacy for anthropologists' presence in the field, and was not only aimed at promoting the relevance of their work for government policy making, it would survive Gluckman's later disillusionment with applied anthropology (discussed in chapter 4).[85]

Although he may have become more cautious about overt political debate with administrators as a result of their attempt to get him banned in the early days of his fieldwork, Gluckman, like Wilson, fiercely defended social anthropology as a profession vital to policy making. In doing this he drew upon the precedents being set by the agricultural sciences, newly arrived in the African field. In both his field behavior and writing, he emphasized the elements of practice and professional ethos shared by anthropologists and agricultural technical officers, using these commonalities to legitimate anthropology as a field science. Moreover, both he and Wilson stressed commonalities in anthropological fieldwork and administrative touring in order to get good conditions of service for RLI researchers. Whenever these practices diverged, both directors justified the differences as due to professional standards entailed by the nature of their discipline and argued for higher field allowances for anthropologists than those given to administrators.[86] In this they also mimicked legitimation strategies used by the agricultural services, which were increasingly asking for higher levels of technological support than those enjoyed by district and provincial administrators. Administrators did not easily accept the demands of these new professions, and in the case of anthropology neither did they acknowledge that the professional expertise being claimed was greater than their own.

Evidence of this battle over claims to expertise can be found in the responses by provincial administrators to drafts of Gluckman's seven-year plan for the Institute's postwar work, which he developed during 1944 and 1945. Three issues emerge from their reactions: what is the proper political identity for anthropologists? what is the disciplinary territory for their expertise? and what is their relationship to the experts already in the field, the technical officers, and the provincial administrators — the administration's so-called practical men?

First, concerns about the political identity of researchers reflected the Second World War context and the defensiveness of the remaining skeleton staff of administrators about their own exemption from military service. The provincial commissioner of Northern Province expressed his fear that the research team Gluckman hoped to recruit would be a team of people who had been unfit for war service, too old, too medically unfit, or, worst of all, conscientious objectors who would be personae non gratae with the officers of the provincial administration — all of whom, he insisted, would have joined up if they had been allowed. Although he did not state it explicitly, this was an attack on the professional importance of anthropology, which Wilson had given as a reason for his own exemption from military service. Other administrators were concerned that the spheres of duty of anthropologists and administrators needed to be carefully defined, with anthropologists not being allowed much scope to criticize government or the administrators' work. Others were concerned that anthropologists should not expect too much assistance from administrators — in response to one of Gluckman's suggestions, that the district officers might participate in some of the research — while still others felt this kind of activity would be appropriate as long as administrators headed the research team. Some of these responses derived from actual experiences administrators had had because of Gluckman's previous attempts to engage them in the work of the RLI.

When discussing all of these issues, the administrators tended to use the term "anthropology," while Gluckman used "social anthropology" or "sociology." As in Radcliffe-Brown's use of the term, Gluckman's use of "sociology" was a rhetorical move intended to stress the scientific character of the discipline of social anthropology and to contrast it with earlier forms of anthropology — evolutionary or diffusionist. In Gluckman's draft of the seven-year plan and in the administrators' responses, one can discern the outlines of an implicit conflict over the professional status of social anthropology and the ways that its practitioners' claims to disciplinary territory differed from those of evolutionists and diffusionists.

For example, District Commissioner Gervas Clay expressed concern about the proper realm of anthropology in terms that reflected older approaches that Gluckman's research plan implicitly challenged. According to Clay, anthropologists should be assigned to tribes rather than to subjects, as the director had suggested: "each major tribe or each province should have its anthropologist." To Gluckman's suggestion that the sociologist could help Africans to formulate criticism of government policy, the provincial commissioner for Northern Province responded that conditions after the war would make the results of such behavior "unfortunate." Clay suggested anthropologists might take on a role similar to that played by information officers during the war, explaining the European to the African, implying that this was needed more than explaining the African to the administrators, who could be expected to already understand "their" people. District Commissioner Munday of Eastern Province echoed these concerns, suggesting that the district officers should head the research teams and that each anthropologist could become a member of a team consisting of "practical men of the area under review."[87]

Two of Gluckman's goals for social anthropology particularly annoyed administrators—that Africans should learn to use the discipline's findings and that RLI researchers should study administrators themselves, as an important aspect of African life.[88] These goals no doubt convinced many administrators that anthropological research needed careful control. Moreover, all of these responses reflected administrators' fears of being displaced as experts on African matters. This fear had emerged not only because of the presence of anthropologists as a new breed of professional experts, but also because of the increasing load of paperwork and time administrators spent on bureaucratic matters in the capital city of Lusaka. These duties prevented them from developing language skills and local knowledge of the rural areas to as great a degree as in the past.[89] As mentioned in the first section of this chapter, language skills and the local knowledge gained from touring figured prominently in the administrative style of fieldwork, and these skills bolstered their claims to be experts on Africans.

Despite this rather unfavorable assessment by the administration, Gluckman's efforts to promote the usefulness of anthropology found more fertile ground in Northern Rhodesia than would have been the case in either South Africa or Southern Rhodesia, because of precedents within the colonial service in that colony. The highly talented agricultural technical officers who found employment in Northern Rhodesia in the interwar period had already developed an interest in African agricultural systems and their efficacy. Some of these men felt that understanding African practices must come before attempting to change them.[90] This attitude was exemplified in the work of the ecologist Colin Trapnell and the agriculturist William Allan, though the latter has been criticized for developing a concept of the "carrying capacity" of land which justified the unpopular anti-erosion regulations of the postwar period.[91]

Nevertheless, although anthropologists and agriculturists might disagree on interventions, they clearly found common ground in their mutual interest in African practices. Gluckman's focus on material conditions affecting African life in the colonial period — exhibited particularly in the decay of subsistence agriculture due to male labor migration — motivated his deep respect for the work of Trapnell, whose ecological survey of the northwestern part of the country critically informed Gluckman's analysis of the Lozi economy of the Barotse Flood Plain.[92]

Furthermore, an experience of actually working in a team with government technical officers gave Gluckman some optimism for the future of anthropology in colonial development work; this experience was the reconnaissance survey of Plateau Tonga agriculture carried out by the agriculture department in 1945.[93] The survey itself reflected the new aggressive approach to development favored by the colonial government after the war. Examples of a transfer of military terminology to agricultural conditions abound in the published text resulting from the study, the title "reconnaissance survey" being but one example. As in a military operation, survey members intended to produce a rapid assessment in a crisis situation, but with the crisis expressed in the subsequent report in the language of ecological deterioration, population pressure, and need for rapid social change.[94]

Gluckman saw this survey as an important model for cooperative research with government and proof that technical officers and anthropologists could work effectively in teams, especially given later signs that his expertise was valued. The agriculturists subsequently asked him to accompany them on another survey and accepted his African research assistant, David Sianga, in his place. The Assistant Director of Agriculture also showed Gluckman around the resettlement area in the Lamba reserve near the Copperbelt, which the director would later choose as the field-training site for the first postwar RLI team of anthropologists who arrived in 1946[95] (see chapter 4). These signs of acceptance of anthropology by the agricultural service were important, for Gluckman had perceived that agriculturists presented a successful model for anthropologists' behavior in the field. And indeed, the colonial government did implement some of the recommendations of the Tonga reconnaissance survey which Gluckman had helped to shape — in particular, the recommendation for communal ownership of farming implements (which ultimately proved unworkable).[96] Being accepted by this group perhaps could ease acceptance by other groups — the rural administrators and white settler farmers, in particular. The presence of agriculturists in the field was also useful for intellectual cross-fertilization. Gluckman's use of Trapnell's ecological research in his own work set the agenda for future intellectual interactions between RLI researchers and agriculturists. As Elizabeth Colson, a member of the first postwar RLI team, recalled, "At one time we swore that we really couldn't do anthropology in an area where there was no agricultural station because there was so much cross-fertilization, so much stimulation."[97]

Imitating elements of agricultural officers' behavior in the field proved for Gluckman to be a useful strategy for gaining legitimacy. Imitating administrators' behavior could also be helpful, but in their choices of models for identification the RLI anthropologists always

balanced uncomfortably between African and government expectations and suspicions, and ultimately RLI researchers would reject
many of the behaviors Gluckman recommended. And Gluckman
never attained the acceptance he hoped for, either from government
policy makers or from the practical men in the field.

Gluckman never completely lost his desire for that acceptance and
the power it would give him to influence government. His description of his final field tour in Barotseland reveals a continuing identification with certain aspects of the administrators' field ethos: "Here,
I'm having a grand time. Nice country when the flood is up. You
have to go to work in a dugout and can shoot duck, and I've had a lot
of riding . . . I like the Lozi and have the best DC I've known—
grandson of Pitt-Rivers, Com. Fox-Pitt, R.N., OBE, (military) etc.
but a good socialist and most helpful and keen on the work."[98]

In this description Gluckman enjoys the sports associated with the
life of the English rural gentry, shooting and riding. Colonial administrators also cultivated these sports as part of an ethos of vigorous
masculinity and chivalrous public service taken on by the colonial
service in the late nineteenth century and fostered subsequently by
the paternalism of indirect rule. Throughout colonial Africa, hunting formed an important part of this ethos and riding was done
wherever conditions allowed it—or demanded it, as was the case in
Barotseland, where the Kalahari sands made other forms of administrative transport, such as bicycles, impossible to use. Gluckman
enjoyed this aspect of fieldwork, but he did not take on other elements of the administrative ethos—authoritarian behavior towards
Africans, for example.

His remarks about the new District Commissioner, Fox-Pitt, may
also reveal a longing to be able to express his political principles
unproblematically in this colonial setting. Fox-Pitt, "a good socialist," was thought by many to be a communist, though his aristocratic
family connections led most critics to dismiss his left-wing point-of-
view as a harmless eccentricity.[99] Nevertheless, he had more power
than Gluckman to promote African interests in his administrative
work, and Gluckman would have been feeling his own powerless-
ness keenly during his last months in Northern Rhodesia. Identifica-

tion with technical officers might have helped anthropologists to be accepted in the field, but it did not ensure that government would implement their recommendations.

Conclusion

In his writing Godfrey Wilson exhibited a clear sensitivity to the role of politics in shaping knowledge. This awareness was not incompatible with his claim to reveal facts; each discipline has standards for the production of what it will accept as legitimate data, and each puts sanctions of a quasi-moral kind on failure to meet these standards. The term "fact" is a product of these processes, unique to each discipline, and built into these facts are the political struggles that have surrounded their making.[100] Wilson was well aware of the contested nature of the assumptions from which he built his case and the likely response to his recommendations.[101] Nevertheless, he delivered his argument with force, actively engaging in the struggles through which the scope for the activism of the social sciences was continually being renegotiated with the objects of that activism — both with governments and powerful industrial interests.

Wilson's arguments and those of later RLI researchers had a positivistic character — in a context in which anthropologists stood accused of introducing politics and religion into the discourse they could hardly have afforded to be tentative.[102] Nevertheless, it is unlikely that they embraced an entirely uncritical positivism, judging from the advice given by a later RLI researcher, Clyde Mitchell, during a similarly contested period of urban research, that one must maintain a *façade* of Victorian objectivity in order to do fieldwork at all.[103] But what is more important in the case of the Wilsons is the dialectical vision of truth that informed their arguments, and that would become a strong and continuing theme in the RLI's (and later Manchester School's) work.[104] Truth emerges from struggle, and the field is the immediate battleground of that struggle. And, if truth be in the field, as Monica Wilson would later entitle her Alfred and Winifred Hoernlé Memorial Lecture for the South African Institute of Race Relations, then the worst fate for the social scientist would be the loss of access to that field.[105]

After Godfrey Wilson left the field, Gluckman continued this struggle through fieldwork strategies intended to gain credibility for anthropology — taking on some elements of the language, dress, and practices of a more successful group, the government agriculturists. Later Mitchell and his African research assistants, too, would take on some of the characteristics of another group that was gaining legitimacy in the urban field — the government labor officers and welfare workers. It was partly through the adoption of this strategy that the early archetypal experiences recounted in this chapter made themselves felt throughout the RLI's history.

These archetypal experiences also contributed to important undercurrents and painful silences in the RLI's work. According to Barnes:

> Gluckman certainly did talk about Wilson's resignation, but my recollection is that this was only after he had moved to Manchester. [In Northern Rhodesia] we were all told to read the Wilsons' book on social change and knew that his death in South Africa was said to have been "on active service," but the details of what went on while Wilson was on the Copperbelt I learned about only years later. Gluckman was always ready to relate anecdotes about his relations with patrol officers and agricultural officers but said little about his relations with Godfrey Wilson.[106]

During his directorship, Mitchell saw a locked box of confidential papers in the RLI office dealing with Wilson's resignation, but he did not open it.[107]

In addition, the early experiences Gluckman and Wilson suffered may have contributed to a political silencing that affected the subsequent work of the RLI. The Marxist strand in the RLI approach, including Gluckman's materialism and Wilson's and Gluckman's dialectical understanding of social processes, may have been less overtly expressed because of the political context surrounding the RLI's development: prewar anticommunism, wartime ambivalence toward the Soviet Union, and subsequent Cold War purges of left-wing thinkers in union, government, and academic circles that went on in

the late 1940s and throughout the 1950s. The tendency to see anthropologists such as Wilson as potentially dangerous outside agita-
tors and the colonial government's response to Gluckman's early
lack of discretion about his political views would be reinforced later
by the growing McCarthyism of the 1950s, which made itself felt
both in Britain and in its colonies. Use of technologies of surveillance
increased dramatically in this period, both in the metropole and the
colonies. The South African academic community, in particular, suffered under political bannings and restrictions on fieldwork that
stemmed from apartheid policies that were often justified in terms of
anticommunism. Gluckman maintained contact with that community and helped some of its members to establish themselves at the
RLI and at Manchester. Thus he would have been in touch with the
concerns of academics there and may have shared in their increasing caution and preference for clandestine activity in response to
repression.

Ultimately Gluckman's absorption into the British academic establishment after he left the RLI may only partly explain his failure to
develop the Marxist aspects of his work.[108] Given the general atmosphere in the 1950s and the conservatism of the higher levels of the
academic hierarchy in Britain, this aspect of his work would have
been actively discouraged and compromises demanded as the price
for any advancement in his career. As it was, Gluckman's activism
did lead to sanctions of various kinds. Because of his involvement in
the Movement for Colonial Freedom, the colonial government prevented him from returning to his fieldsite in Northern Rhodesia until
after Independence, nor was he allowed to go to Papua New Guinea
(then under Australian rule) while staying at the Australian National
University as a visiting fellow. And it is also possible that his and his
wife's earlier membership in the Communist Party may have preju-
diced his chances for an academic post in the United States.[109]

4

The Laboratory in the Field

The second field generation at the RLI set the standard for later RLI teams with its cohesiveness and coordination of research. This team established the distinctive work culture of the RLI during the years from 1946 to 1949 when they were together during preparatory study in Cape Town, during their fieldwork in Northern Rhodesia, and during writing-up periods in Oxford. Teamwork in anthropology did not come easily, however, and the coordinated, comparative nature of RLI research must be seen relative to the dominant image of anthropology as an individualistic endeavor. This chapter will show how the RLI team became a team and how its own network of relationships — social, intellectual, and political — was created and maintained in the field, when members of the group were often far apart and focused on their specific research problems.

Gluckman recruited this team and became the fieldwork supervisor for those who were working for doctorates, as well as for the additional RLI-associated researchers with Colonial Development and Beit fellowships. The group included Max G. Marwick (Colonial Development Fellow); Elizabeth Colson, who had considerable previous field experience; John A. Barnes; J. Clyde Mitchell; the economist Phyllis Deane (Colonial Development Fellow); and J. F. (Hans) Holleman (Beit Fellow), who had previous field experience.[1] New research assistants, interpreters, and clerks in the field included M. B. Lukhero, who worked briefly for Marwick and extensively for Barnes; Benjamin Shipopa (Colson); Rafael Almakio Mvula (clerk-interpreter for Marwick; Marwick employed his wife Joan for most of the research assistant work); Dyson Dadirayi Mahaci (Holleman's interpreter and assistant); and Rajabu Kumpulula (Mitchell's clerk and main informant during his second field tour during this period).

All of the anthropologists except Colson and Holleman got their first taste of fieldwork in the Lamba field training session organized by Gluckman, which included visits by the agricultural officers Trapnell, Peters, and Allan. The anthropologists also gathered for a conference in Livingstone; Colson was visited in the field by Gluckman, and several of the others visited each other's sites and Gluckman's field site. Lukhero and Barnes visited Mitchell in Nyasaland. The economist Phyllis Deane fostered the cohesiveness of this group, for she visited nearly all their fieldsites and had their help in collecting budget data in African villages. Sianga, Suu, Albert Kafunya, and David Kalimosho Maila worked for Gluckman in his Lozi field site or at the headquarters in Livingstone. Colonial administrators and technical officers remained a significant part of Gluckman's social and intellectual network in Livingstone, while still others became part of each researcher's network in the field. Clark continued to direct the Museum, which separated from the Institute in 1946.[2]

"Human Laboratory Across the Zambesi"

The RLI team's cohesiveness derived partly from Gluckman's vision of Central Africa, and Northern Rhodesia in particular, as a laboratory for sociological inquiries relevant to all human societies in southern Africa. Although this vision developed out of his opposition to racial segregation, it was also rooted in the cultural and economic forces that had shaped southern African history. This history had been marked by large-scale migrations of African and European groups northward, some to Northern Rhodesia, where representatives of many ethnic groups rooted in South Africa settled, including the Dutch Afrikaners, the Nguni, and the Tswana. Economic forces in the twentieth century kept migrants from these and other groups in constant flow between north and south. For example, from the 1920s European workers migrated from South Africa to work in Northern Rhodesia's mines and developing industries, just as Northern Rhodesian and Nyasaland Africans had migrated south since the turn of the century, forced by taxation to seek work in South Africa's mines and industries.

Two people who indirectly shaped the RLI through their influence on Gluckman fit this pattern: Clements Kadalie and Roy Welensky. A Nyasaland African, Kadalie migrated to South Africa for work and in 1919 founded the Industrial and Commercial Workers Union (ICU), a multiracial urban and rural union that ignited fears of revolution in the 1920s.[3] Gluckman's father, the prominent Johannesburg lawyer Emanuel Gluckman, defended Kadalie in court.[4] Roy Welensky, on the other hand, came from a Southern Rhodesian Jewish family and migrated to Northern Rhodesia to become head of the railway workers union in 1933. He and Gluckman became close friends while Gluckman stayed in Livingstone, their shared socialist sympathies outweighing their differences on the issue of segregation. Unlike Kadalie's union activism, Welensky's led to a political career carried forward on the postwar wave of white settler demands for autonomy, and he eventually became a prime minister of the Federation of Rhodesia and Nyasaland.

The divergent biographies of these two men say a great deal about the forces that shaped the RLI's research goals in the postwar years. Kadalie's multiracial union may have failed in the 1930s, but World War Two gave hope to Africans, some white liberals, and liberal industrialists throughout southern Africa that the industrial — if not the social — color bar would have to be eased to meet the demands of war and the acceleration of development that was expected to follow the peace. In South Africa these hopes would be destroyed by the Afrikaner Nationalists' rise to power in 1948, but in Northern Rhodesia change did come, though slowly.

During the war years and the years immediately after, however, the direction that events would take in southern Africa was far from certain, and this context inspired Gluckman's approach to the study of social change. He viewed colonial central Africa as a single interdependent society of Africans and Europeans and focused on the universal factors shaping this rapidly changing social situation, such as responses to industrial work and urbanization, rather than on the cultural differences that separated blacks and whites.

The political context for this approach reflected the late interwar questions that faced South African society. The young Max Gluckman did fieldwork in Zululand in 1936–38, during the "high-water point of Hertzog's segregationist 'solution of the Native Problem',"[5] a time when anthropologists' interest in the *differences* between African and European culture could easily be construed as supporting segregation.[6] The majority of English-speaking South African anthropologists followed Malinowski's culture contact theory, which emphasized the importance of these differences for analyzing the problems Africans encountered when they entered the supposedly separate sphere of European industrial and urban culture.[7] Gluckman instead preferred the ideas of the historian William Macmillan, who held that South Africa was a single society, racially diverse but economically and socially interdependent.[8] Macmillan was "bitterly contemptuous" of the anthropologists' interest in cultural difference, and his critique was taken to heart by the South African anthropologist Isaac Schapera, a student of Malinowski.[9] Gluckman followed Schapera in his belief that anthropologists must study colonial society as a racially mixed whole.[10] And he went further in insisting that universals such as the experience of industrial work deserved greater attention, a belief he emphasized in his later statement that an African miner is a miner, an African townsman is a townsman, implying that they should be studied primarily as such.[11] The RLI's enormous contribution to the sociology of work would develop from this goal.

The result of Gluckman's early fieldwork in Zululand was an article published in *Bantu Studies*, "The Analysis of a Social Situation in Modern Zululand."[12] The article dealt with a contemporary situation—the opening of a new bridge in Zululand. In it he described Africans and Europeans in various roles, including himself, the anthropologist, among them. The article took the form of descriptive sections followed by analytical sections, and in both its form and content provided a template for later RLI work. Gluckman's acute perception of the different modern expressions of ethnicity influenced Epstein's and Mitchell's later interpretations of urban ethnicity on the Copperbelt. When they arrived in 1946, all the new RLI researchers familiarized themselves with Gluckman's article — which was popularly known as "The Bridge" — and they thoroughly discussed its implications. As one researcher remarked, it was "The Bridge, the Bridge, all the time the first few years."[13]

The Bridge expresssed Macmillan's and Schapera's approach in terms of its theory of society. But Gluckman also saw Northern Rhodesia as a laboratory for developing a social-scientific critique of trends emerging and spreading from South Africa.[14] He directed this critique at both professional and lay audiences, the former through published criticism of Malinowski's culture contact approach, which he believed encouraged South African segregationism.[15] The lay public he attempted to educate through articles in the South African magazine *Libertas*.[16] In one article, "Human Laboratory Across the Zambesi," he emphasized that the Europeans, Indians, and Africans who lived in southern Africa were "all members of a single community." He used a map of Northern Rhodesia, with arrows showing the flow of laborers from rural areas to the Copperbelt and the Rand, to impress upon the reader the reality of the forces of urbanization and migration that united the region.

Throughout the article Gluckman pointed out features of the "laboratory" that allowed good comparative research on issues of importance in South Africa as well as in the rest of the region, including rural/urban connections and the problems of industrialization and urbanization.[17] The notion of social "problems" that Gluckman held differed significantly from the problems associated with so-called African acculturation, as studied by those who endorsed the culture contact approach. Although his and the RLI's approach to change was not entirely free of concern for the cultural or psychological losses experienced by central Africans who moved to towns and industrial work, their approach stressed more strongly the African potential for healthy adaptation to such changes, the gains to be had from urban life and work, and the attractions that drew Africans to them. Such an approach shared roots with the approach of members of the South African Institute of Race Relations who stressed in the postwar period that the benefits of modernity should be available to all races.[18]

Gluckman also intended to use Northern Rhodesia as a laboratory for comparative research to test the theories of particular anthropological colleagues or rivals. He chose sites for the RLI team partly based on a desire to fill in the blank spaces on the ethnographic map of Northern Rhodesia. Just as important, however, was his determination to check the conclusions of earlier anthropologists, as in the case of his placement of Barnes with the Ngoni to test Margaret Read's ideas[19] or his theory of the relationship between divorce and matrilineality, which was to be tested in the work of the entire team.[20] In this he followed a path suggested by Audrey Richards for understanding the effects of labor migration, as discussed with the members of the first team during an early fieldwork conference at the RLI:

> . . . we selected as our first subject for comparative analysis the relation between kinship and local systems. The importance of this is indicated by a quotation from Dr. Richards' paper on Bemba Marriage and Modern Economic Conditions (RLI Paper, 1940): "We have as yet few accounts of the social effects of migratory labour sufficiently detailed for long-time policies of Native rehabilitation to be based on them. The general similarity of the problems in these different African territories has, I think, blinded us to one important point: viz. that the reactions of the different Native tribes to this particular form of industrialisation are not identical. One type of family structure seems to collapse more quickly than another under urban conditions or in the manless countryside of the reserve . . ."[21]

Gluckman also chose research sites for the individual anthropologists based on the advice of colonial government officials about the places that, in their estimation, would be the most useful to investigate. Contrasting economic and social factors led to his selection of the Ngoni of Eastern Province, the Plateau Tonga of Southern Province, the Lunda of Luapula Province, the Yao of Nyasaland's Southern Province, and the Hera, a Shona-speaking society in northeastern Mashonaland Province of Southern Rhodesia. These groups exhibited high or low labor migration rates, which he hoped to relate to different patterns of marriage and family organization. The economic and social pattern of the entire region would then be analyzed in a macro-study, with the aid of a demographer and an economist. This final part of the plan could not be followed through because funding for the demographer could not be found and the Institute was only able to hire an economist in 1948,[22] one who failed to complete work on the labor migration aspect of the study.

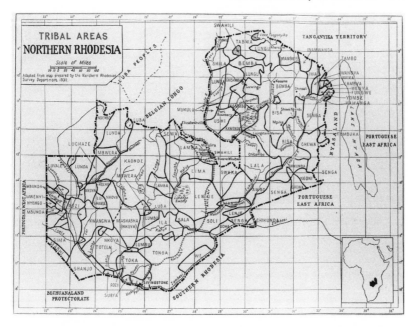

Tribal map of Northern Rhodesia, from Audrey Richards's *Land, Labour and Diet in Northern Rhodesia* published in 1939. (Reproduced by kind permission of the International African Institute, London.)

Major groups already covered by professional studies were not to be included; for example, Gluckman had already done research on the Lozi of the Barotseland Protectorate, a group that in its strong hierarchical government resembled the Zulu he had previously studied, and whose protectorate status presented unusual problems for the colonial administration's attempts at reform. These people also interested Gluckman because of their labor migration to the Rand gold mines of South Africa, which he visited briefly to interview Lozi workers, though he did not carry out extensive research on Lozi urban industrial experiences. And a fine study of the Bemba, useful for the issues of family organization and labor migration, already existed, produced by Audrey Richards in the 1930s. Nevertheless, Richards' work and Gluckman's Lozi study constantly figured in the team's thinking about their major sociological questions.

The government had a particular interest in the Tonga of the plateau along the line of rail between Livingstone and Lusaka. Here

Gluckman and the agricultural officers had carried out a preliminary survey of their agricultural practices and rules of land tenure (discussed in chapter 3). Despite their loss of the land closest to the line of rail to white farmers, these people had resisted labor migration and developed a thriving agricultural economy, adopting the plow with little stimulation from missionaries or government. Colson took on this research site despite her greater interest in the study of fishing economies (from her prior research on a fishing community of Native Americans on the American northwest coast). The government would not countenance a female researcher in the primary fishing area of the colony — the region of the Luapula River which bordered on the Belgian Congo — because it considered this area to be dangerous because of cross-border smuggling activities. Although selected as one of the most urgent sites for study, the Luapula had to wait until the RLI appointed Ian Cunnison at the end of 1947.

Barnes went to the Ngoni area of the country's Eastern Province.[23] Gluckman was interested in that area because he wanted to compare the Ngoni of Northern Rhodesia with those previously studied by Margaret Read in Nyasaland. Mitchell studied the Yao of Nyasaland, partly because of their interesting combination of Muslim religious belief with matrilineality.[24] The government of Nyasaland, like those of Tanganyika and Southern Rhodesia, had also been persuaded to give the Institute funding at its inception, on the argument that it would be a regional research center, and, thus, it was important to do some work outside Northern Rhodesia. Personal reasons also motivated the choice of the particular place: Mitchell's wife and new baby would later join him, and, Mitchell was told, this site had better medical services than the other possibilities, though they were still eighty miles distant.[25]

The Beit Fellow, Hans Holleman, worked on a Shona group called the Hera, in Southern Rhodesia. After clashing with Gluckman over the aims of this study, Holleman was allowed to continue on his own course. This involved doing a basic ethnography without the emphasis on labor migration or other common themes pursued by the RLI team. According to Mitchell, Holleman had a completely different approach to anthropology based on training at Stellenbosch

under P. J. Schoeman and the famous *volkekundige* Van Warmelo —
a training that emphasized "the beauty of African culture. [That
was] completely different from Max — so he was always the odd man
out at the Institute" (see chapter 3).[26] The Colonial Research Fellow
Max Marwick had intended to do a comparative study of Ngoni
(patrilineal) and Chewa (matrilineal) groups in Northern Rhodesia,
basing his choice on Read's mistaken assumption that both spoke the
same dialect, so that he wouldn't have to learn two languages for the
comparative work. After realizing the two groups spoke different
languages, he shifted to doing research on the Northern Rhodesian
Chewa alone.[27] He studied Chewa sorcery beliefs from a social psychology perspective, based on his training in that subject at the Natal
University College. Unlike Holleman, however, he converted to the
RLI approach, becoming more and more a social anthropologist in
his analysis and writing.[28]

Two research assistants who would maintain a long-term relationship with the RLI, M. B. Lukhero and Davidson Sianga, shifted their
research work during this period. Sianga worked for Gluckman in
Livingstone initially, but was seconded to work for D. U. Peters on a
study of agriculture in Serenje District, somewhat east of the Copperbelt.[29] Lukhero began his first work for the RLI as Marwick's assistant for the brief period the anthropologist studied the Ngoni,
chosen by the paramount chief as the most appropriate assistant.
When the Marwicks moved to the Chewa area near Katete and John
Barnes began his study of the Ngoni area, Lukhero became Barnes's
assistant.[30]

In the case of the urban research, which would not take place until
after he left the RLI, Gluckman hoped to question Godfrey Wilson's
ideas about detribalization and intended the research to undermine
the centrality of the use of that concept by administrators trying to
understand African behavior in the towns.[31] The idea of detribalization, like acculturation, carried assumptions about the cultural
losses that would be suffered by Africans who moved to town and
took up industrial work.[32] In response to Gluckman's interest, the
later urban research done by Mitchell and Epstein would pay close
attention to the nature of ethnicity in the towns and to any changes

that had taken place in response to the increasingly stable residence of urban Africans. Much of that work also took note not only of loss, but also of the optimism with which many Africans approached urban life and their delight in the creation of new social patterns and activities.[33]

Gluckman's use of the term "laboratory" when referring to the anthropological field was not unusual at the time, but reflected a widespread phenomenon in the social sciences of borrowing terms from the more established physical and biological sciences in order to gain legitimacy and prestige. For the director, this meant more than the transfer of a metaphor: Governor Hubert Young had intended the Institute to sponsor medical, geological, and other types of scientific research, as well as social anthropology, and in the early days when it seemed likely that medical scientists might work at the RLI, Gluckman hoped for interdisciplinary cross-fertilization. He also justified the construction of new Institute buildings in the same terms used for justifying biological research stations, which were outposts of metropolitan universities — and in a mailing for an impending trustees meeting he emphasized the comparison by enclosing an article by Dr. Frans Verdoorn in *Nature* No. 4007, 17 August 1946 that stressed the biological science model.[34]

At the RLI, the concept of the field laboratory helped to structure the research and standardize the researchers' individual approaches (though each produced a unique monograph and most initiated new developments in theory). In addition to structuring the research, the idea of a shared laboratory aided the emergence of a shared work culture among the team members, not unlike the unique styles that develop in physics and biology laboratories, based on practices specific to each laboratory and passed on as much through apprenticeship as through explicit textbook knowledge or classroom training.[35]

The next two sections of this chapter describe how this process worked in the case of the first RLI team. Surprisingly, the so-called functionalist paradigm — that many subsequent anthropologists have seen as characterizing colonial anthropology and as supplying a strong central core of assumptions — did not seem to these anthropologists at the time to provide the coherence of theory and uniformity of training necessary to guide the comparative research for which the RLI strove. Indeed, the RLI team associated functionalism mainly with Malinowski and his pupils and not with their own approach. Colson, Mitchell, and Marwick had not been trained in functionalism, and Barnes had had little exposure to it at Cambridge. Moreover, Gluckman shared Evans-Pritchard's mistrust of Malinowski.[36] I will argue that shared experiences of apprenticeship and the sharing of a social and intellectual network in the field carried more weight for the RLI's approach than any overarching paradigm that, in retrospect, may have appeared to have existed.

Introduction to the Social Situation in Southern Africa

Even before they arrived in central Africa, the RLI research officers began their education into the ethnography and conditions under which they would work. In letters to the officers who were in England, Gluckman advised on which people to meet, as well as on appropriate reading and appropriate shopping for equipment that could not be supplied in Northern Rhodesia. For example, he advised Barnes that he must meet with Margaret Read, Edwin Smith (a missionary who, with the administrator A. Dale, had produced an ethnography of the Ila that Gluckman judged as close to a professional standard[37]), Evans-Pritchard, Radcliffe-Brown, Audrey Richards, and Raymond Firth (all underlined by Gluckman to emphasize their importance), as well as with Phyllis Deane, E. G. Robinson, Lord Hailey, and sympathetic Colonial Office people like Andrew Cohen. The director also advised Barnes to "work hard" at reading Hailey's *African Survey*[38] and listed what the RLI supplied to researchers: good field notebooks, an African carpenter to make touring boxes for food and kitchen utensils, a "good tent and a bell tent for your servants and interpreter; camp chairs and tables; bath; one stretcher (not for your wife); and if we can get it, at least one power lamp. . . . We also provide a typewriter — again, if we can get it." Because of the postwar shortages in England, he felt that one could buy the necessary clothing as easily in Africa as in Britain.[39] One must not play down the importance of this advice on equipment: the material culture of fieldwork shaped the data that anthropologists collected as meaningfully as did the theories they brought to bear on their experiences. (See the discussion in chapter 8 of the meaning of books and typewriters, and of "being written.")

When Barnes, Mitchell, and Max and Joan Marwick arrived in Northern Rhodesia early in 1946, Gluckman took them for a field-training session in a resettlement area occupied by members of the Lamba people, a group who had lost their best land to the white mining towns of Northern Rhodesia's Copperbelt. He chose the site in accordance with his design for the overall research project: the Lamba area allowed for study of colonial resettlement practices and issues of land tenure, agricultural improvement, local government, and the consequences of changes in settlement on kinship structure. The Lamba people also represented a type of adaptation to industrial society different from that studied by Audrey Richards, who previously examined the consequences of labor migration to the mines for a more distant group, the Bemba. Despite living nearby, Lambas rarely worked in the mines themselves but instead had developed local agricultural production and trade to take advantage of the urban market.[40]

Gluckman and the newly arrived researchers worked together as a group for a few days, visited by the government agricultural officer, David U. Peters, the government ecologist, Colin Trapnell, and the assistant director of agriculture, William Allan. The team was assisted by Davidson Sianga, who had worked with Gluckman on previous studies. It was during this research that the group first discussed what would become the concept of "interhierarchical roles," focusing on the pressures that characterized the position of the village headman as intermediary between the colonial administration and Africans governed under the native administration.[41] They also designed a special form for recording genealogical and other information that could be used by all members of the group. Barnes used the material from this study for his first published article, written later in Cape Town under Schapera's supervision, on the genealogi-

The Laboratory in the Field 87

cal method.[42] While there, he and Mitchell also analyzed the Lamba material and wrote a report.[43]

The agricultural officers showed the researchers how to interpret signs of previous cultivation in fallow land and taught them other practices of reading the landscape that would be helpful in their future land tenure inquiries and mapping of village gardens. "Hobnobbing with the agriculturists was a very valuable experience," Mitchell observed. Trapnell was an expert on the *chitemene* system (a form of agriculture that involves the burning of tree branches to raise the fertility of the soil and which requires long periods of fallow) and showed them how to evaluate the regrowth coming out of the side of cut-off trees to judge the length of time since the last cultivation.[44] By including agricultural officers in the group, Gluckman may have intended to reproduce for his new researchers the kind of teamwork he had experienced in the earlier government survey of the Tonga, which had given him high expectations for future collaboration between anthopologists and government technical officers.[45] And after the Lamba field visit, the team went on to visit the same Tonga area in Mazabuka District where Gluckman had worked, to make general observations for a few days. Social anthropologists as conceived by Gluckman in this period clearly shared the technical officers' professional interest in the problems associated with development. A sample of the reading RLI officers did during this period reveals that they also explored this theme in the anthropological literature while in the field.[46]

Elizabeth Colson joined the RLI team in Cape Town after they arrived there from the Lamba field training session. Holleman had already started fieldwork in Southern Rhodesia and didn't participate in all of the South African study sessions,[47] though he did arrange a visit for the team to the University of Stellenbosch, where his father had been given a professorship.[48] Gluckman arranged the study sessions at the University of Cape Town (UCT) to familiarize the new researchers with African linguistics and sociology, taught through intensive courses given by Schapera and the linguist G. P. Lestrade. Although no urban research was planned for the first team, their training included discussion of the city as a field site. Schapera focused particularly on field methods for rural research and, according to Barnes, gave them a system for classifying subjects which Barnes used all the time — a system "as theoretically unpretentious as possible." Barnes also wrote his genealogy paper for Schapera as part of the work for his course in field methods.[49]

Sites and Scholars

Equally important to this intellectual work was a tour Gluckman suggested of sociologically significant sites, as well as introductions to South African scholars. Because Colson was the most senior, she arranged these introductions using a list the director sent from Northern Rhodesia: "Dr Sonnabend (with whom you will standardise the collection of vital data.), Prof. Marais (Historian), Prof. Gray, Dr Wulf Sachs, Mrs Hoernlé, Brian Farrell, Hilda Kuper, Ellen Hellman, Dr. Biesheuvel, Mr. Rheinallt Jones (s.a.i.r.r.), Prof. Doke, Julius Lewin, Dr. J. N. Reedman, Prof. Macrone, M. D. W. Jeffries (No good but courtesy call), Mr. Glynn Thomas, Mr. Freer (Librarian)."[50]

Many of these scholars were personal friends of Gluckman, as was, for example, the psychiatrist Wulf Sachs, who visited him in Northern Rhodesia; Winifred Hoernlé, who had been his first teacher of social anthropology; and Kuper and Hellmann, who had been students during Gluckman's time there.[51] J. S. Marais was at Wits in History; John Gray was the head of the department of Social Studies and a key figure in social work and community health; I. D. MacCrone and Simon Biesheuvel were in Psychology; Julius Lewin in African Administration; Brian Farrell taught political philosophy and shortly left for a distinguished career at Oxford; Rheinallt Jones was a leading figure in the study of race relations (as was Hoernlé); Clement Doke was professor of Bantu Languages; John Reedman was in Economics; and Glyn Thomas was registrar of the university. Formerly a British colonial administrator in Nigeria, M. D. W. Jeffries had replaced Hilda Kuper as senior lecturer in Social Anthropology at Wits and was much disliked because he changed the focus of the department from the structural-functionalist approach of Radcliffe-Brown to the diffusionist approach followed by some anthropologists in the 1910s and 20s, considered outdated by others in the department at Wits.[52]

A number of other scholars at UCT and Wits participated in the first team's introduction to the South African situation. H. J. Simons, who had done one of the first systematic urban studies in Africa, contributed lectures and took them to see his research site, Langa, the oldest African urban area in Cape Town.[53] Simons published very little because his political involvement with African activists in Langa left no time for writing. Nevertheless, his research focused on topics directly relevant to the RLI's interests, and he and Gluckman shared a left-wing political analysis of the South African situation. Indeed, he called his approach "political sociology," and his controversial openness about the political aspects of sociological work had gotten him thrown out of UCT in 1945.[54] Some members of the RLI team also visited the South African Native College at Fort Hare and met with Monica Wilson, who lectured there, to discuss her fieldwork in Pondoland, the subject of her first book (mentioned in chapter 3 and discussed below).[55]

South Africa possessed a well-established and dynamic intellectual community with its own questions, questions that were relevant to research in any multiracial society.[56] English-speaking South African scholars had provided the context that initially shaped Gluckman's approach to anthropology, as well as his political views. During the interwar period that community had mounted an interdisciplinary attack on South African physical anthropology and its racially determinist elements. Speaking for the social anthropological approach, Schapera had criticized the link physical anthropologists made between race and culture, and the philosopher R. F. A. Hoernlé criticized the concept of "the primitive" and its application to "child-races," a term which implied the superiority of Europeans.[57] The linguist Lestrade, on the other hand, maintained conservative ideas about languages and their connection to race, though he was generally recognized as the leading scholar of African languages. The African Languages chair at UCT had been disestablished by Radcliffe-

Brown because of the conservative nature of linguistic research in South Africa, but reestablished for Lestrade, whose research was later used by the apartheid government to justify separate "Bantu Education."[58]

The department of Bantu Studies at Wits, in particular, reflected the context that had shaped Gluckman's views during his time as an undergraduate there. That department had embraced structural-functionalism after the appointment of Radcliffe-Brown to the chair of Social Anthropology at UCT in 1921. Subsequently that approach was promoted in South Africa by Winifred Hoernlé, who had first studied philosophy at UCT (starting in 1903 while it was still called the South African College) and later studied anthropology and experimental psychology under Haddon and Rivers at Cambridge, Wundt and Kulpe at Leipzig and Bonn, and Durkheim at the Sorbonne.[59] She also mixed with American anthropologists in Cambridge, Massachusetts, while there when her husband was at Harvard.[60] She became Lecturer in Ethnology at Wits in 1923 and began her work with Radcliffe-Brown, whom she had met earlier in Cambridge, England. This joint project would have become a comparative study of African social institutions in southern Africa, if Radcliffe-Brown had not left for the chair of social anthropology at Sydney in 1926.[61]

Hoernlé also promoted Malinowski's approach to fieldwork. Although she took a personal interest in the effects of colonialism on the Nama people she studied during her field expeditions from 1912 to 1923, her published studies focused on reconstructing their pre-colonial society rather than on constructing a theory of change.[62] Nevertheless, students influenced by her interpretation of structural-functionalism focused their research on the contemporary problems of South Africa[63] and took social change as an object of study. Hoernlé also saw public service as an important role for the social anthropologist and resigned from her senior lectureship at Wits in 1938 to pursue a more socially activist career. By the end of World War Two she had become a central figure in that "bastion of liberal thought," the South African Institute of Race Relations.[64]

The first RLI team (and most members of subsequent teams) met with Hoernlé and a number of those who had been at Wits under her supervision when Gluckman studied there, including Ellen Hellmann, Eileen Krige, and Hilda Kuper. Hellmann's research on an African "slumyard" in Johannesburg drew their special attention. She had pointed out the postwar influx of Africans to the city and discussed their increasingly permanent urbanization and its consequences.[65] The RLI team also met with Julius Lewin, the lecturer in Native Law and Administration at Wits, who as a Fabian socialist often critiqued the political stance of the liberals who dominated the university.[66]

The sites they visited illustrated the social processes they would examine in Northern Rhodesia. After discussions with Monica Wilson, some members of the team visited her former field site in Pondoland and met the district officer, the owner of the local trading post, and several Africans who held positions in the native authority.[67] Wilson's book, *Reaction to Conquest*, published in 1936, primarily focused on the rural side of Pondo life but had included one of the first attempts to deal with the urban experiences of an African people.[68] While at Wits the team toured the nearby African areas of Orlando and Sophiatown, the latter a vibrant multiethnic, multiracial suburb that would be demolished under later apartheid policy. They descended into a gold mine to examine miners' working conditions, a visit the researchers found particularly useful because of its timing: "The African strike coincided with our visit, so that all the racial attitudes that one could ask for were on display," John Barnes commented.[69]

When they began their own fieldwork, RLI researchers would soon find all the racial attitudes one could ask for on display in Northern Rhodesia, both among the Africans and the Europeans they intended to study there.

Making the Field

In many ways, the field for anthropological research in Northern Rhodesia had to be made — constructed out of materials provided by prior researchers, as well as routes of access to places and people that others had developed first. Administrators and missionaries were responsible for most of these prior patterns of access to and acquisition of knowledge, but explorers, prospectors, and traders had also affected the variable ways that Africans responded to anthropologists in the field, dependant on what their experiences of these different types of Europeans had been. The RLI anthropologists used these earlier pathways into the field — receiving help and advice from administrators, missionaries, and settlers — but they also distanced themselves from them in the attempt to gain access to information that Africans would not share with these groups. The success of this distancing crucially depended on the help of their research assistants, or "clerk-interpreters," as they were usually called at the time. These men mediated the anthropologists' initial exposure to the societies they studied, through their translation work, introductions to potential informants, smoothing of the way for the researchers' questions, and general management of the researchers' interactions with local people.[70]

One important "rule" for fieldwork, Gluckman advised Mitchell, was not to take one's wife, for this could lead the researcher to live in a "cultural bubble" avoiding contact with the local society.[71] Mitchell, Marwick, Holleman, and Barnes, however, all took their wives to the field. Ultimately, a far more important cultural bubble affected the work of the RLI researchers — one that was deliberately created by the people they studied. Here, the research assistants worked in two ways, interpreting for anthropologists but at the same time protecting the local society and the interests of some of its members. These clerk-interpreters usually came to the anthropologist through local channels of power rather than through the researcher's choosing. African royals or mission-educated elites could play the chief role in their choosing (or act as the interpreters themselves), or the colonial administration could attempt to control the researcher through a hand-picked interpreter.

Gluckman, for example, worked with members of the Lozi royal family, as well as commoners, for his research. Mitchell found his contact with informants seriously compromised during his first field tour because of the length of time he took to rid himself of an interpreter picked by the government, who made it difficult for Mitchell to allay suspicion of his motives — and whose incompetence in collecting data led to angry outbursts in Mitchell's letters to other RLI researchers in the early days of his fieldwork.[72] Association with the government placed an anthropologist on the wrong side of what Gluckman had called the dominant social cleavage, in his Zululand work. As Barnes observed of his own fieldsite: "I can see more cleavages than ties here, and so far it appears that the whole social order is held together only by its common opposition to the Boma, 'the men with small hands.' "[73] Mitchell felt that the main social cleavage was between the Yao and himself until his wife, Edna, arrived with their new baby and broke the ice with Yao women.[74] And the Marwicks were "very depressed initially": "We could see the airliners flying overhead on their way between Jo'burg and Nairobi and felt stuck."[75]

All of the researchers complained about the difficulty in early fieldwork of overcoming the boredom of Africans weary of answering questions, as well as their own experience of tedium and confusion in the early stages of language learning. Some of the locals' boredom with questioning may have been intended to deflect attention from sensitive topics. In her second tour, Colson found that in a village where she had collected demographic data during the first tour, "the people agree quite cheerfully that they lied last year—not all of them, but enough so that the figures weren't at all reliable." She went on to suggest writing a paper on the problems of the reliability of the kind of "snap censuses" that the RLI researchers made—"as Benjamin says wisely, 'If we did this again next year, they might remember some more children they hid this [year].' "[76] Even a sympathetic assistant, like Colson's assistant, Benjamin Shipopa, could not guarantee complete cooperation in an environment where traditions of data collection by colonial administrators were well known to work against local interests. Such was also the case with Mitchell's investigations into sorcery practices, and he was extremely gratified during his second tour when people began to discuss the matter with him and revealed that practices they had earlier described to him as long dead still went on despite decades of mission and government attempts at eradication.[77]

Anthropologists were not, however, naive victims of local manip-

Mitchell's wife, Edna, with their baby, Donald, visited by Yao
women with their babies, in Mitchell's fieldsite in the Yao area
of Nyasaland. (Photo from J. Clyde Mitchell's private collection.
Reproduced by permission of Donald Mitchell.)

ulation. Athough they tried to subvert these defenses in order to get
at protected areas of local knowledge, they also cooperated with
local ways of managing their behavior and activity. In all cases the
relationship between the researcher, the assistants, and the informants had to some degree an antagonistic character, but local people
were aware that anthropologists also represented a useful resource
for battles with other colonial actors, such as the white administration.[78] Their mapping of gardens and interest in land tenure and
property rights could be controversial and was often resisted, as was
also the case with their inquiries into witchcraft and sorcery prac-

tices. But these inquiries were also welcomed in cases where the work could be used to argue the local case against the administration's stand in a territorial dispute. Anthropologists could become allies and advocates in such struggles. Moreover, African societies did not present a united front to outsiders but consisted of groups and individuals with diverse and conflicting interests. While some might be unwilling to give information about certain aspects of local life, others might be happy to do so for any number of reasons, including their own interest in tradition, history, or politics.[79]

Researchers at the RLI usually explained what they were doing as "history" rather than "anthropology," because they felt that Africans understood what history was about.[80] This was not simply because they believed Africans had a nostalgic or proud sense of tribal identity, but because they recognized that Africans in general possessed a long and often unpleasant experience of the use of local history by the colonial administration to create tribes, allocate territory, decide the make-up of the native administration, and impose rigid laws where more fluid rules had formerly obtained. Depending on its results, anthropologists' work might or might not have been useful to particular factions in these disputes, but it nearly always undermined or complicated the colonial administration's views. In cases where local religious or political practices were at stake, anthropologists nearly always aimed their work to counter mission and government attempts to suppress certain activities. Marwick's study of the Chewa *nyau* secret societies and his confidential report to the Nyasaland government, for example, made a case for their continuation under the rubric of their educational function for boys — with Marwick denying government and mission fear that they perverted the young or provided a secret network for political subversion.[81]

That anthropologists' work functions locally in this way has been recognized by current researchers who have observed how their own work is used for the invention of tradition and the creation or regeneration of local identity. This work has produced a growing literature on the politics and preservation of local knowledge. More emphasis needs to be placed, however, on the *very local* character of practices of managing outsiders and the historical factors that influence the development of particular local defenses: much more than a general desire to preserve or enhance local identity is involved. To take one example, a distinctive feature of the early Northern Rhodesian scene was the prevalence of the geologist as explorer. Because of the speculation concerning mineral wealth that characterized the British South Africa Company's colonization of the region, geologists had figured among the earliest arrivals. They practiced a kind of predatory science similar to that practiced by the natural scientists who accompanied early imperial expeditions. In southern Africa the most notorious of these predatory geologists was Carl Wiese. Wiese played a role in the colonial wars that led to the conquest of the Ngoni people — by shuttling between the Ngoni court and the various European powers interested in their land — leaving the Ngoni with a permanent suspicion of the behavior of outsiders.

The Ngoni automatically applied the term *qupe* — spy — or *mwana wa Wiese* — child of Wiese — to any European whose purpose in visiting their territory was unknown or suspicious. When Barnes arrived in Ngoniland, they initially called him *qupe*, though his generous behavior and Lukhero's explanations brought an end to local suspicions relatively quickly in the area where he did most of his fieldwork.[82] Lukhero's connection to the paramount chief's family may also have aided Barnes's acceptance. And as Barnes recalled, giving a beer party and not wearing a hat like other Europeans also helped.[83] Nevertheless, Barnes suffered renewed suspicion each time he went to a new Ngoni area, as he frequently did on his second tour in 1948. (He thought the Tonga in Colson's field site to be more truly friendly in comparison to his Ngoni experiences.) In one of the Ngoni villages he visited, he found that even after meeting the headman and the "drinking population" and attending a church service and meal afterwards, people continued to be suspicious. As he described the scene in a letter to Mitchell: "One of the women said, 'Today we are all eating porridge together, and tomorrow our husbands will be in prison.' There was a delegation afterwards to see my interpreter — 'You are an African like ourselves, tell us what this man is really doing.' "[84]

The RLI researchers used a number of strategies to overcome the problems of suspicion and management of outsiders. Gluckman's advice to avoid staying in chiefs' villages may have stemmed from his own experiences of Zulu and Lozi societies, both of which had powerful royal families who effectively controlled outsiders.[85] But he did not object when Colson decided to live in a chief's village in her field site, for he understood that chiefship was very different in relatively egalitarian Tonga society.[86] And although he avoided living in the Lozi paramount chief's village during his own fieldwork, he himself made concessions to royal control by working with members of the royal family and promoting their interests with respect to the colonial government. These influences unavoidably affected his work.

Nevertheless, both he and the research officers found other ways of entering the societies they studied, ways that could allow them to get a larger view.[87] These strategies relied on two factors: the lengthy and multiple periods of time these anthropologists spent in the field and the movement that was prescribed by the RLI's goals for the research, which required that they spend a length of time in one village during their first tour and then use their second tour primarily to move from one area to another getting a sample of the range of village organizational patterns. The researchers often moved about during their first year, as well, to get a sense of the entire area or to do comparisons based on lengthy stays in a small number of villages that might have contrasting organizational patterns.[88] Returning to the field after being away for a writing-up period also proved a good strategy. According to the Marwicks, "Schapera's advice was good — leave the field and when you come back they'll greet you like a lost tribesman."[89]

The RLI researchers' ability to enter local society in multiple ways was also facilitated by research assistants who could enter local society through their own channels and carry out unsupervised work. Before leaving the field for the first writing-up period, Gluckman advised team members to train their interpreters to keep diaries of births, deaths, arguments, and other incidents in their absence,[90] something he had done with his own assistants in Barotseland. In response, Mitchell argued that such a plan would be impracticable because of the need to supervise the assistant.[91] As mentioned earlier, he had had problems getting a reliable interpreter/assistant, and his letters to Barnes reflected the frustration of his attempts to train one of his interpreters to collect adequate demographic data. Other researchers successfully trained their assistants to keep diaries of events and found them eager to contribute essays on various aspects of their societies. Thus, the researchers were enabled to extend their field of study beyond what they themselves could experience during fieldwork, through this vicarious form of participant-observation.

The overall comparative regional focus of the RLI helped to construct the field not only as a place of interaction with local people, but also as a locus of productive intellectual and social relationships with other professionals. This aspect of RLI teamwork developed out of a cluster of experiences made up primarily of sharing research objectives, observing each other's field practices, and creating communication networks. Gluckman consciously arranged some of these experiences; others took place because of outside factors or physical and social conditions in Northern Rhodesia. The director arranged the initial Lamba field training session and the visit to South Africa, he visited some of the researchers at their field sites, and he required their attendance at a conference where they gave preliminary accounts of their research and critiqued each other's methods.[92] He also set certain overall goals for each study, such as the requirement that all researchers carry out a study of land tenure as first priority, as well as collect demographic data[93] — a goal clearly related to the interests of government. Outside influences that structured the RLI's coordinated work included Lucy Mair's study of marriage and divorce, for which RLI researchers provided data from their own studies, and Phyllis Deane's national incomes study, during which she visited each researcher's field site and used their already established contacts to collect the data she needed.[94]

Conditions of fieldwork in Northern Rhodesia that further shaped communication among the members of the team included the postal service which allowed fairly regular correspondence and a rapidly improving transportation network. The range of transport included buses and trains in a few places. A few of the researchers bought surplus military vehicles, which, despite problems with postwar petrol rationing, made visiting each other in the field easier than would have been the case for anthropologists working in the interwar period.[95] The Institute's Colonial Development and Welfare grant and its considerable local funding also made it possible to enlarge the RLI library, which allowed the researchers as a group to keep in touch with developments in the literature. Recent sociology and anthropology books and journals circulated among the researchers while in the field, where some of them wrote reviews for the the RLI journal.

The journal, started by Gluckman in 1944, and other Institute publications initiated during Wilson's directorship promoted coordinated work among the researchers and meshed them more firmly into the small community of settlers, missionaries, and administrators who saw some value in the RLI's approach.[96] Early issues of the journal were dominated by administrator-ethnographers' work, partly because Gluckman could not call on professional anthropologists to contribute during the war years. Nevertheless, throughout its history the journal's authors and the authors of other RLI publications, such as the *Papers* and *Communications*, continued to reflect the types of people within Northern Rhodesia with whom the researchers could talk about their interests — a mix of administrators, missionaries, and a few scholars from the wider African and British academic networks, as well as some of the African research assistants and other educated Africans with an interest in social research. This mix of authors and the wide range and usually nontechnical nature of the articles reflected the director's goal for the Institute to produce cultural and social knowledge that was accessible to everyone in the colony, including Africans, and he made arrangements for a subsidy that would keep the price of the journal within reach of all.[97]

Examples of local involvement in the journal abound. The government education officer, J. M. Winterbottom (whose department shared accommodation with the RLI after the Institute offices were separated from the Museum) jointly edited the early issues of the journal with Gluckman. The 1947 issue, number 5 — the first to reflect the output of the new team — contained articles by L. Silberman, a former lecturer in sociology at Wits; J. H. R. Shaul,

Mitchell and family at their field camp, standing next to their used military truck, "Sonje Sue." Mitchell captioned the photo " 'Investigator's Tent in a Village,' Chiwalo, April 1947." (Photo from J. Clyde Mitchell's private collection. Reproduced by permission of Donald Mitchell.)

government statistician in Southern Rhodesia; Phyllis Deane; Max Marwick; John Barnes; and E. G. L. Nicholls, an African location superintendent in Lusaka.[98] The journal's mix of authors reflected not only intellectual relations but also the social relations carried on at the RLI's first headquarters at Livingstone.

The RLI Rapids

On arrival in Livingstone the researchers became familiar with the structure of relations that the director had developed around the RLI headquarters, meeting the community of settlers, missionaries, and government officers interested in the Institute's work. The headquarters was at first in the Museum building but later in 1946 it was moved into a ramshackle building with a large verandah, shared with officers of the government education department which had not yet moved to the new capital of Lusaka. The director had developed particularly good relations with the education officers and hired some of their African clerks and messengers for RLI work. The education officers and a few other administrators and technical officers stationed in Livingstone, along with a few local settlers and educated Africans, provided the audience for a series of evening talks that Gluckman had organized to promote the Institute's work.

For the ordinary people of Livingstone drawn to these talks, the attraction would have been rooted in an older understanding of anthropology as a collecting enterprise closely associated with archeology and material culture displays in museums. Indeed, the RLI had originated in a joint archeological/anthropological project envisioned by an earlier governor of Northern Rhodesia, Hubert Young, and used the premises of an already existing museum in Livingstone (see chapter 3). At the beginning of his tenure in 1934, Young had suggested that a museum and institute devoted to archeology, anthropology, and geology should be founded in David Livingstone's memory.[99] A *social* anthropology focus added to this project might have come from Audrey Richards' influence on the government, as well as from the governor's interest in the effects of industrialization on Africans, highlighted by the 1935 strike on the Copperbelt.[100] Young's plans for science in the colony ultimately resulted in a request for funding for a multidisciplinary institute, including the biological as well as the social sciences, and emphasizing the need for research into modern conditions, with a focus on the mining economy of the country. Founded as the Rhodes Livingstone Museum and Institute, the RLI never managed to bring in biological scientists but its early years produced a strong and long-standing archaeological tradition fostered by Desmond Clark, alongside the important social anthropology work.[101]

For local residents, the association with the displays in the museum colored their perception of the RLI long after the formal association between the two halves of the project was ended by Gluckman in 1946. Moreover, Gluckman's championing of social anthropology *included* museum-style collecting and displaying activities, and these would have represented the most visible local image of the RLI to the white public, as well as to the many Africans who collected for Gluckman or brought items to him once his interest became widely known. He purchased numerous objects, masks, and costumes and provided them to the RLI Museum and other museums in southern Africa and Britain; he arranged for traditional dance exhibitions in the museum grounds; and he wrote in the journal on the relevance of sociological research for museum displays.[102]

Despite the current image of structural-functionalist anthropologists as uninterested in material culture because of their differences with the earlier evolutionist and diffusionist approaches, the RLI team members paid close attention to material culture, wrote on it for the museum, and collected objects.[103] Marxist materialism could explain Gluckman's interest in the implements and products of economic activity, as expressed in his article "The Economy of the Central Barotse Plain."[104] Anthropologists at the time also felt that taking some account of material culture was essential when exploring previously unstudied societies, if one intended to provide a thorough account. At the Institute, this feeling was reinforced by the traditional approach to scientific work of the administrator-ethnographers most closely associated with the RLI, who observed, collected, and wrote about every social and natural object within the range of their district tours — including birds, plants, and rare antelope, as well as marriage customs and ritual objects.

Moreover, Gluckman believed that material culture formed a necessary component of social anthropology both as data and as a useful form of participation in the studied society, as evidenced in his requirement that the new research officers collect for the Museum according to the specifications laid out in the article on museum displays he wrote for an early RLI journal: "I wish to point out to you that the collection of exhibits of material culture will be of great assistance to you in your studies both as data and as a means of establishing contact with the people."[105] The curator, Desmond Clark, also initiated a series of material culture pamphlets published and sold at the Museum, to which the researchers contributed.

The aspect of these activities that was most important for the structuring of RLI research, however, was the material culture and data-collecting *network* Gluckman developed, which extended from Livingstone to his fieldsite near Mongu in Barotseland. A group of African assistants and collectors, referred to as "Max's boys," moved between Livingstone and Mongu finding and purchasing objects and providing the director with reports from the field. This practice enabled him to gather information and continue his research in spite of his administrative duties in Livingstone. All of the new RLI researchers would have seen this network in action from the Livingstone side, and some later visited Gluckman at his fieldsite near Mongu and saw the network functioning from that side. Some referred to this fieldsite—"Katongo Camp"—as "Gluckman's big establishment." In this term, admiration for an efficient and comfortable field camp was, for some, mixed with criticism of the size, affluence, and disturbance to local society implicit in such an establishment.[106] The director had personal financial resources and the status acquired from past fieldwork—and his age and position—necessary to make a place for himself in Lozi society that was quite different from that which the new researchers could make for themselves in the societies they studied. The Lozis accorded Gluckman a position similar to that of *induna*, a title given to senior African officials in the Lozi government, whereas the groups that the other researchers studied generally accorded them positions appropriate for younger members of society.[107]

Once established at their research sites, the RLI anthropologists frequently corresponded and occasionally visited each other's and the director's sites, further enhancing their development of similar research networks in the field. Gluckman described some of these field visits in his report on research in 1946–47:

> During the remaining period under review I saw Dr. Colson several times as her field is near Livingstone and she spent two weeks in Barotseland when I was working there. Mr. Barnes visited me there for a week while Dr. Colson was with me. Mr. Holleman worked in Johannesburg and Cape Town before returning to the field. Thus only Mr. Mitchell was completely isolated, especially as he saw Miss Deane and Mr. Marwick (Colonial Research Fellow) [only shortly] before the January conference. Miss Deane visited Dr. Colson, Mr. Barnes, and myself during April-May, and Mr. Barnes also met Mr. Marwick.[108]

These visits also provided the setting for a comparison of field practices that promoted comparability of the data the anthropologists collected, though they functioned just as importantly in establishing the group's social identity. Another contribution to the RLI team's self-consciousness of field practices was the research done by Phyllis Deane. Her economic approach, as she expressed it in an article for the journal describing her proposed research, shared some basic features with Gluckman's style of social anthropology. Her postwar Keynesian approach treated national economies as coherent wholes that could be understood and controlled through planned intervention, a view similar to that of the view of society accepted by functionalism in anthropology. The approach of both disciplines shared political roots in R. H. Tawney's earlier vision of the functional society.[109] As with other facets of the scientific planning movement, national income accounting had been transformed from idea to practice during the war and extended to the colonies in the postwar period.

Despite these very general commonalities, however, the two disciplines' intellectual differences in terms of theory may have been highlighted by Deane's presence in the field — at least for Gluckman, who thought that national incomes was an "arid topic," and for Barnes, who had already become "disenchanted with economics" in 1936 while contemplating a switch from mathematics to economics as an undergraduate at Cambridge.[110]

In addition to intellectual influences, a certain amount of standardization of the research environment had to be attained in order for each researcher's fieldsite to accommodate Deane's set of research questions. This was partly accomplished through each researcher's assistants working with her, translating her questions into the local language, and interpreting the answers. In general, both the researchers' and the assistants' self-consciousness about practices would have been enhanced by her presence, regardless of whether she commented on their practices. For example, Deane showed that Barnes's family's purchases of food and payment of wages represented the single largest source of cash in the local economy,[111] a factor in the anthropologist's impact on his or her studied community that was not often considered at the time. As far as individual research responses were concerned, however, the anthropologists did not necessarily become more interested in questions about the local economy. Barnes reflected, "I probably thought I could neglect inquiries into economic activities, since Phyllis dealt with them."[112] But Colson found that Deane's visit stimulated her to systematically collect data on Tonga crop sales, and she later sent Deane a list of all items she knew had been sold in her field area.[113] At the RLI conference that followed Deane's visits, the group agreed to continue to collect income data for her, as well as demographic data for the South African demographer Henry Sonnabend.[114] Later, Mitchell wrote an article about the methodological problems involved in collecting budgets.[115]

Although her contact with the RLI did not lead to standard budget-collecting activities or a standard intellectual approach that reflected the influence of economics as a discipline, Deane's visits to the fieldsites and her later continuing contact reinforced the group's cohesion. As Barnes recalled, "While we — Max, Elizabeth, Clyde and myself — were in Oxford during 1947–48, Phyllis was living in London. I remember her coming once to Oxford to read a seminar paper, and I think we all visited her in London on various occasions, during that year and later when Elizabeth, Clyde and I were in Manchester. These occasions may have had a positive effect in maintaining our identity as RLI people. . . ."[116]

Not only the motif of economics but also that of demography provided a cohesion-building theme for the group. Gluckman's concern to collect demographic information stimulated the researchers to produce a standard census form for its collection. They used guidelines provided in a seminar presented by the South African demographer Henry Sonnabend, whom Gluckman had invited to the first RLI conference. Like other scholars in Gluckman's South African network, Sonnabend did research that was relevant to political and social policy, including a 1943 pamphlet with Cyril Sofer on the plight of mixed-race children that made the antieugenic point that "miscegenation" had no harmful effects.[117] His relevance for the RLI's work lay in his work to initiate a "fruitful interchange between demography and anthropology" in the 1930s, by demonstrating the connection between differences in the marriage age of men and women and the potential rate of polygyny.[118] Polygyny — the practice of having multiple wives — depended on the availability of women of marriageable age, which increased as the age of marriage for men increased.

While still in the field, the team had been alerted to Sonnabend's visit to the conference by a letter from Gluckman urging them to think about demographic data.[119] Later the director passed on a letter from Fortes urging them to collect statistics on women, especially births and marriages.[120] Thus, during the conference, stimulated by Sonnabend's seminar, Mitchell, Colson, and Barnes developed the census form, relying on a general understanding in anthropology at the time of what was needed, as well as on certain explicit models: Colson, for example, was familiar with the form used by her former supervisor, Clyde Kluckhohn. They also used Audrey Richards's article on the village census, explicit information in Malinowski's published work, and the work of Edward Gifford.[121]

The RLI also became a storehouse for copies of the researchers' fieldnotes, which could be consulted by others and on which the directors sometimes commented. After reading Barnes's fieldnotes Deane suggested that all staff read each other's notes.[122] Similar influences toward the gathering of comparable data continued into the team's second fieldwork period — for example, with Lucy Mair's request for data from all of them for use in her sociological portion of the African Marriage Survey, a study of the effects of modern conditions on marriage and family life sponsored by the International African Institute.[123] In addition, the process of publishing some of their early work while still in the field also drew the team together, corresponding about their contributions to the *Rhodes-Livingstone Institute Journal* and to an edited collection, *Seven Tribes of British Central Africa*.[124]

Of all these influences, the RLI-based conferences functioned for the team as the most important point of intellectual exchange, standardization of practices, and development of a common identity. According to Gluckman's report on the first of conferences: "All the staff met at Livingstone in January–February 1947 to coordinate their work and report on their respective fields. Dr. H. Sonnabend (Acting Head of the Department of Sociology, University of the Witwatersrand), Miss P. Deane (Colonial Research Fellow), and Dr. J. M. Winterbottom (Provincial Education Officer) were also present at most of the sessions, and Mr. L. F. Leversedge (Provincial Commissioner, Southern Province) and Mr. F. J. Passmore (District Officer, Mazabuka) attended when Dr. Colson reported on the Tonga."[125] Each researcher gave a seminar in which he or she presented preliminary findings and suffered a vigorous critique from Gluckman and the others in attendance. According to Mitchell: "Field methods were the most important focus of the seminars — crucial — and this built us into a team, with all having a similar approach. Max emphasized concrete documentation and kept quoting Malinowski to us."[126]

It is worth expanding on Mitchell's view of the function of these seminars and their place in the development of the Manchester School, because he would himself use conferences and seminars to further develop the RLI approach during his period as the RLI's fourth director in the early 1950s:

> The Manchester School was not a school but a set of research studies based on basic procedures: first, meticulous fieldwork; second, Gluckman's Marxist materialism and interest in material conditions; three, quantitative analysis where appropriate; and, four, a case study focus.

Group photo at a 1951 RLI Conference in Livingstone. From left to right: A. J. B. Hughes, J. Clyde Mitchell, Ian Cunnison, Hans Holleman, Elsey Richardson, Victor Turner, unknown man, Bubbles Hyam. (Photo from J. Clyde Mitchell's private collection. Reproduced by permission of Jean Mitchell.)

Gluckman's fieldwork seminars — it was difficult to travel so far! Each had to read a paper and that forced us to systematize data at an early stage. The listeners sought out inconsistencies and thinness in the data, contradictions between data and observations about customs and values. This allowed us to go back to the field to correct gaps.[127]

In the above answer to my question, "What made the Manchester School a school?" Mitchell placed the emphasis on field practices — "basic procedures" — denying that the group was a school in the usual sense which implies adherence to a body of theory. Although it is in the nature of the sciences that some theory would have been implicit in the selection of data and the recognition of inconsistencies and gaps, theory did not form the major topic of discussion in the RLI seminars. A sense of the transitory usefulness of specific theories was likely to have informed this approach, since Gluckman had used the Lamba field-training session to impress upon the group the necessity to collect sufficiently detailed data that would enable one to analyze it later from angles not anticipated while in the field. His later use at Manchester of the reanalysis of famous ethnographies as a teaching technique was also based on this approach — analyzing the same date from a number of different theoretical perspectives.[128] This would have made later students keenly aware of the wide range of information that would have to be collected to support such an enterprise.

The RLI conferences also enabled the formation of a common social identity, equally as important as the development of a common approach to fieldwork. The social side sometimes included the researchers' picnics at the "Institute Rapids," on a bank of the Zambezi River above Victoria Falls, and forays into the surrounding countryside.[129] The sense of an RLI style of behavior that set them apart from the often unwelcoming local white society comes through in the stories the researchers told about these events in later interviews — joking about Gluckman's sometimes eccentric behavior or describing the laughter of African guards who caught some of them skinny-dipping in a reservoir at night.[130]

The pithiness of the groups' banter may reflect the South African element at the RLI, as well as the working-class sympathies of nearly all the members of the group — an earthy straightforward quality that would have contrasted with the courtly and highly ritualistic style of colonial administration and the higher ranks of the white settler community in Northern Rhodesia. This difference resulted in some tension: the administrators and technical officers in Livingstone referred to the team on their first arrival as "Gluckman's Circus," and the director was often hard put to keep his researchers in line.[131] This quality would also distinguish them from the academic community they confronted later in Britain, which in the late 1940s and into the 1950s was still imbued with the upper-middle-class Oxbridge style. As Epstein recalled the situation during his days in Manchester, "When we attended ASA meetings in London, we were referred to as 'the cloth cap boys' — a reference to working class styles."[132]

Their first joint experience of this milieu would come in 1947, when the team went to Oxford for a writing-up period between their two stints of fieldwork, under the direction of Gluckman, who had by then accepted a lectureship there. Mitchell and Barnes joined colleges for their degrees, under the supervision of Gluckman, Meyer Fortes, and Evans-Pritchard.[133] The team as a whole presented seminars, received feedback from members of the "Oxford structural school" (which included John Middleton and Jim and Laura Bohannan, who were also students at the time[134]), socialized together, and gave radio talks arranged by Gluckman to popularize their work. They also took the opportunity to attend seminars given by important scholars nearby in London. Barnes, for example, attended seminars of the sociologist, Morris Ginsburg.[135] And Barnes, Mitchell, Colson, and Cunnison attended Firth's and Forde's combined University College and LSE seminar, where they mixed with Richards, Nadel, Leach, and others.[136]

The time in Oxford was a formative experience for the RLI team, not only for their development of an RLI identity but also for their individual career paths. Academic posts in anthropology could not be taken for granted in the interwar period, and even in the late 1940s the RLI researchers could not have foreseen the boom in anthropology posts that would accompany the 1950s and 1960s expansion of the university systems in Britain, the United States, and Australia. They saw an academic career as highly desirable, even if difficult to obtain, evidenced by Gluckman's concern about his own career and his fight to base the team in Oxford during its first writing-up period. As he reported to the CSSRC on his resignation in June 1947: "I must get teaching experience or I should never be able to return to university life."[137] He was certain that a period at a big university at that stage would "be the making of the members of our team," and defended the decision to send them to Oxford, in preference to the University of Cape Town or, especially, in preference to remaining in Livingstone, where he argued lack of housing and an unhealthy climate — not to mention lack of a university library — would hamper their writing.

The Board of Trustees, the CSSRC, and the Colonial Office reacted angrily to this plan, because it violated the goal of establishing colony-centered intellectual institutions. In response to Gluckman's argument that some team members needed further training to finish doctorates and that they should be allowed to enroll at Oxford to complete their degrees, various members of these bodies saw the writing-up period as an anthropological plot to divert colonial research funds for the purpose of establishing the researchers' academic careers. The researchers, on the other hand, felt disadvantaged by the temporary contracts and lack of adequate pensions that came with colonial research posts.[138] Gluckman and Colson, on the basis of their previous experience, also defended the amount of time needed for analysis and writing up between tours of fieldwork, with the director, no doubt irritatingly, reminding the CSSRC of his original proposal to bind the researchers to two terms of service and to provide a year in, a year out, and a year in as the ideal proportion of fieldwork to writing up during the first half of the first term of service.[139]

In the end, the RLI team got its time at Oxford because of the lack of housing in Livingstone and Schapera's absence from UCT, but the issue of local writing-up periods remained unresolved and would, along with the RLI's status as a colonial research institute that was unattached to a colonial university, again become a bone of contention in negotiations about the Institute's future.[140]

Conclusion

A crucial factor in the thinking of anthropologists about the value of applied research — what effect such work would have on their careers — has been neglected in the literature on colonial anthropology because of the enormous amount of attention given to questions about the morality of anthropologists' involvement in colonial development work and about the relative status of applied versus theoretical pursuits. The latter factors of morality and status played an undeniable role in each researcher's decision making — expressed at the time as disillusionment with the potential role of anthropology in colonial development and in the tension between anthropological interests and the colonial administration's goals. But the failure of the Colonial Office to *support* the development of careers based in colonial research institutes also played an important part, as we shall see in chapter 6 on Mitchell's directorship. The CSSRC exacerbated this failure by insisting on applying academic standards to the RLI research proposals, which limited the RLI's ability to do research immediately relevant to local government concerns, and which might have encouraged them to remain attached to colonial institutes.[141]

Whatever career path a researcher might have desired, the academic route, when available, remained the one most likely to provide security and the time to publish, as Gluckman recognized in his own decision to resign the RLI directorship in 1947.[142] When he subsequently founded the social anthropology department at Manchester in 1949, the former director could then provide RLI researchers with a metropolitan university base from which to pursue academic careers. This did not, however, cause RLI researchers to shift toward a purely academic focus, for they continued to share an intellectual and social network within Northern Rhodesia during fieldwork and to contemplate careers in southern Africa — both factors that kept RLI research focused on more than the development of theories. The journal maintained a mix of local authors, held a place on the shelves of colonial administrators, and became highly regarded among the new generation of administrators that began work in the 1950s, despite the anthropologists' frustration with government's general failure to take account of their work.[143] Subsequent directors continued to foster government connections and planned for the Institute's possible future as the core of a university. After Mitchell moved to the chair of African Studies at the University College of Rhodesia and Nyasaland (UCRN), he sent students to the

Northern Rhodesian field. Some of them worked on topics directly relevant to local government and African concerns — an example of the importance of examining the connections between colonial institutions such as the RLI and UCRN, rather than only the influence of metropolitan institutions on colonial ones. Gluckman's approach and that of other directors would also foster a strong tradition of applied research, both in Northern Rhodesia and other parts of the world, though this strand of the RLI legacy has received practically no attention in previous histories of anthropology. (See chapter 8.)

Before he left, moreover, Gluckman had established a new approach to anthropology at the RLI, which would continue to develop through the work of subsequent directors. This approach emerged from a creative mix of often dissonant elements rather than from the application of a consistent theoretical stance. To the actors at the time, structural-functionalism did not provide a clear template for research. Referring to problems of doing coordinated team research, Gluckman observed: "The problem of achieving co-operative research in *as undeveloped a discipline* as social anthropology is tremendous, since the workers have very varied trainings which are *not co-ordinated by a precise and limiting body of theory*" (emphasis mine). He made this statement as part of an argument for putting a potential new researcher, Ian Cunnison, into the Luapula research site, because he would be available to spend six months in preparation in Oxford while the first RLI team was writing up there and, through this opportunity to share in their experience, become a true member of the team.[144]

"Very varied" is not the view of postwar structural-functionalism that anthropologists hold today. Since the 1970s, most anthropologists have viewed the 1940s–1950s as the high point of a functionalist paradigm — consciously using the term "paradigm" to stress an early Kuhnian model of "normal science" and contrasting it both with an earlier "pre-paradigmatic" stage and the current state of supposed post-paradigmatic (and postmodernist) loss of commitment to a single body of theory. The question of whether or not Kuhn's model is appropriate for the history of anthropology since the war must be addressed, because this is still the most commonly held view of anthropology within the discipline itself, expressed in textbooks, lectures, and most of the memoir/histories produced in recent years.[145]

As shown in the quote from Gluckman, anthropologists in the 1940s were hardly the monk-like devotees to a monotheistic scientific creed that Kuhn found in the natural sciences.[146] The members of the first team came from diverse educational backgrounds, including American anthropology, with its greater focus on cultural and psychological factors. Some arrived with primary training in entirely different disciplines — social work (Mitchell) and social psychology (Marwick), for example. American, British, and South African styles of fieldwork intermingled and clashed. Serious differences in research style is one of the meanings we can draw from Gluckman's description of the variations between sociological researchers: "Sociological research is not like other forms of research where the personal element can very largely be excluded. The type of the work that a man does depends largely on his temperament and also on his training."[147] Holleman and Gluckman, for example, clashed over their divergent South African styles of field behavior, as shown in the preceding chapter when the young Gluckman eagerly joined in the dance and dress of his Zulu informants while Holleman followed the more segregationist style of his *volkekundige* mentor, P. J. Schoeman.

Furthermore, the RLI's creative mix does not fit the retrospective image of social anthropology at its high point as a discipline dominated by the tribal unit of analysis, with little scope for discussing politics or the agency of the individual. In the team's plans for research, as well as in Gluckman's prefaces to the completed monographs, attention to the individual and to psychological and cultural themes enriched the RLI's version of social anthropology. At the first RLI fieldwork conference, they "were all agreed that to prevent our reports being a repetition of the surface generalizations already known from Southern Africa, we must make detailed studies of inter-personal relations of small groups."[148] In a conscious contrast to earlier work, team members focused on the tribe and village as *political* entities in the colonial administration.[149] Individuals figured both as members of lineage systems (drawing on Fortes, Evans-Pritchard, and ultimately Durkheim) and as political actors in modern systems of government from the beginning of the RLI's work — as, for example, in the attention paid to the interhierarchical role of the village head already considered in work that grew out of the Lamba Survey.

What marked the period in social anthropology in general — and the RLI's approach in particular — was not the tribal unit of analysis, but a strong interest in social change, a characteristic that has not been sufficiently acknowledged in the standard picture of structural-functionalism. To get at social change, Gluckman promoted a new approach built up out of Malinowski's style of fieldwork, Radcliffe-Brown's stress on comparative analysis, and Marx's focus on material conditions and dialectical historical processes.[150] He attempted to apply this approach, through the work of the RLI team, to every social problem that troubled central Africa (and, later, the industrial north of England and other parts of the world). In the process he created a research school, but it was one based not on an overarching paradigm but on the tension and divergence of its theoretical elements, as well as endless critique and reanalysis of meticulously collected field data.

Even Gluckman's attachment to an equilibrium model of society did not escape his colleagues' pursuit of the nature of conflict and change, as they increasingly discarded this model in favor of more open-ended views, both of societies and of the forces that held them together or tore them apart. And when they broke new ground as they analyzed their own data, team members often experienced the director's preference for specific approaches as rigid. According to Mitchell, Gluckman insisted he read constantly while doing fieldwork on the Yao, including in particular Fortes's *Dynamics of Clanship among the Tallensi*. Mitchell was also urged to communicate with the Bohannons about their ongoing work on the the Tiv and the Tiv's "lovely" kinship systems — "crystalline in structure" — but the Yaos's shallow genealogies simply would not fit. He chafed under these models and once remarked, to Gluckman's annoyance, that "the Tallensi have been tortured on the rack of clanship." The break that would eventually lead to network analysis derived from these and other dissatisfactions, discussed in conversations and correspondence between Mitchell and Barnes.[151] (For more discussion of network analysis, see chapter 6.)

Thus, it was appropriate that the Manchester School, as it came to be called in the 1960s, was also known as the "Conflict School."[152] Conflict would soon dog the fieldwork of the RLI researchers as they initiated urban studies in the 1950s, but it also lay at the heart of Gluckman's idea of social equilibrium: in his earlier and his later work, he always pointed out—more dialectically than functionally—that equilibrium in South Africa relied on contradictory economic and social motives and that historically this equilibrium was initiated and maintained by force.[153]

5

"A Lady and an American"

Elizabeth Colson directed the RLI from 1947, when Gluckman left, until early 1951, when illness forced her to resign. The third generation at the RLI during this time included Ian Cunnison (who arrived in 1947 and overlapped with the previous team), A. J. B. Hughes, and Marjory Elliot. In 1950, Victor Turner, William Watson, Marion Pearsall, and Lewis Gann were hired on the basis of Colson's seven-year plan but primarily trained and directed by her successor, J. Clyde Mitchell, who also acted as director during her leave in 1951. A. L. Epstein, who came to do a study of urban courts in Northern Rhodesia under a Colonial Research Fellowship, began his work in 1950 supervised by the administrator, Robert Moffat (a descendant of the Moffat mission family), who got on well with the RLI directors. Epstein attended RLI conferences, and when Moffat went on leave Epstein's supervision was transferred to the RLI. Epstein wanted to get rural experience before beginning an urban study, so he spent some time with the Bemba and later with the Lunda in Cunnison's Luapula field site.[1]

Turner studied the Ndembu of Northern Rhodesia's Northwestern Province, with his wife Edith sharing equally in the research; Watson studied the Mambwe (a group near the Bemba but who had a different adaptation to the migrant labor economy); and Pearsall started work on the Lakeside Tonga of Nyasaland but left the field for personal reasons and was replaced by Jaap van Velsen. Gann's post involved researching and writing the history of Northern Rhodesia, vital to the overall RLI project of understanding the region's experience of social change. He spent a year in Oxford looking at archival material before arriving in Africa. Funding for two sociologists to begin the urban study of the Copperbelt would eventually provide the basis for Mitchell's directorship and his social survey, as well as A. L. Epstein's study of urban African politics. Colson's plan also requested a survey team of trained African assistants, but the RLI's board of trustees would not agree to a salary level commensurate with the educational level the Institute required. This ultimately led to the lowering of these salaries and the considerable difficulty Mitchell would later experience in recruiting and keeping the team of Africans he employed for the Copperbelt survey.[2] (See chapter 6.)

The first team's writing-up period in Oxford in 1947 had resulted in the production of a volume of articles, *Seven Tribes in British Central Africa*, four out of its seven articles written by RLI team members Gluckman, Colson, Barnes, and Mitchell and based on seminars they gave at the Institute for Social Anthropology in Oxford.[3] This writing-up period solidified their links with British academia and, from the metropolitan perspective, endowed them with an identity as part of the Oxford structuralist school dominated by E. E. Evans-Pritchard.[4]

Cunnison joined the team while they were writing up in Oxford and came out to Northern Rhodesia in June of 1948, where he had a field training session with Colson in Mazabuka District before beginning his fieldwork on the Lunda in Luapula Province. The economist Marjorie Eliot, who had worked at the British Ministry of Labour and studied economics at Oxford, was recruited in Oxford and began a macrostudy of labor migration intended to place the RLI primary research within that larger context (but which she never published). A. J. B. Hughes took up a Beit Trust grant to work in Southern Rhodesia on the Ndebele people (after a period of training in Britain with Gluckman), administered from the RLI. The Beit Trust also gave Holleman funding for a second research tour among the Hera. In between he had spent a writing-up period in Cape Town with Isaac Schapera. Anne Close became the RLI's administrative secretary. Sianga continued as a research assistant representing Gluckman in Barotseland until the end of Colson's directorship, while Lewanika did the same until he got a job in the Lozi administration in 1949.

Colson and the others from the second generation continued field-work during this period; she visited Barnes in the field and together they traveled to Nyasaland to visit Mitchell. Colson also visited Cunnison in the field. Both Barnes and Cunnison visited Colson at different times. They all met in Salisbury and Bulawayo for conferences because of the housing shortage in Livingstone. Salisbury, the capital of Southern Rhodesia, was also more convenient for Holleman, and Bulawayo, the largest city in the western part of that country, was convenient for Hughes, in his nearby Ndebele fieldsite. Lucy Mair provided an important cohesive factor despite not being in the field herself—by requesting that all the RLI research officers send her comparable data on marriage patterns to help with her part of the African marriage study for the International African Institute.

At least three themes of this book find expression during the period of Colson's directorship—race and gender factors shaping the researcher's identity in the field; research for development as part of the RLI's mission; and intellectual and institutional networks as shaping influences on the RLI's research goals. All of these themes are encompassed in Colson's career, as a female anthropologist, as a long-term researcher whose work has been important in both theoretical and applied anthropology, and as an American in the center of a largely British and South African disciplinary network in southern and central Africa. She also provided the key impetus to solve the RLI's problem of finding a suitable location and adequate funding for administration as well as research—both pressing problems because of postwar inflation and the housing shortage in Northern Rhodesia at the time. Lack of funding for accommodation in Livingstone, as well as for a director's salary, meant that Colson often directed the RLI from her tent in her Plateau Tonga fieldsite while carrying on the research for which she was paid.[5] She was instrumental in relocating the Institute from Livingstone to Lusaka and getting it an adequate headquarters building and houses for researchers. She developed the Institute's new seven-year research plan, which began in 1950. The Colonial Development and Welfare fund agreed to finance the continuing research and provided some money, as well, for the RLI's new buildings. Local support also continued, especially from Northern Rhodesia's then-governor, Sir Gilbert Rennie, who took a personal interest in the Institute and convinced local corporations to aid the building effort.[6]

Reconsidering Women in the Field

During my first interview with Elizabeth Colson, I asked her if she had ever experienced any discrimination as a woman anthropologist, and she replied, "No."[7] I was surprised by this answer and was at first eager to explain it away as I found evidence that her gender had, indeed, made a difference in the perceptions of some of those she encountered during her education and in her career in Northern Rhodesia. Nevertheless, there is truth in her view that has survived my exploration of the roles of women in the history of the RLI and of the current literature on women in the field. In a number of important ways, Elizabeth Colson's career and the careers of other women anthropologists in central Africa critically challenge the often-heard assumptions about gender and anthropology which will be discussed in this section.

Most of the writing on women anthropologists in the field produced over the last twenty years expresses a single-issue focus on, and Eurocentric definition of, gender that is, no doubt, useful to women anthropologists today who are attempting to rise in the metropolitan-based profession. Nevertheless, this literature fails to capture the complexity of the fieldwork situation itself—and its authors fail to appreciate the importance of the interaction between local ideas of gender and more general local practices for the management of outsiders. These local practices often derive from complex precolonial, colonial, and postcolonial interactions among race, gender, and class factors and, especially, from the cultural violence inherent in the imposition of Western gender categories on local societies that led to the enormous changes in relations between men and women demanded by missionaries, governments, and commercial interests. These Europeans interpreted African societies in terms of Western gender categories and, through their interpretations and impositions, created gendered behavior in areas of social interaction where it may not have existed before, while missing entirely other forms of gendered behavior that were alien to Western experience.[8]

Moreover, even the rigid Western gender categories that colonials attempted to impose came blended with other factors, such as class and race. In other words, gender, race, and class were (and are) radically interactive concepts impossible to entirely disentangle even for analytical purposes.[9] Thus, to truly understand the situation of women anthropologists in the field, one must look historically at the complex negotiations and blendings that took place among all three categories. We must not limit ourselves to looking at the actual or perceived dichotomy between local and European notions of the proper place of women.

In the existing literature dealing with the gender of the researcher, three questions predominate. First, do women anthropologists enjoy a special understanding of, or access to, the lives of women in the societies they study? Second, do the societies they study give female researchers a particular status or role primarily because of their gender? And third, what is the woman anthropologist's status within the discipline itself, what are the causes of this status, and how can it be bettered?

In its attempts to answer these questions, this literature often makes generalizations about women's careers but rarely grounds these generalizations in particular case studies, though the authors do use anecdotes from personal experience. Because of this, there is little appreciation of gender as a historically, as well as culturally, constructed category. Moreover, most of those who discuss their personal experiences as women in the field deal only cursorily, if at all, with their relations with the local European communities. These communities usually provide crucial support of various kinds for female (and male) researchers in the field, and their negative evaluation of a researcher's behavior can affect the researcher's access to the field. Historically, too, the indigenous communities that the anthropologists study formed their ideas about Europeans on the basis of experience with local settler communities and usually attempted to "place" a visiting researcher into appropriate categories related to these experiences. Because the literature on women in the field does not deal with this factor, it is necessary to turn to the insightful exploration of gender in European colonial societies made by Helen Callaway and to the groundbreaking work of Ann Stoler on the anthropology of colonialism. These scholars point to the uses of gender within European communities in the colonies,[10] the gendering of relations between the races, the relationship of gender with changing class interests, and the ritualization of colonial social life. This literature informs the following discussion.

Female anthropologists in the colonial period had to deal with the gender rules of small and diverse settler communities before they could get into the field and whenever they encountered Europeans in the field. They had to adopt local styles of behavior or invent acceptable ways of transcending settler-imposed masculine and feminine roles before they could even begin to do fieldwork. In this light, Margaret Read's wearing of riding breeches in the field, mentioned in the first chapter, can be understood as a way of transcending settlers' and administrators' ideas of a woman's proper place.[11] Her choice of dress may have made little reference to expectations or preferences of Africans (though there is no indication from the interviews I conducted that Africans found her dress offensive). The culture of riding in twentieth-century Britain, as well as in the colonies, allowed women to wear a traditionally masculine type of dress. Riding breeches would have been sturdy and comfortable for fieldwork and would have given an impression of self-sufficiency and competence to European observers. They would also have invoked an aura of the English rural gentry, providing the perfect way for a female academic to impress administrators and settlers who had transferred romantic ideas about the English countryside to the form of life they had created for themselves in Africa.[12] Read also had an upper-class background and may have participated in English riding culture, like Thomas Fox-Pitt (mentioned in chapter 3), a member of the aristocracy who was notorious for arranging unsegregated interracial "fox hunts" while in the colonial administration in Northern Rhodesia.

Evoking the ethos of the English rural aristocracy was not a strategy limited to female anthropologists, however, as one can see from

the discussion of Gluckman's dress and hunting activities in Barotseland in chapter 3. Because power itself is gendered, masculine and
feminine styles of behavior can be found even in situations where
only the members of one sex interact. Thus, Gluckman sometimes
found it useful to invoke a particular kind of masculinity—the rural
upper-class image—in the field. At the end of World War Two, this
would have been one of the few strategies open to him, given the
defensiveness and self-consciousness of many colonial administrators about the issue of their own masculinity. Some were men who
had been exempted from military service. They would also have
been experiencing a loss of the frontier style of masculinity they had
previously claimed from experiences of active touring in the bush,
for in the postwar period "men's duties" in "the wilds" had turned
into tame administrative work at desks, the "masculine virtues" into
a "de-sexed existence."[13] Gluckman, too, had been exempted from
active military service, though he had tried to enlist and he drilled
with the Northern Rhodesian Defence force during the war.[14] The
RLI, however, had a reputation as a haven for conscientious objectors. (See chapter 3.) When the new team of RLI researchers arrived
in 1946—many of them decorated veterans—and a new crop of
administrators with war service also returned—like Fox-Pitt—the
politics of masculinity for Gluckman would have been challenging,
indeed.

Gender permeates not just class but other categories, as well, including notions of comfort and ideas of expertise. For women, comfortable, functional, and healthy clothing was rarely considered
fashionable or appropriate, and most of the women at the RLI compromised in various ways with local settler expectations—wearing
ordinary dresses with mosquito boots or donning trousers in the
evening to avoid mosquitoes, in spite of the disapproval of administrators' wives.[15] Mimicking the dress of similar professionals in the
field was also an option not available to them: Gluckman could wear
khaki shorts and shirts similar to those that technical officers wore,
but Read, Richards, and Colson could not. Riding breeches, however, may have also been worn by administrators and technical officers who used horses in the field, which was common in parts of

central Africa. And Colson wore khaki army uniform slacks given to her by her brother-in-law, as well as jeans, which in the 1940s may have been seen as a type of American rural work clothing that did not fit any local category.[16]

To return to the three main questions addressed in the literature on women in the field — first, do women anthropologists enjoy a special understanding of, or access to, the lives of women in the societies they study? Throughout the history of the discipline, anthropologists in general have claimed to have special insight into the lives of the people they study. This has been an essential feature of their claims to expertise, as well as the justification of the method of participant-observation when it was taken up by the discipline. In the literature on women anthropologists as fieldworkers, this claim is given a double edge: not only are women anthropologists gifted with special insights about the female members of the societies they study, but they also have the social skills to gain access to the male realm — while male anthropologists must necessarily be excluded from any deep understanding of the women's side of the societies they study.[17] This resonates with some of the 1980s scholarship on women in science, which emphasized women scientists' unique ways of understanding the biological and physical worlds because of their early socialization, inherited psychological make-up, or position as oppressed members of male-dominated societies. For example, using a historical case study, Evelyn Fox Keller has argued that a female geneticist developed a particularly feminine way of looking at her objects of study, quite different from the masculine style that dominated her field and prevented her work from being fully appreciated at the time it was done.[18]

While it is certainly true that scientific sensibility is critically shaped by gender, the case Keller wrote about involved particular historically and culturally shaped categories of womanhood and scientific knowledge. As well as being historically contingent, gender can be a very fragile construct, constantly in need of reinforcement, and it is also relational, that is, any particular gender can only be understood within the totality of possible genders within a society.[19] So it cannot be assumed that Western women anthropologists always and everywhere have enjoyed special insight into the lives of women of other cultures — it can only be justified by examining the particular commonalities and sensitivities of individual female researchers and their subjects.

When dealing with other cultures and with a science such as anthropology which is dedicated to understanding them, we must reconsider Western categories. Henrietta Moore's "On Sex and Gender" provides a framework for doing so if we use its ideas to look at the researchers, as well as at those whom they researched. If we take Moore's thesis seriously — that not just gender categories but also Western biological sex categories cannot be assumed to be universal — then we must rethink the issues surrounding the role of sex and gender in anthropologists' fieldwork. And this brings us to the second question addressed in the literature on women in the field: Do the societies they study give female researchers a particular status or role primarily due to their gender?

The answer is "not always." The male or female anthropologist's subjects do not necessarily place the same degree or kind of significance on biological sex that is placed on it in Western societies, or they may not recognize the biological differences in the same way at all.[20] This is not to say that people of different cultures do not differentiate male and female anthropologists, or that they don't recognize sex differences — that they can be "fooled" by a female researcher dressed in masculine clothing, or vice versa. It *does* mean that they may place the sex of the researcher on a spectrum different from the mainly dichotomous scheme of many Western cultures and that they may differently construe the relation between biological sex as understood in the West and social gender and/or other important local categories. Among these possible categories are age or position in the life cycle, designation as an adult, as a witch or nonwitch, as slave or free, as a productive or nonproductive member of society, or as some degree of insider or outsider.

Life-cycle events can be important in making such distinctions, but how closely they can be related to gender status, or even biological sex in the Western sense, must remain open for investigation rather than assumed. Particularly relevant here is the collection edited by

Whitehead and Conaway which contains essays on issues of identity, sex, and gender from both male and female fieldworkers' perspectives in a number of different cultures. Although individual women authors sometimes make claims for special gender-based knowledge, the editors' conclusion stresses that these views are debatable, that male fieldworkers' experiences in the area of gender are underrepresented, that gender-role flexibility and the ability to adopt a "neutral professional stranger" role can overcome some of the limitations of gender, and that many more factors besides gender affect the fieldworker's sensitivity to various aspects of the studied culture.[21] The conclusion, however, contains little about the potential effects that the studied community's different categories of biological sex — and any different significance attached to them — might have on the position or insights of the fieldworker.

Nevertheless, the book emphasizes the ways that different gender categories might compare in importance with other crucial factors such as age, experience of key life-cycle events, race, and education. Although this complex field of relations may allow the researcher to negotiate a position that allows him or her greater leeway in terms of gender, the importance of this goes deeper than the idea of conscious negotiation implies. Where the studied community is cross-culturally sophisticated, but the researcher assumes it to be "virgin" to research or outsiders generally, the researcher may not be aware of exactly what is being negotiated. She or he may assume that gender is the central issue, when in fact the key issues of power and access may attach to other features of the interaction. And access to locally gender-restricted activities may be determined on other grounds entirely outside of judgments of the researcher's appropriate place in the local community's gendered or age-specific realms.

One must also remember that, however similarly or differently from Western standards a society may construct sex and gender, all societies are made up of individuals who have varying interests with respect to the anthropologist. In several cases, male RLI anthropologists, for example, gained access to information about the private aspects of African women's lives, while in at least one case a female anthropologist did not. Gluckman, a research assistant recalled, "also asked women about everything, [about] what they do when girls come of age. They showed him even though he was a man. He gave them some money and asked, 'Show me how you do it.' So they disclosed everything. Many people were embarrassed and wouldn't tell him, but others would disclose."[22]

In another example, Ngoni women allowed Barnes and his male assistant to attend a girls' initiation ceremony, though local people recounting the story insist that they made the anthropologist wear women's clothing.[23] In contrast, one RLI woman researcher in the 1950s, Ann Tweedie, was given incomplete information about the Bemba girls' initiation ceremony because local women considered her too immature to have access to such knowledge.[24] Other young, unmarried female anthropologists in the past had had no difficulty attending the ceremony in this area or other parts of Northern Rhodesia, so her immaturity may not have been the real reason. According to a research assistant who accompanied her at the time, "She only pretended to drink [beer in the village], and they thought she was up to something."[25] The tense political situation in 1959–60 when she did her fieldwork, which was reflected in African fears of poisoning by whites, may have been the deciding factor in the local reaction to Tweedie, eclipsing the issue of gender.

To go further than Whitehead and Conaway, one must consider gender in a particular cultural and historical fieldwork situation. In Northern Rhodesia from the 1930s to the 1960s, local African sex and gender categories doubtlessly affected the position and insights of the RLI anthropologists. This chapter cannot answer that question in any detail, since a close look at the sex and gender categories of each of the African societies studied by the RLI is beyond the scope of this book. Nevertheless, a number of examples suggest that while sex and gender were important, other categories were equally so, and many of the RLI anthropologists knew this. What is most important is that during this period of rapidly increasing research activity, African societies developed ways of understanding and accommodating researchers as *researchers*. This process drew on earlier experiences with outsiders—in particular, locally established outsiders such as the administrators and missionaries who visited African villages and studied customs and traditions. The African understanding of research and researchers was influenced by the ethnographic activities of some of these missionaries and administrators, as well as by the increasingly frequent and often widely known presence of professional anthropologists.

Among the most well-known and influential of the latter were women, like Audrey Richards, Margaret Read, and the amateur anthropologist and friend of Richards, Lorna Gore-Browne. Thus from the earliest years of professional anthropological activity, the African perception of the researcher in some parts of Northern Rhodesia would have been based on experiences that mainly involved female researchers. The RLI continued this pattern to some extent. Men may have outnumbered women in the research officer posts at the Institute, but several of the anthropologists' wives participated in the work on a partial or equal basis while in the field. Thus, although the metropolitan scholarly community and white colonial society may have seen the female anthropologist as an anomaly, it is possible that the African societies that they studied did not find them exceptional at all.

This brings us to the third question in the literature on women in the field: What is the woman anthropologist's status within the discipline itself, what are the causes of this status, and how can it be bettered? In the case of Northern Rhodesia, the white settler image of the anthropologist and the position of women within the discipline itself had been profoundly influenced by the concentration of women anthropologists in Africa and the prominence of Audrey Richards, both in central Africa and at the Colonial Office. Thus, women in African anthropology cannot be seen as *necessarily* marginal people. That kind of approach is essentialist in assuming that women are always marginal in disciplines that are predominantly male. Audrey Richards was a central figure in African fieldwork and British anthropology from the 1930s through the 1960s, both because of her intellectual connections (as the most prominent Africanist student of Malinowski) and because of her class status (an important factor in her rise to a position of influence on research matters at the Colonial Office).[26]

In Northern Rhodesia Richards was the first social anthropologist to do fieldwork (1930–31 and 1933–34), and she facilitated the birth of the RLI, setting the agenda for its future relations with government and settlers. The Governor, however, did not allow her to become its first director. As she recalled, "He had 'nothing against women,' he said—a phrase often heard at the time—but he felt it to be too great a risk to appoint someone who was not only a woman but also a woman who was an anthropologist, a word which aroused the greatest possible apprehension in the minds of government officials and settlers at the time." But he later supported her for the directorship after Godfrey Wilson resigned, though she did not want the post at that point.[27] The RLI directors and researchers took her work seriously, and Gluckman acknowledged her influence on his Seven-Year Plan.[28]

Her friendship with the most prominent settler family, the Gore-Brownes, and her sometimes joint fieldwork with Lorna Gore-Browne provided a hopeful model of cooperation and amicable relations between settlers and anthropologists. Her work had impressed the governor who founded the RLI, and she initiated the efforts of social anthropologists in Northern Rhodesia to cooperate with colonial technical officers and make their findings useful to the administration.[29] The flavor of this hoped-for relationship with government is suggested in Elspeth Huxley's novel, *Murder at Government House*, in which the heroine, Olivia Brandeis, is an anthropologist partly modeled on Richards.[30] Brandeis enjoys cordial relations with government officials and gets on particularly well with the District Commissioner in the area where she does research. They discuss esoteric anthropological topics together—which he may have studied at one of the Oxbridge summer courses for colonial civil servants—and he encourages her to do a "systematic study" of the local people.[31] Unlike the later RLI anthropologists, however, Brandeis cooperates with the colonial police by investigating a local African secret society that might be implicated in the Governor's murder.[32] (In the case of the RLI, government did not ask researchers to carry on covert investigations, though individual administrators might sometimes have asked anthropologists about what they had ob-

Frances Barnes in
front of her clinic in
the field. Although she
did not participate
to a great extent in her
husband's fieldwork,
she used her medical
training to treat minor
illnesses and wrote an
article about Ngoni
birthing practices.
(Photo reproduced by
permission of John
and Frances Barnes.)

served of certain Africans suspected of misbehavior.[33] According to
Colson, it was understood from the beginning that the Institute
wrote about "people, not persons," and that they "wrote ethnography, not reports on persons."[34])

Important for the issue of gender is Huxley's portrayal of the seriousness with which Brandeis is taken by the government — especially the administrator in the field who is sympathetic to her work
and impressed by her agricultural knowledge. Neither does Brandeis
feel compelled to present herself as entirely sexless, for by the end of
the novel she is being wooed by a government official. Elements of
this picture surely reflect Huxley's wishful thinking about the position of the woman professional at the time. Nevertheless, Richards's
previous work in Northern Rhodesia and her continuing presence at
the Colonial Office ensured that female anthropologists in central

RLI African survey team with woman researcher. (Photo from RLI poster in author's possession.)

Africa had strong precedents to draw on when claiming a place in the field.

It also set a precedent for Africans' expectations of all anthropologists' behavior. In a letter to Audrey Richards, her former research assistant, the Reverend Paul Mushindo, expressed concern about the behavior of a later male anthropologist whom he helped to get established in the field:

> he [is] a very good young man, but he displeased me very very much. He was approaching any African in the way as if he is his or her slave. I was ashamed very much and felt sad.
>
> According to Bemba custom, a woman should respect men and a common man should respect those above him, but he or her should not forget dignity for himself or herself as a human being. If one is humble

to others, but must not forget himself, as Dr. Richards appeared at [Paramount Chief] Chitimukulu['s] court or anywhere without dispis[ing] anybody but she was Dr. Richards. Whether present people knew about her professor[ship] or not matters nothing.[35]

A research assistant's insistence on the dignity of the anthropologist might reflect self-interest — the desire to be seen as the employee of a powerful patron.[36] Nevertheless, as Stocking has pointed out, relations of "social parity" are not necessarily the best in every fieldwork situation. Among the hierarchical Bemba — as for Malinowski among the socially stratified Trobrianders — Richards asked for, as well as gave, respect.[37] According to Moore and Vaughan, gender and political status were partly cross-cutting systems in Bemba society, and Richards was frequently referred to as a chief, and not simply a chieftainess: "She was, like some senior Bemba women, at times treated as something of a surrogate man."[38]

Academic professions also exhibit many of the features of small-scale, hierarchical societies in which senior women can find themselves treated as surrogate men, as was the case for social anthropology in Northern Rhodesia.

A First-Class Research Man

It was into this context that Elizabeth Colson arrived in 1946. She came from a family in which girls were expected to go to university, and her mother and a maternal aunt had bachelor of arts degrees. Before the war Colson had received a bachelors degree in anthropology at the University of Minnesota and a doctorate at Radcliffe, the women's college associated with Harvard. At the time, women graduate students at Radcliffe could take courses at Harvard that were restricted to male graduate students, though even then the professor could insist that a woman student remain outside the door to take notes. Kluckhohn, Colson's supervisor, allowed women to come inside and join the discussions. Colson pursued anthropology even though there weren't many jobs in the field and "few women got jobs in anthropology." Although she felt that she wouldn't have been allowed to join summer archeological field trips while at Minnesota, she had no difficulty taking part in a summer anthropological field school, the New York University Field Laboratory in Social Science, run by Bert and Ethel Aginsky. Her Ph.D. at Radcliffe in 1945 was based on fieldwork with Native Americans in Washington state, and she had done additional fieldwork at a Japanese-American relocation camp during the war.[39] By the time she reached Northern Rhodesia in 1946, Colson had extensive field experience and possessed the highest qualifications of any of the first team chosen by Gluckman.

During the negotiations over Gluckman's seven-year research plan, the British government requested that the Institute appoint at least one woman, an indication that a commitment to having women working at research institutes existed in the postwar period.[40] But this did not mean that the women chosen would be as unrestricted as men in terms of choice of topic or fieldsite. Although Colson wanted to do a study that would build on her doctoral work, which had dealt with a fishing economy, the colonial government objected to placing her on the Luapula River where she could study this topic. They considered the area too dangerous for a woman because of the presence of smugglers crossing the border with the Belgian Congo (see chapter 4). The Nyasaland government raised similar objections when Marion Pearsall joined the RLI to do research in Nyasaland. She was placed with the Lakeside Tonga because all the other possible fieldsites would have involved work within range of a nearby border.[41]

Colson studied the Plateau Tonga area instead, another of the priority sites for research in the opinion of both Gluckman and the administration. The Director, the Provincial Commissioner, the District Commissioner, and the agricultural officers in the area decided on the general field location in which she would work.[42] Male overprotectiveness made itself felt in pressure on her choice of an initial place to live. In a letter to Mitchell, Gluckman exclaimed that he had to rush off to Monze (the town on the line-of-rail nearest to Colson's fieldsite) "to straighten things for Elizabeth, who is being so well cared for by Hart that he won't let her go and camp where she wants to."[43] An agricultural officer chose her initial campsite but she chose her own campsites after that.[44]

The local settler reaction to Colson's arrival differed somewhat from administrators' concerns about her safety, however. To them, a white woman living alone in African villages aroused suspicion: "her life would be in danger and she would tarnish their reputation — 'let down their side'." She had very few European visitors the first year other than the agricultural officer who helped her get into the field, but the District Commissioner informed her of the local hostility and held out against the settlers' demand that she not be allowed to work in the area. Sensitive to this covert appraisal, Colson accepted a local farm manager's invitation to tea so she could show them that she was not the dreaded anthropologist of local rumor, but only a "quiet unassuming sort of person."[45] The visit led to a lasting friendship with the owners of the farm.

Previous settler relations with Africans may have reflected racial politics more than African concerns about appropriate gender behavior by female anthropologists. The principal role of European women toward Africans in the rural areas was that of settler farmers' wives as "madams" — employers of black domestic workers, nearly all of whom would have been men in this period. Because he preferred not to call Colson *dona* — the local equivalent of "madam" — the Plateau village headman, Chepa, chose the name *Kamwale*, meaning "young woman." This name indicated her status as a learner rather than as a madam giving orders.[46] Despite this local placement in terms of gender, she wore jeans and slacks more often than dresses while in the field, which did not comply with local standards of appropriate female dress. She also used reactions to her style of dress in her analysis of the socialization of children into Tonga society: "So much does appropriate clothing come to be associated with a paricular sex that for children of four or five it becomes evidence for the classification of a person into one sex or another. They need to be reassured again and again that a European woman dresssed in slacks is really a woman and not the man that her clothing indicates."[47]

Local people also worried about the appropriateness of her behavior as a young woman "living alone in the village, just like a man, moving about without other people." According to one young man living in a village Colson studied, "She was both respected and feared because of her respectability and correctness, and not being married and living alone — no man would live like that." Young men in one village where she stayed among the Plateau Tonga watched at night to see if she had male visitors to her tent.[48] This local reaction to a woman researcher shows concern about proper gender behavior but focuses more on issues of respectability and correctness important to local standards of dignity that apply to both men and women. It also hints at a Tonga fear of people who live alone, a behavior that could be associated with witchcraft. As Colson herself observed, people sometimes remarked on the speed at which she walked, getting from one place to another so quickly that one might suspect witchcraft was involved.[49]

Another factor — race — would matter more than gender or age when the Gwembe Tonga allowed Colson to be present at births during her later fieldwork there, which started in 1956. According to her research assistant: "She used to witness child births because there was a general belief among the whites that Africans are born with tails and these are cut at birth. She thought an African child is born like a monkey. So she wanted to prove whether African children are like white children at birth. So, she proved there is no difference."[50]

Although Gwembe people mistakenly attributed her interest to an old evolutionary view of Africans that no European scientist still held in the 1950s, their interpretation of her behavior reflected white settlers' continuing use of this racial insult, rather than the expectation that Colson would be interested in births simply because she was a woman. On the Plateau, as well, reactions to Colson as a fieldworker emphasized characteristics of her behavior that Africans appreciated because of the racial context. According to one, "She was different from other expatriates, not aggressive"; neither was she "demanding and questioning, as a DC would [be]."[51] Respectability and correctness also meant giving respect, and in a general context of colonial disrespect for Africans, Colson's behavior stood out.

Gluckman had a high opinion of her abilities, as well, and recommended to the Board of Trustees that she become assistant director after her first year in the field.[52] The trustees, however, objected to appointing Americans to such posts.[53] Gluckman persisted in his view, and in June 1947, when he received an offer from Oxford, he again recommended Colson, this time as his replacement. In support he cited the difficulty of getting directors for institutes in Africa, her secretarial skills gained while working to support herself as a student at Minnesota, and her status as a first class researcher.[54] The CSSRC did not discuss gender in its deliberations, since the precedent had earlier been set when Richards had been asked to take over the RLI after Wilson's resignation.[55] The reference to Colson's secretarial skills pointed to the difficulty the Institute was having in employing a good secretary and the general dissatisfaction with Gluckman's bookkeeping; a potential director, whether male or female, who could keep the paperwork in order while dealing with inadequate secretarial support would appear as a godsend to Colonial Office bureaucrats. More important were issues of finding someone sufficiently qualified (Colson being the only senior research officer at the time), whether to match the salary to that of the director of the proposed East African institute, whether to continue to pay Gluckman during the transition while Colson was acting director, and to decide who was responsible for choosing the new director.[56] Again and again in the negotiations, Gluckman emphasized Colson's qualifications, and the Council showed its support for Colson for the post.[57]

African and settler reactions to women in the field also point to the need to look more closely at local definitions of race — a problematic and changing category of colonial discourse, discussed in the next section.

True Europeans

Colonial societies' concerns about preserving their racial distinctiveness did not only impinge on women anthropologists. Male anthropologists also experienced restrictions, especially where concerns about the defense of white settler societies became conflated with class and gender issues. As was shown in chapter 3, Godfrey Wilson violated the racial rules of settler society in a number of ways—by fraternizing with African men, by giving lifts to African women, and by visiting the retired colonial administrator, Chirupula Stephenson, and his African wives, who were living representatives of an earlier style of colonial gender relations.

Most scholars have interpreted incidents such as these as the violation of a strict boundary between two separate racial groups. This dichotomous view, however, fails to capture the complexity of the racial politics of the time. Intertwined as they were with considerations of class status and commercial interest, racial categories shifted frequently during the colonial period, though most scholarship has focused only on the shift that came in most colonial societies with the first arrival of significant numbers of European women between the first and second world wars.

Racial categories reflected other important shifts, as well, including the changing status of various European ethnic groups within the colonial setting and shifts in the political power of the imperial and nonimperial nations back in Europe. In the nineteenth century the term "race" referred as much to the spectrum of competing nationalities *within* Europe as it did to globally defined racial types such as "European" and "African." Although in the twentieth century the term "race" itself came to be associated with an image of a strict dichotomy between "white" and "black," the finer gradations of the racial spectrum still made a powerful difference within colonial societies. South African whites, for example, felt a greater concern for the racial conflict between English-speaking and Afrikaans-speaking groups than for that between whites and Africans. Ultimately *class*, as Stoler has pointed out, was the strongest motive behind the policing of the boundary between those categorized as Europeans and those who fell into other groups.[58] Class considerations shifted enormously during the colonial period in central Africa, following the rise and fall of the economy, the need for mine laborers, and the influx of European and South African migrants during and after World War Two.

I would argue further that racial distinctions within the group classified as Europeans reflected hierarchies determined by the application of a climatological north-south scale to nationalities within Europe and by lingering concerns in settler society about physical and mental degeneration potentially brought about by life in the tropics. These ideas continued in popular discourse long after the idea of degeneration lost scientific credibility in the aftermath of World War Two. The importance of colonial rituals and concerns about strict adherence to etiquette, thus, derived from the necessity to place people correctly in these hierarchies, especially when skin color did not conveniently provide a determining feature. Etiquette was an important way of signaling status differences, as well as a method to detect creeping degeneration from European standards. Both of these factors figured strongly in the evaluation of character — a term that like "degeneration" had emerged from a much earlier humoral medical understanding of the relationship between individuals and their environment that was given renewed importance in the nineteenth century debates over acclimatization and colonialism.[59] This discourse re-emerged whenever colonial societies in Africa experienced a new migration of Europeans threatening the established class and racial order.

Anthropologists in the field often diverged from appropriate racial and social etiquette, and they rarely responded to colonial ritual occasions with convincing enthusiasm. Researchers for the RLI noticed the etiquette and rituals and observed them (or violated them) where necessary, as, for example, when John Barnes chose never to wear a hat, to let Africans know that he was unlike all other Europeans.[60] This pattern was already apparent in Gluckman's analysis of the ceremonial opening of a bridge and his careful attention to his own style of dress and behavior in colonial social situations. In his "Analysis of a Social Situation in Modern Zululand," he describes himself as moving between two segregated white and black groups, as well as between the different groups within each of these racially designated groups. In reality, the situation was even more complex. Northern Rhodesia was not made up solely of two segregated racial groups — white and black — between which anthropologists gingerly moved back and forth. In the middle was a small group of Indians and a small group of Coloureds — both official racial categories in the eyes of the government — and small numbers of Africans and whites who failed to fit comfortably into any category. These groups had in common an uncertain or changing identity — in class, ethnic, and racial terms — and could use this ambiguity in status to move across boundaries and profit from unacknowledged economic and social links between white and black, though they did not enjoy the explicit power of the dominant group.

Anthropologists with the RLI had contact with people in these groups but did not often utilize their patterns of access to African societies, though these might have proved useful especially for gaining access to the economic side of village life. Indian, Greek, Jewish, and other traders established outposts in remote villages and often learned the languages and customs and acquired practical knowledge about the economic life of the areas in which they worked. Anthropologists' contacts with traders followed the general pattern followed by settlers with high status, though some struck up friendships with members of these groups. Relations with Indian traders were friendly but mainly over-the-counter exchanges while purchasing supplies.[61] Indian families did not invite white anthropologists to stay with them during breaks in fieldwork as white settlers sometimes did. This may have been partly because of fears that anthropologists might find their living arrangements not up to European standards and partly because of the desire to preserve their own cultural distinctiveness from outside influences.

Ian Cunnison paid particular attention to marginal European groups because of their importance in the Luapula region.[62] Smugglers and other entrepreneurs of what we would today call the "informal economy" profited from the river border between the Belgian Congo and Northern Rhodesia, as did those who attempted to succeed in legitimate trade, business schemes, and formal employment. Cunnison explored both sides of the border, met all manner of Europeans, and described them in his field notes:

> Wangled a night at Katabulwe [on the Belgian Congo side of the Luapula River]. . . . There are 3 whites at K — Ongaretti, Italian, about to make a canal somewhere. Leon Meyer, the richest of the lot, a

Turkish Jew. And Paschael, a Belgian, as poor as a church mouse, unhealthy and broken in spirit. It was he who offered me hospitality. They all live in the utmost squalor. . . . I could see Paschael struggling to offer me a slice of bread and a cup of tilleul. . . . He came out as a railway inspector in 1923, soon left it and started trading and has been around all the provinces. Dogged all the way by misfortune. . . . Sympathetic with Africans, probably half the cause of his failure here. Had wanted to cross to NR [Northern Rhodesia] and had written away but suddenly felt a change of heart. *Je suis fatigue de l' Afrique.*[63]

Although Northern Rhodesia more effectively policed smugglers, traders, and other dropouts from white society than the Belgian Congo in the postwar period, this picture suggests the conditions that obtained earlier in both colonial territories and that provided the rationale for the policing of social and racial boundaries. In Northern Rhodesia white traders, often of non-British ethnic groups, still usually failed to meet colonial British society's standards and found themselves outsiders because of their class, economic failure, or failure to preserve racial distinctiveness. The Jews, Greeks, Italians, and other groups who predominated among traders also fell into European categories that those of British descent considered racially inferior. The white traders who entered Northern Rhodesia in the 1940s and 1950s, in contrast to the traders who arrived earlier, also had to move into territory unclaimed by earlier whites and often lived in economically and socially precarious circumstances. Marriage or concubinage with local women was part of this pattern, as it had been for the first traders and British South Africa Company (BSAC) administrators in the early days of colonialism, but this practice was now frowned upon by the more established groups.[64] The more recent arrivals, too, had to compete with African traders on terms that could not be counted upon to be favorable to them, especially if a local administrator was attempting to foster African entrepreneurship.[65] Like Indian traders, the less affluent white traders worked alongside their children and their African help, another factor that lowered their status in white society. Thus, the category of "trader" was racialized, regardless of the skin color of the individual.

In Cunnison's perceptive account of the whites of Katabulwe, the characteristics of this excluded category emerge, along with some of the reasons for its marginality:

> We went to Meyers place. He was there with his African (half caste) mistress, *trez trez decolletee*, who was eating fish with her fingers and not speaking. . . . After her meal, a large tumbler of *lutuku*, which sent her silently below the table, and she was assisted away. Ongaretti was there too, with the bearing of an officer, except when he walked in a sort of slouch, hands in pockets. . . . These three people say that we are *des congolais, oui, mais nous sommes les Katabulwistes* . . . and that they had a language all of their own. This language was really no worse French than the jargon of Kasenga or Eville [Elizabethville].
>
> I got off in the morning after a reluctant cup of coffee from P. Katabulwe was a cold place, a bitter wind blowing down Luapula. . . .[66]

All had failed economically except Meyer, but Meyer found himself on the margin because he was a Turkish Jew with a half-caste mistress. Ongaretti, on a government development project, was already showing signs of decline, his officer's bearing deteriorating into a slouch. Their degeneration from ideal standards of character becomes clear in their reference to the "language all of their own"— supposedly worse than the French of the larger colonial towns of Kasenga and Elizabethville — and their contrary pride in identifying themselves as *les Katabulwistes*. Sympathy for Africans or too close relations with them may have also been "half the cause" of their failure, as Cunnison noted in his earlier observation of Paschael.

Although the Belgian side nourished more of these marginal groups than the British side,[67] similar people could be found in Northern Rhodesia, and concern to know more about their trading and smuggling activities had partly motivated the colonial government to support RLI research on the Luapula area. Such research was initially suggested by a local administrator, and, when asking the CSSRC to fund the study, Gluckman argued that Luapula was worthy of study for several reasons, not least of which was that "Middlemen of all races flourish."[68]

John Barnes also closely observed the complex hierarchies in colonial society in his research area and believed that racial, ethnic, and class groupings could be called "castes" because of the lack of mobility between them. He despaired of the possibility of ever doing research on the towns, because of the language problem involved in dealing with so many groups of diverse origin. He listed them: the British English-speakers — the "*Azungu ngako*," or true Europeans; the Afrikaaner farmers; the wartime Polish refugees who weren't British subjects and therefore had civil liberties on the order of Coloureds and Africans (and who could only go "submissively" into European shops). Indians could also go "submissively" into European shops, and Coloureds and Africans could go "submissively" into Indian shops.[69] Generally in Northern Rhodesia Africans and Coloureds could buy from European shops but only if served from a hatch in the back.

Barnes's observation of behavior in shops carried particular significance: etiquette in shops was related to a person's recognized class (or consumer) status. In Northern Rhodesia, African buying power never overcame racial barriers. On the contrary, Europeans of British descent frequently employed racial and ethnic distinctions to police class boundaries and limit access to commodities, in a process similar to the "exclusion and enclosure" described by Stoler.[70]

The language problem Barnes mentioned may not have been the most compelling reason why he could not do research in town. At one point, he noted that in shops he was being greeted by Africans in Polish. Although he did not go on to discuss the implications of this, it might indicate that his status as a *muzungu ngako* was getting shaky, perhaps due — as in the case of Paschael — to too much sympathy for Africans and a failure to strictly follow the etiquette of European colonial society.[71] Although Africans noticed the social/racial categories he mentioned, ultimately it was the British who had decided the ranks within that hierarchy, which had existed in roughly similar form since British colonial rule had been established in South Africa. People of British and, sometimes, Dutch descent invariably stood above Africans, while Indians, Coloureds, and non-British whites occupied shifting layers below them, sometimes even falling below specific African groups that were perceived by the British as superior in civilization.[72]

Other RLI anthropologists got direct experience of colonial racial rules, both written and unwritten. Edith Turner remembered the disapproval and threats of legal action when local settlers discovered that her family lived in a "grass camp" made up of African-style temporary shelters, instead of a large cottage tent of the kind used by Europeans.[73] And Ruth van Velsen remembered the distaste with which she and her husband were approached by visiting administrators in Nyasaland, because of her husband's Dutch name and lack of British nationality, as well as their living situation in the midst of African society.[74] Suspicion of his possible Afrikaner origin may have figured in this evaluation because Afrikaaners often have Dutch names. Partly through such experiences, RLI researchers were convinced early on of the difficulty of doing what Gluckman's seven-year plan had originally set out for them to do — to study Europeans, as well as Africans. Some research was done on Europeans, but the researchers always found this work presented them with enormous problems due to their own vulnerability and discomfort in settler communities.[75]

This vulnerability affected not only individual researchers. Because the RLI had been founded partly on the basis of local interest and support, criticism from settler society could threaten the continued existence of the Institute itself.

A Future University

In the deliberations of the CSSRC in 1947 and 1948 over the hiring of Colson first as acting director and later as full director, the worth of the RLI and the direction of its work came up for consideration, and not only by the Colonial Office. Settler opinion in Northern Rhodesia also intruded. In a minute to J. G. Hibbert, Secretary of the Colonial Research Council and Andrew Cohen, head of the Colonial Office African Division, Sir Thomas Lloyd quoted a minute by Rees-Williams on a Northern Rhodesian press article and asked that they look into it.[76] Canham replied at length, quoting the *Central African Post*: "[The article] accuses the Colonial Office of wasting money on research by Rhodes Livingstone Institute. There are already masses of information about tribal customs and trends which for lack of time have never been adequately studied." In response, Canham gave a short history of the work of the RLI, mentioning its very able young director, Colson—"a lady and an American"—and its prestige in academic circles, and he emphasized the Northern Rhodesia governor's enthusiastic support for its new grant.[77] Others agreed with this evaluation, especially Andrew Cohen (discussed in chapter 2), who dismissed the *Central African Post* as "not a particularly serious paper."[78]

Aside from the criticism directed at the Institute from local settlers, at this point in the RLI's history the Colonial Office had three major reservations about continuing its work: the inadequate housing for researchers at the headquarters in Livingstone; "a certain want of confidence in the policies and abilities of those in control" based on disagreements with Gluckman;[79] and the larger problem of the overarching policy for colonial research institutes—that they should be sited near colonial universities. They judged Gluckman to be a poor administrator because of his lack of what they considered sufficient attention to paperwork, which had burgeoned at the Colonial Office while Creech Jones was Colonial Secretary. This was why Colson's secretarial skills figured in their positive evaluation of her for the directorship.

They also disagreed with many of Gluckman's ideas about the proper relationship between colonial governments and research institutes and the role of the sociologist in policy making—a longstanding disagreement which had erupted at various points during his directorship. His acceptance of a lectureship at Oxford and his fight to get the RLI team there for their first writing-up period had also left the lingering suspicion that he was using Colonial Development and Welfare funding to launch anthropologists into academic careers, which would also make it more difficult to get them to remain in colonial research posts. He was also accused of changing his mind about the importance of local colonial institutes, which he denied.[80] This concern may have been based on the suspicion of many at the Colonial Office that Gluckman wanted to continue to control the Institute from his new post at Oxford, which would violate the principle that colonial institutes should be locally controlled.[81]

The Northern Rhodesia governor, Gilbert Rennie, supported both Colson and the Institute, and this proved to be the critical factor in the CSSRC's continuation of its funding. According to Rennie, the RLI was the only colonial research institute for the social sciences that was "a going concern" (the East African and West African institutes still being largely on paper at this stage), and he reassured them about local support for solving the Institute's housing problem.[82]

The decision to move the Institute to Lusaka developed as a solution to the housing problem, as well as from the need to get closer to the Copperbelt for the proposed urban research. During her directorship Colson dealt with the RLI's affairs mainly from her tent in the field in Mazabuka District, partly because the government no longer honored its commitment to supply housing for the RLI. Postwar expansion of the civil service had led to a serious housing shortage: Gluckman's house had been given to a civil servant; the RLI headquarters had to share office space with the Department of African Education; and even the hotels in Livingstone were crowded with newly arrived civil servants.[83] Colson also began writing up her material in the field, preferring this to working from a hotel room. Directing involved more than administrative work, because Colson kept up the tradition of RLI conferences and visiting researchers in the field.[84]

One of the tasks facing Colson as director was the development of a new seven-year research plan to fund the Institute and another team of anthropologists, as funding for Gluckman's plan drew to a close. She attempted to negotiate longer contracts for RLI research officers and the funds for more African research assistants at higher salaries, a pressing issue since the Northern Rhodesia government had recently raised its African staff salaries and assistants would leave the RLI for these higher-paying jobs. She pointed out that the Institute desperately needed assistants for the collection of quantitative material. She also pressed for an urban sociologist to complement the rural studies and for continuing the effort to attract researchers from other disciplines, in particular, history.[85] This pressure facilitated the hiring of Gann, though the CSSRC and Board of Trustees continued to block significant change in the area of research officers' conditions of service and African assistants' salaries.

Because of Gluckman's move to Oxford (and later Manchester), the RLI began to lean more toward Britain in its institutional network, but other African developments would have as strong a role to play in shaping its intellectual — and political — character in subsequent years. The most significant of these were the transfer of its headquarters to Lusaka and Mitchell's and Fosbrooke's directorships there. Although Mitchell clearly found the prospect of urban research an exciting intellectual challenge likely to make his career, both of these directors also kept the RLI's research relevant to colonial planning and supported major research initiatives that got substantial funding from the CSSRC and local sources (the Copperbelt Survey and the long-term Kariba Dam resettlement study, discussed in chapters 6 and 8). The establishment of other social science research institutes in British Africa, unlike the RLI associated with developing colonial universities, also kept up the pressure on the Institute to link itself with a colonial university.

Gluckman had the latter development in mind already in 1947 when reporting on the Institute's budget prior to his departure and requesting more funding to balance it in 1948:

> I would emphasize that [though] the Institute has perforce diverged from the policy of the Council, it has never been granted the sums granted in West and East Africa, where similar Institutes are related to incipient Universities. But it has a major piece of research under way, and under way successfully. . . . I understand that I am said to have changed my mind about the importance of local Institutes. This is not so, though I do consider that the balance to be struck between the local Institutes, especially in Central Africa, and the universities is a major problem still to be tackled.[86]

Gluckman expressed this concern (that the RLI received less generous funding) at a time when the East African institute was hardly more than an idea in postwar planners' minds.[87] This state of affairs reflected issues of control over the RLI that undoubtedly affected the CSSRC's attitude toward funding it. The RLI had independent sources of funding, locally derived from central African colonial governments and the mines, and thus it enjoyed greater freedom from CSSRC control, and it had the ability to use CSSRC support to limit local government control. This balance of power had ramifications for the RLI's research program, as well as for its place in the larger political context of central Africa.

One factor in this larger context was the RLI's relations with the Northern Rhodesia government as it increasingly moved its own operations to the new capital, Lusaka. Another was the possibility of political amalgamation among the three central African countries that figured in the RLI's mandate for research—Northern Rhodesia, Southern Rhodesia, and Nyasaland. It would be efficacious for both research and political reasons to move the RLI headquarters closer to the center of the combined territories or to the capital of a future federation. High among research-related reasons for a move was the impending urban research, which would focus on the Copperbelt. The latter reason figured high in the CSSRC's deliberations about funding the move. In a report of 2 November 1948 on the RLI's work and needs, Keyston, Research Secretary to the Central African Council, noted the greater interest the Northern Rhodesia government had shown in the RLI's research but stressed the need for even closer cooperation. This could be facilitated by appointing special government administrative officers to advise the governments of the three territories on their "practical sociological problems." He emphasized in his report that the Institute's buildings in Livingstone were "shocking" and "no sort of home for a field investigator." Instead of remaining in Livingstone, which also had a "bad climate," he recommended the RLI should move to Lusaka or Salisbury.[88]

A number of potential sites were considered in addition to Salisbury and Lusaka, including Kitwe or Ndola on the Copperbelt, and Broken Hill—halfway between Lusaka and the Copperbelt and the former site of Godfrey Wilson's research.[89] Choosing Salisbury would cause difficulties because the Northern Rhodesia government had a greater interest than the Southern Rhodesia government in the RLI and administered not only the local funding for the Institute but also the CSSRC funding.[90] The RLI's identity as a "Northern Rhodesian institution" was recognized and confirmed even after plans were begun to site the future central African university in Salisbury.[91] Moreover, Colson expressed concern that if the Institute had to mount its urban social surveys in Southern Rhodesia at the same time as it was starting them in Northern Rhodesia, the researchers would be spread too thinly during the crucial early period of their work.[92]

Racial politics may have also weighed against Salisbury in the eyes of the anthropologists, because its stricter color bar would have made collaborative work at headquarters more difficult for both the researchers and African assistants. The Copperbelt, on the other hand, would have been too distant from the center of gravity of a future federation, and choice of such a site may have given the impression the RLI was not sufficiently interested in doing Southern Rhodesian research. Thus, Lusaka emerged as the site most reflective of these various interests. Although set aside for the moment, the issue of association of research institutes with colonial universities would arise again in the 1950s.

Colson had reservations about siting the new headquarters in Lusaka because she feared the Institute could be dominated by Northern Rhodesian government interests. Nevertheless, she saw advantages in associating the RLI with a "pro-African" institution at the Lusaka location — the recently founded Munali African Secondary School, which she thought might become the site of a future university. Along with its potential as a source of educated Africans to work as assistants, a location near Munali would also provide an intellectual community of European and African teachers who lived on the grounds and which included the few university-educated Africans in the country.[93] Because of the presence of a group of highly trained Africans, Colson hoped the RLI would eventually be able to appoint African research officers on equal terms with the European officers. This, too, could foster the growth of a future university in Northern Rhodesia.

Unfortunately, settler political aspirations and a growing African opposition would lead to conflicts that would deflect these plans. During Colson's directorship, the Victoria Falls conference on the political amalgamation of Northern and Southern Rhodesia and

The Institute buildings in Lusaka shortly after construction. (Photo from RLI poster in author's possession.)

Nyasaland caused acrimonious debates among settlers agitating for self-rule, Africans of all kinds who were opposed to white domination, and colonial administrators often divided in their loyalties. Although amalgamation failed at that point, the Federation that was established in 1953 would radically alter the political and economic balance of central Africa, redirecting the resources of Nyasaland and Northern Rhodesia in favor of the larger white settler society in Southern Rhodesia. As a result, the hoped-for future university would be placed in Salisbury, reopening the debate on the RLI's location.

The aspirations of another white group, Afrikaner nationalists in South Africa, would also influence the RLI's future. The growing importance of apartheid policies after 1948 and the changes forced on the liberal universities there led to the flight of many South African academics. Some of these left by way of the RLI and Manchester, where South African exiles joined Gluckman and others in antiapartheid and anticolonial activities in the 1950s, keeping alive there and at the RLI many of the political issues that had informed Gluckman's original seven-year plan and its vision of central Africa.

Conclusion

Colson left the directorship before the new RLI buildings in Lusaka were started. Mitchell became acting director and eventually full director of the RLI while working on his Copperbelt study. He would direct the Institute from Luanshya, his fieldsite on the Copperbelt, until the buildings in Lusaka were finished. Meanwhile Colson took up a senior lectureship in the social anthropology department that Gluckman founded in Manchester in 1949.

Gluckman's prior move to Oxford and an academic career in England not only led to Colson's RLI directorship and later lectureship in Manchester but also affected other key areas. These included the position of the RLI in the career paths of anthropologists, its role in the development of a group of researchers into a research school, and the Institute's own position in the geography of political and intellectual institutions in British Africa, South Africa, and Britain. When Gluckman moved to Oxford in 1947, and especially when he became the chair of social anthropology at the University of Manchester in 1949, he strengthened the Institute's and its researchers' ties with the metropolitan universities and funding organizations. Colson's subsequent lectureship there pioneered the kind of career path that several former RLI researchers would follow. Gluckman also provided at Manchester a firm base for initial training and writing up of research results for new groups of RLI fieldworkers. The fact that many of the original team and subsequent students obtained posts at Manchester contributed to the interaction necessary to produce the related body of theory and method that earned them recognition as the Manchester School.

This, however, has given rise to a picture of the relationship between Manchester and the RLI that is far too simple — that of Manchester as the intellectual center and the RLI as a dependent fieldwork outpost available for occasional outdoor relief for a group of intellectuals whose development of theory necessarily depended on the intellectual stimulus of the university setting. Anthropology's own self-histories usually produce stories of this sort, where the field might be a source of revelation and insight but not the setting for the serious work of theory development. Gluckman's own published description of the process also follows this way of looking at the relationship of fieldwork to theory construction, for already in 1947 he felt it was time for the new crop of fieldworkers to "forsake the savage for the study" and devote themselves to using the data they had collected for developing new anthropological theories.[94]

Although Gluckman's move to England helped to foster the Manchester School as a group involved in the development of their characteristic theories, what the previous chapters have shown is that this research school's emergence and group character had already evolved in the field. Indeed, it was the RLI experience that created Manchester's social anthropology department, according to Gluckman, who in 1949 told Mitchell he intended to "build a new RLI" at Manchester. He felt that the core of researchers already trained at the RLI provided him the means to compete with older schools in bigger universitites.[95] And, confirming the CSSRC's suspicions, he indeed intended to use Manchester's social anthropology department as a means of supporting the further work of the Institute, for he saw the RLI as "an important experiment in sociological research — and it will further that experiment if I can keep a nucleus of RLI people in association at Manchester."

In general, RLI researchers did become more oriented toward careers in metropolitan universities and toward developments in theory. But their commitment to locally useful research continued to be strong whenever their conditions of service made that kind of work both possible and attractive.

6

Atop the Central African Volcano

During J. Clyde Mitchell's directorship from 1952 to 1955, the RLI initiated a full-scale program of urban research. Although rural studies continued, the urban research inspired an extraordinarily productive period of work at the Institute for a number of reasons.

First, the fact that urban and rural studies were proceeding at the same time stimulated a new type of interaction among the researchers, many of whom were now able to benefit from experience in both settings, as well as from the insights of colleagues in one or the other. This type of interaction provided the data necessary for researchers to begin to see patterns of African rural and urban experience that would not have been as easily discerned if the researchers themselves had been limited to one setting or the other. Second, this period saw the first serious funding for training a team of African research assistants. This team not only helped in the collection of statistics but also provided an essential qualitative dimension to the Institute's work. This may have been the first time in the history of anthropology that a large number of indigenous researchers worked together for a lengthy period of time doing studies of their own communities and society. The effect of their insights and their style of research practice would be profound (see chapter 7). In addition, their interactions with the RLI research officers, like that between urban and rural researchers, provided yet another level of intellectual stimulation and yet another network — this time of African intellectuals and their friends, families, and work and school contacts — that facilitated and influenced the Institute's research. Third, the Manchester connection, and the contemporary RLI researchers' continuing correspondence with former RLI researchers there and in new non-African field sites, became stronger during this time.

The published output from this period at the RLI is so large that it cannot be discussed in detail, though Mitchell's "Kalela Dance," like Gluckman's "Analysis," will be considered in its role as a model for later work. Although he only published the paper in 1956, Mitchell discussed his ideas with his colleagues, including the African survey team members, and presented the paper at an RLI conference much earlier. The paper itself drew together information from a number of surveys that figured in earlier discussions, as well as observational work by Mitchell and his assistant, Sykes Ndilila, that took place early on in the Institute's urban research. Epstein's development of the case study method for urban fieldwork and his other innovations in method and theory will also be discussed at some length.

In general, the theoretical innovations that developed out of the RLI and Manchester School fieldwork in urban anthropology have been masterfully described by Ulf Hannerz — in particular, network analysis, which had a major impact on scholarship across a number of disciplines in the 1960s.[1] Richard Werbner has also considered the impact of other strands of RLI research based on fieldwork carried out at this time, especially that of Turner, Watson, and van Velsen.[2] Watson's work emphasized the relationship between dual spheres of country and city, showing structurally how the Mambwe had achieved a different and more positive adaptation to the money economy than had their neighbors, the Bemba, studied by Audrey Richards.[3] Van Velsen further developed Mitchell's use of micro-histories to analyze Yao village politics, in his work on the Lakeside Tonga of Nyasaland. He paid particular attention to informal political processes and strategies that did not rely entirely upon formal political offices or traditional practices of succession.[4] Turner's study of the Ndembu represented path-breaking work in the areas of transactionalism and symbolic interaction, as well as further developing the methods of microhistories and processual analysis.[5]

Karen Hansen has discussed the urban work of Hortense Powdermaker, an American anthropologist partly trained at LSE, who did a study in the RLI urban fieldsite of Luanshya while affiliated with the Institute and supported by a trained RLI assistant, Frederick Phiri.[6] This work contained valuable insights about the lives of urban African women.[7] Lewis Gann's historical work continued in earnest during this period, as RLI anthropologists familiarized him with the use of local archival sources often neglected by the imperial-focused historians but which the RLI researchers had already used extensively for the historical contextualization of their own work.[8] In addition, my own historical/sociological approach to this study of the RLI has been influenced by later developments in the history of science, the sociology of work, and the sociology of the professions that began with the RLI/Manchester School innovations.

Mitchell continued the tradition of taking new researchers out into the field for a training session, but because many of the new researchers arrived at different times he was unable to take any large group out at one time. Researchers also left the field at different times, according to when their contracts ended. Those who remained for a second contract saw many of their contemporaries leave long before they did — Epstein, for example, felt like the "last of the Mohicans" at a point when nearly all of those with whom he had worked had moved on, including Mitchell, the director.[9] Nevertheless, the series of productive RLI conferences continued, supplemented by the Manchester seminar, as researchers moved from one institution to the other. And interaction continued to be most intense for those researchers who did fieldwork at the same time. Researchers continued to visit each other in the field, with urban researchers, in particular, doing rural work and language learning before they started their urban work and sometimes doing those preliminary rural studies near the sites of the rural researchers. The cohesiveness of the RLI researchers as a group was also enhanced by the team of assistants, who could be called upon to visit as a team and do survey work for the rural researchers. This survey work and the continuing plan to produce a joint volume on the industrial revolution in central Africa kept Gluckman's vision of comparative regional research alive until Mitchell left in 1955.

Some of the studies begun during Mitchell's directorship spilled over into the subsequent directorships of C. M. N. White and Henry Fosbrooke. Moreover, Mitchell, from his new post as chair of African Studies at the University of Rhodesia and Nyasaland (UCRN), began to send students for fieldwork. During his directorship Fosbrooke kept the African urban survey team for a number of smaller studies, and researchers arrived to do poverty datum line studies that employed the team. He continued the RLI conferences and argued for a large-scale, long-term project—the Kariba Study—that not only kept up the Institute's involvement in applied anthropology but also brought Elizabeth Colson back for a major piece of rural research.

Because of the large numbers of people at the Institute and the diversity of the work done there, the usefulness of the idea of a field generation diminishes somewhat for analyzing this period. Thus, in this chapter and the following one I will discuss the RLI's history thematically, dividing my attention between two interconnected aspects of the Institute's work in this period—its urban studies and the emergence of the RLI's African urban survey team.

The Bridge to the City

Many of the concerns that RLI anthropologists brought to their work in Central Africa originated in the concerns of South African society in the years from 1919 to 1936, as delineated by liberals, social scientists, and politicians. The rapid migration of Africans to the cities, caused by rural poverty and the attraction of industrial work, triggered the concern of white scholars and laymen about the so-called native problem. Mining companies generally maintained the traditional policy of keeping African workers in a state of labor migration because they felt South Africa's gold was a wasting asset that would not assure jobs for a permanently urbanized black workforce. This policy became even stronger when the 1929 world economic slump led to a surplus of African labor.[10] Politicians used these worries to erode or delay political rights and better working conditions for Africans, with General J. B. M. Hertzog, founder of the Afrikaner-based National Party and Prime Minister between 1933 and 1939, being "particularly adept at transforming the idea of black political advancement into a generalised sense of panic."[11]

Emerging from this context of anxiety about Africans in the city, segregationist thought in the 1920s and 1930s affected even the liberal anthropologists' thinking about African culture. In the 1920s, "the reconstitution of a 'primitive idyll'" as part of segregationist thinking found a parallel in anthropologists' seeking to "uncover the essence of 'primitive mentality' and to proclaim the integrity and inherent worth of different 'cultures.'" Whether or not they agreed with segregationist policy or had any effective influence on the government, anthropologists found their ideas about African culture being used to support segregationist ideology.[12] In this context, Malinowski's "culture contact" theory, which became dominant in South African anthropology from the mid-1930s, could be construed as supporting segregation because of its emphasis on the damaging effects that contact with a modern urban industrial society could have on a "primitive" society. Ellen Hellman, the leading South African exponent of this theory, who pursued the first urban anthropological studies in the mid-1930s, however, disagreed that segregation should be the solution for the psychological problems Africans suffered as a result of bridging the gulf between cultures.[13] For her M.A. thesis at the University of Witwatersrand (Wits), she did a study of a Johannesburg slumyard in 1933, the research intended to parallel, in an urban context, that of Monica Wilson in Pondoland,[14] which had itself included a brief look at Pondo migrants in town. The importance to the RLI of her urban study can be judged from Gluckman's interest in republishing it in 1948.[15]

Gluckman's "Analysis," though it did not deal with an urban situation, also provided a model for the RLI's urban research in its use of situational analysis and attention to the larger industrial context of southern Africa. It also signaled the importance of ethnicity, not in the form of a tribal unit of analysis, but as interpreted and employed by Africans attempting to deal with rapid social change. This aspect, too, would be further developed in the RLI's urban work. Gluckman also set the agenda for undermining the idea of detribalization for understanding the lives of urban Africans. This was partly based on a critique of the view that towns were an unnatural setting for Africans, an idea used to justify labor migration in South Africa. But it was also both a critique of and further development of Godfrey Wilson's use of the term.

Gluckman's South African heritage was far from being the only source of the RLI's goals and methods for urban research. The late nineteenth-century British movement that originated from reformers' interest in the causes of poverty in Britain's fast-growing cities also provided inspiration. Anthropologists at the RLI received this influence in a number of ways. For example, the genealogical method that they, like other social anthropologists, commonly used, derived in part from early surveys of the British poor conducted by Charles Booth and Seebohm Rowntree in the 1880s that focused on family or household. British anthropologists began using the genealogical method during the 1898 Cambridge Expedition to the Torres Straits.[16] The practice had become a standard method soon after.

Although the genealogical method first used in British poverty studies had become standard practice, the RLI work on assessing poverty itself derived from other more local sources. Godfrey Wilson's early RLI work, though not focused on poverty, produced data relevant to the issue because Wilson looked at wage levels of migrant workers and stressed that they were often inadequate.[17] Attention to poverty-related—though nonurban—subjects also came from Phyllis Deane's economic study of the rural RLI fieldsites. In addition, the influence of Booth and Rowntree found its way indirectly into the later Copperbelt survey through Mitchell's familiarity with the work of Edward Batson, who had been trained by A. L. Bowley at the London School of Economics. Batson's social survey of Cape Town, begun in 1936, was the first survey of poverty in an African city. He later conducted "poverty datum line" surveys—that is, surveys to determine the minimum income necessary for an adequate standard of living—in other parts of Africa, including Salisbury, the capital of Southern Rhodesia, in 1944. He also experimented with ways of taking culture into account in determining minimum needs.[18] Batson's influence continued in the work of later human geographers, such as David Bettison and George Kay, who conducted poverty datum line surveys for the RLI in the late 1950s.

Missionary interest in African cities emerged slowly and had little influence on social scientists' ideas about urban research until the late 1930s. (Some of these issues are described in chapter 3.) Missions in southern Africa nearly always based themselves in the rural

David Bettison with urban survey team. In the late 1950s, Bettison and the team did the first poverty datum line studies in central Africa. (Photo from RLI poster in author's possession.)

areas and treated the cities as white enclaves.[19] Ironically, starting in the nineteenth century, missions to rural Africa had provided a model for metropolitan-based mission work among the urban poor in Britain because of the Victorian tendency to equate the poor with savages.[20] Interest in the effects of industrialization on Africans in the interwar period, however, stimulated some research, for example, the World Council of Churches study of conditions on the Copperbelt in 1932.[21] This study influenced Wilson's hiring, and his approach, as discussed in chapter 3, owed much to ideas of Christian sociology. Other studies by missionaries or under the auspices of missions followed the World Council of Churches' study and Wilson's work in Broken Hill. The first study of poverty in Southern Rhodesia was a survey carried out in 1942–43 by the secretary of the Native Welfare Society, the Reverend Percy Ibbotson. This study compared wages with the cost of food in urban areas. In Northern Rhodesia, R. J. B. Moore studied family budgets on the Copperbelt after the 1940 miners' strike and found that half were receiving less than what was required for basic needs.[22] The mining companies did not accept these findings, and the later poverty datum line work done by Bettison for the RLI also would stir up controversy because of its potential use by African miners to justify their wage demands.

The South African mining companies had long shown an interest in African laborers' characteristics, initially focusing on ethnic traits that supposedly suited different groups for different kinds of work. Later, in Northern Rhodesia, the mines sought further (nonethnic) data to help with policy decisions about labor stabilization on the Copperbelt, where—unlike the Rand—the companies competed with each other and with the copper mines in the Belgian Congo to attract African workers and, thus, had to improve living and working conditions to do so.

Other differences from the South African situation shaped mining company policies on the Copperbelt. The initial focus on ethnic traits had led South African mines to base labor policies such as hiring, supervision, and housing in South Africa on the managers' practical experience and their belief in a hierarchy of tribes well or ill suited for various kinds of work. On the Copperbelt, however, tribal identity did not shape workers' experience as rigidly as on the Rand,[23] though an ethnic hierarchy of job categories still characterized some mine work and other work that was available to Africans in the towns. In addition, in South Africa (but only much later in Northern Rhodesia), the mining companies, though interested in research on Africans, favored psychological research over anthropology and its possibly disturbing methods.[24] Industrial psychology, unlike anthropology, focused on the worker as worker, rather than as a member of an African society either urban or rural, and thus promised to help in the maintenance of an efficient and harmonious work situation through attention to workers' psychological needs and their fitness for specific tasks. (Gluckman's approach, as discussed in chapter 3, also stressed treating African miners as miners, first and foremost, but he equally stressed the importance of comparative research that would link urban studies with rural studies to elucidate the total picture of labor migration, rural life, and industrial urban society.) British industrial psychology had made similar arguments for its usefulness between the wars, going so far as to argue that the mere presence of psychologists showed management's concern for workers and made them happier and more productive.[25] Both of these reasons may have figured in mine managers' preference for psychological over anthropological research. The research methods used by psychologists could also be more easily employed in a segregated society than those of anthropology.

The Rand mines' history of interest in ethnicity as a means of classifying labor led these companies, in 1929, to hire a psychologist from the National Insitute of Industrial Psychology in Britain to help them increase efficiency through the differentiation of labor. The psychologist, A. Stephenson, placed workers on a continuum from the primitive to the civilized based on levels of "self control" and suggested that such characteristics as adaptability, cheerfulness, and willingness to work might be determined by tribe.[26] A more sophisticated variety of industrial psychology emerged following the Second World War, along with occupational testing and the professionalization of occupational and industrial psychology through the auspices of the South African National Institute for Personnel Research (NIPR),[27] whose director, Simon Biesheuvel, formed part of the southern African network of the RLI. (He later did research on white miners on the Copperbelt on the eve of Zambian independence, in conjunction with Holleman.[28])

All of the concerns discussed in this section — about the responses of Africans to urban industrial life — came to be focused primarily in the RLI's work on the cities of the Copperbelt.[29] Thus it is necessary to consider the nature of the Copperbelt towns and what they represented to the Africans and whites who settled there, as well as to the professional groups — administrators, missionaries, mine managers, and anthropologists — who found their livelihood bound up with this new and rapidly changing environment.

"Nothing Is Pure in the Copperbelt"

The location of Northern Rhodesia's Copperbelt towns had been initially determined by white interest in the copper deposits, but Africans — and the need to attract, accommodate, or discourage their presence — played a decisive role in determining the *nature* of the urban areas. For Africans, the Copperbelt represented a place to get money — for taxes, for modern consumer goods, or for investment in the equipment needed for rural enterprises such as fishing or farming. It also increasingly represented a more comfortable and sophisticated (or so-called civilized) way of life to Africans who had been exposed to mission education and Western commodities in the rural areas, and who aspired to modernity. Many also found themselves driven from the rural areas by poverty. The initiating factor in these needs was the demand for labor on the mines and the government's collusion in a tax policy designed to force rural Africans to sell their labor in the towns. But as the rural areas suffered increasing poverty from the effects of the migration of large numbers of young men, more and more Africans of all kinds, including women, moved to the towns in hope of a better standard of living.

From the beginning, urban Africans had diverse motives for being there and for seeking the jobs they acquired in towns. Many moved to the towns, not as potential mine laborers, but to provide services for the miners through prostitution, beer brewing, or growing and selling food. Some also worked for whites as domestic servants, employees in shops, construction workers, or clerks for government and the mines.[30] An ethnic hierarchy ruled the allocation of jobs, partly enforced by white ideas of tribal differences, but also determined by the migrants' dependence for employment on the experience and connections of previous migrants from their home areas, a dependence that led to the clustering of certain ethnic groups in certain jobs, such as the Luvale in night soil removal.[31] Africans from Nyasaland made up the majority of clerks because of their greater educational opportunities in their home area and they got a reputation among mine managers as being more intelligent than local Africans.[32] The Bemba, who equated work on the mines with their former warrior roles, got a reputation for bravery and, thus, the highest paying jobs as deep underground miners.[33] Colored people and ethnic groups that Europeans believed had originated from earlier racial mixing, such as the Kunda of the Northern Rhodesia/Mozambique border area, often got jobs as mechanics because of the general belief of settlers that European blood gave them greater skill with machinery.[34]

The mines' policies on housing and pay responded to African preferences to some degree, though changing economic conditions were always the more powerful factor. African miners had to be attracted to the mines from other labor centers, for example, the Belgian Congo Katanga mines, where working and living conditions were better,[35] and the Rand and Southern Rhodesian mines, both on labor migration routes that predated the emergence of the Copperbelt and thus continued to attract Africans. Local mine conditions also determined patterns of African movement into the towns. Broken Hill and Bwana Mkubwa mines, not located directly on the Copperbelt, competed with the Copperbelt mines, and Africans preferred them because management allowed miners' families to live there.[36]

Africans also influenced the nature of the towns by refusing to leave when employers decided their labor wasn't needed. Government and mines labeled this phenomenon the "loafer problem" and continued into the 1950s to express the vain hope that redundant laborers would return to the rural areas, as most, but not all, of them had done during the slump of the 1930s.[37] Thus, the government and mine policy of "stabilisation without urbanisation" instituted at the end of the 1940s failed to provide sufficient social services for permanently urbanized Africans, though it called for greater support for laborers whom they expected to spend a significant portion of their life cycle in the towns.[38]

The nature of the towns also derived from white migrant labor and its demands, as well as government and mine policy concerning white settlement and the provision of social services for this segment of the population. The Copperbelt towns began as prospectors' towns — temporary settlements designed for the exploitation of a resource that was recognized as finite. Accordingly, the mining companies paid high salaries and at times a "copper bonus" to attract skilled white labor into a difficult frontier environment. This produced an inflationary economy that made life difficult for other Europeans and Africans, as well as for government administrators, who did not have salaries equal to those of white miners and managers. The Copperbelt cities' aura of impermanence also derived from the boosterism (the aggressive self-advertising) that the mines engaged in as part of their campaign to attract white labor.[39] A promotional film produced in the 1950s focused on features of white life in the Copperbelt reminiscent of tropical pleasure resorts, with smiling black waiters, swimming pools, and year-round golf greens. African villages appeared as exotic curiosities, much as they appear in films promoting popular tourist destinations today.[40] White society on the Copperbelt put into practice this temporary, pleasure-seeking ethic in behavior that emphasized excessive consumption as a compensation for temporary hardships, which were endured only to gain the financial means for permanent settlement elsewhere.[41]

Other segments of Northern Rhodesia's white population, however, wanted to remain in the country. These settlers sought self-determination and hoped for eventual independence from British colonial rule.[42] Booster campaigns on the Copperbelt thus also reflected the desire of some whites to increase their numbers and their political strength. Even limited social services for Africans — involving sanitation and health care — sometimes gained the support of these Europeans who saw such policies as a way to make the cities healthier and more attractive to future white immigrants.[43] Interest in African housing, for example, stemmed partly from these concerns, originally stimulated in South Africa by the 1919 influenza epidemic that revealed the slum conditions under which urban Africans lived, conditions that could endanger the white population through the spread of disease.[44] Settlers also tried to reduce outside control, both by the colonial government with its supposed favoritism toward blacks, and by the externally based mining companies that took the copper profits out of the country. The mines responded to white settler resentment of their failure to invest locally in a number of ways. For example, when in the 1930s Governor Hubert Young questioned the legality of mine royalties, this may have motivated the mines to donate money for the RLI, the governor's pet project.[45]

Members of the white miners' union also resented their treatment by companies that, in difficult economic times, always attempted to replace them with cheaper black labor.[46] Roy Welensky, a railway workers' labor leader and the leader of the drive for white self-determination in Northern Rhodesia, (discussed in chapter 3), attempted to win mineral rights away from the British South Africa Company (BSAC) — a policy that could have forced more investment of copper profits in the country. For the same reason, he supported amalgamation with Southern Rhodesia as a way of strengthening Northern Rhodesian settlers in their struggle against outside control by the mines and colonial government.[47] Northern Rhodesian settlers felt ambivalent about the policy of amalgamation, however, because of the possibility of their losing power to the greater white population in Southern Rhodesia. Nonetheless, a looser economic and political federation received sufficient suppport both in Britain and the Rhodesias to become a reality in 1953.

The nature of the Copperbelt city was also determined in no small part by colonial government policies that suppported or checked the different African and white forces that shaped its development. As a result, the colonial administration was resented both by Africans because it limited their movement into towns and by whites because it limited their local domination. The colonial government seemed anachronistic to both whites and blacks, especially in the midst of the 1950s' struggles for self-determination launched by each of these groups. Administrators often found themselves ignored or resented in this context, a situation described by one of them as follows: "It was appropriate at that time to tour the town and Mine Compounds by bicycle, accompanied by two or three Messengers and dressed in khaki. . . . We were, after all, the 'Queen's men' and if we chose to be a little old-fashioned, perhaps it was fitting. It was the sight that the people were used to in the villages. Besides, we could take the temperature as we rode along, and enter to some extent into the African's feelings as we were borne over to the side of the road by a succession of badly driven motor-cars coming up behind us."[48]

In the booming and increasingly modern Copperbelt towns, the district officer on his bicycle represented the inadequacies of the colonial government in urban Africa. As Epstein observed at the time, "The office of the District Commissioner has its origins in the conditions of rural administration."[49] And government had since done little to modernize administrative practices to meet urban needs on the Copperbelt largely because the powerful mines discouraged government interference in issues affecting their operations. District Officer Robin Short, who is quoted above, may have been the victim of "munt-scaring," while touring the workers' compounds on his bicycle, a common practice among Copperbelt whites, many of them miners from South Africa, who enjoyed driving their cars as closely as possible to Africans on bicycles wobbling along the bad township roads.[50] Such whites generally considered colonial officers to be "Negrophiles" who stood in the way of white self-determination in Northern Rhodesia. Africans also saw colonial government in the towns as inadequate and set about organizing their own welfare societies, unions, and political parties.

In terms of policy, the colonial government accepted African urbanization after World War Two, but did not change its administrative practices significantly in the colonial period. Until the early 1960s, the residents of the Copperbelt found themselves assigned to the native authorities in the rural areas from which they or their parents came.[51] The focus remained on the policy of "stabilisation without urbanisation" favored by the mines, which supported government plans to make the rural areas more attractive as places of retirement for labor migrants. This policy allowed the colonial administrators, as opposed to technical officers, to retain a view of African development that saw the countryside, and not the city, as the appropriate locus of progress. As Heissler contends, "The Provincial Administrators . . . perceived their colonial duty to be the generation of a 'civilised' society out of the bush and [the] primitive technologies of pre-contact Zambia. These civil servants in the main did not believe that urbanisation was the right path towards 'civilisation.' "[52] Government plans to improve urban social services accordingly involved considerable footdragging, for administrators feared that providing services in the towns would stimulate more urbanization at the expense of the development of the countryside.

Government technical officers, however, pushed different ideas of development based on their areas of specialization and, in the case of labor, received the backing of the Colonial Office. In 1938 the Colonial Office got its first Labour Advisor and began to urge colonial governments to found native labor departments.[53] The Northern Rhodesian government, as in other colonies, did not take up this suggestion eagerly and hesitated to transfer responsibility from district officers to a specialist department.[54]

In this contested urban setting, government was not the only actor with an interest in understanding and controlling African workers. The mining companies had a history of collecting minimal basic statistics on their labor force and experimenting with management practices, though practices most often were based on managers' experience rather than on systematic research. Payroll statistics and statistics on output could be used to roughly determine the efficiency of the workforce, and an awareness of low productivity as well as economic pressure to reduce labor costs was what stimulated the introduction of so-called scientific management techniques, pioneered in the United States much earlier. It was partly because of these concerns that the growing influence of industrial psychology on the Rand found its way to the South African-owned companies on the Copperbelt.

Often in contrast with the South African-owned companies, the American and British-owned companies inherited a management culture associated with the "company town," which led to their greater willingness to stabilize African labor.[55] The creation of the company town in Britain and the United States had also involved experiments in social engineering, and this heritage added to the tendency to use the Copperbelt towns as experimental sites for trying out new management policies. The American/British-owned mine, Roan Antelope, also became the first—both on the Copperbelt and in the entire southern African region—to mechanize its payroll using early statistical technology. Eventually an in-house research department used this new technology to gather statistics relevant to management policy. Systematic in-house research did not begin, however, until after the mines experimented with the use of external researchers—the urban researchers of the RLI.

The mines also shaped the nature of the urban areas through the constant supervision and control of African miners, requiring them to live in mine housing areas (called "compounds" or "locations") and encouraging them to use their leisure time in mine compound beer halls and other facilities. During most of the colonial period, the mines and government controlled African workers' movements and access to labor through a pass system, requiring each African worker to carry a *citupa* — an employment history card signed by employers, which made it easy to blacklist so-called undesirables.[56] Within the housing areas, the compound managers exercised authority over almost every aspect of life, helped by white supervisors of welfare, maintenance, and other departments, each with a complement of African assistants of various kinds — clerks, laborers, and police — in a system not unlike that of the rural government administrator.[57] Although overall company policies determined basic conditions in the mines, individual managers themselves could create urban environments that were more or less attractive to workers. Some managers had a liberal and egalitarian reputation, while others beat or abused workers or instituted unpopular scientific management practices.[58]

The major 1935 strike by African miners, however, revealed the weaknesses in the mining companies' organization and control of the Copperbelt cities. Indeed, the general "Strike Wave," which hit Africa in the mid-1930s and continued into the 1940s, led to dramatic changes in labor and urban policies on the part of the British government.[59] After the Copperbelt strike of 1935, Governor Young pointed to industrialization and detribalization as the most important problems in Northern Rhodesia.[60] Young was already in the midst of a struggle with the Colonial Office to get funding for his research institute, and after the strikes he argued the case for the future RLI on the basis of its usefulness for studying the problems the 1935 strike had highlighted.[61]

In general, this continuing labor unrest strengthened the hand of government in dealing with the mines and strengthened the technocrats within government who, in turn, may have looked more favorably on the employment of experts like themselves to study these problems. As a result, the early RLI research focused on urban African labor, though Godfrey Wilson's study from 1939 to 1940 dealt only with Broken Hill, and he was not allowed to continue with his intended study of the Copperbelt. After this failure, and a second wave of strikes in 1940, the government continued to press for research and funded A. L. Saffery in 1943 to do a study of mine labor conditions on the Copperbelt, which strengthened the government's argument that the mining companies must increase African wages and avoid future strikes.

Ultimately what the 1935 strikes demonstrated to both government and the mines was that—like it or not—urban Africans had their own effective methods of organization and control within the urban, industrial environment. Africans had organized the strikes despite the absence of any formal union, through a system of communication based on informal networks of African clerks, the *Mbeni* dance associations, and the Watchtower church (Jehovah's Witnesses) groups.[62] African welfare societies, political parties, and unions gradually evolved in the urban environment in similar ways— in the case of the welfare societies, to fill the gaps in government and mining company social services for urban Africans. In the case of the other organizations, however, Africans consciously developed alternatives to mine or government structures of control that they found objectionable. African women organized strategies for beer brewing and other illegal money-making activities, subverting government attempts to remove them from, or control them within, the urban environment.[63] Unions developed out of African miners' attempts to channel their grievances through nontribally based organizations, reflecting their growing consciousness of class and recognition of the weakness of mine-imposed types of organization based on rural models. And political parties, beginning with the Northern Rhodesian African National Congress (ANC or Congress) founded in 1948, rose in response to the threat of federation and developed a campaign that eventually led to African independence.

In one way, however, urban Africans agreed with the government and the mines—they viewed the Copperbelt environment as less healthy than rural life and during this period frequently used appeals to the purity of rural conditions and traditions when arguing with Europeans over living and working conditions. Both Europeans and Africans used the idea of tradition selectively to defend different practices or shore up opposing arguments. This was not only because of the inherent power of appeals to tradition. It also derived from the history of the Copperbelt as a place of boom and bust, where both the white and black populations fluctuated with economic extremes.

As RLI researchers discovered, access for researchers sometimes had to be negotiated with Africans who felt that urban life was too ephemeral to be worth studying. For example, in October 1950 an RLI research assistant, Ivor Kalima, encountered some resistance when he went to observe a mourning ceremony for the paramount chief of the Lunda, who had died in rural Luapula Province. Miners from Luapula had arranged to hold the mourning ceremony at Roan Antelope African Township for Lunda people who lived in Luanshya and could not return to Luapula for the mourning. The Luanshya mourners told Kalima not to bother with the urban ceremony:

> In the evening I spoke to Mr. Tuba and Mr. Musumbulwa that I would like to observe the mourning of Mwata Kasembe in connection with the Social Study directed by Dr. Mitchell. *Mr. Tuba*: What has Dr. Mitchell to do with mourning of Mwata Kasembe? We know only one person in this country—Kalanda Mikowa [the Lunda name for RLI anthropologist, Ian Cunnison] who is at Kawambwa [in the Luapula district]. Tell him to go to Kawambwa if he really wants to know something about [the mourning ceremony]. *Mr. Musumbulwa*: In fact nothing is pure in the copperbelt. People will not take the mourning in the way it will be taken at home. Therefore Dr. Mitchell must record the real things about the mourning ceremony at Kasembe's Village."[64]

Africans' interest in the "real things" that could only be recorded in the village stemmed from the past usefulness of arguments based on tradition for influencing the colonial government on any number of matters from chieftainship to marriage law.[65] Even urban Africans employed strategies based on appeals to rural custom for organizing and controlling their urban environment. But in the course of the 1950s Africans would increasingly turn toward other strategies and, to do that, began to show interest in other ways of understanding the city, going beyond the simple negative comparison of urban society with rural society.

Indeed, Africans, the mines, and government all responded to the

strike wave of the 1930s and 1940s with fresh attempts to understand, organize, and control the Copperbelt city — Africans with a
sense of new possibilities gained from the success of some of their
strikes, while mines and government with the sense that a degree of
African urbanization had to be accepted. *Whose* methods of organization would dominate and what shape they would take, then, became the object of struggle in the 1940s and 1950s. Despite, or
perhaps because of, these struggles for control, the African city that
was developing was in many respects an unknown quantity. The
colonial government possessed a vision of what the rural African
was supposed to be and become, but because of its rural bias it had
no strong vision of the future of the urban African. The mining
companies also clung to a rural vision of Africans, even when they
accepted that the workforce must be stabilized in the urban areas for
a portion of its life cycle. Africans, too, maintained ties to the rural
areas as long as their urban lives were made uncertain by government and mining company policy, but they created structures for
urban survival that, though often expressed in traditional language,
constituted new urban ways of understanding and organizing themselves that also affected the ways they organized and understood
themselves when in the villages.

Therefore, throughout British Africa the decade from 1935 to
1945 represented a "break point in colonial thinking: the idea of
'tribal' Africa was losing its usefulness and officials were casting
about for conceptual tools to regain their sense of control." According to Cooper, the British began to apply the model of metropolitan
industrial relations to their colonies, introducing labor departments,
trade unions for African workers, and social welfare programs intended to produce a responsible African working class and to limit it
to a manageable size — a policy of stabilization bolstered by development of housing, health care, and other social services.[66]

Because understanding and organizing were important to all the
parties in the struggle for control of the African city, social scientists could make arguments for the usefulness of their work that
would appeal to Africans, mines, and government. Indeed, by the
1950s when the RLI launched its first successful Copperbelt study, it

wisely offered the use of its data to all concerned, including Africans who had come to control access to the African city on a nearly equal basis with the mines and government. Thus, the Institute presented itself as responding to the needs of all those groups who were trying to make the Copperbelt towns their own. This strategy worked to produce ground-breaking research, but it only partially and very slowly gained acceptance among government and mining company planners.

Finding a Frame

The RLI's urban research in the 1950s became possible because of a number of factors that had changed since Wilson's earlier work, even though government and mining company anxiety about the political position of the researcher continued. More strikes and labor disturbances, as well as something of a sense of obligation to demobilized African soldiers, motivated government to consider development plans that included city life for Africans and more social amenities than could be offered in the villages. The likelihood of federation also motivated British and local government interest in certain kinds of development, including a focus on African welfare that might make the idea of so-called racial partnership — used to persuade Africans of the advantages of federation — seem viable. Social research played a key role in these plans. Research of any kind was a relatively inexpensive way for the British government to demonstrate concern for the colonies. Research results also had potential usefulness in government disputes with mining companies over labor policies. Moreover, in the postwar years the Colonial Development and Welfare Fund actively sought research projects appropriate for its funding, including those in the social sciences, and the RLI was initially the only social science research institute in the colonies that was already a "going concern," as discussed in the last chapter — both willing and able to utilize these funds.[67]

Despite his frequent mention of plans to begin urban studies himself whenever the hiring of an urban sociologist was delayed, Gluckman never did urban research other than a brief visit to Lozi miners on the Rand. He found his ability to do any kind of fieldwork hampered in later years by the demands of his job as director. Moreover, he was reluctant to begin work himself, or to allow another researcher to enter the field, without a guarantee that he would not share Wilson's fate. The RLI Board of Trustees refused him this support despite his outline of a plan of attack on the urban areas designed to prove his ability to conduct noncontroversial research before he reached the Copperbelt:

> The Board was unable to agree to the Director's formula of support for any worker undertaking urban research, though it appreciated his point of view. The Board discussed the difficulties of this type of work, and the Director explained that he planned to begin work in Livingstone and proceed to other townships up the railway line before tackling the mining areas. . . . Any research plans in any area would be referred to the competent authorities. The Board agreed that plans for research in urban areas should be laid before the Government and other relevant authorities before the research was undertaken.[68]

As he later complained to the CSSRC, he would not do the urban research under such conditions for a number of reasons. Wilson's experience loomed large, as expressed in this statement of Gluckman's disappointment: "The request that the urban-worker be underwritten against the treatment accorded the late Godfrey Wilson in Broken Hill, as set out in my plan, has been deemed unacceptable."[69] Later, after Gluckman established the department at the University of Manchester, he was himself discouraged from returning to Northern Rhodesia because of his involvement in anti-Federation politics.[70] If anything, the government and mines became more suspicious of researchers and their political motives after the war and into the 1950s, as would become clear in their treatment of Epstein when he later did research on the Copperbelt.

Nonetheless, before he left, Gluckman ensured that the RLI had something of a mandate for its work from the CSSRC and the Northern Rhodesia government. He based this mandate on the fact that the CSSRC had earmarked funds for urban research. In addition, the mining companies — through the urging of Rheinalt Jones, a South African liberal and friend of Gluckman who worked for the Anglo-American mines in South Africa at this time — had also contributed funds to this project and, thus, had a stake in its success.[71] The chief problem that remained was to find an anthropologist or sociologist willing and able to do urban fieldwork.

In 1950 A. L. Epstein had received a Colonial Research Fellowship to conduct a study of Northern Rhodesian urban courts.[72] This fellowship meant that he was directly responsible to the CSSRC, but he also developed contacts with the RLI and attended one of their conferences. After his court study he went to Manchester and began doctoral work. He then returned to Northern Rhodesia as a research officer at the Institute and began a study of African urban organization in Luanshya. Mitchell, who had already done a rural study for the RLI in Nyasaland and was the acting director of the RLI, agreed to become its senior sociologist in 1950 and do the social survey of the Copperbelt, which he started in 1951. As it turned out, he also took up the directorship after Colson's resignation and ran much of the Copperbelt survey from the RLI's new headquarters in Lusaka. While director, he spent part of 1953 on leave in Manchester, where he shared an office with Barnes in the social anthropology department, continuing their exchange of ideas about theory.[73]

Mitchell lived on the Copperbelt when he began his urban research, however. From his house in Luanshya, in an area of town populated mainly by white government and mine employees, Mitchell could hear the distant booming of drums that invaded the white residential area when Africans in the Luanshya Management Board Location (the municipal African township) danced on Sunday afternoons.[74] White residents sometimes went to the African township to watch the dancing, and when Mitchell went for a look, he noticed that while the traditional dances of the individual ethnic groups were often poorly attended, the Kalela dance — which involved coordinated teams of male dancers in smart European dress — drew the biggest and most enthusiastic African audiences.

Mitchell did not join the dancing as an anthropologist in a village might have done, for white members of the audience would have frowned on such behavior as damaging to a dignified European image they felt was esssential for white dominance in Africa. But Mitchell returned with a research assistant, Sykes Ndilila, and recorded the features of the dance. He observed, took photographs, and talked with the dancers, while his research assistant wrote down and translated the songs. Mitchell looked into the history of the dance and sorted out the various connections among the members of the dance team in terms of ethnicity, housing area, work, and leisure, as well as their positions in relation to other Africans in the town. The resulting paper, "The Kalela Dance," which he consciously modeled on the situational approach of Gluckman's "Analysis," became one of the seminal works for the RLI's study of urban African society.[75] Its focus on a contemporary activity in an urban setting announced the RLI's intention to study urban African society on its own terms rather than in reference to some purer, untouched rural state.

This did not mean, however, that RLI work ignored past models and practices, rural or urban. The continuity in personnel from the earlier rural research ensured that established models and practices would be tried out and modified for use in the urban setting. And the Copperbelt city itself offered models and practices useful for research. Mitchell had done previous research in both urban and rural settings: for example, his Yao study for the RLI had been decidedly rural, but his first degree, a B.A. in Social Science from Natal University College, had included a specialization in social work. For this he had done a quantitative study of illegitimate births among various categories of African women at a hospital where he worked as a civil servant doing clerical work. In his application for a job at the RLI, Mitchell sent the paper resulting from this study. The paper was "full of chi squares," which impressed Gluckman, and he got the job.[76]

Epstein, who had been trained in law, did his first fieldwork in an urban setting after a brief period of language study in a village where he had familiarized himself with rural life. Continuities with earlier RLI research also included some of the research assistants chosen for the urban studies. One of Gluckman's assistants, Davidson Sianga — who had considerable experience with rural surveys — tried out the

RLI's new census cards for a random sample in Livingstone run by the RLI administrative secretary, Bubbles Hyam, before the main survey began.[77] Sianga participated in a later rural field training session for Victor Turner in Lambaland, arranged by Mitchell, and then worked for Epstein briefly in Livingstone during the urban courts study.[78] M. B. Lukhero, who had worked with Marwick and Barnes in rural fieldwork in Northern Rhodesia's Eastern Province, also joined the urban survey team. The plan of the Copperbelt study itself was modeled on Wilson's original plan and was to contain three parts: a sociographic survey to gather basic statistical data (to be done by Mitchell), a study of family economics and nutrition (to be done by Elsey Richardson), and a study of social structure that Mitchell planned to do but that was ultimately done by Epstein after Mitchell became the director of the Institute.[79]

Aside from Godfrey Wilson's study of Broken Hill—which was not a quantitative sociological survey but a study of wages and budgets and an assessment of degree of urbanization—there were few models for what Mitchell wanted to do. He had learned survey methods as an undergraduate and had read a number of sociological studies, including *Rooiyard* and *Middletown*. He had read some of the sociological work of the Chicago School of sociology and was interested in their general approach. He, Colson, and Barnes had discussed Moreno's work on social dynamics, charting people's interactions, as well as George Lundberg's sociographic approach.[80] He was also familiar with Batson's work, which he used as something of a guideline, though Batson's work focused on poverty only. What Mitchell had in mind was "straight demographic stuff" focused on measuring the effects of the colonial situation, that is, the growth of towns, changes in marriage, and labor migration. In other words, he "wanted to quantify what Wilson had done on migration" and extend it to other urban social phenomena.[81]

Evolving methods for the study proved challenging. When developing urban survey practices the RLI anthropologists sometimes employed elements of earlier nonsociological information-gathering practices. Using these, researchers could get access to information in the initial stages by using approaches the informants had already experienced. Thus Mitchell considered following a local district commissioner's procedure at the beginning of the Copperbelt study: "We might be able to cash in on a tradition which is followed here — that the DC sends out a private census form each year — we might be able to get some valuable stuff from sending out a similar one."[82]

Generally, however, government did not conduct true censuses in this period. Administrators made rough estimates using the district commissioners' tax books and multiplying by a factor to account for women and children.[83] The RLI censuses would be much more sophisticated. Nevertheless, Mitchell found that the tools necessary for analysis of the resulting statistics could be found on the Copperbelt itself, where the mines had already invested in early computer technology. Mitchell used the Hollerith machine owned by the Anglo American Copperbelt mines, which were in the process of putting all their staff records onto punchcards. The mines had already gathered so much data that Mitchell initially hoped to base an article on his analysis of it.[84] He also later acquired for the Institute a Powers-Samas machine for doing basic statistical analysis, and the African assistant Edward Mbewe became proficient in its use.

Mitchell arrived on the Copperbelt and began the sociographic survey approximately a year before Richardson and Epstein began working for the RLI. Recruiting the team of research assistants for the social survey occupied a great deal of time in the beginning. He found it difficult to hire well-educated Africans for the work, especially for the post of the senior assistant who was to supervise the daily work of the team. The RLI's Board of Trustees would not allow him to offer salaries high enough to compete with those offered by mines and government, in a situation where Africans with clerical skills were in high demand. Government security officers also checked the background and possible political activities of applicants for the assistant posts and found many of them unsuitable for employment on these grounds.[85] But by December 1950, despite government delays, Mitchell had managed to pull together a team of "odd bods and sods" from the local welfare departments and began surveying a nearby location in Luanshya.[86]

Mitchell and the team found getting sufficient cooperation from informants for filling in the survey questionnaires initially very difficult, and the director waxed nostalgic about rural research conditions, compared to urban research: "Its [sic] bloody work. The point about the village is that you get hold of the village headman and spill the beans about what you are up to. Here there is no such handy lance-corporal and each visit to a hut means the same battle — the same suspicions etc. The refusal rate is high."[87]

He also encountered problems devising a way to organize the urban field to make it amenable to quantitative research. During the year he spent in the field before Richardson and Epstein began their work, Mitchell set out to "design samples," a task difficult to accomplish without a "sampling frame" — that is, without a list of addresses or names for the African population, something from which to build a structure for the fieldwork. In the municipal and mine housing areas the houses had numbers, thus providing a frame, but in the sprawling industrial housing areas — where housing for African employees was provided by the numerous different businesses they worked for — things were chaotic, according to Mitchell. Thus, he devised procedures to number the houses himself and then select the required number randomly, using a different "raising factor" for each different housing section for multiplying to get a population estimate.[88] At first Mitchell and the team of assistants used a form he devised himself, but soon they switched to using Hollerith punch-cards that the interviewer punched with a hand punch while in the field.

Although it was a sociographic study, unlike many such quantitative studies the Copperbelt survey did not completely separate the quantitative data from its qualitative context. Evidence of this *embedding* of the quantitative within the qualitative can be found in the work process that the assistants and Mitchell developed for gathering information in the African housing areas. There the team interviewed and punched cards for the inhabitants of the randomly selected houses, but they supplemented this formal procedure with informal visits to observe urban activities, answer the questions of residents, conduct open-ended interviews, and generally gather information. The assistants then used this information to write es-

The King
was in the
Counting House

Counting out money has ever ranked high on the list of man's tribulations. His schooldays are clouded with vexatious purchases at so-much and elevenpence farthing per gross. Leaving school, he is like as not set to work on day book, journal and ledger; and woe betide him should a perverse penny play hide-and-seek among his long tots and cross tots!

All honour, then, to CHARLES BABBAGE, whose 'Difference Engine' was probably the first machine ever designed for the mechanical solution of arithmetical problems; and to Dr. HERMAN HOLLERITH, whose Punched Card method of electrical accountancy has been so developed as to perform incredible feats in the solution of general accounting, book-keeping and statistical problems, at speeds that would seem fantastic in any other than a jet-propelled age.

HOLLERITH Punched Cards and Equipment, long in general use throughout the United Kingdom, are already installed in India, South Africa and Australia, and enquiries are invited from other overseas territories. Moreover, the machines that compute sterling can be adapted for other currencies.

"HOLLERITH"

THE BRITISH TABULATING MACHINE CO. LTD
Head Office: Victoria House   ·   Southampton Row   ·   London   ·   W.C.1

Branches at: BOMBAY, CALCUTTA, NEW DELHI, RANGOON, COLOMBO, HONG-KONG, MELBOURNE, SYDNEY, JOHANNESBURG AND CAIRO.   REPRESENTATIVES IN THE PRINCIPAL TOWNS THROUGHOUT INDIA, AUSTRALIA, SOUTH AFRICA, RHODESIA AND KENYA.

RPL/P.50

Advertisement for Hollerith Machines. Note that the advertisement points out their distribution to dominions and former colonies of Britain. The Northern Rhodesian mining companies used this early computing technology to mechanize their payrolls. (From the Colonial Office List, 1948 [Rhodes House Library shelfmark .010.r.92. 1948; p. 579]. Reproduced by permission of the Bodleian Library, University of Oxford.)

Edward Mbewe operating the Powers-Samas machine purchased by Mitchell to aid statistical analysis of the urban survey data. (Photo from RLI poster in author's possession.)

says, producing a series of short analyses of African urban life.[89] Like the RLI research officers, the assistants had also read Gluckman's "Analysis," and its influence can be discerned in their essays.

This process of embedding the quantitative in the qualitative also revealed itself in the physical characteristics of the punchcards used to collect the quantitative data, which became "rather well thumbed and a bit dog-eared from much handling by the interviewers." This was because the interviewers, Mitchell included, often scribbled observations on the backs of the cards—"qualitative material" that Mitchell did not try to quantify.[90]

The qualitative aspect of the study was further reinforced by the collection of information sufficiently detailed to allow for future analysis. In this respect, the urban survey may have been shaped by the Lamba survey experience, the early training session in which Gluckman introduced Barnes, Mitchell, and Max and Joan Marwick to rural fieldwork and the collection of data (discussed in chapter 4). In their report on the Lamba study, Barnes and Mitchell pointed out that the extensive amount of detailed information Gluckman urged them to collect was what allowed them to carry their analysis into areas they had not anticipated while in the field. This collection of detailed information that went beyond the basic categories was not standard procedure in anthropology or in sociological surveys at the time. For example, while Mitchell directed the Copperbelt survey, another survey was being carried out by J. R. A. Shaul of the Southern Rhodesian department of statistics in Salisbury. Although Shaul was the first to use sampling procedures for a population study in Southern Rhodesia, his study lacked detail. "Shaul's study used very limited categories, broad age groups, [he was] mostly interested in numbers," according to Mitchell, while Mitchell saw himself as attempting to get a "social profile of the people" by collecting extensive information on work, marriage, children, and other topics as background for a study of social structure and the effects of colonialism.[91] This insistence on the collection of detailed information so prominently characterized the RLI method that when Lukhero went to observe Shaul's survey, he wrote back to express disappointment at the lack of detail, concluding, "Our RLI way is the only one."[92]

While Mitchell and the assistants gave the qualitative side of the research its due in the context of the quantitative survey, Epstein carried the qualitative aspects even further through his transfer of the rural method of participant observation into the urban setting. This process had begun with his urban courts study.[93] He felt that his background had given him no models for an urban study. Seminars at LSE, where he was supervised by Audrey Richards, "had nothing to do with urban courts; [there was] no literature and no model for urban fieldwork," so he "could only fall back on case method" derived from his background in law.[94] So he visited the courts in Ndola, one of the Copperbelt towns chosen for the study, and, with an assistant, sat with the court members and took notes on the cases. Interest in the attitudes of local people to courts and court members led him to experiment with an idea he had gotten from a Nyasaland African education officer he had met in London — to form a discussion group made up of educated Africans. It was from this group that he began to realize the political dimension of the court and the selection of its members. He also learned of the educated Africans' perspective — that the courts were "an intrusion of tribal government into the towns . . . a dialogue of norm and counter-norm, custom vs. the urban situation."[95]

Epstein's work for the RLI's urban survey stimulated him to still more creative responses to the problem of urban fieldwork. Choosing an overtly political topic, he moved from Ndola to Luanshya shortly after Mitchell moved to Lusaka to become director.[96] In Luanshya Epstein began studying the development of African political organizations in towns, including the miners' union and the ANC. For this study even the case method was inadequate, and, though he was familiar with Wilson's Broken Hill survey, he felt it looked too much at external factors and lacked local detail. So Epstein decided to "recreate as closely as possible the conditions of an anthropologist in a village living with the people." Because of the restrictions imposed on his access to an urban fieldsite, he could not live in African locations himself, so he placed his research assistants and their wives in different parts of the town and set them to observing urban life. He spent time teaching the men to write reports and produce texts on union and political meetings and to conduct informal interviews. The women, similarly, "dropped in" on other women rather than conducting formal interviews and they kept diaries of their own daily activities and observations.

Epstein himself attended meetings of political organizations and used his rural connections — developed during his training and language study period in a part of the countryside from which many Luanshya miners came — to develop good relations with Robinson Puta, vice-president of the ANC and notorious for hating whites. His visits to union meetings led to a friendship with Lawrence Katilungu, the African miners' union leader. He also started a "Drama Club" modelled after an African-designed soap opera that was broadcast from the Lusaka radio station, so that he could learn about attitudes to urban life from the members' script writing.[97]

Thus, in spite of the mining company's sudden withdrawal of Epstein's and his assistants' permission to do research in the mining company's African housing locations early in the study, he managed to get a picture of African urban life and the development of political organizations based on his own and his research assistants' participant observation in other areas, and occasionally through assistants' private visits to friends on the mine.[98]

Before starting her urban research Elsey Richardson spent some time in villages in Luapula and Northern Provinces — one the home village of her assistant, Joachim Lengwe, who later joined the urban survey team.[99] There she learned the Bemba language, did censuses, collected genealogical information, and tried to get some budget data, though the time she spent in the rural villages was too short to gather extensive data.[100] In October 1953 she began her urban work, studying family budgets in the Copperbelt town of Kitwe, where she continued to work until 1955. She took particular interest in the effect that visiting relatives and lodgers had on urban families' income and expenditure and related these to urban families' growing class status, as well as continuing links to the countryside.[101]

The RLI's institutional place in the African colonial context changed dramatically during the 1950s, a shift which had ramifications both for its research and its administration. Mitchell's duties as director involved dealing with the rapid growth of the metropolitan-based colonial research bureaucracy, stimulated by the relatively generous funding provided by the Colonial Development and Welfare Fund but punctuated by periodic British government belt-tightening exercises in the postwar years. Negotiating the Institute's unique position as other institutes, attached to new universities, sprang up in east and west Africa proved increasingly difficult. The local political situation also became more complex as a new layer of Federation government was created in 1953 and the "unofficials" — representatives of the white settler population who were often unsympathetic to the RLI — gained more seats in the Northern Rhodesia legislative council as part of the Federation plan for greater devolution of power to local whites.

The larger network of African-based institutions within which the Institute was placed also began to change dramatically in the 1950s, leading the director to make choices in the use of his time and energies based on the covert political mission of the RLI. Confiding in former director Colson, Mitchell explained why he decided to work for a local government training scheme for social workers:

> We've got to turn into a university one day. Let's corner the market in social science now. Let's try to hasten our development that way. (University of SA has turned into an apartheid institution — [it] says Central African territories are going to look after Africans [so it does not have to admit them]. Union has closed S. A. universities to Central Africa as from beginning of 1954.) Hence our library plus technical staff could be the beginning in NR. . . . For the meantime I have agreed to give the lectures on Sociology and social psychology to the trainees.[102]

Both professional and political reasons motivated Mitchell's decision to teach in spite of his already heavy duties as director. As a liberal South African he worried about the changes in the climate of the universities in the southern African region that would make it difficult for Africans to obtain higher education, and the natural move of many liberal South Africans at the time was to pin hopes on the development of education in the less segregation-oriented environment of Northern Rhodesia. Furthermore, he saw this as an opportunity to claim future academic territory for social science — a motive especially strong in his case since he contemplated a local career in an African or South African university. He clearly felt at this time that a career at a new university in Northern Rhodesia would be an attractive option.

Political developments soon altered the context of these long-range plans, however, as African opposition to the Federation gained strength in the latter half of the decade and the territorial governments took a more rigid stance against Africans at the behest of powerful white minorities.[103]

Conclusion: Anthropology and the Struggle for the City

The difficulties that anthropologists and their assistants encountered while doing urban fieldwork stemmed from two main sources: African and European political suspicions. The particular fieldwork practices of anthropology aroused these suspicions, but in the long run the anthropologists' image of the city proved to be troublesome, as well.[104] Anthropological practices shaped — and were shaped by — changing images of the city, and the anthropologists' methods of organizing research had implications for urban social and political policy that government and mines found threatening.

In dealing with the mines and with miners, RLI researchers found participant observation increasingly difficult to pursue, and their attempts to compensate by using other practices also met with difficulty. An already established pattern of interaction between whites and blacks in the mines and mine compounds limited what anthropologists could do in this situation. Mining company officials expected researchers to follow company patterns of interaction with miners and were willing to provide offices for them to interview and question informants. This was the pattern followed by compound managers when they interviewed Africans seeking mine employment, and Africans answered often very intrusive questions in such a setting in the hope of gaining employment.

Researchers for the RLI refused the offer of offices on mine property, however, partly because they feared surveillance by mine officials but also because this style of information gathering approximated the old "verandah ethnography" of an earlier period. It also paralleled the method of using interviews with carefully chosen informants favored by the South African *volkekundige* (see chapter 3). In this and other respects the style of interaction used by European staff at the mines deliberately put distance between them and the African workers as a way of enforcing a racial hierarchy. Even whites who spoke the local language often used translators when interviewing workers or hearing their complaints, again, to stress their authority and distance from African workers.[105] To the social anthropologist this mode of interaction was uncomfortably reminiscent of prefunctionalist methods. The compound managers also resented the anthropologist's fluency in the local language, perhaps seeing this as an expression of solidarity with Africans or a way of usurping the managers' own role as experts on Africans and intermediaries between them and other Europeans.[106]

Researchers and assistants at a RLI conference at the Lusaka headquarters. Note the more casual attire of the researchers. Pictured from left to right are Ackson Nyirenda, William Watson, unknown, Simon Katilungu, and A. L. Epstein. (Photo reproduced by permission of Merran [McCulloch] Fraenkel.)

As had been made abundantly clear during Wilson's urban work, both mining companies and the government discouraged anthropologists from publicly commenting on policy. As a result, though the government encouraged Epstein to write a report on his earlier urban court study and asked for recommendations, when they published the report they left out his recommendations section.[107] Government and the mines also kept close watch on anthropologists' public discussions with Africans. A false report that Epstein had spoken in favor of a bread boycott at a union meeting — that he had attended only to explain his research to the union membership — gave the mines an excuse to ban him from their property, including the African miners' compounds on which his study depended. His refusal to cooperate with a "special branch type" (a government agent) who wanted him to report on African political activities may have also contributed to the government's refusal to intervene in the mining company's decision to ban him. Although the report of Epstein's speaking in favor of the bread boycott was false, the mines and government did have reason to be suspicious that his activities promoted African nationalism, for ANC and union leaders sometimes met at his house in Luanshya, and his research assistant, Ackson Nyirenda, used Epstein's postbox to distribute ANC communications.

When the mines banned him, Robinson Puta suggested that the miners should strike in protest.[108] Mitchell, like Wilson before him in his defense of Gluckman's access to the Lozi field, argued with government and the mines in defense of Epstein, but the mines remained adamant. Epstein suffered enormous anguish from the loss of his fieldsite and from the increasingly tense atmosphere on the Copperbelt in the final years of his study, especially after Mitchell and many of the other RLI researchers in his field generation moved on to academic careers. The rising coerciveness of the colonial government's responses to African civil disobedience campaigns, such as the initial campaign based on economic boycotts, led to increasingly violent responses from African nationalists, leading eventually to the 1961 "Cha Cha Cha" campaign of stone throwing, roadblocks, and riots that marked the last phase of the liberation struggle that led to independence in 1964.

The atmosphere of repression affected the Institute headquarters, as well as the researcher in the field. Both mines and government kept track of the RLI's activities in official and unofficial ways during the period of the Copperbelt survey. While living in Luanshya, Mitchell found his files disturbed and requested the Institute to supply him with a filing cabinet in order to lock them "away from prying eyes," suspecting government agents had been at work.[109] The newsletter that the administrative secretaries, Merran McCulloch and Janet Longton, circulated among the researchers — which contained frank discussions of fieldwork problems — may have also fallen into the wrong hands. McCulloch issued a warning to researchers to keep the newsletter to themselves.[110]

Africans also criticized the activities of the RLI both as individuals and as members of local union branches that suspected researchers and their assistants of pro-Federation sympathies. Nonpolitical objections, such as the familiar one that urban life and customs were not a proper subject for research, however, led the assistants to invoke the usefulness of history to Africans in their struggle for equality with Europeans. As one assistant argued, at a meeting at which he was called upon to justify the RLI's research:

> I told the meeting that the information we are seeking [about urban customs] may look stupid but things that are happening today may not happen in the next thirty or fifty years and people living at that time will want to know what is happening now. And the only way they can know this is by reading the records we are making now, "Europeans have been making records about themselves and other peoples," I told them, "and that is why they are able to tell about things that happened hundreds of years ago."[111]

History had long proved itself to be useful to Africans in arguments with provincial administrators about chiefly succession and the legitimacy of tribal claims to land or to the right to pursue their own customs. The assistant used this general knowledge to invoke the usefulness of history in the urban situation and also may have been referring to the knowledge that educated Africans in the audience would have of the way British history was taught in colonial schools and its importance to European identity and claims to being more civilized than Africans.

Effective as they could sometimes be, researchers' arguments about the historical usefulness of research had to be bolstered by political arguments, because fieldwork itself had become politicized. As discussed above, this politicization of fieldwork stemmed partly from white suspicions that fieldwork practices themselves undermined segregation and raised African expectations. But African responses also contributed to this politicization. The political activities of Africans and Europeans who sympathized with Federation and created multiracial political parties—the political "fieldwork," so to speak, of the Capricorn Africa Society and the Federal Party—bore some similarity to RLI field practices. Both the RLI and these pro-

Federation parties consisted of whites and blacks working together, and both sent teams of Africans into the townships to ask politically significant questions and write down names on cards — party cards in the case of the political groups and punchcards in the case of the RLI. So it was understandable that Africans increasingly responded to researchers with suspicion.

Indeed, earlier in the 1950s, Simon Zukas, a white member of the ANC, himself questioned the RLI survey team about its activities in the townships when it first started work on the Copperbelt. After Epstein left for his break between the urban courts study and his Luanshya study, the discussion group he had started as part of his research method became caught up in controversy about its own political stance and relation to Zukas's more radical activities. Soon after, the Northern Rhodesia government charged Zukas with sedition and deported him.[112] African concern about the RLI's activities continued to be one of the themes of African response to the urban survey and to the other RLI research studies that followed it and continued up to Zambian independence in 1964. The national political parties and union leaders, however, frequently took on the task of justifying the Institute's work to hostile local branch members. And the model of Zukas — a Jew, a communist and sympathizer with African nationalism who had been deported by the government — might have seemed appropriate to apply to Epstein, by the mines that banned him and by the Africans who wanted to strike in his support.

The politicization of fieldwork revealed itself in the rural areas, as well, where Africans saw researchers as Federal agents, as possible avenues of complaint against Federation, or as means of getting attention for local problems. As Epstein observed of his census work in Northern Province in early 1953 during the period of African opposition to the impending Federation:

> It's been pretty quiet here since I returned from Abercorn [today, Mbala] [where he had been visiting Watson]. I have been working two villages this month and census cards are both completed and exhausted. . . . The most interesting thing perhaps was the differential response I got in each village. At the one it was the usual story these days of the villagers taking to the bush as soon as they heard us ap-

proaching; at the other the people wouldn't let us leave until they had "been written." At the end of one day, when I had completed about fifteen cards, I was so worn out that I was confusing the sexes of the people being interviewed.[113]

Ultimately, in the later 1950s and early 1960s, the usefulness of the anthropologist's method of framing the urban environment for understanding the city would be eclipsed by political events after the United National Independence Party (UNIP) became a force in African politics. Rivalry between ANC and UNIP further complicated fieldwork, and the continuing intransigence of white settlers toward African self-determination led to more violence. What distinguished UNIP from the ANC was its greater ability to organize and mobilize the urban population, a process of *framing* not unlike that of the social scientists, but for a different purpose. As expressed by later political scientists: "UNIP constructed a tightly articulated party organisation which was a phenomenon of the high-density housing areas in both council estates and mine townships. The basis of the structure was a system of cells, or sections, in groupings of twenty houses, through which the party politicised existing social relations, and in the process created networks of social as well as political control."[114]

The miners' union supported nationalism but resisted UNIP's efforts to establish hegemonic control over miners in the urban areas, a practice that would continue in the postcolonial period in resistance to the state's attempts to control miners' wages and the dominance of mining in the national economy.[115] Thus the union managed to remain a separate contender in the struggle to organize the Copperbelt towns.

Despite the increasing perception by Africans that social research was irrelevant to these political struggles,[116] the RLI's research left its mark in images of the city that would continue to form a backdrop for thinking about urban policy. The importance of these ways of understanding the Copperbelt still reverberates in current debates about the nature of urbanization in Zambia.[117] How much these ways of understanding African societies, urban and rural, were the product of an African perspective is the subject of the next chapter.

7

Africanizing Anthropology

This chapter discusses the work of the RLI's African research assistants and the effects their diverse backgrounds and goals had on the Institute's rural and urban research practices.

The previous chapter dealt with the development of the African survey team during Mitchell's directorship. Members of that team continued to work together or in smaller teams during the subsequent directorships of Charles White (1955–56 and 1960–62) and Henry Fosbrooke (1956–1960). White, a Northern Rhodesia colonial administrator, had long been publishing his research on the Luvale through the *Rhodes-Livingstone Journal* and *Papers* and continued to do so during two periods as the RLI's acting director. Watson, Epstein, and van Velsen continued their research during his first directorship. Raymond Apthorpe also worked as a research officer during White's second directorship. Epstein completed his work during Fosbrooke's directorship. During that directorship Colson and a new researcher, Thayer Scudder, began the Kariba Study, a project focused on the effects of resettlement on the Gwembe Tonga people who would be moved to make way for the Kariba hydro-electric project—a massive Federation-based development scheme. Fosbrooke was instrumental in arguing with the colonial government for the necessity of this study, which became a long-term project that continues today.

New research officers and affiliates who arrived at the Institute during Fosbrooke's directorship included David Bettison and George Kay, who carried out poverty datum line studies, Raymond Apthorpe, Peter Rigby, Robert Sutcliffe, John Argyle, J. Matthews, and G. Clack. Audrey Richards returned for a brief stint of fieldwork in

1957. In addition to the urban survey team, Munali School students did vacation work for the Institute. They included David Phiri, Edward Shamwana, Rhupia Banda, Lazarus Mwanza, Roger Mumbe, Crispin Nyalugwe, Peter Siwo, P. P. Banda, Jacob Mwanza, and Lyson Tembo, among others.[1]

Biographical information on many of the assistants is incomplete because of the destruction of most of the Institute's personnel files. The information included here has been gleaned from what remains of the files, from other archival sources, and from interviews with many of the former assistants and anthropologists and some of their informants, family, and friends.

Sundry Africans

Advances: Sundry Africans. It has been the practice for the past few years to make petty advances to African staff from month to month of amounts from 5/- to 1. This causes much confusion and difficulty in the accounts, and should, I consider, be stopped.

Although in the above quote[2] it is not applied solely to research assistants, the phrase "sundry Africans" provides a way to approach the emergence of the type of research assistant who worked at the RLI between the Second World War and Zambian independence. As the word "sundry" suggests, the category of research assistant started as an all-encompassing one, marked by the flow of a variety of people of differing age, gender, class, education, and ethnic background, who played a number of different roles with respect to the researchers. Considerable movement took place among staff positions at the RLI, with clerks or interpreters becoming research assistants, or research assistants being shifted into positions as library assistants, statistical analysts, or even gardeners during Henry Fosbrooke's directorship. Researchers' terms for their assistants also varied, with some anthropologists calling them "research assistants" while others called Africans doing essentially the same work "clerks" or "clerk-interpreters." Indeed, the only continuity was that all research assistants in the RLI's history *were* Africans. No European ever held that position, though there were plans almost from the beginning to have Africans and Europeans with undergraduate degrees in equivalent junior research officer posts (see below).

Despite causing "much confusion and difficulty," advances to African staff continued to appear on future RLI balance sheets. This practice reflected the conditions of the Central African political and social environment. The directors of the Institute found themselves repeatedly frustrated in their attempts to raise staff salaries, and in particular the salaries of research assistants, to match or rise above those of the Northern Rhodesian government's African employees. Thus, the Institute's research assistants along with other African staff continued to ask for advances in order to meet needs these low salaries could not cover. The resulting problems with the budget reflected a larger confusion and difficulty both in the place of the RLI and of its research assistants in the surrounding society.

Both the RLI anthropologists and their assistants occupied a middle ground in Northern Rhodesian society that was politically and socially uncomfortable but highly productive in terms of method and theory. Researchers moved between Africans and government, more sympathetic to the former, while assistants moved between African society and European society, getting access to the latter through their employment and education. Because they occupied a middle position, researchers and assistants accomplished their work by acting in some respects as culture brokers — but, even more importantly for the later urban survey team, they also acted as political brokers, pointing to a variety of African aspirations to justify sociological research in the highly politicized environment of the Zambian independence struggle. As a result, the researchers, as well as the assistants, had to be sensitive to the political repercussions of their work and its consequences both for themselves and for the local groups they studied. This sensitivity, however, enhanced their studies, particularly in cases where these studies focused on understanding the emergence of African political, union, and other forms of organization.[3]

Induna Francis Suu acting as translator for the Provincial Commissioner at the Barotseland Agricultural Show. Suu also assisted Gluckman in his fieldwork. The photo illustrates a "culture broker" role that some Africans assumed during the colonial period and that shaped the background of a few of the early RLI assistants. (Photo no. 30165 in Gluckman Collection, Royal Anthropological Institute. Reproduced by permission of the Royal Anthropological Institute.)

Although I will sometimes use the term "culture brokers" for RLI assistants, I will also discuss intellectual and professional aspects of their behavior that do not necessarily characterize all culture brokers. As discussed in the first chapter, all terms that have been used for indigenous research assistants are problematic in some way, but the term "intellectuals" allows for a more symmetrical analysis of their relationship with social anthopologists. The intellectual and professional features that stand out in such an analysis were what became the crucial elements in the career paths of both anthropologists and assistants during the watershed years preceding and following independence. During that time the Institute underwent a complete change of character; academic careers rather than lengthy research officer or director posts became the norm for the anthropologists, and the assistants recruited in the 1950s for the most part joined other educated Zambians in taking positions in government and industry.[4] Although they did not pursue careers as social scientists, the assistants had created a clientele for anthropological expertise that allowed many of them, even after independence, to continue to function in a somewhat professionalized culture broker role — in the area of local politics, reviving traditional ceremonies and enhancing local ethnic projects to achieve recognition and resources from the postcolonial state for the regions from which they came, or, in the area of national politics, taking a more sociological perspective on the administrative or development-planning work they did after independence.

The RLI assistants came from a variety of social and ethnic contexts, but most shared the advantage of having a level of education attained by few Africans in Central Africa in the late colonial period. Nearly all of the assistants, and particularly members of the urban survey team, had a few years of secondary school education. Africans who had advanced through primary school and acquired some secondary education were in demand, especially those who had acquired typing skills. The extent of their education marked this group out for skilled work as clerks for government, the mines, and white businesses, or as assistant social workers in the mines' housing areas. They could also afford to move from job to job seeking higher wages or better working conditions. Thus, conditions of work were an important motivation for Africans to work at the RLI, for though the Institute often had difficulty matching mine and government salaries for African clerks, it offered a relatively egalitarian working environment not to be found elsewhere.[5]

Like other African men whether educated or not, most of the assistants had either served in the military in World War Two in various parts of Africa or the world, or had labor migration experience that had taken them far from Northern Rhodesia. This meant they had often directly observed developments in other parts of Africa and especially in South Africa, where African urbanization, labor unions, and political parties had advanced further than in Northern Rhodesia. In addition, they had often migrated in order to get schooling. Africans had to travel for secondary education because of the scarcity of secondary schools in Northern Rhodesia before independence. Some assistants had traveled from their home areas to the few secondary schools in Northern Rhodesia or to Southern Rhodesia or Nyasaland. For tertiary education, there was little choice but to go to South Africa or take a correspondence course.

The RLI recruited and trained over fifty assistants of various kinds in the course of its rural and urban research, spanning the period from 1938 to 1964. The urban survey team alone employed six to twelve people at various times. Some urban assistants had previously worked for individual anthropologists in the rural areas. The RLI recruited others in the Copperbelt towns as the urban surveys got under way. The Institute also recruited senior assistants with university training, who would act as team supervisors, through RLI contacts with universities in South Africa. After the Institute moved to its Lusaka headquarters near the African secondary school at Munali, RLI directors encouraged Munali School students to do research work during their vacations.[6] Several of these students worked on the urban surveys and some wrote essays for the Institute on subjects such as rural tribal traditions and ethnic relations in the towns. But to understand the role of the research assistant and the perspective of assistants on the work of the RLI, one must begin with the earliest employees of the Institute, the clerks and interpreters who worked for individual anthropologists in the rural areas.[7]

Makapweka the Witchfinder[8]

In the rural areas, African assistants may have chosen their anthropologists as often as their anthropologists chose them. Anthropologists frequently took on assistants suggested by local chiefs, village heads, or colonial administrators. The pool to choose from consisted of African mission school teachers, native authority clerks, and others who had proficiency in speaking and writing English, and who thus could enable the anthropologist to begin research while still in the process of learning the local language. In some ways the anthropologist's assistant resembled the colonial administrator's district messenger.[9] Like the district messenger, the assistant acted as a handy informant, being asked for explanations of local behavior as well as the meanings of local words. Also like the district messenger — who was steered to the administrator by chiefs or village heads seeking to protect their own interests — the assistant was often chosen by local leaders with an interest in controlling the activities and perceptions of the anthropologist. Unlike district messengers, however, the assistants had more education and did not suffer from the stigma of being associated with tax collection and law enforcement. But they nevertheless controlled the anthropologist's perceptions in subtle and not-so-subtle ways. One former assistant took pride in telling me how he had mistranslated villagers' statements for the anthropologist. He had done it because he was ashamed of the vulnerability and eagerness with which members of his own ethnic group responded to the anthropologist's interest in local customs usually frowned upon by administrators and missionaries.[10]

Those chosen to be assistants often had a facility for the work that should not be surprising given the long-standing necessity for indigenous groups to shape the perceptions of the colonial administrators governing them — a task that called forth local culture brokers.[11] Anthropologists often saw this interest in culture as parallel to their own and considered particularly gifted assistants or informants to be indigenous anthropologists, as when Victor Turner compared his favorite informant to a university don.[12] Indeed, cultural sensitivity may be a characteristic displayed by certain members of any society, and especially of societies experiencing contact and conflict with neighboring groups as was the case in central and southern Africa in the precolonial and colonial periods. The assistants themselves often described their attraction to the work in terms of an understanding of culture that mirrored the anthropologist's. As the assistant Jacques Chiwale[13] observed of his first contact with an anthropologist: "I could see what Cunnison was interested in and that inspired my own interest. I could understand what was in the back of his mind."[14]

The assistants came to the work, however, with more than donnish and disinterested motives. Like other brokers in colonial situations, they intended to gain personal profit from their activities. For some research assistants, attachment to an anthropologist meant not only a relatively high-paying job and enhanced local prestige. The most important feature attracting some Africans to this position was the opportunity to play a role in the creation of tribal history and ethnic identity, processes that were of vital interest to Africans in this period.[15]

In the rural areas, African agency and the anthropologist's vulnerability had already combined to bring about a degree of Africanization to the discipline and its practices. In much the same way that administrators had adopted some African models of authority, anthropologists complied with certain African practices in order to conduct research. In practical matters, anthropologists' housing, their contacts in indigenous societies, and their patterns of movement could be partly determined by local people. In terms of methodology, their commitment to participant observation required them to live with their informants and observe their daily life instead of, or in addition to, the more formal questioning that had characterized earlier anthropological methods. Participant observation made anthropologists more amenable to pressure to adopt local practices and encouraged them to identify with local interests, whether or not they managed to attain the ideal of a total immersion in and understanding of the local culture.

Africans also had expectations of Europeans largely based on their experiences with colonial administrators and missionaries, and they attempted to make anthropologists conform to these expectations in such matters as housing location or patterns of movement, thus restricting anthropologists' perceptions of local activities. The anthropologists of the RLI combatted these expectations with a deliberate attempt to distance themselves from administrative and missionary practices, usually by initially financing a beer party and joining in the dancing.

How assistants perceived themselves as employees at this early stage depended more on their own original status and on the local perception of the anthropologist's status than on any pre-existing idea of what a research assistant should be. Models of black/white relationships were nearly always of the employer/employee type, and this influenced the assistant's relationship with the researcher. Those who became assistants had usually had jobs as government clerks, native authority clerks, or similar posts, and in some respects their work as research assistants consisted of similar practices — typing and translating, counting people or asking questions of villagers, or preparing for their employer's visit to a village. Anthropologists, however, wanted something more. The information that assistants gathered had to be systematized in the form of censuses, genealogies, or diaries of events. The assistant was also expected to act as a kind of *superinformant*, being asked for explanations of local behavior in addition to the meanings of local words.

The work practices of RLI assistants usually differed significantly from those of other African employees, such as government district messengers and clerk/typists, in that they were more systematized and were structured by the anthropologists' theoretical goals. District officers, for example, might want assistants to collect census data or data for a rough assessment of crop yields in a particular area. In contrast, social anthropologists tried to perceive the underlying structures of African societies, and their questions, though they might be superficially similar, demanded a different kind of answer — in the form of data collected systematically and/or placed in a framework that systematized it in a way that revealed social structure. Even former RLI research assistants today structure information in a similar way in response to the questions of a visiting researcher — in my case, a historian rather than an anthropologist. When informed that I wanted to know about the kind of work done by RLI research assistants, a former assistant of Gluckman, David Kalimosho Maila, listed and explained the roles of each of Gluckman's assistants, including himself, in our first interview.[16] At the next interview, informed that I wanted to know what Gluckman himself had done while in the field, the assistant opened the interview with the systematic definition of the various kinds of witchcraft practiced in the area: "Number one: charms that you step on and your leg swells — *kanjate*, brought by the Luvale and Luchazi; Mack Gluckman asked but failed to find a proper person to tell him and bring him the medicine for some money; they were too afraid that he would turn them in, since this was a very bad medicine. . . . Number two: a bad medicine called *muhole* . . ."[17]

This description continued until I asked more questions about Gluckman's purpose for being in Barotseland. I received replies that invariably indicated that Gluckman's primary interest was in witchcraft and the systematic collection of data concerning it, data often construed by the research assistant as evidence for court cases against witches. As he continued:

> at that village they found a piece of a pot . . . Dr. Gluckman knew the pot was there because once there were 26 cows and a herdboy killed by lightning and he wanted to know why so many cattle were killed. . . . and the people said there were people there using magic, so he sent men to look. . . . The DC didn't believe the witches would send lightning, so that was why I was sent by Mack Gluckman to investigate and I got the pot and brought it to the *boma*. . . . The DC collected the *indunas* and talked to them at Katongo Camp [Gluckman's camp outside of Mongu in Barotseland]. The DC sent them all to Gluckman to decide the case together with him, to decide if witchcraft had been involved.[18]

This example shows that research assistants, like other Africans, interpreted anthropological research as an activity similar to other culturally and socially interested behavior they observed in Europeans or in themselves. Those Europeans most interested in rural African culture and society would have been administrators and missionaries. Both collected ethnographic data and examples of local crafts. Both groups wanted to eradicate certain behaviors — polygyny, witchcraft accusations, and the like. And their interest was both invasive and coercive.

On this model, collecting material culture artifacts, as Kalimosho did for Gluckman, could be interpreted as collecting evidence to be used in court cases against witches. In the above quote from the second interview, Kalimosho painted a picture of the anthropologist as witchfinder, cooperating with the Lozi *indunas* and going further than the DC was willing to go in pursuing witches. The assistant's attitude toward this pursuit was positive, for he portrayed Gluckman as a knowledgeable expert, finding and turning in witches to the government (which would then prosecute if the witch's medicines could be produced in evidence — thus the importance of finding the pot buried in the floor of the hut which the research assistant himself retrieved for Gluckman). Being both a Christian and a Lozi, the assistant interpreted Gluckman's interest in witchcraft — which the Lozi considered an activity practiced by other ethnic groups — and his payments to witches for their medicines as a mission to capture and convict witches.

Gluckman was, indeed, interested in local ideas about sorcery and witchcraft held by members of the numerous ethnic groups that lived in Barotseland. He had also had a great interest in understanding male initiation rituals and the array of *makishi* spirit dancers associated with these and other ritual events. To a Lozi assistant, and particularly one with a Christian education, these aspects of other local cultures might have been categorized with sorcery, as well. Gluckman's close association with the Lozi *indunas* also would have reinforced his image as a defender of the dominant group, at least in the assistant's eyes, as may also his similarity in dress to government administrators and association with the government, which was responsible for the prosecution of witchcraft cases. Missionary behavior in Barotseland had also been construed by the Lozi in a similar way, and Lozi in the early days saw missionaries as the rivals of witches, beginning with Livingstone whom the Lozi considered a powerful magician.[19]

Kalimosho's active role in this story reveals something else about early African perceptions of the job of assistant. In this case the assistant did not act as an informant or as an interpreter of cultural knowledge to the anthropologist. Instead his role was more like that of a *boma* messenger going out to gather up malefactors for the district administrators. The assistant gathered evidence of witchcraft to deliver both to Gluckman and the *indunas*, hoping that by way of them the government would prosecute the witches responsible for the lightning strike. As a Lozi Christian, Kalimosho identified with the government's campaign and what he perceived the anthropologist's role to be in it. His behavior also revealed his own cultural and political interests, which he expressed through his work for the anthropologist, gathering evidence against rivals — the supposedly less Christianized Luvale, Luchazi, and other ethnic groups under Lozi domination. This was a common feature of culture brokers in the colonial period, including guides and interpreters who found themselves in a position to influence their European employers' views of and pathways through the local political and social terrain. Indeed, the European employer could be used as a resource in local power struggles simply by managing his or her movements and perceptions. Research assistants, likewise, played a key role in managing the movements and perceptions of anthropologists, though this does not imply that anthropologists saw only what assistants wanted them to see.

As with Holleman's story about Gluckman in Zululand, however, another story lies behind Kalimosho's interpretation of the anthropologist as witchfinder. During 1957 and 1958, long after Gluckman had left Northern Rhodesia, an upsurge of witchcraft accusations, as well as incidents of witchfinding and the killing of suspected witches, came to the attention of the colonial administration. Reynolds's *Magic, Divination and Witchcraft among the Barotse* describes the 1957–58 events and the artifacts sent to the Rhodes-Livingstone Museum where Reynolds was then keeper of ethnography.[20] The government began a campaign to prosecute both practicing witches and witchfinders, by arresting those accused and gathering what evidence could be found of necrophagy, poisoning, and the use of magical devices with the intention to kill.

When he returned for a short visit to the area in 1965 after independence, Gluckman found it difficult to ask questions about many of the topics of his previous Lozi law research that he had hoped to follow up. He found people still disturbed by the witchcraft-related events, and he refrained from carrying out census and genealogical investigations and "enquiring into past quarrels, lest these awaken fears that I was hunting for deaths and witches responsible for these deaths."[21] He did, however, listen to the stories that local people told about their experiences of that time, including their accounts of the mistreatment of those accused as witches by the district commissioners' staff or the police of the minor Barotse courts.[22]

Moreover, Gluckman believed that a district officer who misappropriated his nickname, *Makapweka*, had triggered the witchcraft accusations.[23] I have not been able to discover the name of any person who used Gluckman's nickname, and former administrators whom I have asked about this have denied knowledge of such a person. Gluckman inserted his nickname into the title page of the 1967 edition of *Judicial Process* because young people in Barotseland then knew him by that name but also, it seems, as an attempt to reclaim it from this misappropriation.[24]

Nevertheless, the interpretations of the assistant, Kalimosho, and of other people with whom I spoke in the main area of Gluckman's work are interesting because of what they say about the variety of local responses to anthropological research and the limits of the anthropologist's power to affect those interpretations. Kalimosho's descriptions of his work with Gluckman show that he interpreted the research work as witchfinding and saw his employer as a powerful and knowledgeable figure to whom the Lozi royal family and government authorities would come for help in prosecuting witchcraft cases. Although it is possible that the assistant subsequently worked for the district officer who used the anthropologist's nickname, Kalimosho never referred to Gluckman as Makapweka and, indeed, used the name "Dr Gluckman" to indicate his special relationship as assistant. He also gave detailed descriptions of routine collecting work and knew the names of the other assistants who worked for Gluckman. He was, however, a minor assistant, working for the anthropologist only during one year of collecting and translating, though they kept in touch after Gluckman left Northern Rhodesia. Gluckman did not, of course, engage in witchfinding in the sense meant by Kalimosho, but he did enquire about artifacts and practices that the assistant associated with witchcraft and he no doubt questioned people Kalimosho and other people in the area considered to be witches or potential witches.

The later 1957–58 events, as Gluckman recognized, had long-term consequences and, given the insecurities and conflicts caused by subsequent periods of sudden political shifts and/or economic downturns — at the time of Gluckman's return visit, as well as at the time I did my own research in the early 1990s — the issues occasioned by that historical event continue to arise. Unlike the Ngoni attitude toward spies (discussed in chapter 4), however, the Lozi attitude toward witchfinders was positive, though the people who were accused by them no doubt felt differently about the case.[25] Before I interviewed Kalimosho I interviewed a number of other Lozi people in the area about Gluckman's work, and many, though not all, portrayed the anthropologist's work as witchfinding. This was also the case with the entirely unsolicited stories about Gluckman that were told to a Norwegian anthropologist working in the area just before I arrived. These stories were told by younger educated people, who felt that Gluckman had been very popular with their parents because of these witchfinding activities.[26]

The events of 1957–58 and the activities of a district officer who may have used Gluckman's nickname thus show that subsequent events can reshape the local memory of an anthropologist's work. This would also be the case with Colson's work in the Gwembe Tonga area in 1956, which she studied immediately before the people were resettled — with some violently resisting the move — to make way for the Kariba hydroelectric project and the creation of Lake Kariba in 1959. Her subsequent fieldwork on the people's responses to resettlement was at first very difficult, according to one of her later assistants, because people thought she might have had a role in the government's plans (though she persisted in her work until her own good behavior allayed these suspicions).[27] In cases like this, the returning anthropologist is not greeted like a lost tribesman.[28]

Kalimosho also interpreted his own role of assistant in terms of his previous work experience as a government tax collector, which points to the importance of understanding the models that assistants themselves bring to the work they do for researchers. In Kalimosho's case his local identity as a Christian Lozi shaped his attitude to Gluckman's work and interactions with non-Lozi people. Accordingly, it is important to consider the particular nature of the assistants' local connections when considering their roles in the research. Anthropologists in rural areas usually hired assistants who came from the ethnic group they studied in order to employ the assistant's local connections and local knowledge. Some assistants in the rural areas, however, did not have local connections but came to the anthropologist through other channels that reflected the assistant's own skills and interests. This was the case with Benjamin Shipopa, who worked for Colson during her research in the Plateau Tonga area in 1947–1950. He had come from the Ila area just north of the Tonga area and had a Standard Three education, army experience, and training as a driver. Gluckman met him in Kenya in 1947 (while the director was there visiting Audrey Richards) and offered him a job at the RLI. According to Colson, he did well as a research assistant despite the lack of local connections because he was "a man of integrity who could make friends and win respect."[29]

This would also be the case with many members of the urban survey team, who, though they may have lived in some of the urban areas they studied, could not possibly have had local connections in all of them nor with the numerous rural areas from which the Copperbelt residents came. Instead, they usually had connections to the emerging African political and union organizations, as well as membership in the growing informal network of educated Africans who worked as clerks, teachers, and welfare officers in the urban areas. And their cosmopolitan experiences and their activities in emerging African organizations would prove to be a particularly useful form of indigenous knowledge for the urban work.

Walking with Europeans

During the RLI's initial program of rural research in the late 1940s, assistants' work in rural areas established practices that could be imported into the urban research situation. One reason for this was the quantitative aspect of the RLI's research program, which required gathering demographic information both in rural and urban areas. Assistants walked around with the anthropologist when he or she counted heads, at first playing the role of translator but eventually participating in the counting themselves. For larger survey projects members of the first RLI team of researchers sometimes employed government survey workers known as "African enumerators." For example, in his Malemia survey in Nyasaland, the government provided Mitchell with African government clerks to do a census of that "semi-urban" area.[30] Another rural practice that would become crucial for urban anthropology was the assistants' continuation of research when anthropologists left the field. The RLI required researchers to leave the field at regular intervals — for in-house conferences approximately every six months, for larger yearly conferences with outside experts on certain aspects of the research, and for study or writing periods in South African universities, Oxford, and, later, Manchester. In advance of the initial writing-up session for the first team of researchers, Gluckman suggested that the anthropologists train their interpreters (as he called the assistants then) to keep diaries of births, deaths, arguments, and other significant events during the researchers' absence.[31] Through this practice, rural assistants gained a fair amount of autonomy in conducting the research.

Assistants in the rural areas also provided the anthropologist with guidance about local customs and expectations, smoothing the way for life in the village until the anthropologist learned enough to manage successfully. Urban researchers, however, required more than this initial guidance from their assistants. In the urban areas anthropologists dealt with a more Westernized population of Africans with different expectations of Europeans. Moreover, the mines and white society prevented anthropologists from living in the urban African locations and constrained their research visits there. These constraints limited their contacts with ordinary Africans, making them more dependent on assistants for their knowledge of urban African society. And although anthropologists tried to transpose their own rural patterns of research onto the research assistants' activities, the assistants' own status and contacts in the urban areas shaped their patterns of research, sometimes in other directions, as explained in a later section of this chapter.

Gluckman and Colson planned to attract highly qualified Africans from across southern and central Africa for the survey team jobs, especially at the senior assistant level. For example, the salaries and contracts Colson asked for in her research plan reflected the RLI directors' general aim to encourage African scholars to pursue careers in sociology: "The appointment of a team of African Assistants would also enable the Institute to train a small number of Africans in scientific procedures. The Senior Assistants at the end of their five year contracts would undoubtedly be trained sociologists competent to work independently. They would attend all conferences of the Institute staff and would be encouraged to write reports for publication."[32]

The salaries she requested were based exclusively on qualifications and did not reflect the color bar, for she hoped eventually to take on European and African staff at all levels, with high enough salaries to compete for the very few Africans in the region who possessed some tertiary education. For example, an urban sociologist with a D.Phil. was to receive £1700 (not including additional expenses), a senior assistant with B.A. or M.A. would get £1200; a junior assistant with a Standard Eight or higher secondary school qualification or previous experience would get £812.[33] The RLI Board of Trustees, reflecting government concerns about competition for educated African staff, refused to allow such high salaries for the assistant positions, as noted in the previous chapter.

Because salaries remained generally lower or at best comparable with those offered by mines and government, the question of what motivated Africans to take work as research assistants becomes more interesting. In the towns what attracted African assistants to anthropological research often differed from what attracted them to the work in rural areas. The work practices — conducting interviews and writing reports — did not differ enough from those of clerks and welfare assistants to compensate for the sometimes lower salaries offered by the Institute. The subject matter — statistics and observations of urban African life — however, proved attractive because of its potential for use by Africans to change government policies. Assistants believed they were joining a profession critical of government and white settler dominance. They also saw themselves as learning a method for analyzing European, as well as African, society.[34] The RLI assistants, as well as some informants, pointed out these uses in the course of the research and used them to justify the work to potential informants (see below).

The egalitarian aspects of the RLI work culture also enhanced the assistants' modern urban self-image. For example, not the least of the attractions of working for anthropologists in the towns was that it allowed one to get a good drink when at RLI conferences in Lusaka. For elite urban Africans in Northern Rhodesia, access to alcohol had become an issue of symbolic importance. Although access to bottled beer and wine had been liberalized in 1948 in response to the modernizing aspirations of returning African soldiers, the consumption of spirits by Africans remained illegal until shortly before independence.[35] This prohibition exacerbated Africans' anger at the urban color bar. Judged by the regularity of its mention in interviews with the former assistants, the invitation to drink spirits with the anthropologists at RLI headquarters was highly valued as a symbol of equality.[36] Nevertheless, the context of work and social activities at the Institute was only free of color bar restrictions relative to the larger racist context, which constantly impinged upon it.[37] While an assistant might value the equality of sharing a drink at one anthropologist's house, at another's he might find himself confined to the verandah while the anthropologist's family took tea inside, as one assistant bitterly recalled.[38] And different directors established different practices at the Institute headquarters, some of them welcomed and others resented by the assistants (see below).

Being seen in association with anthropologists was also a mixed blessing. As discussed previously, Africans in the late colonial period viewed anthropologists and assistants with suspicions based on their experiences with other Europeans and their African employees — in the rural areas, the colonial officer and his district messengers, and in the urban areas, the mining compound manager and his African

police. These suspicions increased during the anti-Federation struggle as African political parties and unions came under intense government and mining company surveillance often carried out by African collaborators who attended the meetings of nationalist and
union organizations and reported their activities. As the tensions
escalated all whites came to be stereotyped as spying on African
activities, an idea that could easily bring observing anthropologists
under suspicion. Moreover, Africans who appeared to cooperate
with whites could be found guilty of "walking with Europeans."[39]
The RLI assistants faced these political suspicions as they carried out
the urban surveys.

Beginning in 1950 the RLI's fourth director, Mitchell, recruited
and trained the team of research assistants and began a series of
demographic and social surveys in the major towns on the Northern
Rhodesian Copperbelt and the line-of-rail. The first assistant recruited for the urban survey was Sykes Ndilila,[40] employed at first
individually by Mitchell. At that time Mitchell resided in the town of
Luanshya on the Copperbelt during the early period of the RLI's
urban research in 1951. His first piece of urban research concerned
the Kalela dance, which he observed in the Luanshya Management
Board Location.[41] As mentioned in the previous chapter, Ndilila
translated Mitchell's questions and wrote down and translated the
songs that figured prominently in Mitchell's analysis of the dance.

Another of the RLI's earliest urban assistants was Davidson Sianga[42]—who, as mentioned in previous chapters, had worked for
Gluckman and who had considerable experience with rural surveys.
He tried out the RLI's new census cards in a random sample in
Livingstone run by the RLI administrative secretary before the main
survey was begun. Sianga participated in a later rural field training
session for Turner in Lambaland, arranged by Mitchell, and then
worked briefly for Epstein on his urban courts study.[43] Like Sianga, a
few assistants who had previously done rural research or research
for a single anthropologist in town became early members of the
survey team. Because the RLI researchers usually had nationalist
sympathies and research interests in African political organization,
they preferred assistants who were politically aware and sensitive to

the issues that would be important in an urban study. These assistants were "in the games — they knew what we were about," according to Mitchell, and they picked up other potential assistants with similar awareness. Mitchell selected assistants for their literacy and their "social skills for dealing with suspicion" — because "people always thought they were government and doing a census to throw people out of towns." He also ensured a mix of ethnic backgrounds because of the tribal sensitivities in the towns and the frequent need to interview informants in their own languages, though all assistants had to speak "town Bemba" — the Copperbelt lingua franca.[44]

Using punchcards, each assistant filled in questionnaires for the inhabitants of five houses per day. On days when this "card work" was impossible, they conducted open-ended interviews with informants or observed local events such as dances and football matches, gathering qualitative data for their own research reports. In the early days, Mitchell supervised the interviews and corrected the assistants' procedures. He also checked the punchcards for inconsistencies at the end of the day, and the assistants had to interview the informants again to correct any inaccuracies or gaps.[45] Later the assistants themselves did much of the work independently, as well as the recruitment and training of additional team members, under the direction of senior research assistants who had university qualifications.[46]

Mitchell helped to set up the surveys in each new town, however, because of white compound managers who were "always suspicious [and who] never understood what he was doing."[47] As Ndilila reported to him on his own successful attempt to bring around a recalcitrant compound manager: "I have managed to get permission from another two contractors['] compound[s]. I had a long talk with the Manager of the Northern Builders who at first was very difficult & yet anxious to know much about Research. He fired dozens of questions at me: such as: 'What is Research? Whom do you Represent? What statistics for?, Isn't the Gov't doing?' etc. I managed to answer his questions."[48]

On other occasions the assistants' explanations did not satisfy white authorities, resulting in failures that must have been galling to their sense of independence and professional status. As Ndilila re-

The urban survey team in Kitwe, on the Copperbelt, in April
1952, with Senior Assistant, Simon Katilungu, standing on the
right and M. B. Lukhero, in hat, standing on the left. (Photo from
J. Clyde Mitchell's private collection. Reproduced by permission
of Jean Mitchell.)

ported of some other contractors, "They say they would not allow
anybody to enter into their compounds unless one produced a note
of introduction from one's master."[49]

Gender, as well as race, became a source of trouble in conducting
the surveys because of working men's fears concerning their wives'
opportunities for adultery while they were away at work. From the
start the Institute attempted to recruit African women for the general
urban surveys and for special surveys of women's issues. These re-
cruits didn't work out because interviewing clashed with women's

domestic work and with the prohibition on their movements enforced by their husbands. As a supervising male assistant commented on a female trainee's evaluation form: "*Remarks. Is unable to do research—has baby on back all the time. Likes to learn but seems to have no way out.*"[50]

On the other hand, some research assistants' wives carried out participant observation research which allowed them to continue with their normal domestic routines and, in the evening, write a diary of the day's events. Women didn't join the urban survey team until the late 1950s, at about the same time that women in UNIP began doing political organizing that challenged their restricted roles. And then only one woman joined the RLI, Possenta Akapelwa, who worked on urban surveys during Fosbrooke's directorship.[51]

The growing professionalization of the research assistants found expression in the standards they applied to themselves and others based on intellectual attainment and membership in a meritocratic elite, as indicated in the male assistant's approval of the female trainee (above) when she showed that she "like[d] to learn." In a late colonial context in which African achievement was measured by academic grade and level of autonomy on the job, the RLI assistants had gained an unusually privileged position. Some, like Godfrey Mukonoweshuro,[52] who served for a time as senior assistant, or Simon Katilungu,[53] the longest-serving senior assistant, considered themselves professional sociologists on career paths that would lead to academic posts.[54] Both men organized seminars for the other assistants and assigned them reading and research topics. Mitchell encouraged them and others on the team to pursue their education, attempted to arrange funding for the purpose, and published the best of their papers in the RLI journal or cited their work in his own published papers.[55]

Ethnicity, as well as race and class, became an object of study that the assistants dealt with in their work.[56] In "The Kalela Dance," Mitchell cited a survey of beer-drinking habits carried out by one of the assistants which showed that the drinking clubs were divided along tribal lines.[57] Mitchell himself carried out a social distance study for inclusion in "The Kalela Dance." To determine the social distance between the members of various tribes in the urban areas, the study used such questions as "Would you willingly agree to close kinship by marriage with a Lozi?" and "Would you willingly agree to share a meal with a Bisa?" The study was done at an African secondary school by Mitchell rather than in the Copperbelt towns by the survey team because of the need to administer the questionnaire to a literate group.[58] Mitchell drew on the assistants' views of ethnicity, particularly in deciding the content and order of the questions.[59]

Ethnicity figured to a small degree within the team itself, as its members divided up the resources allotted them for research. Until he put a stop to it—Mukonoweshuro complained—"tribalism" dominated the allocation of the team's two typewriters.[60] Tribalism, however, was not an important factor relative to other factors such as resentment of the senior assistants' university education and the team's solidarity along racial lines.[61] At one point Ndilila wrote to Mitchell to advise him of a potential rebellion of the team over late salary payments, led by Mukonoweshuro and Katilungu.[62] In another letter, Mukonoweshuro denied the charges, and Ndilila later left the team.[63] It is not clear from the sources whether this conflict had an ethnic dimension.

The fact that Ndilila broke ranks with the other team members, however, indicates that racial solidarity against the white director was not the only issue. The struggle may, indeed, have been over *control of* the white director, with Ndilila using his best civil service language and speaking of Mitchell as his "master" to curry favor in letters he wrote during the conflict, while Mukonoweshuro used a more professional tone and references to his academic colleagues at Ft. Hare College when anwering the charges.[64] Formerly Mitchell's sole assistant, Ndilila may have resented his loss of control over the anthropologist's perceptions, indicated by the greater status given to assistants with university qualifications. Katilungu, who came from a Bemba area, may have been resented by Ndilila even more than Mukonoweshuro, who came from a Shona area in Southern Rhodesia, because people from Katilungu's area—because of the relative lack of secondary schools—rarely managed to obtain the educational qualifications necessary for clerical and other white-collar occupations, and Katilungu had managed against the odds to do so.[65]

The assistants' research reports revealed that racial politics was ultimately the most important issue for them in their engagement with anthropology. In a report on the Robinson Puta trial, Katilungu discussed the ethnic behavior he observed in the African Mine Workers' Union during its conflict with the mine compounds' tribal representatives — a case in which Puta, an official in the union, was charged with threatening the tribal representatives for their collaboration with mine management.[66] At the end of the report Katilungu stressed that, though "tribal feelings" could be found in everyday relations among Africans, "black nationalism [was] more pronounced" whenever Africans interacted with whites.[67] Indeed, his report itself often analyzed mine management's motives and behavior in maintaining the tribal representative system, and in the report he concluded, "It is this European employer element in an African organisation that is significant from the sociological point of view,"[68] an African view that resonated with the older RLI theme of crosscutting ties between European and African groups.

Max Gluckman, the RLI's second director, had stressed the need for a sociological analysis of European society together with African society. His "Analysis of a Social Situation in Modern Zululand" had provided a model of this kind of study for later RLI work, though RLI research on the whole did not treat European institutions as thoroughly as African ones. The assistants in their seminars discussed Gluckman's work and found the idea of analyzing white society attractive. One of the assistants, Joachim Lengwe,[69] seems to have consciously applied Gluckman's method in a report on an athletic meeting attended by a racially mixed audience, which he observed for his research. In the report, Lengwe commented on the voluntary segregation between African and European spectators, enforced mainly by the African women. He focused also on the contrast in gender relations between the races: "Tea was given to [the African women] by their husbands, whereas on the European side women served men. Another interesting incidence I noticed was the time when the guests found that the waiters were few, European women helped the waiters whereas African women just remained in their chairs drinking and eating."[70]

Lengwe's focus on the racial dimension of gender roles may have been a conscious response to the colonial attitude toward race and gender. Administrators, missionaries, and settlers adhered to an earlier evolutionary view of African societies that saw their apparent treatment of women as "beasts of burden" as an indication of savagery. Lengwe used his report to point out that this was not the case as far as elite African women were concerned and, moreover, that European women voluntarily took on the role of waiter, joining African men in this task. Thus he may have been implying that, by their own evolutionary scale, Europeans ranked below the so-called savage African.

Lengwe's report illustrates a process occurring in many of the assistants' reports, of a reworking of anthropological material and methods to fit African purposes. Jomo Kenyatta's *Facing Mount Kenya* is perhaps the best example of this process of reworking anthropology, in his case for the purpose of imagining Gikuyu nationhood.[71] In both cases the goal was political—to provide a critical analysis of the colonial racial situation. The crucial difference between them was that the RLI assistants were not primarily reimagining ethnicity as Kenyatta was—though some of them would take up that project in the post-independence period.[72] Another difference from Kenyatta was that the RLI assistants involved in the survey used a different kind of anthropology, a quantitative anthropology that focused on modern urban life rather than the cultural focus favored by Kenyatta, who was partly trained by Malinowski. Thus the material the RLI assistants had available for their political purposes was often statistical and concerned with contemporary problems rather than with traditional customs and local histories.

Statistics, as well, had the power to impress or annoy the government, and the assistants were not unaware of this. They promoted the idea that social research would help to improve living conditions and provide ammunition for debates with colonial officials, a strategy that they employed to get informants to cooperate with their work. And this strategy was successful. First, Africans did, indeed, use the data collected by the RLI for political debates at the time.[73] Second, the assistants themselves acted "politically," in the sense in which Zambians often employ the term—strategizing to advance their own personal goals — which in this case, was doing their paid work for the RLI. Thus, when to my question about his political affiliation a former assistant replied by exclaiming, "We were all politicians!" he meant not only that he had been a member of a political party, which he had, but also that he had used his political network strategically to get his paid survey work done.

"We Were All Politicians!"

While singing the praises of the loyal and unspoiled district messengers who served them, most colonial administrators reviled those they called "African politicians," who made governing difficult, especially in the towns. In keeping with the Cold War atmosphere of the day, they suspected politically conscious Africans of being communists, though one administrator noted ironically in his memoirs that when security officers searched for communist literature in the house of an arrested union leader, they were disappointed to find only "Professor Tawney."[74]

Government agents checked the political background of all African applicants for jobs in government, a procedure that also applied to the RLI because of the government's role in its funding. This greatly increased the director's difficulty in finding assistants to work for the Institute, since many of the applicants engaged in politics.[75] Despite this government scrutiny, most of the Africans who eventually got work on the urban survey team had been politically active before their employment or clandestinely engaged in such activities during their employment. In an interview, one former assistant emphasized that their political involvement was what made the urban research possible at all.[76] Their membership in the miners' union, in the Northern Rhodesian ANC, and later in UNIP — or their contacts with friends in these organizations — gave the assistants access to urban compounds that were increasingly coming under nationalist or union control.[77]

Before undertaking a survey in a particular town, the assistants contacted union and political party leaders, who then introduced them at the next union or party meeting. There they would be grilled as to the politics and the value of social research. Lukhero,[78] the administrative assistant for the Copperbelt survey, described such an event in one of his reports to Mitchell: "We were asked to climb on top of the table one by one in order to be seen by people. The [Union Branch] Secretary introduced our work and told people that it was of great importance & that our Department was not 'connected' with the government. One question was put to me by one man 'Do you belong to government?' I said 'We have nothing to do with the Boma and we do not belong to them at all. We only ask for cooperation from every concerned organisation, such as the Mines, contractors and even the government itself if we want to do our work in the Compound where their people live.' "[79]

The assistants' association with European anthropologists — and as it was sometimes assumed, with government — became more problematic as African resentment of the Federation increased in the mid-1950s. The accusation that assistants were "walking with Europeans" carried with it specific political connotations as well, for Africans used this epithet to describe the African members of multiracial groups such as the Capricorn Africa Society or the Federal Party. African members of the latter party usually came from Southern Rhodesia and toured Northern Rhodesia at Federal Party expense to gather African support for the Federation. Assistants for the RLI found themselves frequently accused of being "Capricorns" or "Federal agentsi."[80]

At one point a man making this accusation beat up the team's senior assistant.[81] When the assistant took his assailant to court, however, the man refused to pursue his political accusation about the assistant and insisted that he had beaten the assistant for "interfering with" his wife, possibly because he would be more likely to get sympathy for this charge from the white magistrate. This shift in accusation was not, however, a shift entirely away from politics. Well-dressed and relatively highly paid, the research assistants fit the image of the emerging class of African white-collar workers. Resentment against them increased on the Copperbelt after the African Salaried Staff Association broke from the mineworkers' union in order to represent the interests of the educated and higher paid clerks on the mines. The union suspected the new association of collaborating with management against the other African workers. Whatever their actual union sympathies, RLI assistants dressed and talked like members of the breakaway staff association and, like them, sometimes expressed contemptuous attitudes toward miners. The RLI assistants found the miners' compounds the most difficult areas to survey, for miners were hostile because they had become accustomed to visits by African compound personnel who were "not on friendly missions." The research assistants also saw miners as among the least "enlightened" of urban Africans, "kept back" by mine management in order to make them easier to control as workers.[82]

When talking about their fieldwork at the time, research assistants used words like "invading" and "persuading," words that reveal their response to this difficult environment. Particularly rough compounds would be "invaded" by the entire team in order to provide safety in numbers. At particulary unsettled times, a compound might be left out of the survey until strikes, boycotts, or rumors about Federal agents had subsided. If nothing else worked, in the early days the team sometimes called on the African police to encourage cooperation through their presence. The senior assistant may have had misgivings about this practice when, in a report to the director, he wondered if some of the assistants' problems were caused by a lack of tact.[83]

But neither tact nor the African police alone was enough to get the work done. Ultimately, African informants had to be persuaded of the usefulness of research. Accordingly, the assistants developed the practice of talking individually with difficult informants in the hope of persuading them that the RLI's work could better their lives. Assistants went in pairs after work to meet with informants who had refused to "be written" — that is, refused to respond to the survey questions — or those who simply had questions about the research. In one case — of a man whose wife had been interviewed while he was at work — the assistants found that he wanted the punchcard back, probably because he feared it might be used to show he had joined the Federal Party.[84]

In other cases, informants welcomed the assistants and readily gave information, sometimes asking to talk to them at length as in the following example: "Before Mr. Chansa [one of the assistants] finished explaining [why we were there], [the informant] told him to start writing without wasting his time. He said, he was pleased to see us at his house for he was longing for the work we do so as to be able to present his problems also."[85]

This informant responded as though to a commission of inquiry which he expected would bring about changes in the treatment of Africans. Indeed, part of the "tact" that the assistants' acquired in the course of the survey may have consisted of learning how to present their work as contributing to African arguments for better living and working conditions, on the model of the government commissions that often followed strikes and disturbances on the Copperbelt. After one strike, the administrative research assistant described the people's reaction to the survey as unusually positive: "When we go in the compounds, people have a hope that we are 'bringing' them good wages when we ask them what work they are doing, and what type of houses they live in! Some say their wages shall go up after we finish our work on all four mining centres!"[86]

Soon Africans, however, lost confidence in the ability of colonial commissions to address their grievances. By the time of the Monckton Commission, which sought to gauge African opinion of Federation, nationalist leaders condemned any cooperation with the commission as giving support to the Federation. The urban survey team, which continued its work throughout the resulting boycott of the Commission, experienced considerable resistance, with people expressing the fear that being written would in itself lead to their being counted on the side of Federation.

Other informants became skeptical when changes in working and housing conditions did not follow from their cooperation with other surveys. Once when Ackson Nyirenda called at a house, the man living there said, "I've been interviewed before and nothing good came of it—push off!"[87] Resistance to the survey could express Africans' disillusionment with the government's commitment to improve living conditions and their increasingly sophisticated skepticism about the usefulness of research into those conditions. Katilungu encoun-

An informant "being written" by members of the urban survey team in
Mufulira on the Copperbelt. This photo is one of a collection of
"sociological snaps" taken by the survey team to supplement their data
collection. Team members captioned these with descriptions of social
situations and the research process. The caption for this one states: "Here is
a picture of two Research Assistants getting information from their
informants in Murambe Compound. As you see them here they are very
interested with their work of research. The two men [the informants] are
staying in a poor hut as you can see by yourself. One informant is standing
up while the other one is s[it]ting down. This man is trying to go and get
something from the roof of the two informants', and behind him you can see
a Research Assistant writing one of his informants." (Photo taken by L. L.
Bweupe. From J. Clyde Mitchell's private collection. Reproduced by
permission of Jean Mitchell.)

tered this attitude after explaining the purpose of the survey to a
union executive meeting: "In concluding I invited questions from the
meeting which were poured at me like tropical summer rains. Some
of the most difficult questions concerned the benefits which the survey would bring to the African population. It is not easy to say
anything to this group about social planning, as they would tell one,

and they told me 'The Government is the social planner, but since it is not interested in facts it cannot improve things. District Commissioners and District Officers have for many years asked how many children this man has and how [many] has the other and so on, but what have they produced?' they ask. 'Nothing' is the answer they gave themselves."

Ultimately Katilungu won the approval of the meeting by explaining the potential *political* usefulness of the survey: "Our publications contain useful information which could be used for arguing their case in negotiations. I was supported in this direction by Mr. Chapoloko who seemingly heard [someone?] quoting written evidence in their arguments."[88] (James Chapoloko was the Branch Secretary of the union at Roan Antelope Mine in Luanshya.) In this case, Africans' recognition of the power of *written* evidence led them to accept the process of "being written" by the RLI survey team.

Even when local branches proved difficult to persuade, the previous contacts *national* union and political leaders had had with the Institute often saved the day. Harry Nkumbula (from 1951 the president of Congress) spent time reading at the RLI library, was familiar with its publications, and had even been suggested for a job as research assistant.[89] Lawrence Katilungu, head of the miners' union, knew of the RLI's work through friendship with one of the anthropologists, Bill Epstein. Both could be called upon to persuade the local branches to cooperate with the assistants or to dispel rumors about their work.[90] The union management, in particular, expressed an interest in social research and at one point requested that Epstein conduct a study of its organization.[91]

Along with stressing the usefulness of their research to all groups, including Europeans, Africans, unions, nationalists, and government, RLI researchers and assistants developed a professional stance of neutrality to protect themselves from public scrutiny. Reacting to attacks on the RLI in the local white press, as well as to the assistants' difficulties, Mitchell wrote to the administrative secretary: "The fact that we are attacked by both African and European seems to indicate that we are about in the right place — in the middle. And that's where we must stay. Things are likely to become more and more difficult as time goes on and I think I should say that I think it would be wise if we were to refrain from falling into the trap of expressing any political opinions whether to government or settler or African. In our public relations, at least, I think we ought to present the façade of the Victorian 'objective' scientist."[92] Here Mitchell recognized that the RLI's appearance of objectivity was a façade for the purpose of public relations, for both researchers and assistants realized that the assistants' ability to argue for the political usefulness of social science was what allowed them to carry on research in a highly politicized environment.

Indeed, when the struggle for independence intensified in the early 1960s, and the conflict included rivalry between the two nationalist parties — Congress and UNIP — the assistants had to declare their political allegiance openly in order to gain access to informants in compounds dominated by one or the other party. Some assistants resorted to carrying membership cards from both parties. Nothing guaranteed safety, however, in a time of suspicion so intense that "even your wife would suspect you for belonging to the wrong party and would report you to your party," as the assistant Jacques Chiwale put it.[93]

In this atmosphere, the assistants' *professional* stance may have been useful to them, because it allowed them to distance themselves from political commitment in a situation in which some may not have yet decided where their personal interests lay. Open affiliation with a political party carried with it dangers — first, of losing one's job if the government caught wind of it, and, second, of attracting the hostility of members of the other competing political party, who might include neighbors or kin. Coupled with this may have been a genuine, but certainly not entirely disinterested, interest in the political situation for its intellectual and social complexities. Standing back as professionals, observing and experimenting with the situation, may have allowed some assistants to gain an understanding of it that would be useful for their future survival in a post-independence state. An example of this professional distancing is contained in one of Katilungu's reports to Mitchell, in which he comments on nationalist political activity: "Incidentally Mr. Dixon

Konkola President of the African Railway Workers Union, and District Chairman of Broken Hill branch of the Congress, has been imprisoned with [an]other six African congress leaders and followers for taking part in an unlawful procession which demonstrated at the police station here, carrying banners which read 'Our Ultimate End is Self Government' and 'No Colour Bar.' These uprisings are the most interesting to study."[94]

In another case, Epstein commented to Mitchell on an assistant's apparent attitude to a Congress boycott: "[The boycott] is due here in Ndola next wk, and I wouldn't be surprised if Nyirenda isn't giving it every encouragement just to have something interesting to follow up: not meant seriously of course. N is a bit fed up with Congress' antics, but rubs his hands in anticipation of having 'a real social situation' to deal with."[95]

This kind of professional distancing clearly received approval from the assistants' employers — which may have been a factor in its adoption by the assistants — but it also proved useful in dealing with the painful instances of racism that confronted the assistants in their work and social lives. Describing a time when the white owners refused to let him enter a restaurant in Southern Rhodesia with Mitchell while he worked as Mitchell's assistant at UCRN, Lukhero brushed off the incident by saying to Mitchell, "It is all research." Later Lukhero participated in anticolor bar protests by entering whites-only hotels and businesses to — as he put it with some humor — "conduct sociological experiments."[96] For the assistants, then, social research had become a versatile strategy for dealing with the political situation and with the daily humiliations of a racist society. It was not, however, a strategy that always succeeded.

Conclusion: Savagery and Social Science

The later stages of the independence struggle saw a devaluation in the usefulness of negotiation in the political arena and, thus, less interest in social research as a means of arguing for change. On the defensive because of Hastings Kamuzu Banda's return to Nyasaland in 1958 and the aggressive independence campaign he initiated there, the Federal and Northern Rhodesian governments followed the Nyasaland government's lead and cracked down on African protest and began preemptive arrests of nationalist leaders. The new style of political organization favored by UNIP also brought more effective forces into play on the African side. Along with mobilizing women and the masses, UNIP organized youth brigades that proved their usefulness in the violence that increasingly became the nationalist response to government recalcitrance, culminating in the violent "Cha Cha Cha" campaign of July to October 1961 to bring pressure for constitutional change.[97]

Being menaced by a group of stone-throwing youths while driving into a housing location in 1956 convinced Epstein that urban fieldwork was no longer possible for white anthropologists, and he left Northern Rhodesia for Manchester shortly thereafter. With the end of the first urban survey in 1955, Mitchell had already left for UCRN in Southern Rhodesia, where he had been offered the first chair in African Studies. With the future takeover of the RLI by UCRN (as part of an overall Federation plan for centralization of services), the RLI was supposed to become the university's research wing, and it was hoped that Mitchell's presence at UCRN would benefit the Institute. As the assistants put it in their farewell message to Mitchell: "As a matter of fact, we are soothed by the fact that by leaving this place you are not cut off from the Institute and its science but that you are going to an upper chamber where you can render your services to the Institute to a greater extent in these troubled days than you have hitherto done. We therefore have all hope that some of us will be with you in the nearest future either as students or as your assistant lecturers or even in other capacities — all of which are admittedly pretty hard."[98]

Their farewell message showed the assistants' interest in advancement in social science, though at the same time they expressed the anxiety that it would be difficult to attain. Ackson Nyirenda,[99] for example, had been strongly encouraged to continue with his studies and had already produced published and unpublished work of high quality, but, like most of the other assistants, did not continue in sociology or anthropology.

The Board of Trustees replaced Mitchell with Henry Fosbrooke, a colonial administrator who had previously worked as a government sociologist and district commissioner in Tanganyika. Through this move the government intended to make it easier to control the Institute's controversial research.[100] Politically, however, Fosbrooke supported African nationalism and engaged in a number of activities that demonstrated his sense of racial equality and strong objection to the color bar. He also objected to the degree of control exercised over the Institute by government and used its research capacity, as well as his government contacts, to advance the issue of social security measures for Africans. Ultimately, he resigned in protest of the RLI's takeover by UCRN because he felt the reputation of Southern Rhodesia for its segregationist policies would make the Institute's work impossible among Africans. He further objected to UCRN's dominance as the only university in the Federation — again because its location in a segregationist country made it an inappropriate training ground for the "future leaders of independent African states," and his letters to Northern Rhodesian students attending that university expressed sympathy for them because of the racism they encountered.[101]

The survey team continued working on a number of projects, including a government housing survey and a family budget research project that established the poverty levels of the three capital cities of the Federation. During this time the assistants encountered trouble not only in the field but also at the Institute itself where staff relationships changed dramatically under Fosbrooke. Under Mitchell, the Institute headquarters had stood out as one of the few nonracial institutions in the Federation. For example, assistants had argued for, and succeeded in getting, their title — "African Research Assistant" — changed to the nonracial "Research Assistant."[102] Although he didn't find Africans to fill the higher posts, Mitchell encouraged some of the assistants to continue their schooling and publish their research.[103] He also embarked on a building project for the headquarters which gave the assistants' and other African staff housing the highest priority.[104] The houses were situated behind the main buildings and in some ways replicated the so-called African quarters found behind the government *bomas* in each district administrative center, where the clerks and *boma* messengers lived. Despite this spatial segregation, the staff quarters influenced the atmosphere of the RLI in no small measure. As in a village, chickens wandered everywhere, and the assistants and anthropologists carried on noisy discussions of field methods whenever they stayed at headquarters together.[105]

Under Fosbrooke, however, the RLI changed in ways that disturbed both the assistants and anthropologists. Anthropologists resented what they saw as a government ploy to control their research, and new researchers arriving at the Institute, eager to join its "pro-African project," felt betrayed.[106] Assistants resented Fosbrooke's misunderstanding of their established practice of getting together to discuss field methods, analyze theoretical articles, and debate sociological points — "He thought we were just making noise," Katilungu recalled.[107] In addition, the assistants criticized Fosbrooke for not being "progressive," meaning that he maintained the strict practices associated with district commissioners rather than the more culturally sensitive practices of the previous directors, who happed to include a culturally sensitive administrator, Charles White.

In particular, Fosbrooke objected to the wandering chickens. At one point a clerk at the Institute accused him of killing a rooster that had wandered too close to the director's office and annoyed him with its crowing.[108] The senior research assistant, Katilungu, saw Fosbrooke strangling the chicken and "told [the director] he was behaving like a savage instead of a director of a social research organization."[109]

The recriminations that followed this incident increased the tension between the director and the African staff to the point that Katilungu resigned. His resignation statement accentuated the seriousness with which he took giving up social science as a career: "If when I was born I was meant to work for the Rhodes-Livingstone Institute only, and if I was unable to work for it I would perish, [then] I am prepared to perish!"[110]

The end of Katilungu's career as a social scientist, however, preceded by only a short time the end of the RLI's existence as a center primarily focused on anthropological research. Despite the director's own resignation in 1960, the Institute was handed over to UCRN in 1962 and then quickly handed back upon Northern Rhodesia's independence in 1964. In the process it lost its research focus on social anthropology and most of its personnel, including the research assistants who were much in demand for other work in the soon-to-be-independent nation.[111]

The contrast that Katilungu pointed out—between a savage and the director of a social research organization—indicated for him the difference between authoritarian colonial administrative practices and the more egalitarian work relations that had previously prevailed at the Institute. The social researcher's professional stance represented a practice of distancing and maintaining neutrality incompatible with Fosbrooke's behavior, and Katilungu took this opportunity to turn the standard colonial criticism of Africans back onto the European, by comparing the director's behavior to that of a savage. Thus, he reinterpreted the professional stance of the social scientist into a critical stance on the failings of colonial practice.

His reinterpretation notwithstanding, Katilungu found himself out of a job as a social scientist. The colonial administrative practices that drove Katilungu to resign signaled a break in the RLI's program, for both its overt sociological aims and its covert political goals. The Institute did not become the nucleus of a Zambian university, though it would later be absorbed into one. Neither did its coordinated anthropological research continue, being displaced by a coordinated research program in psychology in the period immediately before and after independence. An RLI anthropologist, Jaap van Velsen, again headed the Institute in the early 1970s, the University of Manchester continued to publish some of its research, a number of Manchester students continued to do fieldwork in Northern Rhodesia, and Max Gluckman maintained an interest in the Institute's fate well into the 1960s. But the institutional culture fostered by the RLI no longer flourished, except during a few periods when later Manchester School researchers overlapped during fieldwork or while holding posts at the University of Zambia, as occurred for a time during van Velsen's directorship.

The nature of that institutional culture and its relationship to the culture of fieldwork developed by the RLI anthropologists will be explored in the concluding chapter.

8

The Culture of Fieldwork

Four ideas have driven this account of anthropology as a field science in Africa: networks, cultures of research, the coproduction of scientific knowledge, and the field as a constructed and negotiated space for the production of knowledge rather than as a mere source of data. In this concluding section I draw out some of the larger implications of these ideas for understanding the RLI and its place in the history of science in Africa. I begin with the enormous changes that occur when the members of a network established in the field move into academic careers. Because this happened for different RLI researchers at different times and also involved the transition of the RLI itself from a colonial to a postindependence institution, this shift in networks raises the question of what is an appropriate endpoint for the RLI's history.

The Ends of Histories

A history of the RLI could end at many different points, and each alternative endpoint could be used to say something meaningful about the nature of RLI fieldwork and its legacy. Each alternative endpoint changes the story, as well. One could end with Mitchell's resignation and use that endpoint to stress that academically minded anthropologists no longer controlled the Institute and its research agenda. But that would give less importance than it deserves to the continuing use of the RLI as a field center with strong academic connections that included future fieldworkers sent from Manchester, UCRN, and other universities, which had been or would become part of the RLI's institutional network. This use of the RLI as a field center continued even during the subsequent directorships of administrator-ethnographers such as White and Fosbrooke.

Such an ending would also distract from key aspects of Mitchell's directorship — his promotion of applied anthropology and the work he did to establish demographic and poverty datum line studies at the RLI, as well as to continue the fostering of links with government. It would also leave out Jaap van Velsen's later directorship (1971–73) and the strong continuity of the *sociological* vision of the RLI's work, which led, as well, to the founding of the Department of Sociology at the University of Zambia, the first professor of which would be the Manchester School medical sociologist Ronald Frankenberg in 1966.

Alternatively one could end with Fosbrooke's resignation and use that endpoint to emphasize the loss of the RLI's coordinated program of anthropological research. Indeed, the RLI as an institution might not have survived the subsequent uncertain period during its transfer to UCRN and then almost immediate return to Northern Rhodesia when the Federation came to an end. As one former Munali School student, who worked for the RLI during his vacations, put it, "The Institute went into a black hole at that time."[1] Continuities of many kinds seemed broken, and when a research program was started again at independence, it was a program devoted to cross-cultural and occupational psychology. Despite the complete change of research personnel, however, many continuities with earlier work persisted. Previous RLI directors, and especially Mitchell, had attempted to get psychology onto the Institute's agenda, and many of the researchers — and especially Marwick, Epstein, and Biesheuvel and Holleman — had included elements of social psychology, Freudian analysis, or occupational psychology in their work. In addition, the psychologists who began work at independence — Robert Serpell, Jan Deregowski, Alastair Heron, and Donald Munro — took some aspects of the previous anthropological studies into account in their own research. They also continued to use a few elements of the material basis and social networks for fieldwork established by the previous researchers, and they employed a few of the same clerks and assistants who had worked for the earlier anthropologists and demographers. As director from 1963 to 1967, Heron worked with the Zambian government and mines, carrying on the RLI tradition of applied research relevant to local needs. In his later directorship (1978–1983), Serpell did the same.[2]

The best endpoint, of course, would be a constantly moving one, following the Institute up to the present day and considering the changes in personnel and research focus that have taken place over the years. The first African director, Philip Nsugbe, came from Nigeria (1968–70).[3] Mubanga Kashoki became the first Zambian director (1973–1978), followed by Serpell and then Steven Moyo (1983–1988) and Oliver Saasa (1989–2000). Each new director set a research agenda for the Institute that reflected local as well as multidisciplinary concerns. The Institute's name also changed to reflect concerns about its place in Zambian society and its goals — first being renamed the Institute for Social Research (1965), with the Centre for African Studies added (1966–1971), and then being renamed the Institute for African Studies.[4] In 1998, it was again renamed the Institute for Economic and Social Research (INESOR).

Debates about its colonial legacy arose at various points in the Institute's postcolonial history, with Zambian directors, researchers, and observers often divided over the significance of the Institute's disciplinary focus on anthropology during the colonial period. The most prominent case was Bernard Magubane's critique of anthropology as a colonialist pursuit (in articles published in 1969 and 1971). He focused on the urban ethnography of the RLI — and, in particular, Wilson's, Mitchell's, and Epstein's work — for its supposed emphasis on Africans' "aping" of Western ideas and dress and its failure to address the oppression of colonialism.[5] Magubane's critique relied largely on quotations taken out of context and misinterpreted, as was pointed out in some of the contemporary responses to his 1971 article. In addition, he ignored overt critiques of the colonial system in Wilson's and Gluckman's work (discussed in chapter 3) and the unusually strong focus in Mitchell's and Epstein's urban work on African agency (rather than mere victimhood) in response to the colonial context, a focus that appeals to scholars working in anthropology and history today. What is most interesting about Magubane's critique, however, is that, despite its flaws, its general theme was taken up as typical of the African point of view on colonial anthropology, and it was used by a subsequent generation of largely non-African anthropologists and historians as ammunition in a territorial move for the displacement of British social anthropology from the African field. (See the discussion of the "handmaidens of colonialism" critique in the first chapter, and see below for discussion of the nature of professional territoriality on the part of the social anthropologists in an earlier case, carried on against the administrator-ethnographers.)

Magubane's critique was not the only African response in Zambia to the Institute's work, for, as mentioned in chapters 6 and 7, Zambian nationalists and union organizers had a favorable view of the work of the very researchers Magubane finds wanting. And Zambian academics coming from more theoretically informed positions held a variety of opinions in the postindependence period. For example, in 1984 Kashoki defended previous RLI directors against charges of maintaining the colonial legacy, charges made by Moyo when he became director. In this defense, Kashoki prefigured the critiques that have since been made of the simplistic handmaidens-of-colonialism analysis of colonial anthropologists:

> As you [Moyo] perceive it, their [the RLI directors'] contribution was in essence designed to further the colonial objectives of penetration, occupation and oppression. . . . I myself suffer from a serious doubt as to whether any one of us, even with the hindsight of history, has sufficient evidence to justify our conclusions that research workers in the Rhodes-Livingstone Institute slept in the same bed as the colonial Governor in terms of the conceived ends and use of social science research. I doubt even more that we have such evidence to conclude in categorical terms that the Gluckmans, Colsons and even "air force officers" like Wilson saw their research primarily or consciously as a direct contribution to the hidden motives of the colonizer. For one thing, didn't some of these same people we are indicting today actually resign their directorships when they didn't see eye to eye with the colonial administrators who wanted them to behave in a certain way?[6]

Kashoki subsequently developed a critique of the problems for the development of Zambia created by so-called academic tourism — the practice of doing research only for very short periods, which had become typical of rural development studies by both expatriate and local researchers in the 1980s. In his critique he pointed to the RLI tradition of long-term fieldwork, "the tradition of the tent, the candle and the camp bed," which allowed for a greater understanding of rural conditions, and which few contemporary researchers practiced.[7]

Kashoki's critique, unlike Magubane's, pointed to the difficulties of carrying on meaningful research under the conditions imposed by postindependence international development agendas and agencies. And the Institute, indeed, has often been shaped powerfully by those agendas despite some of its subsequent directors' efforts to promote strong local interdisciplinary research programs. The name the Institute carries today, the Institute of Economic and Social Research, still shows the broad scope that the Institute's directors have always envisioned for its work. Unfortunately, funding for its local work has shrunk in the last two decades, and much of the work going on at the Institute since the early 1980s has been done by individual expatriate researchers with their own research agendas. Although no longer cohesive, the work culture of the Institute has continued to be stimulating, as researchers from around the world congregate at various times and mix with local researchers, but the disparities in local and outside resources for research work and opportunities for local scholars to publish have been crippling to any overall local agenda that might potentially coordinate research in the country. Moreover, the results of expatriate studies usually go back to the home country of the researchers when they leave, where they are published and help to establish the researchers' careers. Although some of the work has been put into application through its effects on development planning and the donor countries' views of Zambia, the entire body of work done by expatriates has not been coordinated or even collected together in one place where results could be compared and utilized in a comprehensive fashion.[8]

As a result, many of the researchers working in Zambia today have no idea of the former studies done at the Institute either during its colonial past or in the subsequent postindependence decades. Nevertheless, the colonial work and subsequent work have some little recognized links. Ideally a constantly receding endpoint for an RLI history would allow one to follow the work of the former RLI researchers up to the present and trace the Institute's legacy into current work being done in a wide and diverse range of disciplines and endeavors. One could follow this work from anthropology and sociology into their legal, medical, industrial, urban, ethnomusicological, and applied subdisciplines (to name only a few). One could also follow it into new research initiatives, such as the Israeli school of sociology/social anthropology founded by Gluckman in the 1960s or into the work of a group of sociologists of science and medicine at the University of Delhi inspired by J. Singh Uberoi's later work on the history of science, or into the shop-floor ethnographies carried out in Manchester, Zambia, and elsewhere.[9]

The theoretical advances of the Manchester School are but one aspect of this legacy — and not necessarily the most important one. A significant strand of development anthropology (with theoretical and applied dimensions) originated in the work of the RLI and continues to the present in international development research networks founded by Scarlett Epstein and Norman Long.[10] Moreover, these scholars have fulfilled the early RLI directors' mission to train indigenous scholars to the doctoral level in sociology and anthropology. The demographic strand of the RLI's work has also had a significant impact on both theory and application, both within Zambia today and in an international context in the emergence of the research agendas of population studies and refugee/forced migration studies. The pioneering work in these areas was the long-term Gwembe-based Kariba Study initiated during Fosbrooke's directorship and pursued by Elizabeth Colson and Thayer Scudder from the 1950s to the present, now joined by a new generation of fieldworkers who began work in Gwembe in the 1990s.[11]

Further, the research assistants who played a vital role in developing the culture of RLI fieldwork have, in some cases, carried on with that culture of fieldwork long after most of the anthropologists had left the field. Although they did not transplant the institutional culture of the RLI headquarters into any of the postindependence organizations they worked for, at least two of them — M. B. Lukhero and J. C. Chiwale — continued with anthropological fieldwork and became key culture brokers for their ethnic groups in the 1980s.[12] This work remains an important legacy of the RLI, a continuation of its work in an Africanized version. That these former research assistants continued the RLI style of fieldwork when reconstructing the history and customs of their ethnic groups reveals the impact of the RLI on the history of indigenous cultural interpretation in central Africa.

The legacy of the RLI for the ordinary people they studied, however, is much more diffuse and difficult to pinpoint. Government and the mines may have responded to suggestions from the researchers for changes in African urban housing and working conditions or rural land tenure and resettlement issues, but they did not broadcast the fact, nor would it be easy to disentangle RLI research influences on African living conditions from the many sources from which administrators and planners drew their inspiration. New administrators who arrived in the 1950s had a more positive assessment of the RLI's work than the majority of those who had worked in the 1930s and 1940s; an administrator who began his career in the 1950s told me that the *Rhodes-Livingstone Institute Journal* and *Papers* were highly respected, displayed and read at every *boma*, and he included as "RLI" the work of agriculturists like Allan and Trapnell.[13] But, again, these administrators drew on the work in a general way and did not footnote the sources they used for making policy.

Among Africans themselves, as has been suggested at several points in the previous chapters, RLI work has been diversely interpreted, sometimes used and sometimes forgotten. Munali School students who went on to government jobs in the postindependence government had a largely positive assessment of their RLI experience, but most either felt it had been irrelevant to their subsequent work or influenced their thinking only in a general "sociological" way.[14]

Among the subjects of the research, the former RLI informants whom I interviewed exhibited a wide range of perspectives.[15] Many in the old RLI fieldsites who had been young at the time had forgotten the research, and in the urban areas, few people who experienced the research remained in the same place. But always I found some people, both in the urban and rural fieldsites, who had vivid memories of the researcher's stay and who placed that visit in the context of other events in the cultural history of the area. For some, the RLI research had become part of a sophisticated local consciousness of culture and its uses, developed through multiple experiences of negotiation with RLI and later researchers, as well as from previous experiences of cultural investigations by administrators and missionaries. Anthropologists of the RLI were themselves aware of this process, already underway before they arrived, and they speculated about their own impact on the emergence of later cultural forms. While in the midst of her Plateau Tonga fieldwork, Colson made a short visit to the Gwembe Valley, which, although she did not know it at the time, would be the site of her future long-term fieldwork:

> Despite the isolation, it was still impossible to get explanations for many of their [Gwembe Tonga] customs, even for customs which the Plateau Tonga could provide with an explanatory myth. They have for instance a clan joking relationship, as do the [Plateau] Tonga. After digging and digging for some myth explaining the clan tieups and failing to get anything save "perhaps they knew long ago but when we were young and asked the old about this, they said it was only custom," we proceeded to tell a little group of men about the Tonga myths. They were fascinated. And now perhaps at some future date another anthropologist will really work the area and perhaps find myths of this type and then discover to his great horror that some European first told them.[16]

In the same vein, Gluckman proudly recounted the following story in the reprint of the second edition of his *Judicial Process*: "Mr. Philip Silverman [a subsequent researcher] of Cornell University wrote to me that when he asked questions about law at the Barotse southern capital, Nalolo, the SAMBI asked him why he was wasting their time asking questions about their law when they had written a book about it. And the SAMBI produced this book [*Judicial Pro-*

cess]."[17] (It is interesting, too, that the SAMBI said that they—the Lozi legal experts—had written the book, perhaps indicating their estimation of the degree of their own local input to Gluckman's work.)

This observation suggests that some of the books produced by the RLI, as well as the fieldwork, have a local history quite different from their history in the development of academic anthropological theory (see below).

Diaspora and Return

The question of the possible histories that could be told about the RLI relates closely to the use of the concept of networks to understand its history. Much of my work on RLI history involved tracing the networks of interaction that enabled the fieldwork to be accomplished. In this study I have not used the concept in any of the technical senses worked out during the heyday of Manchester School network analysis, but have, rather, returned to a less technical sense of the term.[18] "Network" is also a term that has been transformed through its use in a large number of fields, including history of science, where the related notions of "thought collectives" and "social geographies" also help to map out intellectual and social/political connections among scientists and between them and the multiple human contexts that shape their work. (In this book on RLI history, I have employed the concept of network largely as it has been transformed through its use in history of science, but with strong influences from the sociology of the professions and the sociology of work, also fields in which the Manchester School anthropologists played pioneering roles.) As in the original Manchester School studies, however, the concept of networks is most useful for dealing with unbounded units of analysis, though one must always make a somewhat arbitrary decision about where to stop when following the links in any network or in pursuing its shifting character over time. Time constraints and the multicentered nature of the fieldwork and archival research required to trace RLI researchers, assistants, and informants, both in the former fieldsites and in the many places to which their subsequent careers brought them, have limited the scope of my study, and many important people and connections have been neglected in this book (but will be taken up in subsequent work).

Nevertheless, this far-flung research can say something about the kinds of interactions that took place in the RLI's history that led to the researchers' particular anthropological understandings. To discuss the genesis of particular theories and relate each to particular researchers' networks and experiences is beyond the scope of this book. I instead, limit the discussion to the significance of the field in the shaping of these networks and in the development of the general characteristics of the RLI approach.

Thus, I would argue that the unusual rootedness of the RLI research in a field-based institution, along with the mobility of the researchers in their individual fieldsites and between each other's fieldsites, produced a different anthropological perspective and, ultimately, a different *field* from that which is produced when anthropologists work individually. Many of the insights they gained derived from this difference, and these insights were enhanced by their subsequent experiences of the lifting and shifting of their own intellectual network to Manchester and beyond. The first major social and spatial translation of the researchers' network, from the RLI to Manchester—which Gluckman "colonized" with RLI people—in some respects also paralleled an earlier social and spatial translation that took place in Central Africa itself—the adaptation of rural methods to a new urban environment and the move from rural to urban fieldsites and field relations experienced by some of the researchers and assistants.

The subsequent diaspora of RLI researchers into new posts around the world would eventually turn their "tight-knit group" into a "loose-knit network," as Werbner has argued.[19] An exceptional number became professors or heads of departments, many newly established, in social anthropology or sociology.[20] But equally important to this diaspora are the instances of *return* that occurred in the later careers of RLI researchers. These include, most famously, Colson's and Scudder's long-term research on the Gwembe Tonga project, but they also include later books by Mitchell and Epstein that allowed

Max Gluckman's return to Zambia in 1965, after independence. He is pictured at the Institute headquarters in Lusaka. (Unaccessioned photo from RAI Box "Supplementary Gluckman Material," in Gluckman Collection, Royal Anthropological Institute. Reproduced by permission of the Royal Anthropological Institute.)

them to return to their central African material, much of which still remains to be analyzed.[21] If one considers yet another kind of "return," it also includes the method of reanalysis, encouraged by Gluckman, which became an element in the teaching style of many of the former RLI researchers after they moved into academic posts — and which encouraged the reappraisal of their own work, as well as other anthropologists' work, by a new generation of students.

Research Culture

Another theme of this book has been that small groups of scientists develop unique cultures of research and/or styles of field practice that shape the results of their work. The term "work culture," as it has been used here, is intended to capture the way that a hetero-geneous group of people drawn together for a long-term project develops a shared identity and style of practice and uses these to produce knowledge. A work culture is not a thought collective nor a style of thought, for though some members of the group may share a thought style and training in a particular discipline, the group in-cludes people who do not explicitly take part in writing or theory making and who may have entirely different interpretations of the collective project. What the concept of work culture does is to show how a science connects with its context through the partly overlap-ping networks of the people involved in the research. It shows how a field science becomes a part of its field context while at the same time distingishing itself from other activities within that context, produc-ing a group identity. The identity of a scientific project and the people involved in it are constructed from what is available in the field context in addition to what particular members bring from their background and training.

The notion of a work culture also focuses attention on the scien-tific group as a small society engaged in maintaining itself for the duration of the project. This small society develops rules and rituals, practices of inclusion and exclusion, and traditions and customs, some of which carry on into other settings after the group disperses. Despite often great differences in individual members' interpreta-tions of the overall project, a work culture like that of the RLI pro-duces a cohesive group with a strong collective identity, often antag-onistic to others within the same discipline or fieldsite. Thus, an RLI director might critically examine the political position of a new re-searcher, an anthropologist might insult a director imposed by the colonial government by calling him an ethnographer, an administra-tive secretary might deflect government surveillance of research as-sistants' political activities, a research assistant loaned to another project might disparage their data gathering methods as not "the RLI way," and a gardener at the RLI headquarters who never actively does research might nevertheless feel himself to be part of an exem-plary interracial project within a hostile colonial society.

But these examples only begin to capture the individual motivations and interpretations of its goals that would draw diverse people into the RLI project. The cohesiveness of the group derived from different individual sources but also from common experiences of living and working together and the group's harmonies and dissonances with the larger society. The analysis of the culture of this group should resemble the uses of anthropological analysis to study colonial societies, but on an even smaller scale, like the study of a small band of researcher hunter-gatherers living in uncomfortable symbiosis with a larger society of colonial farmers and herders.

I do not want to give the concept of work culture too much theoretical weight nor clarify its fuzzy edges, but rather use it primarily to suggest the importance of aspects of field research that are missed by studies of the research of individual anthropologists — studies which, until recently, have failed to deal with the *collective* processes that are involved in fieldwork even when only a single researcher is in the field. Although the RLI project was a rare instance of team research in anthropology, my analysis of its work processes can help us to understand the work of individual anthropologists supposedly working alone, because anthropological work always involves the cooperation of a group of people with diverse backgrounds and interests.

Each anthropologist in the field becomes an employer with dependents attached to him or her, whether or not exchanges for food, shelter, and assistance are transacted in currency. Each anthropologist, too, becomes the center of a production process that she or he does not entirely control. The metaphors I am using to understand ethnographic fieldwork are very different from others more common in the literature on ethnographic method — those being of the self as a research instrument and of the anthropologist as a sensitive and intuitive observer and participant, coming to understand a society by being socialized into it, both observing the society and observing its practices, and reflexively observing the self's responses to its new environment. Although these metaphors are not entirely wrong, they focus too much on the individual experiences and psychology of the researcher and fail to capture the joint nature and materiality of the processes through which fieldwork yields knowledge. And so the metaphors I have chosen to emphasize are metaphors of the factory, of production teams, of employer/employee relations, and of apprentices and master craftsmen.

Territorial Wars and Disciplinary Frontiers

I have also found another set of metaphors useful for capturing the professional strategies that anthropologists use to align themselves in their fieldwork and their texts. These are metaphors of territorial expansion and combative skill. Perkin's view of the professions as vertically organized hierarchies cutting across class strata, like modern versions of warring feudal fiefdoms bound by codes of honor, is an image I find appropriate here.[22] The academic disciplines and schools within them, like feudal fiefdoms, create research frontiers and do battle over research territory. Within the discipline of anthropology, this process took place when Gluckman theoretically and politically positioned the RLI researchers to challenge the intellectual descendants of Malinowski, based on his own intellectual descent from Radcliffe-Brown, Schapera, and Winifred Hoernlé. Gluckman also challenged Malinowski directly in his texts, critiquing the culture contact approach, using language heavily freighted with moral and political censure.

But the rivalry between Radcliffe-Brown's and Malinowski's intellectual descendants was a mere academic skirmish compared to the territorial war social anthropologists fought with another less recognized but more significant rival — the administrator-ethnographers.[23] (Or compared with the war that a subsequent generation of postcolonial anthropologists would fight to discredit colonial anthropologists; see above.) This battle receives little attention in anthropology's histories of itself because it was not carried on (overtly, at least) in the realm of theory, but mainly took place in the field and over the appropriateness (and moral/political worth) of differing field methods and relations with the subjects of research.

The outcome of the battle, on anthropology's side, was the denial that administrator-ethnographers even *had* a method or any kind of professional status — and anthropologists labeled them with the names "amateur" or "ethnographer," in a use of the latter term that pointed to administrators' links with earlier, disparaged types of anthropology focused around the collecting of customs and artifacts. In addition, a rhetoric that invoked theory could play a role in the field as part of a strategy for demonstrating professional superiority. As Barnes recalled of their time in Cape Town, Schapera advised him and Mitchell and Colson, that "if and when we encountered administrators or missionaries who claimed to know all about the culture of the natives, to direct the conversation to the topic of kinship, where it would be easy for us to show our superior understanding."[24] And anthropologists contested not only field territory in this battle, but academic territory as well. They founded the British Association of Social Anthropologists in 1946 specifically to protect the interests of professional anthropologists with respect to getting university posts that might otherwise have gone to retired colonial administrators.[25]

This process of differentiation between social anthropologists and administrator-ethnographers can be used to illustrate how what scholars have called "incommensurability" works in the field sciences. Thomas Kuhn originally used this concept to emphasize the dramatic nature of scientific revolutions, which he saw as producing entirely incompatible worldviews that left scientists on one side of the revolutionary moment unable to speak to scientists on the other side. Kuhn's view has since been challenged by numerous scholars who believe such changes are more gradual. In the case of the history of anthropology, it is not a radical incommensurability, but a gradual misrecognition of categories and loss of the ability to communicate that explains why administrator-ethnographers disappeared from anthropology's self histories or were exiled to a "prescientific," "pre-paradigmatic," or "pre-professional" past along with the Enlightenment-tradition travel writers whom anthropologists today sometimes recognize as distant ancestors. In truth, however, administrators and administrator-ethnographers worked contemporaneously with the social anthropologists, sometimes had training in functionalist approaches, and were the social anthropologists' chief rivals and mentors in the field.

In central Africa the process of making distinctions between administrator-ethnographers and anthropologists began in the inter-war period and was well advanced by the 1950s. This process took place during precisely the key years in the development of the RLI's identity and characteristic methods. As pointed out in the earlier chapters of this book, Gluckman and Wilson used the talk and dress of administrators to establish the RLI's credibility with the colonial government and to gain access to the resources needed to conduct research. The first team of anthropologists arriving after World War Two depended to a great extent on advice from and good relations with administrators and technical officers in the field. In everyday field practices the two groups shared a great deal initially, though the RLI's pioneering use of comparative statistical methods quickly dif-ferentiated this aspect of their work from field administrators' rough estimates (though not from the mines' adoption of statistical meth-ods and machines and, somewhat later, the government's adoption of such methods). Similarly, both administrators and anthropolo-gists used the genealogical method, but anthropologists had already considerably refined and extended the practice.

In the area of interviewing informants and in their work relation-ships with Africans, anthropologists and administrators also often used similar practices or were constrained by informants who ex-pected certain methods to be used. Examples discussed earlier in-clude Gluckman's "big establishment" at his fieldsite and the pres-ents he gave his workers and informants, the visits he received from Africans selling crafts, and his reputation as a witchfinder. The latter image combined the adjudicative and protective functions of the local *induna* with attributes of the colonial district commissioner. Gluckman's generosity went far beyond that of most administrators, however, and derived from his background as the son of a wealthy liberal family in South Africa, generous to its servants and depen-dents, feeling this as a moral duty imposed by their position in an unjust society. In another example, Hans Holleman combined both administrator and anthropologist roles, trained as a social anthro-pologist and doing research both as an autonomous researcher and as a government sociologist. His research methods very closely fol-lowed those of administrators, and other RLI researchers criticized him for calling informants to come to his *boma*-style bush camp. There he also adjudicated local disputes, so that in the eyes of his informants he may have been little dissimilar from Gluckman in the latter's locally perceived role as witchfinder.

Although social anthropologists increasingly differed from administrators in their actual practices, what is equally important is that the criticisms that pointed to differences in practice formed part of a process of consciously *creating* distinctions. These consciously distinguished distinctions were necessary because the differences between anthropologists and administrator-ethnographers were not always obvious, the territories marked out by their expertise nearly coincided, and their methods always overlapped.

As political tensions escalated in the years immediately before federation, anthropologists consciously distanced themselves more and more from the administration — though not always from individual administrators, some of whom shared their political views. Distancing took place in talk and dress, as well as in field relationships, and it was a distancing that was demanded of them by the growing power of their African informants and assistants in this period. Administrator-ethnographers also changed their behavior during the 1950s — more paperwork and more centralization of administrative work in Lusaka meant less time for touring and performing ethnographic tasks. In the Cold War context, too, political surveillance became an increasingly important part of the colonial government's activities, and the atmosphere created by this led to greater wariness in relations between administrators and researchers. Some anthropologists (though not all) shifted their attention toward academic careers and away from the discipline's earlier interwar project to become the field of expertise essential to the running of colonial administration. This was exemplified in Gluckman's career in the 1940s, but a similar pattern also shaped Mitchell's career in the 1950s.

One of the most important aspects of this differentiation process took place in sites developed for shared disciplinary communication, such as the RLI publications and especially its journal. With its first issues in the 1940s, this journal established an international reputation as a scholarly publication in the field of social anthropology. In its first half dozen issues, articles by administrator-ethnographers and technical officers figured prominently, as they did in other important anthropological journals of the interwar and early postwar period. Gluckman initially invited administrators and technical officers to contribute to the journal because he was himself the only professional author available during the war.[26] Nevertheless, some of those he invited, such as the agriculturist William Allan, shared his interests and influenced his work and would, no doubt, have been invited to contribute regardless of the lack of availability of professional authors in social anthropology.

Behind these published acts of communication between administrators and anthropologists lay RLI conferences that often included administrators who joined the discussions and presented papers, as well as occasional research reports from anthropologists to administration. All three of these types of communication suffered from changes in the last years before independence, however. Articles by administrators continued to appear, but in smaller numbers. A few administrators continued to attend the conferences, especially when encouraged by Mitchell and by the administrator-ethnographer, Fosbrooke. At a conference during Fosbrooke's directorship, however, an angry debate broke out between the conservative administrators he had invited and an openly Marxist researcher — an incident that revealed growing disparities between anthropologists and administrators at a point when the power of the African independence movement had both hardened the colonial government's responses and emboldened researchers to make public statements of their support for the nationalists.[27]

In some respects this analysis of administrator/anthropologist relationships could be framed using Biagioli's reinterpretation of the Kuhnian notion of incommensurability.[28] Incommensurability is not a sudden shift of perspective that renders two groups of scientists incapable of communicating with each other. It is, rather, a complex process of persuasion and repositioning, of interacting with some and refusing to interact with others, of speaking to some and refusing to speak to others. Languages differentiate into dialects in this way, as do ethnic groups. The differentiation takes place along cultural lines, first through noticing or creating differences in style and then by emphasizing them. The failure to speak eventually leads to the failure to comprehend, as when dialects of a language become mutually incomprehensible among groups of people who share the same physical space but whose interests radically diverge.

Possibilities for eventual cultural differentiation evolving from initial stylistic variations hold the key to this model of incommensurability, and the history of the RLI and its relationship to the colonial government clearly illustrates the process. Looked at as cultural groups, RLI anthropologists and administrators in central Africa diverged from the start in one prominent feature: administration in Africa was a highly ritualistic and courtly affair, abounding with strictly observed (though largely recently invented) traditions intended to legitimate European authority. The courtliness of administration derived from the culture of the public school, though many administrators by the 1940s and 1950s did not have a public school education. It also derived from the New Chivalry of the late nineteenth-century British civil service, concerned to foster a new vigorous masculinity needed in an industrial, imperial age.

Although anthropologists were no sluggards in inventing disciplinary rituals, and despite the fact that their love of the rigors of fieldwork was strongly shared with administrators, they did not share the courtly aspects of administrative style. Indeed, the RLI may have diverged from that style more than most groups of anthropologists in developing a work culture that expressed an antiauthoritarian style. Despite his elite background, Gluckman admired proletarian values, and at the Manchester social anthropology department, he promoted a "working class" style, with colleagues frequenting a laborers' pub near the university and occasionally holding seminars in the stands during Manchester United football games. Gluckman exerted significant pressure on his staff and students to attend the games.[29] But this style ultimately derived from the work culture at the RLI headquarters, where, in the RLI Circular Newsletter of July 1954, the secretary printed the "odd utterances overheard during our June Conference," including Edith Turner's remark: "I'd rather see a blast furnace than a ballet."[30]

Differences of style affected more than the relations between anthropologists and administrators, as important as that differentiation process was. The study of national and subnational styles of practice in anthropology is an area where much more needs to be done for understanding fieldwork and its history; here I have only made a beginning. The RLI style developed in conscious distinction from the South African volkekunde style, as discussed in chapter 3. There, I compared three styles — volkekundiges' fieldwork, administrators' touring practices, and Gluckman's own evolving style. A comparison of the RLI's fieldwork style with further examples of anthropological fieldwork styles is difficult to do at this point, though one can speculate that RLI field practices were quite different from the contemporaneous styles of French, German, or Portuguese anthropological fieldwork. One can speculate, however, that the RLI style may have shared some features with that of Georges Balandier, who admired Gluckman's approach and was also interested in industrial and labor migration studies.[31] On the other hand, it differed sharply from Marcel Griaule's expedition style of fieldwork in North Africa and his concern to capture the essential features of African philosophy and religion, which he believed differentiated the African worldview from that of Europe. Moreover, as more research is done on the history of anthropological fieldwork, as opposed to the history of theory, we may find that national differences are not as important as differences within national traditions. South Africa alone supported at least three different styles of fieldwork — those of the volkekundiges, the administrator-ethnographers, and the social anthropologists. All of these expressed crucial political and theoretical conflicts among South African anthropolgists, reflecting the wider social and political context within that country.

Coproduction and Efficacious Relationships

Despite the comparatively better housing and greater status the RLI provided its African staff, the layout of the Institute headquarters, with its *boma* design and African quarter at the back, showed that the architecture of colonial institutions still constrained the relationships between RLI researchers and assistants. Nonetheless, the Institute presented an image of colonial structures breaking down — in the enthusiastic discussions of the research assistants, as well as in the roosters crowing outside the director's office. The most striking image of this breakdown is that of the research assistants presenting their papers at an RLI conference dressed formally in suits, while the anthropologists watched, dressed casually, some in colonial-style khaki (or *kabadula*)[32] — an image filled with the dissonances of the late colonial period itself. In this image, the research assistants appear as Africa's so-called new men, apprenticed in a field that they see as having the potential to improve the condition of Africans and, in the hopes of some of them, leading to successful individual careers. In it as well, the anthropologists assert themselves as Europeans dressed for comfort in a tropical climate or as fieldworkers evoking the ethos of the bush. Yet despite these dissonant elements, the practices of fieldwork that lay behind these images — both in its urban and rural dimensions — gave the institutional culture of the Institute an egalitarianism exceptional in Northern Rhodesia in the late colonial period.

This was not a culture associated *necessarily* with anthropological fieldwork, nor necessarily with a participant-observation style of fieldwork, but was a unique product of the political and social background of a particular group of anthropologists working during a watershed in southern African history. Because of contingent historical factors, this group stretched to the limit the possibilities inherent in social anthropology's field methods and developed theories that often challenged the tenets of what is today called the functionalist paradigm. In the process they created an institutional culture that became an experiment in black/white relations unequaled by the few other mixed race institutions, such as the nearby Munali Secondary School or the white pro-Federation political parties that recruited Africans using the propaganda of racial partnership.

Unlike the pro-Federation political parties and the rhetoric of interracial partnership that masked the drive for a white-dominated dominion, the Institute relied on a different kind of partnership between Africans and Europeans for the success of its fieldwork.[33] This is not to say that the assistants had equal status with anthropologists nor that they shared all of the goals of anthropology; they were undeniably employees and apprentices and sometimes chafed at these roles. They did not possess the administrative or academic/ professional power of their employers, and they related to anthropologists in a larger context of European dominance and African subjugation, which affected the behavior of both researchers and assistants. But in the field, they often had greater power than the anthropologists to gain access to various aspects of African society and determine the kind of information collected, while as interpreters of culture their influence pervaded every aspect of the RLI's work, from the anthropologist's language learning to the framing of survey questions and the analysis of results. The anthropologists depended upon and acknowledged the assistants' power in these spheres.

What made the RLI's practices different from other examples of black/white relations at the time was the culture of fieldwork that informed the institutional culture of the RLI headquarters. This was not, however, a case of there being something special about anthropological fieldwork in itself that necessarily led to a more egalitarian institutional culture. Some have claimed that anthropological fieldwork — and participant-observation as a method — is itself subversive of established hierarchies. This subversive character supposedly stems from anthropologists' reflexivity, which leads not only to the analysis of the self as well as the subject, but also leads to the analysis of the so-called customer of anthropological knowledge. In the case of development anthropology, the customer is a government or development organizations, or, perhaps also, the academic or disciplinary institutions of the anthropologists themselves.[34] This kind of reflexivity can, indeed, be subversive, as in the case of Gluckman's focusing attention on the role of the colonial administrator, an activity that made the colonial government uneasy and resulted in its often strict control and limitation of anthropological fieldwork.[35]

Anthropological reflexivity is not *necessarily* subversive, however, for it can be limited to the anthropologist's observation of the self as a participant in another culture — the minimum amount of reflexivity (seeing the self as a research tool) necessary to make participant-observation work as a method at all. Or, some anthropologists may see the people they are studying as the customers of the research — that is, as the beneficiaries of development projects made more sensitive to local needs through social research or as the beneficiaries of anthropologists' work as culture brokers, writing about local history and customs, or as advocates for change or resistance to dominant forces. At least some members of local communities or ethnic groups may benefit from these activities, but this does not necessarily make anthropology's method a subversive one and may, indeed, mask support *for* certain local hierarchies and certain preferred cliques in local structures of domination.

Rather, what is interesting about the role of fieldwork in anthropology is not if it is necessarily subversive.[36] What is interesting about fieldwork has to do with *relationships* — between anthropological method and anthropological theory, and between anthropologists and the people they study. Here, the history of the Rhodes-Livingstone Institute can provide an example, not of subversion, but of the development of particularly efficacious relationships in both areas. In certain cases these relationships went some small way toward subverting the colonial system, but their greater importance lies in their usefulness for anthropological activity continuing both outside of colonial boundaries and after the end of colonialism, and in their usefulness for anthropology as an activity done by and meaningful to Africans.

As I am using it here, the word "efficacious" refers to relationships that work *effectively* to produce knowledge and at the same time are useful to each person involved, though the people involved might have different and even contradictory ideas of the goals of the activity. Antagonistic relationships can be as fruitful as friendships in the field; mistakes and misunderstandings can lead to important insights, despite the danger of the researcher being shut off from certain areas of local life. But what is most important to recognize is that the goals of each person involved are usually multiple. In the case of the RLI, the goals of the research assistants exercised a profound influence on the development of the anthropologists' characteristic practices because of the vulnerability of the researchers in politically or racially charged settings. This was true of the rural research, where local attitudes to outsiders had led to the development of specific defenses and management strategies, and it was even more true of the urban research, which took place in a period of rapid change, struggles for independence, and growing African control of the towns.

The origins of the relationships developed by the RLI anthropologists also lie in the three contexts described in chapter 2 and the place of the anthropologists and assistants within them. By showing three important contexts of RLI research—British, American, and African—the intention was to challenge a simple center/periphery understanding of how scientific research was carried out in the colonies. The RLI researchers had a complex relationship to anthropology as a discipline centered in the British universities. Some were academically centered elsewhere throughout most of their education and careers, in Africa or the United States. Although Central Africa acted as a periphery to South Africa as center—just as it functioned for the British academy as a convenient field outpost—the white and black societies in which the South African-centered RLI anthropologists lived and worked while in the Central African field shared much with the South African society from which many of them came. In terms of class as well, RLI anthropologists—including those born in Britain—often came from marginal groups, but those which were experiencing new mobility and opportunities. Some RLI researchers were part of the influx of lower-middle-class students into British universities in the postwar period, others were Jews, women, South African colonials, and people of Britain's Celtic fringe, who were also able to exploit new opportunities for advancement. The African assistants also experienced marginal status, as educated and/or urban Africans kept on the margins of white economic and political hegemony. Marginality alone, however, fails to explain the culture these researchers developed at the RLI nor their individual success in their careers. Membership in these social groups did not render each individual marginal in all settings nor in all of the activities they aspired to join.

Instead of marginality, the characteristic theories of the Manchester School anthropologists find their roots more in the identity of the researchers as hopeful migrants entering — not established and hierarchical social situations — but rapidly changing and contested settings in which migrants could make a telling difference and in which researchers could find purchase for their own skills of defining and analyzing novel situations. It was this novel quality of their situation that resulted in their attention to movement across boundaries and within contexts organized, defined, and contested by others.[37] Network theory bears a clear relationship to the strategies of newcomers in complex and rapidly changing situations — African assistants attempting to get their research (and political) work done in an urbanizing, decolonizing society; or RLI anthropologists attempting to rise through the British academic hierarchy in the postwar period. Home boy or old school (or RLI) ties helped in both cases. Moreover, situational analysis, attention to cross-cutting ties, the dominant cleavage, and intercalary roles are ideas that emerge even more clearly from the African context — both the colonial indirect rule context of Central Africa and the racially segregated context of the central and southern African region.

That political context also explains to a large degree the RLI focus on history and process. Gluckman brought to the work an overarching view of southern African history based on his view of colonialism, segregation, and industrialization as its key processes. Furthermore, his interest in Marxism as an approach to research made historical arguments essential to the program he developed to make the RLI's work politically and socially relevant to the major issues facing southern Africa at that moment in its history — a watershed that led to both the rise of apartheid and the emergence of independent African nations.

But the characteristic RLI theories also have their roots in the more local context of fieldwork, in the work conditions and relationships discussed throughout this book. Attention to intercalary roles and the micropolitics of interracial and interethnic situations would have been necessary on practical grounds alone, in the context of late colonial Northern Rhodesia. The RLI researchers had to be sensitive to the political situation in order to negotiate permission for their research from a number of groups, and they also found themselves occupying intercalary positions between government and settlers, settlers and Africans — or in the case of the assistants, between anthropologists and informants. A characteristic method of the RLI, the extended case method, has obvious precedents in the legal and social work training of Gluckman, Epstein, and Mitchell. It also, however, could hardly have been used effectively outside of the work conditions provided by the Institute — the lengthy periods of fieldwork, the requirement for two periods of fieldwork with a break in between, and the continuity of the researcher's interest allowed by this. This continuity of interest also stemmed from the initial expectation of some of the researchers that they might continue their careers (and not just their fieldwork) in Central Africa and, after the move by many of them to Manchester, the continuing commitment of the Manchester department of social anthropology to Central Africa as a fieldsite where they might hope to return or to send their students.[38]

It is important here to distinguish between two aspects of the culture of fieldwork. The characteristics of fieldwork discussed earlier constitute the material culture of fieldwork — the objects, physical locations, and work relations necessary to do research in the field. But there is another sense in which fieldwork has a culture, and that is in the way that members of a particular discipline speak about the field, value it as part of a range of scientific activities, and use it programatically to advance within the academy. An example in the case of the RLI was Gluckman's construction of the Manchester School *as a product of* the Central African fieldwork, as he presented it in a history of the Manchester School that he used to convince the University of Manchester of the need for a grant for the further development of research in the department of social anthropology there.[39]

In this document, Gluckman describes the development of the famous seminars at Manchester as deriving from seminars he held for the RLI researchers at Oxford, when the group took a field break there in 1947. These, in turn, he describes as a continuation of the first conference held at the RLI headquarters in Livingstone. He speaks of it in almost biblical terms as the "conference where we all came out of our tribes and met at Livingstone, [where] we worked out a coordinated attack on common problems by similar methods and techniques."[40] He continues the story by describing the diaspora of RLI people into professorships around the world, the spread of its method into numerous subdisciplines, and the hoped-for return to Central Africa where — given sufficient funding — their fieldwork could be resumed "on the former scale" under the supervision of Mitchell at UCRN.[41]

Behind this mythic charter, however, lay field experiences that did, indeed, involve coordinated teamwork. Critics of anthropology have pointed out that the discipline bases its claims to intellectual authority on fieldwork that is largely invisible to all but the individual researcher and that the descriptions of fieldwork contained in published ethnographies and texts on method bear little resemblance to the field experiences on which they are based.[42] But RLI fieldworkers, in contrast, often set out to make some aspects of fieldwork visible. This is not to say that RLI publications more directly conveyed the true character of the fieldwork or provided some closer representation of the social realities they attempted to explain. The published material did, however, result from the researchers' use of a more public method, unavoidably subject to both friendly and hostile scrutiny from local government, industry, settlers, informants, assistants, and fellow researchers. In the case of the latter, Gluckman encouraged the kind of wide-ranging data collection that would allow for reanalysis of a researcher's work by other researchers. To this end he encouraged the researchers to deposit copies of fieldnotes at the RLI headquarters, insisted upon the writing of detailed ethnographies that could be reanalyzed by others, and led the Manchester seminar in conducting the reanalysis of other classic enthnographies.[43] And RLI field methods continued to be taught, talked about, observed, and modified through a collective effort as directors like Colson and Mitchell trained new teams of researchers and ventured into new fieldsites.

In the urban context, public pressure on RLI fieldwork intensified these collective efforts to develop and modify research practices.

Urban Africans, including the research assistants, exerted more control over the research and presented the researchers with a field situation full of unavoidable conflict. This conflict was often irresolvable, as well, during the preindependence period when settler intransigence met every move for African self-determination. This dominating factor of racial tension permeated even the most well-intentioned of relationships, including those at the RLI. Scholars have pointed to the RLI's characteristic attention to conflict and conflict-resolution, but one of the strongest features of its later work was the incorporation of ongoing conflict in its picture of society, *without* the certainty of resolution into a new state of equilibrium — an important break with Gluckman's own work.[44]

But even in the urban field, the culture of rural fieldwork could be imported as a means of keeping conflict to a manageable level, compatible with research. Epstein, for example, did not engage in formal interviews with informants and trained his urban assistants in open-ended methods of questioning as a way of avoiding the inegalitarian structure of the interviewer/interviewee relationship. He always tried to "keep relationships egalitarian as a way of recreating the position of the anthropologist in the [rural] field."[45] Moreover, he based this view of the anthropologist's role on an important distinction between anthropologists and other professionals. "A doctor is a professional offering a service; an anthropologist isn't" and so must respect people's right to privacy. "The anthropologist is not privileged to explore and must observe limits." The situation in the rural field is, ideally, one where people *can* tell the anthropologist to "go to hell, but wouldn't."[46]

Given the colonial situation, however, Africans would have felt coercion in any relationship with whites, a coercion that would prevent the ideal fieldwork situation from being achieved. Nevertheless, villagers could, and in at least one instance did, resort to running away when researchers approached. Even racial coercion was mediated through local rulers in the rural areas and Africans could have resisted field research through an appeal to colonial authorities or other white groups who were sometimes hostile to the RLI. Even more in the urban areas in the 1950s, Africans challenged implicit and explicit coercion on the basis of race, to the point of preventing whites free entry to the African townships. Epstein's last fieldwork experience on the Copperbelt was of being threatened and told to leave by young Africans who did not know who he was. Thus, although the relationship between researcher and informant could not be egalitarian in a colonial setting, that relationship was negotiated in the context of struggles between colonial and anticolonial forces. That conflict placed RLI researchers in insecure positions that demanded constant realignment and that, despite their efforts, sometimes broke down irreparably, as was the case when the mines prevented Epstein from doing fieldwork in mining townships.

The Field as a Knowledge-Making Machine

One of the major arguments of this book has been that the field is not simply a source of data that is then organized in the mind of the researcher to create theories. Instead I have discussed the field as a constructed and negotiated space that through its very structure produces knowledge. Other scholars have made this argument about the natural history museum, arguing that this institution (through its collectively developed practices) organizes the work of many diverse professionals and laypersons; processes and stores the objects they collect; and associates these objects in novel ways that produce new knowledge.[47] This analysis of theory production focuses on collaborative processes of collection and association rather than on what happens in the mind of an individual scientist who simply directs the activities of others.

The insights provided by this approach are relevant to anthropological fieldwork because this approach reveals the multiple influences — including all kinds of human and nonhuman actors — that shape scientific knowledge. Museums were the original organizers for fieldwork across all of the natural history disciplines, including anthropology in its earliest forms. In the interwar period, social anthropology made a significant break with its own museum tradition, but it also retained some aspects of that tradition in the structuring

256 Africanizing Anthropology

of its fieldwork. The new method of participant-observation may have changed the relationship of the researchers to their informants in significant ways, by bringing the researchers down off the verandah and into the midst of the village, but this new method did not replace, but rather nested among, earlier practices of information- and artifact-gathering and the relationships that had sustained them, none of which completely disappeared.

The types of information and artifacts associated with the period of museum ethnography played different roles in social anthropology than they had in diffusionist or evolutionary anthropology. The relationships in the field that had sustained these older types of anthropology also took on different meanings and did different kinds of work for the professional social anthropologist. And although anthropologists still sent the artifacts to a museum, the museum no longer functioned as the central organizing institution for the knowledge-making enterprise of anthropology, once it became *social* anthropology. Similarly, the base for the relationship between researchers and their fieldsites also shifted from museums to other institutions — to university departments and research institutes.

In the case of the RLI, a social anthropology research institute initially existed in close conjunction with a museum. Gluckman engaged himself theoretically and practically with both sides of this institute/museum project, writing articles on the relationship between museum displays and social anthropology research and collecting artifacts for the museum displays. He also adapted these collecting practices and networks for his anthropological research, as discussed in previous chapters. He was, in addition, a strongly visual and spatial thinker in his planning of the RLI's research, a skill that expressed itself in his vision of Northern Rhodesia as a human laboratory. His seven-year plan of research provided a structure for the comparative, coordinated work that followed, in which researchers were carefully placed at points in the flows of activity that allowed Northern Rhodesia's multiracial society to function. Gluckman intended this placement of their research studies to reveal important features of the processes going on, and all of these processes were to be elucidated as a whole in a final jointly written volume on the industrial revolution in central Africa. This book itself represented a structuring process that created new knowledge — the characteristic RLI methods and theories — despite the fact that the intended book never materialized.

Today, the individualism of the monographs produced by the RLI researchers dominates our view of the entire project, so that it seems that only a characteristic method united the group as a whole. Nevertheless, in many ways, that intended volume functioned as an organizing structure to which all the many different researchers and the many different pieces of research could relate, despite their diverse goals and results. This industrial revolution book provided the focus of discussion at some of the conferences, it reappeared in subsequent research plans sent to the funders, and it kept Gluckman and the later directors in communication over its shape and contents — deciding what topics and field studies should be included and which people should contribute. In some respects this book that was never written functioned as an objective that united the diverse work of the researchers at the RLI. It was a unifying project, yet it did not demand complete conformity of vision, disciplinary background, or approach from each of those expected to contribute to it. Historians, demographers, economists, and administrators, as well as anthropologists, appeared on various lists of potential contributors made up by Gluckman and Mitchell.[48] Like the directors' research plans themselves, the book contributed to the cohesiveness and standardization of RLI research but did not impinge constantly upon the researchers' autonomy.

This unwritten book, and other books associated with the RLI, functioned in some ways as so-called boundary objects, that is, as objects that can be used to translate between the different social worlds of the diverse actors who must cooperate to produce scientific knowledge.[49] In the case of the industrial revolution book, the differences between the social worlds of the actors were very small and consisted only of the differences in training, discipline, or research interest that marked the RLI researchers as individual scholars. In the case of the overall work of the RLI, however, many different objects served to translate between the very different social worlds of the anthropologists, the assistants, and the informants. Here I can only describe one set of objects, books, but many others, such as vehicles, punchcards, artifacts of material culture, and so on, could and did function in such a way in the RLI's research.

Books had many meanings in central Africa during the late colonial period. A number of different books impinged on Africans' consciousness — the bibles brought by missionaries, the books associated with Western education, and the tax books carried ceremonially by a *boma* messenger when district officers toured the villages to collect taxes and stamp a unique yearly mark next to each taxpayer's name. Each anthropologist also strove to produce a book, and anthropologists' books became part of the cultural history of many former RLI fieldsites. The case of Gluckman's book on Lozi law has already been cited. Actual books, however, did not have to be present in the fieldsite to play the role of boundary object, for the processes associated with the researching and writing of books could by themselves play this translation role. Thus, local Africans asked one RLI anthropologist why he was not typing every evening, as a previous anthropologist had done. Similarly, research assistants and their informants who participated in the process of interviewing and filling in data on punchcards, called this process "being written." For rural research, too, the assistant Lukhero told me he always carried the same notepad, essential in his mind for writing fieldnotes (see epilogue). And in the Gwembe Valley, the corpus of demographic information that has been collected by Colson's and Scudder's project over the past forty years is referred to as "the book" by Gwembe people, who play a significant role in inducting new researchers into the practices associated with its ongoing production.[50]

The field and the informants, in the case of the Gwembe "book," have shaped the anthropological project into a locally meaningful endeavor. Ultimately, it is these localized projects and their capture of the objects and processes of research — and sometimes of the researchers themselves — that create anthropological knowledge.

Carrying on one of the traditions of the "RLI way," John Barnes has written an introduction to the last book of his former Ngoni research assistant, M. B. Lukhero, which I will use to end this chapter. As in previous introductions written by Gluckman, Colson, or Mitchell, this one places the author's work in the context of other anthropological studies and raises key issues. In this case the context is that of the anthropologist as fieldworker. As Barnes writes of Lukhero as researcher and author:

> Lukhero's positive sentiments about the traditional social order should not surprise us. However a tendency to favour unduly an Ngoni point of view . . . is not confined to the Ngoni themselves. . . . My Ngoni informants told me approvingly that [Margaret] Read had real tears in her eyes at the funerals she attended. I was more dry-eyed and thought that I was more balanced in what I wrote. Nevertheless both of us have been criticised. . . . Lukhero's essay forcefully raises the question of the extent to which ethnographers, and in particular indigenous ethnographers, can gain access to the sentiments of the people they study without being captured by them. This empirical question is perhaps not as important as the disciplinary query: should the committed ethnographer solicit capture or try to avoid it?[51]

As this book has argued, it is not only ethnographers, but anthropology itself that has been captured by Africans.

EPILOGUE

The local people also started to understand her work. [Colson worked] as you are now doing, by visiting people in different parts. You visit people in Siameja and also visit their relatives who work [in town]. They [the local people] were pleased to know how people live, those that have died or have left the place or arrived in the place. This showed the people [that] she was concerned with their problems and way of life. In 1978 when she departed they were happy [with her visit]. [When she came again] they no longer asked such questions as what Kamwale wanted, but [instead asked] whether Kamwale knew each one of them. Kamwale would acknowledge saying she knew them. "You are such, such. You are Tom's son, you are Galantia's son," and so on.
(Kaciente Chifumpu, speaking to Lisa Cliggett,

a new Gwembe project researcher)[1]

I remember going to mass with Blackson at the White Fathers' mission. We were kneeling, and at some point I noticed Blackson scribbling away in his notebook. (John Barnes, recalling

M. B. Lukhero's devotion to fieldwork)[2]

Elizabeth Colson at the Lusitu Agricultural Show, in a Gwembe Tonga resettlement area, August 1992.

M. B. Lukhero with notepad, preparing for fieldwork with author, May 1991, Chipata, Zambia.

(Both photos taken by author.)

NOTES

Abbreviations: Archives and Papers

IAS/UNZA   Institute for African Studies, University of Zambia,
            Lusaka, Zambia
JCM   J. Clyde Mitchell Papers, Rhodes House, Bodleian
            Library, Oxford
NAZ   National Archives of Zambia, Lusaka, Zambia
PRO   Public Record Office, London
RH   Rhodes House, Bodleian Library, Oxford
ZCCM   Archives Zambia Consolidated Copper Mines Archives,
            Ndola, Zambia

1. "The Water Follows the Stream"

1 Read, like Audrey Richards, worked in central Africa prior to the establishment of the Rhodes-Livingstone Institute. See her early article "Traditon and Prestige among the Ngoni," *Africa* 9 (1936): 453–84. J. A. Barnes, who worked in the area later for the RLI, recalls people speaking approvingly of her visit because she attended funerals. (Personal communication with author.)

2 M. B. Lukhero, interview by author, fieldnotes (29 May 1991) held by author.

3 See Richard Werbner's account of their accomplishments in the area of theory, "The Manchester School in South-Central Africa," *Annual Review of Anthropology* 13 (1984):157–85 (and the version in Richard Fardon, ed., *Localizing Strategies: Regional Traditions of Ethnographic Writing* [Smithsonian Institute: Scottish Academic Press, 1990, 152–81]). Richard Brown discusses the role of patronage and politics

in the establishment of the RLI, "Anthropology and Colonial Rule: Godfrey Wilson and the Rhodes-Livingstone Institute, Northern Rhodesia," in *Anthropology and the Colonial Encounter*, ed. Talal Asad (New York: Humanities Press, 1973), 173–98, and "Passages in the Life of a White Anthropologist: Max Gluckman in Northern Rhodesia," *Journal of African History* 20 (1979): 525–41. See also the substantial sections on the Manchester School in Adam Kuper's, *Anthropology and Anthropologists: The Modern British School* (London: Routledge & Kegan Paul, 1983); Ulf Hannerz's, *Exploring the City* (New York: Columbia University Press, 1980); and Joan Vincent's, *Anthropology and Politics* (Tucson: University of Arizona Press, 1990).

4 For a case in the history of British anthropology see Henrika Kuklick's discussion of the diffusionist school, in *The Savage Within: The Social History of British Anthropology, 1885–1945* (Cambridge: Cambridge University Press, 1991).

5 For a study of colonial settler culture that contains insights important for this approach, see Helen Callaway's, *Gender, Culture and Empire: European Women in Colonial Nigeria* (Oxford: Macmillan Press, 1987). For the importance of mission and administrative practices for the development of anthropology, see Peter Pels's and Oscar Salemink's "Introduction: Five Theses on Ethnography as Colonial Practice," *History and Anthropology* 8, nos. 1–4 (1994): 1–34; and Lynette Schumaker, "A Tent with a View: Colonial Officers, Anthropologists, and the Making of the Field in Northern Rhodesia, 1937–1960," in Henrika Kuklick and Robert Kohler, eds., "Science in the Field," *Osiris* 11 (1996): 237–58.

6 George Stocking's work exemplifies this approach, as does that of most of the contributors to his edited series, *History of Anthropology*.

7 See Kuklick's review article, "Speaking with the Dead" (*Isis* 89 [1998]: 103–11) for a comparison of Stocking's "multiple contextualization" in *Victorian Anthropology* and his narrower contextualization in *After Tylor* (104). (George W. Stocking Jr., *After Tylor: British Social Anthropology, 1888–1951* [London: Athlone Press, 1995])

8 "In commemorating the fiftieth anniversary of the foundation of the Rhodesias in 1890 and the centenary of the arrival of Livingstone in Africa, the appeal balanced the widely different associations evoked by the two names." (Brown, "Anthropology and Colonial Rule," 181)

9 Mainza Chona, interview by author, fieldnotes (13 August 1992) held by author.

10 For discussions of the literature in sociology of science that focus on the social forces that shape science, see Michael Mulkay, *Science and the Sociology of Knowledge* (London: Allen and Unwin, 1979) and Kuklick, "The Sociology of Knowledge: Retrospect and Prospect," *Annual Reviews in Sociology* 9 (1983): 287–310. See also Bruno Latour's, *Science in Action: How to Follow Scientists and Engineers through Society* (Cambridge: Harvard University Press, 1987).

11 The history of the field sciences is growing rapidly. Examples of this approach include George W. Stocking Jr., "The Ethnographer's Magic: Fieldwork in British Anthropology from Tylor to Malinowski," in Stocking, ed., *Observers Observed: Essays on Ethnographic Fieldwork* (Madison: University of Wisconsin Press, 1983), 70–120; Alex Soojung-Kim Pang, "Spheres of Interest: Imperialism, Culture, and Practice in British Solar Eclipse Expeditions, 1860–1914," (Ph.D. diss. University of Pennsylvania, 1991); Martin J. S. Rudwick, "The Emergence of a Visual Language for Geological Science, 1760–1830," *History of Science* 14 (1976): 149–95; several essays in the collection *Cultures of Natural History*, ed. N. Jardine, A. Secord, and E. C. Spary (Cambridge: Cambridge University Press, 1996); and the volume, "Science in the Field," *Osiris* 11 (1996), edited by Henrika Kuklick and Robert Kohler.

12 For an analysis of the ways RLI anthropologists reacted to the administrators' and missionaries' construction of the racial and ethnic landscape of Northern Rhodesia, see Schumaker, "Landscaping Race," in Peter Pels and Oscar Salemink, eds., *Colonial Subjects: Essays in the Practical History of Anthropology* (Ann Arbor: University of Michigan Press, 1998).

13 Brown, "Passages," was an early example. For more recent examples see Kuklick, *Savage Within*; Stocking, ed., *Colonial Situations: Essays on the Contextualization of Ethnographic Knowledge*, History of Anthropology 7 (Madison: University of Wisconsin Press, 1991); and Pels and Salemink, *Colonial Subjects*.

14 For an overview of the anthropology of colonialism, see Pels's "The Anthropology of Colonialism: Culture, History, and the Emergence of Western Governmentality," *Annual Review of Anthropology* 26 (1997): 163–234. Some examples include Nicholas Dirks, ed., *Colonialism and Culture* (Ann Arbor: University of Michigan Press, 1992); Anne Stoler, *Race and the Education of Desire: Foucault's "History of*

Sexuality" and the Colonial Order of Things (London: Duke University Press, 1995); and Nicholas Thomas, *Colonialism's Culture: Anthropology, Travel and Government* (London: Polity Press, 1994).

15 See John A. Schuster, "Methodologies as Mythic Structures: A Preface to the Future Historiography of Method," *Metascience*, nos. 1–2 (1984): 15–36; and Schuster and Richard R. Yeo, eds., *The Politics and Rhetoric of Scientific Method* (Dordrecht: D. Reidel, 1986).

16 Megan Vaughan compares this approach with the rich ethnographies produced by the anthropologists of the colonial Zambian Copperbelt, "that provided us with a mass of empirical observations which constantly threaten to escape the frameworks of analysis." ("Colonial Discourse Theory and African History, or has Postmodernism passed us by?" *Social Dynamics* 20, no. 2 [1994]: 19, 1–23)

17 Judith Okely and Helen Callaway, preface, in Okely and Callaway, eds., *Anthropology and Autobiography* (London: Routledge, 1995), xi. The essays in this volume address the neglect of the experiential side of fieldwork.

18 This concept has its roots in E. P. Thompson's work, but by way of numerous studies in the history of technology that show how manufacturing processes were resisted and shaped by workers rather than simply imposed according to technical rationales. See, in particular, Merritt Roe Smith, *Harpers Ferry Armory and the New Technology* (Ithaca, N.Y.: Cornell University Press, 1977). The sociology of the professions and recent ethnographies of laboratory science have also contributed to my understanding of work and institutional cultures. Important examples of the latter include Bruno Latour and Steve Woolgar, *Laboratory Life: The Construction of Scientific Facts*, 2d ed. (Princeton, N.J.: Princeton University Press, 1986), and Sharon Traweek, *Beamtimes and Lifetimes: The World of High Energy Physicists*, (Cambridge: Harvard University Press, 1988).

19 Some examples include Steven Feierman's *Peasant Intellectuals* (Madison: University of Wisconsin Press, 1990), John and Jean Comaroff's *Ethnography and the Historical Imagination* (Boulder, Colo.: Westview Press, 1992), and David William Cohen and E. S. Atieno Odhiambo's, *Siaya: The Historical Anthropology of an African Landscape* (London: James Currey, 1989).

20 For an example of a historical ethnography that also functions as a restudy, see Sharon Hutchinson's *Nuer Dilemmas* (Berkeley: University of California Press, 1996).

21 An example of this is Megan Vaughan and Henrietta L. Moore's use of the work of Audrey Richards and other anthropologists in their book *Cutting Down Trees: Gender, Nutrition and Agricultural Change in the Northern Province of Zambia, 1890–1990* (London: James Currey, 1994).

22 "Anthropology's Hidden Colonialism: Assistants and their Ethnographers," *Anthropology Today* 9, no. 2 (April 1993): 13–18. Sanjek also provides an overview of more recent anthropologists' writings about their assistants. The invisibility of the anthropologist's assistant is characteristic of the role of the "hidden technician" found in the sciences more generally. See Steven Shapin's "The House of Experiment in Seventeenth-Century England," *Isis* 79 (1988): 373–404.

23 "On Ethnographic Authority," in *The Predicament of Culture* (1988), 49.

24 In *The Forest of Symbols: Aspects of Ndembu Ritual* (Ithaca, N.Y.: Cornell University Press, 1967). See Jules-Rosette, "Decentering Ethnography: Victor Turner's Vision of Anthropology," *Journal of Religion in Africa* 24, no. 2 (1994): 160–81. Turner did not use the term "indigenous anthropologist," but he did compare Muchona to a university don.

25 This is in contrast to the position taken by Jules-Rosette ("Decentering Ethnography," 168–69).

26 See Leroy Vail's use of the concept in Vail, ed., *The Creation of Tribalism in Southern Africa* (London: James Currey, 1989). See also Moore and Vaughan's *Cutting Down Trees* for a discussion of the numerous local African and administrative influences on Audrey Richards' portrait of Bemba culture.

27 See Ivan Karp's *Museums and their Communities* (Washington, D.C.: Smithsonian Institution Press, 1992); and Karp and Steven Lavine, eds., *Exhibiting Cultures* (Washington, D.C.: Smithsonian Institution Press, 1991).

28 See Eric Hobsbawm and Terence Ranger, *The Invention of Tradition* (Cambridge: Cambridge University Press, 1983); and Ranger's "The Invention of Tradition Revisited," in Ranger and Olufemi Vaughan, eds., *Legitimacy and the State in Twentieth-Century Africa* (London: Macmillan, 1993), 62–111. The idea that traditions are developed to serve current political purposes has several anthropological antecedents, including Malinowski's idea of myth as charter. Max Gluckman

developed this idea in his early work on Zulu identity; see 57–59 and 62 in Hugh Macmillan's "Return to the Malungwana Drift—Max Gluckman, the Zulu Nation and the Common Society," *African Affairs* 94, no. 374 (1995): 39–65. The RLI anthropologists further developed the concept into an analytical tool that could be applied to the varieties of history-telling they found in the societies they studied. See J. A. Barnes, "History in a Changing Society," *Rhodes-Livingstone Journal: Human Problems in British Central Africa* 11 (1951): 1–9; Elizabeth Colson, *Tradition and Contract: The Problem of Order* (Chicago: Aldine, 1974), and "Contemporary Tribes and the Development of Nationalism," in J. Helm, ed., *Essays on the Problem of Tribe* (Seattle: University of Washington Press, 1968); and I. G. Cunnison, "History on the Luapula," *Rhodes-Livingstone Papers* 21 (1951).

29 The particular sense in which I will be using the concept "intellectuals" owes much to Steven Feierman's ground-breaking work, *Peasant Intellectuals*.

30 *Power in Africa: An Essay in Political Interpretation* (London: Macmillan, 1994), 201. This is essentially different from the kind of Africanization of anthropology that Sally Falk Moore discusses, by which she means the significant impression on general Anglo-American anthropological theory made by theories developed out of African fieldwork from the 1930s through the 1950s. See her *Anthropology and Africa* (Charlottesville: University Press of Virginia, 1994).

31 See Arjun Appadurai, "The Production of Locality," in Richard Fardon, ed., *Counterworks: Managing the Diversity of Knowledge* (London: Routledge, 1995), 207.

32 Examples include Joe Cain, "Intimate Working: Collaborations between Husband and Wife in the Early Scientific Careers of Anne Roe and George Gaylord Simpson," n.d., manuscript, University College London; Andrea Cornwall and Nancy Lindisfarne, eds., *Dislocating Masculinity: Comparative Ethnographies* (London: Routledge, 1996); and Helen Callaway, "Ethnography and Experience: Gender Implications in Fieldwork and Texts," in Okely and Callaway, eds., *Anthropology and Autobiography*.

33 This debate has been carried on by James Ferguson and Hugh Macmillan in various issues of the *Journal of Southern African Studies* (*JSAS*). See Ferguson's, "Mobile Workers, Modernist Narratives: A Critique of the Historiography of Transition on the Zambian Copper-

belt. Part One," *JSAS* 16, no. 3 (1990), and "Part Two," *JSAS* 16, no. 4 (1990), and Macmillan's response, "The Historiography of Transition on the Zambian Copperbelt — Another View," *JSAS* 19, no. 4 (1993): 681–712. See also Ferguson in *JSAS* 20, no. 4 (1994) and *JSAS* 22, no. 2 (1996) and Macmillan in *JSAS* 22, no. 2 (1996).

2. Contexts and Chronologies

1 Functionalist anthropologists studied societies as organic wholes characterized by harmonious systems of relationships and institutions that could be elucidated through scientific methods of observation based on fieldwork.

2 Henrika Kuklick, *The Savage Within: The Social History of British Anthropology, 1885–1945* (Cambridge: Cambridge University Press, 1991), 25.

3 See G. R. Searle, *The Quest for National Efficiency* (Berkeley: University of California Press, 1971). See also Frank Whitehead, "The Government Social Survey," in Martin Bulmer, ed., *Essays on the History of British Sociological Research* (Cambridge: Cambridge University Press, 1985), 83–100.

4 Arthur Marwick, *A History of the Modern British Isles, 1914–1999* (Oxford: Blackwell Publishers, 2000), 198.

5 Peter Weiler, *British Labour and the Cold War* (Stanford, Calif.: Stanford University Press, 1988), 12.

6 Marwick, *A History of the Modern British Isles*, 197.

7 Morgan, *Labour in Power*, 303–4 .

8 Morgan, *Labour in Power*, 228–31, 201. Also see Frederick Cooper, *Decolonization and African Society: The Labor Question in French and British Africa* (Cambridge: Cambridge University Press, 1996), 64–66.

9 Morgan, *Labour in Power*, 86. See Cooper, *Decolonization and African Society*, for the problems of the Colonial Office vision of African development in the late 1940s (214–16).

10 Cooper, *Decolonization and African Society*, 394–95.

11 Colonial resistance to nationalist movements led to violent liberation struggles despite the rhetoric of gradual devolution of power. See Frank Füredi, *Colonial Wars and the Politics of Third World Nationalism* (London: I. B. Tauris, 1994).

12 Morgan, *Labour in Power*, 202–6.

13 Morgan, *Labour in Power*, 189–90.

14 Several of my informants mentioned this.

15 Elazar Barkan, *The Retreat of Scientific Racism* (Cambridge: Cambridge University Press, 1992). Authors in the *Rhodes-Livingstone Journal: Human Problems in British Central Africa* 12 discussed the UNESCO statement.

16 For a description of the movement, see Fenner Brockway, *The Colonial Revolution* (London: Hart-Davis, MacGibbon, 1973). The Aborigines Protection Society was founded in 1838 after British parliamentary hearings on the so-called Kaffir Wars in South Africa.

17 See Anthony Low, "The End of the British Empire in Africa," in *Decolonization and African Independence: The Transfers of Power, 1960–1980*, ed. P. Gifford and W. Roger Louis (New Haven, Conn.: Yale University Press, 1988), 33–72; and William Roger Louis and Ronald Robinson, "The United States and the Liquidation of the British Empire in Tropical Africa, 1941–1951," in *The Transfer of Power in Africa: Decolonization, 1940–1960* (New Haven, Conn.: Yale University Press, 1982), 31–56.

18 Weiler, *British Labour*, 14, 30.

19 This is the argument of David M. Anderson in "Cow Power: Livestock and the Pastoralist in Africa," *African Affairs* 92, no. 366 (1993): 124, 121–34. In *The Hidden Hippopotamus: Reappraisal in African History, The Early Colonial Experience in Western Zambia* (Cambridge: Cambridge University Press, 1980), 80 and 269, note 121, Gwyn Prins claims that when Gluckman "wrote [about Lozi not really being a cattle people], his ideas were cast within the restrictive framework of Herskovits's 'cattle complex'." See Herskovits's "The Cattle Complex of East Africa," *American Anthropologist* 28 (1926): 361–88, and "The Culture Areas of Africa," *Africa* 3, no. 1 (1930): 59–77. The RLI researchers, however, did not consider the idea relevant to any part of Africa, and Gluckman was actually contemptuous of it. (Elizabeth Colson, personal communication with author; J. A. Barnes, personal communication with author.) Gluckman often took the ideas of other scholars and attempted to test their relevance through his and other RLI researchers' studies. Testing previous frameworks is not the same as being restricted to them.

20 William Beinart, "Introduction," in *Conservation in Africa: People,*

Policies and Practice, ed. David M. Anderson and Richard Grove (Cambridge: Cambridge University Press, 1987), 17, 15–19. See also David Anderson, "Depression, Dust Bowl, Demography and Drought: The Colonial State and Soil Conservation in East Africa during the 1930s," *African Affairs* 83, no. 332 (1984): 321–43.

21 See Ulf Hannerz, *Exploring the City* (New York: Columbia University Press, 1980).

22 Mapopa Mtonga, interview by author, fieldnotes (11 July 1991) held by author.

23 Carnegie funded Lord Hailey's *An African Survey* (Kuklick, *Savage Within*, 215). Stocking discusses Rockefeller support for anthropology in "Philanthropoids and Vanishing Cultures," in Stocking, ed., *Objects and Others* (Madison: University of Wisconsin Press, 1985), 112–45 (also cited in Kuklick, *Savage Within*, 205).

24 See Roberta Balstad Miller's, "Science and Society in the Early Career of H. F. Verwoerd," *Journal of Southern African Studies* 19, no. 4 (1993): 642, 634–61.

25 Stocking, "Philanthropoids," 123–24. The American model of a government ethnological bureau motivated some of those who argued that anthropology would be useful for empire (123).

26 Brown, "Anthropology and Colonial Rule: Godfrey Wilson and the Rhodes-Livingstone Institute, Northern Rhodesia," in *Anthropology and the Colonial Encounter*, ed. Talal Asad (New York: Humanities Press, 1973), 184; "Anthropology and Colonial Rule" cited in Stocking, "Philanthropoids," 139.

27 20 December 1948, PRO, CO 927/41/6. See Henry Fosbrooke, "From Lusaka to Salisbury, 1956–1960," *African Social Research* 24 (1977): 321, 319–26, for mention of the arrival of affiliates. For a more general discussion of American academic interest in Africa, see K. C. Wylie and Dennis Hickey, *An Enchanting Darkness: The American Vision of Africa in the Twentieth Century* (East Lansing: Michigan State University, 1993).

28 Duncan Innes, *Anglo: Anglo American and the Rise of Modern South Africa* (Johannesburg: Ravan Press, 1984), 92. Beatty had been a colleague of Hoover while initiating mining development in Russia in 1911. (Innes, "Sir Alfred Chester Beatty," *Horizon* 11, no. 3 [1968]: 18–21.)

29 Jane L. Parpart, *Labor and Capital on the African Copperbelt* (Philadelphia: Temple University Press, 1983), 19–46.

30 See Brown, "Anthropology and Colonial Rule." This article and his later article on Gluckman's directorship also deal with the directors' problems with white society in Northern Rhodesia, but little attention is given to the reactions of Africans to the Institute and its work.

31 Brown has dealt with the Northern Rhodesian governor's mobilization of local forces to support the founding of the RLI. I explore these local forces in greater detail in chapter 3.

32 See Brown, "Anthropology and Colonial Rule," 183.

33 As A. B. Cohen at the Colonial Office expressed it in a minute to Raymond Firth, 13 March 1945 (concerning an upcoming CSSRC decision about additional funding requested by Gluckman), "I do not think that we ought to press the point about connection with a university in this case. There will probably be room for an African university or at any rate university college in Central Africa. The Institute must then become part of it and would no doubt have to move for the purpose. But we cannot afford the money for such a higher education institution at the present time, nor is the educational standard of Africans in either Northern Rhodesia or Nyasaland anything like high enough yet to justify setting up such an institution. But it would be a thousand pities to deny the Central African Territories of the benefit of this necessary sociological research station, with its valuable cultural influences so greatly needed in these Territories, just because they cannot have a university." (PRO, CO 927/8/7.)

34 Saul Dubow, *Scientific Racism in Modern South Africa* (Cambridge: Cambridge University Press, 1995), 52–53. Dubow quotes J. H. Hofmeyr's phrase "South Africanisation" and articles in the *Cape Times*, 7 and 28 August, 1925, on Hrdlicka's responses to a visit to the country.

35 Saul Dubow, *Racial Segregation and the Origins of Apartheid in South Africa, 1919–36* (Oxford: St. Antony's College/Macmillan, 1989), 4.

36 See Richard Elphick's "Mission Christianity and Interwar Liberalism," in *Democratic Liberalism in South Africa: Its History and Prospect*, ed. J. Butler, R. Elphick, and D. Welsh (Cape Town: David Philip, 1987), 64–80.

37 Elizabeth Colson to Monica Wilson, 23 March 1948, PRO, CO 927/64/3.

38 See Hugh Macmillan's paper on Gluckman's attitude to cultural difference and similarity in the South African context, "Return to the Malungwana Drift — Max Gluckman, the Zulu Nation and the Common

Society" (paper presented at the conference on "Ethnicity, Society and Conflict in Natal," University of Natal, Pietermaritzburg, 14–16 September 1992), 4.

39 Balstad Miller, "Science and Society," 642.

40 Gluckman, "Human Laboratory across the Zambesi," *Libertas*, 6, no. 4 (1946): 38–49.

41 For a view of African university education at Fort Hare, see H. R. Burrows, A. Kerr, and Z. K. Matthews, eds., *A Short Pictorial History of the University College of Fort Hare, 1916–1959* (Alice: Lovedale Press, 1961). I have not been able to determine the precise numbers of research assistants who achieved different educational levels, because the RLI personnel files have been lost and I was only able to interview approximately twenty of the former assistants.

3. Archetypal Experiences

1 Richard Brown, "Anthropology and Colonial Rule: Godfrey Wilson and the Rhodes-Livingstone Institute, Northern Rhodesia," in *Anthropology and the Colonial Encounter*, ed. Talal Asad (New York: Humanities Press, 1973), 173–98, and "Passages in the Life of a White Anthropologist: Max Gluckman in Northern Rhodesia," *Journal of African History* 20 (1979): 525–41.

2 "Return to the Malungwana Drift — Max Gluckman, the Zulu Nation and the Common Society," *African Affairs* 94, no. 374, (1995): 39–65.

3 Gluckman's fieldnotes, however, are available at Emmanuel College, Cambridge.

4 The idea of archetypal experiences that shape anthropologists' behavior in the field is George Stocking's. See George W. Stocking Jr., "Philanthropoids and Vanishing Cultures," in Stocking, ed., *Objects and Others: Essays on Museums and Material Culture* (Madison: University of Wisconsin Press, 1985), 136–37, 112–45. See also his further discussion of the case of Paul Kirchoff, whom the Colonial Office prevented from going to Northern Rhodesia, and later New Guinea, because of suspicion that he was a communist, in George W. Stocking Jr., *After Tylor: British Social Anthropology, 1888–1951*, (London: Athlone Press, 1995), 411–12.

5 These include, most recently, an Indian historian of medicine, Harish

Naraindas, who traced his intellectual lineage back to the Manchester School through J. Singh Uberoi, a student of Gluckman and Cunnison. (Personal communication with author.) At Manchester, Uberoi did a restudy of the work of Malinowski, *The Politics of the Kula Ring: An Analysis of the Findings of Bronislaw Malinowski* (Manchester: Manchester University Press, 1962).

6 George W. Stocking Jr., "The Ethnographer's Magic: Fieldwork in British Anthropology from Tylor to Malinowski," in Stocking, ed., *Observers Observed: Essays on Ethnographic Fieldwork* (Madison: University of Wisconsin Press, 1983), 70–120.

7 "Max Gluckman, 1911–1975," *Proceedings of the British Academy* 61 (1975): 492–93, 478–96.

8 Holleman received a Beit Fellowship (funded by the Beit Trust, the philanthropical arm of the British South Africa Company) and was attached to the RLI because it was the only social science research institution in central Africa at the time. Gluckman was not involved in choosing Holleman for this work. When describing to me his first meeting with Gluckman at the RLI, Holleman glossed over some of the tensions, which came out later in the interview. Interestingly, the clash over field methods that resulted in Gluckman allowing Holleman to "go his own way" came out of a general discussion of their ideas and an exchange of anecdotes about fieldwork and not from any explicit discussion of methods, according to Holleman. This points up the likely role of anecdotes for teaching students appropriate field behavior even in university settings where fieldwork practices (as opposed to methodology) are not explicitly taught. (Holleman also resisted becoming part of Gluckman's coordinated comparative scheme; see chapter 4 and his RLI colleagues's encouragement to make his work more theoretical; see the author's note (p. v) to his "Accommodating the Spirit among Some North-Eastern Shona Tribes," *Rhodes-Livingstone Papers* 22 [1953].)

9 Published originally in *Bantu Studies* (*African Studies*) in 1940 and 1942, the article was republished as *Rhodes-Livingstone Papers* 28 in 1958, with a foreword by J. Clyde Mitchell. Page numbers in the following footnotes refer to the 1958 publication. Subsequent RLI researchers read and discussed the original article and dubbed it "The Bridge."

10 Gluckman, "Analysis," 5. Gluckman used the term *i beshu*.

11 Gluckman, "Analysis," 19–20.

12 Holleman, interview with author, fieldnotes (5 November 1993) held by author.

13 Robert Gordon, "Apartheid's Anthropologists: The Genealogy of Afrikaner Anthropology," *American Ethnologist* 15, no. 3 (1988): 535–53, 536–37.

14 For discussion of Schoeman, see Gordon, "Apartheid's Anthropologists," and W. D. Hammond-Tooke, *Imperfect Interpreters: South Africa's Anthropologists, 1920–1990* (Johannesburg: Witwatersrand University Press, 1997).

15 Stocking, *After Tylor*, 425–26.

16 Robert Gordon, "Early Social Anthropology in South Africa," *African Studies* 49, no.1 (1990): 30–31, 15–48.

17 Gordon, "Apartheid's Anthropologists," 549.

18 According to Raymond Firth, Gluckman lived with a Zulu family and joined in the dancing, beer-drinking, and other activities of daily life, at a time before apartheid made this kind of participant-observation impossible. ("Max Gluckman, 1911–1975," 481) Whatever the truth of Holleman's story, Gluckman probably wore European clothing most of the time and especially when interacting with Europeans in the research settings described in "Analysis."

19 Macmillan believes this experience may have led to the importance of the issues of conflict and cohesion in "Analysis" and his later work. ("Return to Malungwana Drift: Max Gluckman, the Zulu Nation and the Common Society," *African Affairs* 94, no. 374 [1995]: 43, 39–65.)

20 Gordon, "Early Social Anthropology," 32. Hugh Macmillan discusses the reasons for his banning in "Return to Malungwana Drift" (41–43). Gluckman offended the Zulu Regent by attempting to protect a drunken man who was being flogged for disagreeing with the regent at a meeting. The regent had also complained about Gluckman's wearing *bheshu*. Some administrators also voiced concerns about his behavior in the field and his possible communist sympathies. Gluckman had joined the South African Communist Party at about that time. See Macmillan, "Return to Malungwana Drift," 51.

21 David Welsh, "Social Research in a Divided Society: The Case of South Africa," *Social Dynamics*, no. 1 (1975): 21, 19–30.

22 Hammond-Tooke, *Imperfect Interpreters*, 137. Holleman, interview with author, fieldnotes (6 November 1993) held by author.

23 See chapter 4 for the challenge to this style of anthropology mounted by social anthropologists.

24 Holleman, interview with author, fieldnotes (6 November 1993) held by author.

25 *Land, Labour and Diet: An Economic Study of the Bemba Tribe* (London: Oxford University Press, 1939).

26 Administrators frequently employed African symbols of authority to legitimate colonial rule. (See Lynette Schumaker, "A Tent with A View: Colonial Officers, Anthropologists, and the Making of the Field in Northern Rhodesia, 1937–1960," in Henrika Kuklick and Robert Kohler, eds., "Science in the Field," *Osiris* 11 [1996]: 241, 237–58.)

27 Brown discusses some of these attacks, as does J. Clyde Mitchell in his article on the history of the RLI during his directorship. (Brown, "Anthropology and Colonial Rule," 182; Mitchell, "The Shadow of Federation, 1952–55," *African Social Research* 24 [1977]: 309–18.)

28 This was reported in several interviews.

29 There are also deeper resonances that they may not be aware of, having to do with Rhodes's purported homosexuality.

30 Jan Vansina, *Paths in the Rainforests: Toward a History of Political Tradition in Equatorial Africa* (London: Currey, 1990).

31 Brown, "Anthropology and Colonial Rule."

32 Mufalo Liswaniso, "The Livingstone Museum — Storehouse of Zambian Culture," *Horizon* 11, no. 11 (1968): 15, 13–17.

33 Monica Wilson, "The First Three Years, 1938–41," *African Social Research* 24 (1977): 282, 279–84. Wilson is wrong, however, in her observation that "archeological research carried no political implications" at the time. Particularly in white settler societies, archeology had been used well into the interwar period to shore up beliefs that Africans had not developed culture except when stimulated by outside influences. (See Henrika Kuklick, "Contested Monuments — The Politics of Archaeology in Southern Africa," in George W. Stocking Jr., *Colonial Situations — Essays on the Contextualization of Ethnographic Knowledge* [Madison: University of Wisconsin Press, 1991], 135–69.)

34 Audrey Richards, "The Rhodes-Livingstone Institute: An Experiment in Research, 1933–38," *African Social Research* 24 (1977): 275–78, 275. Brown discusses the unique local conditions that led to the founding of the RLI — despite Colonial Office obstruction — before any of the other African social science institutes. ("Anthropology and Colonial Rule.")

35 Livingstone, however, had long before lost the battle to become the major tourist center of central Africa to Victoria Falls Town, which enjoyed a position immediately on the Southern Rhodesian side of the Falls. (Winston Husbands, "Nature, Society, and the Origin of Tourism at Victoria Falls [Zambia]", unpublished paper, 1994) The Museum established in 1934 may have been intended, like most developments in Livingstone, as a means to tempt tourists to cross the border and travel the 12 km distance from the Falls to the town.

36 While conducting research in Zambia, I explained my project by saying that I was doing a history of the Rhodes-Livingstone Institute and of anthropology in Northern Rhodesia. Local whites of long residence would usually respond by talking about the Rhodes-Livingstone Museum and its archeological work and collections. The word "anthropology" was generally taken to mean archeology by all but a handful who had actually been acquainted with the anthropologists and their work. Black Zambians never made this mistake. The discipline of anthropology only divided into "discrete subfields" — social anthropology, physical anthropology, and archeology among them — in the 1930s. (See Kuklick, *The Savage Within: The Social History of British Anthropology, 1885–1945* [Cambridge: Cambridge University Press, 1991], 12.) According to Stocking, the collection of artifacts, both archeological and contemporary, gave anthropology meaning during the "Museum Era" prior to Malinowski's winning of Rockefeller support for functionalist fieldwork-oriented anthropology. The older anthropology "tended to be conceived as a study of the human past as it was embodied in collectible physical objects, rather than an observational study of human behavior in the present; its important relationships were to the biological sciences represented in museums of natural history, rather than to the social sciences." (Stocking, "Philanthropoids and Vanishing Cultures," 140–41.)

37 The first director of the RLI, Godfrey Wilson, acknowledged the Museum's importance to the white public when he called for both the Museum and the Institute to be called by the same name, so that the Institute could get the "credit of the Museum." (Letter to the RLI Board of Trustees Secretary, 18 August 1939, National Archives of Zambia, Lusaka, RC/1384.)

38 Brown, "Anthropology and Colonial Rule," 182.

39 Moore was an atheist. (J. A. Barnes, personal communication with author.)

40 Monica Wilson, "Lovedale: Instrument of Peace," in *Outlook on a Century: South Africa 1870–1970*, ed. Francis Wilson and Dominique Perrot (Lovedale: Lovedale Press, 1973). Lovedale was a Scottish Presbyterian mission. As a child, Hunter was educated along with African pupils there and would have been in touch with what happened to them and their families in their Ciskei and Transkei homelands. (Elizabeth Colson, personal communication with author.) Fort Hare Native College developed from Lovedale in 1916.

41 *Reaction to Conquest: Effects of Contact with Europeans on the Pondo of South Africa* (London: Oxford University Press, 1936).

42 *The Analysis of Social Change: Based on Observations in Central Africa* (Cambridge: Cambridge University Press, 1945). The Wilsons' backgrounds are discussed in Brown, "Anthropology and Colonial Rule," and in Hammond-Tooke, *Imperfect Interpreters*, 77–83.

43 Monica Wilson was an early critic of some aspects of culture contact theory (Gordon, "Early Social Anthropology," 31).

44 H. J. Simons, interview with author, Cape Town, South Africa, May 1992, fieldnotes held by author.

45 Macmillan, "Return to Malungwana Drift," 62.

46 "Return to Malungwana Drift," 49. Gluckman's use of the concept of "tribe" contained complexities that have not been appreciated by more recent scholars who know little of his political and social background and who conflate his use of the word with the ideas of colonial administrators. (For this view see Kate Crehan, *The Fractured Community: Landscapes of Power and Gender in Rural Zambia* [Berkeley: University of California Press, 1997], 55–62; also cited in James Ferguson, *Expectations of Modernity: Myths and Meanings of Urban Life on the Zambian Copperbelt* [London: University of California Press, 1999], 27.) Administrators' views were far more functionalist in conceiving (and creating) bounded tribes, while Gluckman and other RLI researchers defined the term as a political unit in the colonial government's construction of the native authority. Gluckman's use of the term also reflected Marxist ideas about modes of production.

47 Hammond-Tooke concludes that the Wilsons' ideas about increase of scale were not taken up by later anthropologists. (*Imperfect Interpreters*, 81). This idea may not have been used in research on South Africa, but the Wilsons' concern with the ways that Africans coped with large-scale Western systems resonates with later RLI strategies for

understanding African urban life through network analysis, which can be used for looking at unbounded social systems.

48 Frederick Cooper, *Decolonization and African Society: The Labor Question in French and British Africa* (Cambridge: Cambridge University Press, 1996), 63.

49 Stocking, *After Tylor*, 409, 417.

50 Parts I and II, *Rhodes-Livingstone Papers* 5 and 6 (1941) and (1942).

51 "Anthropology and Colonial Rule," 195. Brown calls this position "a marriage of Marx and Malinowski" (195).

52 See Hugh Macmillan's article "The Historiography of Transition on the Zambian Copperbelt — Another View" for a discussion of the anti-imperialist influences on Wilson, which included Marx, J. H. Hobson, and, especially, Lenin (*Journal of Southern African Studies* 19, no. 4 [1993]: 696, 681–712).

53 See Richard Elphick's article "Mission Christianity and Interwar Liberalism" for a discussion of the overlap between missionaries and liberals in South Africa and the network of religious and social institutions that made up this benevolent empire (in Jeffrey Butler, Richard Elphick, and David Welsh, eds., *Democratic Liberalism in South Africa: Its History and Prospect* [Cape Town: David Philip, 1987], 64–80).

54 See Reinhard Henkel, *Christian Missions in Africa: Zambia* (Berlin: Dietrich Reimer Verlag, 1989); Roland Oliver, *The Missionary Factor in East Africa*, (London: Longmans, Green & Co., 1952); and Robert I. Rotberg, *Christian Missionaries and the Creation of Northern Rhodesia, 1880–1924* (Princeton: Princeton University Press, 1965). See Leon de Kock's "English and the Colonisation of Form," *Journal of Literary Studies* 8, nos. 1–2 (1992): 32–54, on the importance of Lovedale Mission's school for Africans and its printing press in shaping African literacy and consciousness throughout the southern African region. See also his " 'Drinking at the English Fountains': Missionary Discourse and the Case of Lovedale," for a discussion of some of the ways Africans internalized or subverted the missionaries' linguistic orthodoxy (*Missionalia* 20, no. 2 [August 1992]: 116–38). The RLI used Lovedale Press for its earliest publications.

55 G. B. Masefield, *A History of the Colonial Agricultural Service* (Oxford: Clarendon Press, 1972), 6.

56 See Henrika Kuklick's "Professional Status and the Social Order," unpublished manuscript, n.d.

57 See Frank Füredi's *The Silent War: Imperialism and the Changing Perception of Race* (London: Pluto Press, 1998); Hugh Macmillan, "The Historiography of Transition," 691; R. H. Tawney, *The Acquisitive Society*, (London: Bell, 1921).

58 *Africa* 13, no.1 (1940): 43–61.

59 Francis Wilson, interview with author, fieldnotes (6 May 1992) held by author. Chess playing could also prove to be an ambivalent encounter; Wilson made the mistake of beating the Governor at chess at their first meeting. (Brown, "Anthropology and Colonial Rule," 186)

60 Francis Wilson, interview with author, fieldnotes (6 May 1992) held by author.

61 J. Merle Davis (London: Macmillan, 1933). Davis came from an American missionary background.

62 Brown, "Anthropology and Colonial Rule," 186. See also Füredi, *Silent War*.

63 See also Füredi, *Silent War*.

64 R. J. B. Moore, *These African Copper Miners* (London: Livingstone Press, 1948).

65 Powdermaker, *Stranger and Friend: The Way of an Anthropologist* (New York: W. W. Norton, 1966), 293.

66 M. Wilson, "The First Three Years," 279.

67 T. R. Pickard, General Manager, The Rhodesia Broken Hill Development Company, to Wilson, 15 August 1940, University of Cape Town, Social Anthropology Department, Wilson Papers, "Labour Troubles and Ban on Anthropological Work." Some of these papers are now in the archives of library in the UCT African Studies Centre.

68 "Notes — Friday April 12" (notes Wilson took of the meeting on that date with Pickard and compound managers, Emans and Young) University of Cape Town, Social Anthropology Department, Wilson Papers, "Labour Troubles and Ban on Anthropological Work."

69 M. Wilson, "The First Three Years," 280.

70 J. Moore, Secretary, Broken Hill Management Board, 11 April 1940, University of Cape Town, Social Anthropology Department, Wilson Papers, "Labour Troubles and Ban on Anthropological Work."

71 Wilson to J. Moore, 15 April 1940, University of Cape Town, Social Anthropology Department, Wilson Papers, "Labour Troubles and Ban on Anthropological Work."

72 Brown, "Anthropology and Colonial Rule," 192.

73 "Conscientious Objectors Appear Before Man Power Committee," *Livingstone Mail*, 27 (1940), ZCCM Archives, Ndola, Zambia, 14.2.3B.

74 14 October 1940, ZCCM Archives, Ndola, Zambia, 14.2.3B.

75 Wilson to the Governor, 26 April 1940, quoting correspondence from T. R. Pickard, General Manager, Rhodesia Broken Hill Development Company, University of Cape Town, Social Anthropology Department, Wilson Papers, "Labour Troubles and Ban on Anthropological Work."

76 This was a concern because of the drive to recruit Africans for military service.

77 Confidential minutes of 14th meeting, 27 October 1940, National Archives of Zambia, Lusaka, B1/4/MISC/6/3.

78 Brown, "Passages," 529.

79 Secret letter, 19 (?) August 1940, University of Cape Town, Social Anthropology Department, Wilson Papers, "Labour Troubles and Ban on Anthropological Work."

80 A. L. Epstein, personal communication with author.

81 J. Clyde Mitchell, personal communication with author.

82 Mitchell, as stated above, knew about it before going to the RLI. Barnes did not remember it being discussed while he was at the RLI, though it may have been discussed later in Manchester. (Personal communication with author.) Norman Long, much later, remembered that everyone at Manchester knew about it but did not discuss it because they knew Gluckman was sensitive about it. (Norman Long, interview with author, fieldnotes [11 April 1995] held by author.)

83 "Passages," 534–55.

84 Brown, "Passages," 528. Gluckman himself recalled some of the administrators in Zululand and Barotseland as sharing his sympathy for African interests but working under difficult conditions, which he analyzed in terms of their interhierarchical position. ("Inter-hierarchical Roles: Professional and Party Ethics in Tribal Areas in South and Central Africa," 69–93 in *Local-Level Politics: Social and Cultural Perspectives*, ed. M. J. Swartz [Chicago: Aldine, 1968].)

85 This disillusionment resulted from the government's hostile response to his attempts to influence their reform of the Barotse Native Authority, as well as his and government ecologist Trapnell's insistence that land tenure reform in Northern Rhodesia be carried out only after a detailed scientific study. Both were removed from the Native Land Tenure Committee. See Brown, "Passages," 536–39.

86 See Schumaker, "A Tent with a View," 246–47.

87 These various responses are in National Archives of Zambia, Lusaka, SEC 1/131, 1944.

88 Both of these are discussed at length in Schumaker, "A Tent with a View."

89 In *African Sunset* (London: Johnson, 1973) Robin Short expresses many of these frustrations, which increased in the postwar period.

90 G. B. Masefield, *A History of the Colonial Agricultural Service* (Oxford: Clarendon Press, 1972), 44, 82–93.

91 For a recent discussion of carrying capacity and its varied interpretations by agricultural experts in Zambia, see 30 ff in Megan Vaughan and Henrietta L. Moore, *Cutting Down Trees: Gender, Nutrition, and Agricultural Change in the Northern Province of Zambia, 1890–1990* (London: James Curry, 1994). See also W. Allan, "Studies in African Land Usage," *Rhodes-Livingstone Papers* 14 (1949).

92 C. G. Trapnell and J. N. Clothier, *The Soils, Vegetation and Agricultural Systems of North-Western Rhodesia* (Lusaka: Government Printer, 1957); Max Gluckman, "Economy of the Central Barotse Plain," *Rhodes-Livingstone Papers* 7 (1942), and "Essays on Lozi Land and Royal Property," *Rhodes-Livingstone Papers* 10 (1944).

93 Brown mentions this experience as highly instructive and rewarding for Gluckman ("Passages," 538).

94 "Land Holding and Land Usage among the Plateau Tonga of the Mazabuka District: A Reconnaissance Survey," William Allan, Max Gluckman, D. U. Peters, and C. G. Trapnell, *Rhodes-Livingstone Papers* 14 (1948).

95 Temporary Report of Director to Trustees on Work of Year 1945, 10 December 1945, National Archives of Zambia, Lusaka, SEC 1/130.

96 K. R. M. Anthony and V. C. Uchendu, "Agricultural Change in Mazabuka District, Zambia," *Food Research Institute Studies* 9 (1970): 222, 215–67. Colson had pointed out problems with some of Gluckman's and Allan's assumptions. (Marcia Wright, "Technology, Marriage and Women's Work in the History of Maize-Growers in Mazabuka, Zambia: A Reconnaissance" *Journal of Southern African Studies* 10, no. 1 [1983]: 80, 71–85.)

97 Elizabeth Colson, interview with author, fieldnotes (6 September 1990) held by author.

98 Gluckman to Barnes, (?) May 1947, Barnes Papers, Cambridge, Box 1

(or 201), "RLI Central Office, 1944–1948." Fox-Pitt later became secretary of the Aborigines Protection Society in London. (J. A. Barnes, personal communication with author.)

99 Schumaker, "Tent with a View." When Fox-Pitt started using a surplus military Jeep for his field tours, it was nicknamed "The Yellow Peril." (John Blunden, interview with author, fieldnotes [15 November 1993] held by author.)

100 What is important is not to condemn disciplines or professions for using the concept of "fact," but to understand what constitutes fact in each discipline and what historical experiences have shaped the standards for their construction. For approaches of this kind, see Ludwik Fleck, *The Genesis and Development of a Scientific Fact* (Chicago: University of Chicago Press, 1979); Steven Shapin, *A Social History of Truth: Civility and Science in Seventeenth-Century England* (Chicago: University of Chicago Press, 1994); Mary Poovey, *A History of the Modern Fact: Problems of Knowledge in the Sciences of Wealth and Society* (Chicago: University of Chicago Press, 1998).

101 " 'The Economics of Detribalization,' Part 1," 3–4.

102 Gordon makes this point about South African scholars and the South African Institute of Race Relations. ("Early Social Anthropology in South Africa," 25.)

103 Mitchell to McCulloch, 6 June 1953, Rhodes House, Oxford, JCM 2/2.

104 The work of the Comaroffs exemplifies the current development of this Manchester School theme. See John L. Comaroff, "Dialectical Systems, History and Anthropology: Units of Study and Questions of Theory," *Journal of Southern African Studies* 8, no. 1 (1981): 143–72; and Jean and John L. Comaroff, *Ethnography and the Historical Imagination*.

105 The title was ". . . So Truth Be in the Field . . . ," published in Johannesburg by the South African Institute of Race Relations as a pamphet in 1975. The title quote is from Milton. In the essay Wilson emphasizes that the clash of ideas is what leads to truth: "Thesis, antithesis, synthesis is the perennial intellectual process" (9). Her positivism is also apparent in passages where she compares the great scientists to saints (8). See also *Truth Be in the Field: Social Science Research in Southern Africa*, Pierre Hugo, ed. (Pretoria: University of South Africa Press, 1990).

106 J. A. Barnes, personal communication with author.

107 Mitchell, personal communication with author.

108 Some have interpreted it this way, according to Raymond Firth. ("Max Gluckman, 1911–1975," 493–94.) See also Ronald Frankenberg's discussion of Gluckman's Marxist approach in "A Social Anthropology for Britain?" in Frankenberg, ed., *Custom and Conflict in British Society* (Manchester: Manchester University Press, 1982), 1–35.

109 Tim Jacob Gluckman, personal communication with author.

4. The Laboratory in the Field

1 Mitchell and Marwick had known each other previously in South Africa, where Mitchell had been a student at Natal University College while Marwick was working there as a part-time lecturer in psychology. (Max Marwick, personal communication with author.) Marwick and Gluckman also met previously there, when the psychologist Ella Pratt-Yule invited Gluckman to deliver a lecture on witchcraft to the second-year psychology class. (Marwick, interview with author, fieldnotes 25 November 1992.) Barnes had met Gluckman in 1939 in Oxford, while there to meet Evans-Pritchard, who was the examiner for his undergraduate work at Cambridge (where he was supervised by Driberg). (Barnes, interview with author, fieldnotes 12 August 1993.)

2 Elizabeth Colson, "The Institute under Max Gluckman, 1942–47," *African Social Research* 24 (1977): 287, 285–95.

3 Primarily composed of African and colored workers, the ICU also had 250 white members and ultimately had more influence in the countryside than in the cities. Leonard Thompson, *A History of South Africa* (New Haven:Yale University Press, 1990), 176; see also William Beinart and Colin Bundy, *Hidden Struggles in Rural South Africa* (London: James Currey, 1987).

4 Richard Brown, "Passages in the Life of a White Anthropologist: Max Gluckman in Northern Rhodesia," *Journal of African History* 20 (1979): 525–41, 528.

5 Hugh Macmillan, "Return to Malungwana Drift: Max Gluckman, the Zulu Nation and the Common Society," *African Affairs* 94, no. 374 (1995): 51, 39–65. Macmillan also quotes from Gluckman's

posthumously published "Anthropology and Apartheid": "It is possible in the cloistered seclusion of King's College, Cambridge (or Merton College, Oxford) to put the main emphasis on the obstinate differences: it was not possible for 'liberal' South Africans (in the 1930s) confronted with the policy of segregation within a nation into which the 'others' had been brought and treated as different — and inferior." (In M. Fortes and S. Patterson, eds., *Studies in African Social Anthropology* [London: Macmillan, 1975], 29, 21–40.)

6 See Saul Dubow, *Racial Segregation and the Origins of Apartheid in South Africa, 1919–36* (Oxford: St. Antony's College/Macmillan, 1989), for a discussion of this (5, 34–35).

7 See Saul Dubow, "Wulf Sachs' Black Hamlet — A Case of 'Psychic Vivisection'," *African Affairs*, no. 369 (1993): 519–56; Malinowski, *The Dynamics of Culture Contact* (New Haven, Conn.: Yale University Press, 1938), republished in L. Mair, *Methods of Study of Culture Contact in Africa*, Memorandum 15 of the International African Institute (London: International African Institute, 1946).

8 See Macmillan, "Return to Malungwana Drift"; Richard Brown, "Passages in the Life of a White Anthropologist: Max Gluckman in Northern Rhodesia," *Journal of African History* 20 (1979): 540, 525–41; Shula Marks and Hugh Macmillan, eds., *Africa and Empire: W. M. Macmillan, Historian and Social Critic* (London: Temple Smith, 1989); and Christopher Saunders, *The Making of the South African Past: Major Historians on Race and Class* (Cape Town, South Africa: David Philip, 1988).

9 Dubow, "Black Hamlet," 37.

10 "Schapera had written of the emergence of 'a specifically South African culture, shared in by both Black and White.' " Hugh Macmillan, " 'Paralyzed Conservatives': W. M. Macmillan, the Social Scientists and 'The Common Society,' " in Hugh Macmillan and Shula Marks, eds., *Africa and Empire*, (London: Temple Smith, 1989) 72–90, 87, citing Schapera in Lucy Mair, ed., *Materials for the Study of Culture Contact* (London, 1938), 26.

11 "Social Anthropology in Central Africa," *Rhodes-Livingstone Journal: Human Problems in British Central Africa* 20 (1956): 17; "Tribalism in British Central Africa," 57. Quoted in Macmillan, "Return to Malungwana Drift," 61.

12 Republished by Manchester University Press in 1958, Gluckman's paper first appeared in *Bantu Studies* 14 (1940): 1–30 and 147–74.

13　Cunnison, interview with author, fieldnotes (3 August 1993) held by author.

14　Macmillan says of the "radicalism" of Gluckman's "Analysis," "It would be difficult to find any social scientific writing on South Africa from 1942 to 1970 which was as radical in its critique of South African society." ("Return to Malungwana Drift," 55.)

15　Hugh Macmillan, " 'Paralyzed Conservatives'," 87. See also Stocking's description of Malinowski's visit to South Africa in 1934 and the divergent messages of his talks to white and black audiences. (George W. Stocking Jr., *After Tylor: British Social Anthropology, 1888–1951* [London: Athlone Press, 1995], 413–15.)

16　Later, in Manchester, he would produce talks for the BBC, published in *The Listener*—talks that pointedly applied anthropological theories and methods developed in Africa to British social situations.

17　*Libertas* 6, no.4 (1946): 38–49. Macmillan's point that Gluckman's ideas were radical in their historical context is especially borne out by the contrast between his articles for *Libertas* and its standard fare, which was usually liberal but paternalistic. In the June 1946 issue (vol. 6, no. 7), an article on Africa's future in the "Atomic Age" describes the Bushmen as "living human fossils" and outlines the "duty and the mission of the white man's civilisation in Africa." (8)

18　Hammond-Tooke, *Imperfect Interpreters*, 55. Nostalgia for pure African cultures also featured in the thinking of many other South African liberals, including some who were close to Gluckman. In 1940, R. F. A. Hoernlé, husband of Gluckman's beloved teacher, Winifred Hoernlé, supported segregation only if it could be "true and just"—that is, economic as well as political, and if it allowed Africans to achieve an "adequate economic life," but he did not feel that such could be achieved in reality (Hammond-Tooke, *Imperfect Interpreters*, 126).

19　Read saw the Ngoni in Nyasaland as heroic because of their warrior past, which Gluckman did not believe could be true of the Ngoni in eastern Northern Rhodesia, where she had spent only a short time. Moreover, between Read's departure and Barnes's arrival, many Ngoni had suffered resettlement. (Barnes, interview with author, fieldnotes [12 August 1993] held by author; and Barnes, personal communication with author.) For this aspect of Read's work see Henrika Kuklick, *The Savage Within: The Social History of British Anthropology, 1885–1945* (Cambridge: Cambridge University Press, 1991), 268–69. The heroic view of the Ngoni constituted only a part of Read's work, which covered topics from child-rearing, education, marriage, and divorce, to migrant labor and standards of living. Her published work in the 1930s and early 1940s included "Tradition and Prestige Among the Ngoni," *Africa* 9 (1936): 453–84; "The Moral Code of the Ngoni and Their Former Military State," *Africa* 11 (1938): 1–24; "Native Standards of Living and African Culture Change," *Africa* 11, Supplement (1938); and "Migrant Labour in Africa and its Effect on Tribal Life," *International Labour Review* 45 (1942): 605–31.

20 Mitchell, interview with author, fieldnotes (29 September 1993) held by author.

21 "Report on Research, 1946–47, 16 Nov. 1947," PRO, CO 927/64/2.

22 Colson, "The Institute under Max Gluckman," 290–91.

23 J. A. Barnes, *Politics in a Changing Society*, 2d ed. (Manchester: Manchester University Press, 1967).

24 J. Clyde Mitchell, *The Yao Village: A Study in the Social Structure of a Nyasaland Tribe* (Manchester: Manchester University Press, 1956).

25 Mitchell, interview with author, fieldnotes (31 October 1990) held by author.

26 Mitchell, interview with author, fieldnotes (10 August 1994) held by author. Schoeman and N. J. Van Warmelo played important roles in the development of volkekunde after the takeover by the Nationalist government in 1948. The beauty of African culture that they celebrated was used to justify the apartheid policy of separate development and the creation of the Bantustans. Holleman should not, however, be equated with his teachers, and he responded to the RLI approach in his later work in Rhodesia, producing a sensitive and sophisticated study of interhierarchical administrative and African roles in a contemporary political clash. See his *Chief, Council and Commissioner* (Assen, The Netherlands: Royal Van Gorcum, for Afrika-Studiecentrum, 1969).

27 Marwick, personal communication with author.

28 Max Marwick, *Sorcery in its Social Setting: A Study of the Northern Rhodesia Ceŵa* (Manchester: Manchester University Press, 1965).

29 D. U. Peters, "Land Usage in Serenje District," *Rhodes-Livingstone Papers* 19 (1950).

30 Lukhero, interview with author, fieldnotes (30 May 1991) held by author.

31 Gluckman, "Seven-Year Research Plan of the Rhodes-Livingstone In-

stitute of Social Studies in Central Africa," *The Rhodes Livingstone Journal* 4 (1945): 12, 1–33.

32 This reflected Gluckman's seven-year research plan, submitted in 1943, in which he emphasized that he did not "view the social processes at work [urbanization and labor migration] as entirely disintegrative. . . . The problems set for the urban areas alone indicate my awareness that new groupings and relationships, perhaps torn by conflicts, are emerging." ("The Seven-Year Research Plan," cited on 289 in Colson, "The Institute under Max Gluckman.")

33 In the 1950s, when much of the urban research took place, urban Africans experienced rising economic expectations often partly fulfilled by the boom created by the copper industry. Political disappointments were many — especially the imposition of Federation — but Africans also became increasingly able to organize political opposition and public demonstrations of strength in this period. One must take into account that some of the chief ethnographies of the interwar period, in contrast, reflected the consequences for Africans of the worldwide depression of the 1930s and the lingering aftereffects of their exploitation for military service in East Africa during World War One.

34 Gluckman's agenda for the RLI trustees meeting, 16 Nov. 1946, Barnes Papers, Cambridge, box 1 (or 201), "RLI Central Office, 1944–1948."

35 See Jonathan Harwood's *Styles of Scientific Thought: The German Genetics Community, 1900–33* (Chicago: University of Chicago Press, 1993). I would like to extend the idea of style to field practices, as well as to intellectual approaches and laboratory practices.

36 Barnes, personal communication with author.

37 *The Ila-Speaking Peoples of Northern Rhodesia*, 2 vols. (London: Macmillan, 1920).

38 London: Oxford University Press, 1938.

39 Gluckman to Barnes, 8 September 1945, Barnes Papers, Cambridge, box 1 (or 201), "RLI Central Office, 1944–1948."

40 See Brian Siegel, "The 'Wild' and 'Lazy' Lamba: Ethnic Stereotypes on the Central African Copperbelt," in Vail, ed., *The Creation of Tribalism in Southern Africa* (London: James Currey, 1989), 372–94.

41 J. A. Barnes, J. C. Mitchell, and M. Gluckman, "The Village Headman in British Central Africa," *Africa* 19 (1949): 89–106.

42 "The Collection of Genealogies," *Human Problems in British Central Africa* 5 (1947): 48–55. (Barnes, interview with author, fieldnotes [12

August 1993] held by author.) His later genealogical work in Ngoniland, where genealogies tended to be remembered in great depth, led
him to develop a new form for recording them. In a letter to Mitchell,
he mentioned having done one village so far and the sheet was already
19 feet long: "I am therefore trying to evolve a new technique of
draughtsmanship, as I have no way of coping with such a huge document except by spreading out on three camp beds, where it stays until
the next dust devil comes along, and we have to begin again." (16 Oct.
1946, Barnes Papers, Cambridge, box 5, "Official Letters.")

43 "The Lamba Village: A Report of a Social Survey," *Communication
(New Series)* 24 (Cape Town, South Africa: School of African Studies,
University of Cape Town, 1950).

44 J. Clyde Mitchell, interview with author, fieldnotes (31 October 1990)
held by author.

45 "Land Holding & Land Usage among the Plateau Tonga of Mazabuka
District: A Reconnaissance Survey, 1945," *Rhodes–Livingstone Papers*
14 (1948).

46 After the team went to Oxford in 1948, the Institute librarian wrote to
Mitchell about returning the books he had borrowed, listing Gluckman's *Economy of the Central Barotse Plain*, Linton's *Acculturation in
Seven American Indian Tribes*, Malinowski's *Coral Gardens*, Richards's *Land, Labour and Diet*, and Read's *Native Standards of Living
and African Culture Change*. (8 March 1948, Rhodes House Library,
Oxford, box 1, "JCM Papers.")

47 Colson, "The Institute under Max Gluckman," 292. Marwick remembered Holleman attending for part of the time. (Marwick, personal
communication with author.)

48 Barnes, personal communication with author.

49 Barnes, interview with author, fieldnotes (12 August 1993) held by
author.

50 Undated letter from Gluckman to all in Cape Town, Barnes Papers,
Cambridge, box 1 (or 201), "RLI Central Office, 1944–1948."

51 Gluckman to Barnes, from Livingstone, 23 July 1947, announcing that
Wulf Sachs had suddenly turned up from America for few days' visit.
(Barnes Papers, Cambridge, box 1 [or 201], "RLI Central Office, 1944–
1948.")

52 Most of these descriptions come from Bruce K. Murray's, *Wits: The
'Open' Years* (Johannesburg: Witwatersrand University Press, 1997).

53 For a description of Langa and its history, see Monica Wilson and Archie Mafeje, *Langa: A Study of Social Groups in an African Township* (Cape Town: Oxford University Press, 1963).

54 Simons, interview with author, fieldnotes (7 May 1992) held by author. Simons later spent two years at Manchester, where he participated in the social anthropology seminar. He and his wife, Rae, wrote *Class and Colour in South Africa, 1850–1950* (London: International Defence and Aid Fund for Southern Africa, 1983). Simons had gotten his degree in London, attended Malinowski's seminars and wrote some of the chapters for Hailey's *African Survey*. Schapera originally suggested Langa for his study.

55 Colson, interview with author, fieldnotes (6 September 1990) held by author.

56 The history of South African social anthropology, as well as the Afrikaner volkekunde, illustrates that colonial social science, like the natural sciences, might better be studied from a polycentric viewpoint rather than from the metropolitan/periphery approach that has characterized much of the historiography of science and imperialism. Centers of science in the colonies did not merely function as field outposts for metropolitan theorists but were usually rooted in local concerns and influenced as much by other colonial centers as by the institutions and scientific organizations of the imperial power.

57 Dubow, *Scientific Racism*, 54–55.

58 Howard Phillips, interview with author, fieldnotes (14 May 1993) held by author.

59 Peter Carstens, Gerald Klinghardt, and Martin West, eds., *Trails in the Thirstland: The Anthropological Field Diaries of Winifred Hoernlé* (Centre for African Studies Communications No. 14, University of Cape Town, 1987), 3–4.

60 Elizabeth Colson, personal communication with author.

61 Carstens et al., *Trails in the Thirstland*, 9.

62 Ibid., 12.

63 Murray, *Wits: The Open Years*, 235.

64 Carstens, et al., *Trails in the Thirstland*, 11.

65 In 1946 this was a community of scholars in the process of being displaced. In that year Hilda Kuper left for the University of Natal, being replaced by the former British colonial administrator, M. D. W. Jeffreys, a diffusionist, who turned the department away from contem-

porary sociological concerns. Gluckman later played a role in restoring social anthropology to Wits through his support for Max Marwick, who became that university's first professor of social anthropology in 1957. (Murray, *Wits: The Open Years*, 255) During the uncertain time before his appointment Marwick derogatorily referred to Jeffreys as a "museum man" — because he was more interested in linguistics, archeology, and physical anthropology than sociology and social anthropology. (Marwick to Mitchell, 23 January 1956, Rhodes House, Oxford, box 7, file 1, "Mitchell Papers.")

66 Murray, *Wits: The Open Years*, 256.

67 Colson, interview with author, fieldnotes (6 September 1990) held by author.

68 London: Oxford University Press, 1936.

69 Barnes to Max Marwick, Barnes Papers, Cambridge, Box, box 1 (or 201), "RLI Central Office, 1944–1948."

70 Lynette Schumaker, "A Tent with A View: Colonial Officers, Anthropologists, and the Making of the Field in Northern Rhodesia, 1937–1960," in Henrika Kuklick and Robert Kohler, eds., "Science in the Field," *Osiris* 11 (1996): 237–58.

71 Mitchell, interview with author, fieldnotes (31 October 1990) held by author. Gluckman's wife, Mary, and their children lived most of the time in Livingstone. She stayed in Mongu and occasionally joined him in nearby Katongo where he based himself during fieldwork before he became director and before the children were born. (Elizabeth Colson, personal communication with author.) Mary participated in some of the fieldwork, according to stories remembered by her children. (Tim Jacob Gluckman, personal communication with author.) Evans-Pritchard may have been the source of this rule about fieldwork, for, according to Barnes, he was opposed to researchers taking their wives to the field and to women anthropologists in general, though his married students did not follow his advice. (Barnes, personal communication with author.) He did, however, send women to do fieldwork in Africa — Eleanor Machadden and Jean Buxton to the Sudan and Mary Douglas to the Congo — and he backed Laura Bohannon to work among the Tiv with her husband. (Elizabeth Colson, personal communication with author.)

72 On the other hand, his language skills developed rapidly because he needed to avoid the interpreter's interference. (Barnes, personal communication with author.)

73 Barnes to Mitchell, 16 October 1946, Barnes Papers, Cambridge, box 5, "Official Letters." In a later letter he complains more about the local whites than about the Ngoni: the English are "bloody awful colonists" and Fort Jameson, the closest town, is "the dead end of Western civilization." (Letter to Mitchell, 10 October 1948, Rhodes House, Oxford, box 4, file 1, "Mitchell Papers.")

74 Letter to Barnes, 12 December 1946, Rhodes House, Oxford, box 4, file 1, "Mitchell Papers." Mitchell, interview with author, fieldnotes (31 October 1990) held by author.

75 Joan Marwick, interview with author, fieldnotes (25 November 1992) held by author.

76 Colson to Barnes, 7 November 1948, Barnes Papers, Cambridge, box 1 (or 201), "RLI Central Office, 1944–1948." Benjamin Shipopa worked as Colson's driver initially, and his work developed into that of assistant, as was the case with many of the clerk-interpreters for the RLI researchers.

77 Mitchell, interview by author, fieldnotes (11 December 1990) held by author.

78 On the antagonistic element in fieldwork, Barnes recalled that Watchtower informants (members of the Jehovah's Witnesses) used to parry his questions by asking the same questions of him. (Personal communication with author.)

79 RLI researchers were aware of the diversity of local interests and its effect on research. See Elizabeth Colson's "Competence and Incompetence in the Context of Independence," *Current Anthropology* 8 (1967): 92–100, 108–9.

80 J. Clyde Mitchell, interview with author, fieldnotes (11 December 1990) held by author; J. F. Holleman, interview with author, fieldnotes (7 November 1993) held by author.

81 Max Marwick, interview with author, fieldnotes (25 November 1992) held by author.

82 Lukhero, interview with author, fieldnotes (29 May 1992) held by author. According to Lukhero, Barnes was unaware of this at the time. Not only Africans thought anthropologists might be spies: when Barnes began his later research in Norway during the Cold War, he recalled, "there were three theories about my identity—that I was a spy for the British, a spy for the Russians, and a spy for the Norwegian Labour Party government, whom my Pietist informants regarded as anti-Christian." (Barnes, personal communication with author.)

83   Barnes, personal communication with author.

84   Letter to Mitchell, 10 October 1948, Rhodes House, Oxford, box 4, file 1, "Mitchell Papers."

85   Several of the former RLI researchers, when interviewed, mentioned "Gluckman's dictums" or other advice of this sort that they received before entering the field. Barnes's papers also include a long list of instructions and practical advice for fieldwork, including the suggestion to meet the chief initially but then to stay away from him. (undated letter from Gluckman to Barnes and Mitchell, Barnes Papers, Cambridge, box 2, "RLI Central Office, 1949–1951"; although undated, this list is clearly intended to provide advice for new fieldworkers and must have been misfiled in this box instead of the 1946–48 box.)

86   Elizabeth Colson, personal communication with author.

87   Gluckman's fascination with circumcision rituals and the *makishi* masked dancers involved in these and other events doubtless gave him insight into the perspective of non-Lozi groups under Lozi control.

88   Colson, for example, lived in four different villages during her first year (personal communication with author).

89   Max and Joan Marwick, interview with author, fieldnotes (25 November 1992) held by author.

90   RLI Secretary to Mitchell, 14 May 1947, Rhodes House Library, Oxford, box 1, "Mitchell Papers."

91   3 June 1947, Rhodes House Library, Oxford, box 1, "Mitchell Papers."

92   Other anthropologists visited students or colleagues in the field before this, but not on the scale that Gluckman was able to do, given his post at an institution located in the research area. Malinowski, for example, visited Audrey Richards and other students of his doing fieldwork in Africa. (Audrey Richards, "Malinowski," *New Society* 41 [1963]: 16, 16–17.)

93   Colson, "The Institute under Max Gluckman," 290.

94   The work for Mair's study was done after Gluckman left the directorship, but while the first team was still doing fieldwork.

95   One could also travel by plane to Mongu in Barotseland, as Gluckman sometimes did, or catch lifts on lorries, as Deane did. None of these modes of transport was reliable. Mitchell referred to the main bus company, Thatcher and Hobson, on which he sometimes traveled and transported — and lost — his field equipment, as "Fleeces and Robsem." (Mitchell to Barnes, undated October or November, Barnes Papers, Cambridge, Official Letters, box 5.)

96   Contrary to James Ferguson's view, the RLI anthropologists did not "hate" white settlers or treat them as a kind of "other" while leaving Africans themselves out of the debate over African interests. The RLI anthropologists recognized the diversity of white society in Northern Rhodesia (see, especially, quotes from Barnes and Cunnison, in the section "True Europeans" in this chapter) and made common cause with those with whom they got on, either in terms of social or political affinities. As for leaving Africans out of the debate, this would have been difficult at any time, because the RLI assistants from the start tended to come from the more politically active groups and, in the urban survey teams, saw sociology as potentially useful for achieving their political or historical goals (see chapter 7). By the 1950s, African union and political activists were quite capable of arguing their own case, though they certainly did not discourage any who cared to join them, even those who came armed only with statistics. For Ferguson's view see *Expectations of Modernity: Myths and Meanings of Urban Life on the Zambian Copperbelt* (London: University of California Press, 1999), 32–33.

97   Colson, "The Institute under Max Gluckman," 288.

98   *The Rhodes-Livingstone Journal* 5 (1947).

99   Richard Brown "Anthropology and Colonial Rule: Godfrey Wilson and the Rhodes-Livingstone Institute, Northern Rhodesia," in *Anthropology and the Colonial Encounter*, ed. Talal Asad (New York: Humanities Press, 1973), 177.

100 Brown discusses these founding issues in greater detail in his 1973 article.

101 See J. Desmond Clark, "Digging On: A Personal Record and Appraisal of Archaeological Research in Africa and Elsewhere," *Annual Review of Anthropology* 23 (1994): 1–23.

102 "The Use of Sociological Research in Museum Display," *The Rhodes-Livingstone Journal* 4 (1945): 66–73.

103 Barnes also collected items for the South African Museum in Cape Town, at the request of a curator, Margaret Shaw, whom he had met while at UCT. (Personal communication with author.)

104 *Rhodes-Livingstone Papers* 7 (1942). But see Ronald Frankenberg's assessment of Gluckman's Marxist approach, "Economic Anthropology or Political Economy? (I): The Barotse Social Formation — A Case Study," in Clammer, ed., *The New Economic Anthropology* (New York: St. Martin's Press, 1978).

105   Letter to all research officers, 7 March 1946, Barnes papers, Cambridge, box 1 (or 201), "RLI Central Office, 1944–1948." The article, "The Use of Sociological Research in Museum Display," appeared in an issue dominated by articles on the museum.

106   Nearly all of my interviewees referred to Gluckman's camp and his advice about living in the field. The Marwicks felt the size of his camp may have affected the research. Joan and Max Marwick, interview with author, fieldnotes (25 November 1992) held by author.

107   Some of my informants believe the Lozi treated Gluckman as an *induna* because of his age and seniority, while others, such as Elizabeth Colson, have pointed out that the Lozis had decided in general to treat Europeans as chiefs in order to minimize problems with them. (Colson, personal communication.)

108   "Report on Research, 1946–7, 16 November 1947," PRO, CO 927/64/2.

109   Deane, in *Rhodes-Livingstone Journal* 5 (1947): 24–43, 25.

110   Barnes, personal communication with author.

111   Barnes, personal communication with author.

112   Barnes, personal communication with author.

113   Colson, interview with author, fieldnotes (6 September 1990) held by author.

114   "Staff Conference Report from Gluckman to CSSRC: January 1947 Conference in Liverpool, 20 February 1947." PRO, CO 927/64/2.

115   "The Collection and Treatment of Family Budgets in Primitive Communities as a Field Problem," *Rhodes-Livingstone Journal* 8 (1949): 50–56.

116   Barnes, personal communication with author.

117   *South Africa's Stepchildren* (Johannesburg: South African Institute of Race Relations, 1947–48).

118   Monica Wilson, "Development in Anthropology," *Race Relations Journal* 22, no. 4 (1955): 10, 6–11. She cites Sonnabend's 1934 article in the *South African Journal of Economics*.

119   Gluckman to Mitchell, 12 December 1946, Rhodes House Library, Oxford, box 1, "Mitchell Papers."

120   With 8 March 1947 letter, Rhodes House Library, Oxford, box 1, "Mitchell Papers."

121   Colson, interview with author, fieldnotes (6 September 1990) held by author.

122   RLI secretary to all staff, 19 May 1947, Rhodes House Library, Oxford, box 1, "Mitchell Papers." The RLI is an unusual case of anthropologists routinely having access to each others' fieldnotes. See Roger Sanjek's discussion of fieldnotes and their place in the work of anthropologists, "On Ethnographic Validity" and "The Secret Life of Fieldnotes," in Roger Sanjek, ed., *Fieldnotes: The Makings of Anthropology* (Ithaca: Cornell University Press, 1990), 385–418 and 386–418.

123   Director Colson to all research officers, 7 November 1948, Rhodes House Library, Oxford, box 1, "Mitchell Papers."

124   Edited by E. Colson and M. Gluckman, (London: Published on behalf of the Rhodes Livingstone Institute, Northern Rhodesia by Oxford University Press, 1951).

125   "Report on Research, 1946–7. 16 November 1947," PRO, CO 927/64/2.

126   Mitchell, interview with author, fieldnotes (19 November 1990) held by author.

127   Mitchell, interview with author, fieldnotes (31 October 1990) held by author. Theoretical elements of Marxist analysis in Gluckman's work should not be exaggerated; Marxist materialism contributed to his work, but as Epstein recalled, "Max himself used to say he could not read Marx, only Engels" (personal communication with author).

128   Gluckman called for a greater attention to theory after he founded the department in Manchester, and the seminars became the testing ground for former RLI researchers' theoretical innovations.

129   The phrase appears in a letter from Mitchell to the RLI secretary, 17 March 1947, shortly after the first conference. (Rhodes House Library, Oxford, box 1, "Mitchell Papers.")

130   The stories were gathered from several interviews.

131   When Marwick and Mitchell wore shorts for the occasion of being introduced to the Provincial Commissioner of Southern Province, Gluckman told them, "You can't go and see the King's bloody representative dressed like that. Go and put on suits." (Marwick, personal communication with author.)

132   The *anthropological* academic community, however, was not dominated by this style. (Barnes, personal communication with author.) The element of South African pithiness in the RLI group, which is also reflected to a degree in their work, was pointed out to me by William

Beinart. On the courtliness and ritualistic character of colonial society there is much good recent literature. And on the gentrified nature of Northern Rhodesian settler society a good source is Robert Rotberg's biography of Sir Stewart Gore-Browne, *Black Heart: Gore-Browne and the Politics of Multiracial Zambia* (Berkeley: University of California Press, 1977). Although Gore-Browne was not a typical settler—having an aristocratic background and a personal fortune—he represented the ideal to which many would have aspired. (Epstein's comment is from a personal communication with the author.)

133 Gluckman to Evans-Pritchard, 6 July 1947, Rhodes House Library, Oxford, box 1, "Mitchell Papers."

134 Mitchell, interview with author, fieldnotes (27 November 1990) held by author.

135 Barnes, personal communication with author. With L. T. Hobhouse and G. C. Wheeler, Ginsburg had produced a quantitative analysis of all known information on the world's cultures, *The Material Culture and Social Institutions of the Simpler Peoples: An Essay on Correlation* (London: Chapman & Hall, 1915). See Kuklick, *Savage Within*.

136 Elizabeth Colson, personal communication.

137 Gluckman to CSSRC, 13 June 1947, PRO, CO 927/64/2.

138 The idea of getting his research officers eventual employment at universities because of the lack of pensions for RLI service appears in his agenda for the RLI trustees meeting, 16 November 1946, which also links this goal to their getting a write-up period in Oxford. (Barnes Papers, Cambridge, box 1 [or 201] "RLI Central Office, 1944–1948.") Years later, former RLI researchers who got subsequent posts in Britain found their pensions were reduced because the RLI had not been university-based at the time of their appointments. The UK Universities Superannuation Scheme (USS) refused to recognize the RLI despite its later adoption by the University of Zambia. In addition, the USS gave credit for years of military service in World War Two as equivalent to university service if there was no gap between discharge and a university post. Appointments at the RLI constituted a gap according to this ruling. (Barnes, personal communication with author.)

139 Gluckman to Secretary of Colonial Research Committee, 28 August 1947 (and additional correspondence and minutes in this file from July through October), PRO, CO 927/64/2.

140 Holleman spent his initial writing-up period in Cape Town with Schapera, because he preferred to be near his relatives there.

141 Mitchell, interview with author, fieldnotes (31 October 1990) held by author.

142 Mitchell came to the same conclusion in the list he made of his options in a letter of 3 June 1948 to Director Elizabeth Colson in which he prioritizes an academic job over renewal of his RLI contract, but recognizes that academic jobs are scarce. (Rhodes House Library, Oxford, box 1, "Mitchell Papers.")

143 John Hudson, interview with author, fieldnotes (3 November 1992) held by author.

144 "Report on Research, 1946–7, 16 November 1947, " (Gluckman to the Colonial Research Committee at Colonial Office), PRO, CO 927/64/2.

145 For just one example, see Hammond-Tooke's *Imperfect Interpreters*. For a sophisticated and historically contextualized use of the term, see George W. Stocking Jr., "Paradigmatic Traditions in the History of Anthropology," in Stocking, *The Ethnographer's Magic and Other Essays in the History of Anthropology* (Madison: University of Wisconsin Press, 1992), 342–61.

146 How appropriate this image is to the natural sciences has been the subject of much controversy, starting with the initial publication of Kuhn's *The Structure of Scientific Revolutions* (Chicago: University of Chicago Press, 1962). Kuhn today appears to embrace a more dynamic model. Evolutionary models of theory change have emerged since the 1980s; see Stephen Toulmin's *Human Understanding* (Oxford: Clarendon Press, 1972) for a particularly fine example. And one of the chief tenets of Kuhn's paradigm model — the notion of incommensurability, or the inability of scientists to communicate across paradigm shifts — has been undermined by much subsequent work; see Mario Biagioli's "The Anthropology of Incommensurability," in his *Galileo: Courtier: The Practice of Science in the Culture of Absolutism* (Chicago: University of Chicago Press, 1993; 211–44. It is also appropriate that anthropologists' current use of a Kuhnian model should be reconsidered in this history of the Manchester School, responsible for the development of network analysis. Network analysis has influenced current approaches to the history and sociology of science at least as thoroughly as Kuhn's approach.

147 "Staff conference report from G to CSSRC, 20 February 1947," PRO, CO 927/64/2.

148 "Report on Research, 1946–7, 16 November 1947," PRO, CO 927/64/2.

149 In a letter of 22 October 1948, Barnes explained to Betty Clarke at the Museum his views on the tribal map for his area: "I have taken the tribal affiliations on a political rather than an ethnic or ancestral lands basis. . . . I haven't the information to show what might be regarded as an ethnic affiliation, and indeed I don't think it is possible to identify any single ethnic affiliation for many of the villages under Ngoni chiefs." (Barnes Papers, Cambridge, box 5, "Official Letters.")

150 Mitchell observed of this period that "Gluckman rammed history down our throats," though this history must be understood in the Marxist sense of historical process, opposed to the earlier evolutionist or diffusionist styles of historical analysis. (Mitchell, interview with author, fieldnotes [27 November 1990] held by author.)

151 Mitchell, interview with author, fieldnotes (27 November 1990) held by author. Mitchell also emphasized the usefulness of the case study approach for looking at human behavior in real-life situations. This approach derived partly from legal models, but also had roots in Mitchell's social work background.

152 Hammond-Tooke, *Imperfect Interpreters*, 17

153 Macmillan, "Return to Malungwana Drift," 53, quoting Gluckman's "Analysis," 42 (Lusaka: Rhodes-Livingstone Institute, 1958 edition).

5. "A Lady and an American"

1 Robert Moffat at the Secretariat in Lusaka to Elizabeth Chilver, 15 December 1949, PRO, CO 927/64/4; A. L. Epstein, personal communication with author.

2 Colson, "From Livingstone to Lusaka, 1948–51," *African Social Research* 24 (1977): 302–3, 297–308.

3 E. Colson and M. Gluckman, eds. (Oxford: Oxford University Press, 1951).

4 Werbner, "The Manchester School in South-Central Africa," *Annual Review of Anthropology* 13 (1984): 158, 157–85.

5 Colson, "From Livingstone to Lusaka," 298–99.

6   Colson, "From Livingstone to Lusaka," 302.

7   Colson was, however, aware that discrimination made it more difficult for women anthropologists to get jobs and that she had not been allowed to do fieldwork in the Luapula area because she was a woman. (Colson, personal communication with author.)

8   An example of the latter is the still commonly asserted idea that homosexuality did not exist in Africa until introduced by Europeans. This is true in a sense; nothing like the Western idea of homosexuality existed precolonially in most of sub-Saharan Africa. Nevertheless, same-sex sexual practices did (and do) exist, as recent work is beginning to show.

9   See Nancy Leys Stepan, "Race and Gender: The Role of Analogy in Science," *Isis* 77 (1986): 261–77.

10 In general this point is correct. In the immediate postwar period and especially the 1950s, however, gender roles were exaggerated in the metropole, as well. The new emphasis on feminine dress and behavior and the desirability and responsibilities of motherhood formed part of a cultural campaign to get women out of the workplace so that there would be jobs for demobilized soldiers and a return to an idealized prewar normality. This 1950s context is relevant to the particular case of women in the field at the RLI, some of whom had experienced war work and the masculinizing of women's dress and behavior during the war in their home countries.

11 Settler opinion did not cause problems in areas where there were few of them. Some areas, such as Barotseland and Luapula, had no settler population, while others, such as the line-of-rail in Southern Province, the Copperbelt, and the tobacco-growing areas of Eastern Province, had relatively large numbers.

12 It is also possible she rode a horse in her fieldwork, though bicycles were more commonly used by the administration in eastern Northern Rhodesia and Nyasaland.

13 Helen Callaway, *Gender, Culture and Empire: European Women in Colonial Nigeria* (Oxford: Macmillan Press, 1987), 243–44.

14 Richard Brown, "Passages in the Life of a White Anthropologist: Max Gluckman in Northern Rhodesia," *Journal of African History* 20 (1979): 531, 525–41.

15 Joan Marwick, interview with author, fieldnotes (25 November 1992) held by author.

16 The slacks were much envied by local people, Colson recalled. (Personal communication with author.)

17 Some examples include essays in M. Rosaldo and L. Lamphere, eds., *Woman, Culture, and Society*, (Stanford: Stanford University Press, 1974); Manda Cesara, *Reflections of a Woman Anthropologist: No Hiding Place* (London: Academic Press, 1982); Ruth Behar and Deborah A. Gordon, eds., *Women Writing Culture* (Berkeley: University of California Press, 1995); and Edith Turner, "Changes in the Status of Senior Women Anthropologists After Feminist Revisions," paper for the Association for Feminist Anthropology, panel entitled "Through a Gendered Looking Glass: Women Doing Ethnography Before and After 1974," American Anthropological Association Meetings, 1995.

18 *A Feeling for the Organism: The Life and Work of Barbara McClintock* (San Francisco: W. H. Freeman, 1983).

19 Michael Roper and John Tosh, "Introduction: Historians and the Politics of Masculinity," in Roper and Tosh, eds., *Manful Assertions: Masculinities in Britain Since 1800* (London: Routledge, 1991), 1–24; 15, 2.

20 One need only look at the history of European concepts of biological sex to see the great variety of ideas that are possible concerning what physical differences truly make a difference.

21 Tony Larry Whitehead and Laurie Price, "Summary: Sex and the Fieldwork Experience," in Whitehead and Mary Ellen Conaway, *Self, Sex, and Gender in Cross-Cultural Fieldwork* (Urbana: University of Illinois Press, 1986), 289–304.

22 Alfred Simakando Chimuka, interview with author, fieldnotes (14 September 1992) held by author. RLI anthropologists paid for material-culture artifacts but did not usually pay for information. Most gave gifts, though not directly, for information, and they paid the local people who worked for them. Gwyn Prins criticizes Gluckman for paying for information and generally evaluates his fieldwork practices as producing suspect data, but given that Gluckman had numerous and diverse sources of information, in addition to paid informants, the case is not so simple as Prins makes it out to be. See Prins, *The Hidden Hippopotamus: Reappraisal in African History, The Early Colonial Experience in Western Zambia* (Cambridge: Cambridge University Press, 1980), 245.

23 Lukhero, interview with author, fieldnotes (27 February 1992) held by author. Barnes does not recall wearing women's clothing to the event. (Barnes, interview with author, fieldnotes [12 August 1993] held by author.) He and Lukhero were only allowed to attend part of the ceremony. (J. A. Barnes, personal communication with author.)

24 J. C. Chiwale, interview with author, fieldnotes (24 January 1992). Tweedie did a study of Bemba nutrition during April 1959 and July 1960, gathering food consumption data from February through March 1960, with additional work done by research assistants keeping income and expenditure accounts for one year for individuals included in the survey. Her work resulted in an unpublished thesis, "Change and Continuity in Bemba Society," (D. Phil., University of Oxford, 1966). See Megan Vaughan and Henrietta Moore, *Cutting Down Trees: Gender, Nutrition and Agricultural Change in the Northern Province of Zambia, 1890–1990* (London: James Currey, 1994), for discussion of her work, especially 64, 240, and note 16.

25 J. C. Chiwale, interview with author, fieldnotes (24 January 1992) held by author.

26 She was the daughter of a knighted Oxford professor of law, who served on the Viceregal Council, and granddaughter of a barrister and public servant. (Henrika Kuklick, *The Savage Within: The Social History of British Anthropology, 1885–1945* [Cambridge: Cambridge University Press, 1991], 318)

27 Audrey Richards, "The Rhodes-Livingstone Institute, 1933–38: An Experiment in Research," *African Social Research* 24 (1977): 277, 277–78.

28 This was despite the opposition that existed between some students of Malinowski and Evans-Pritchard. Although Richards identified herself with Malinowski and Gluckman identified himself with Evans-Pritchard, Gluckman was much readier than Evans-Pritchard to recognize that Richards's work had to be taken seriously. (Barnes, personal communication with author.)

29 For a more detailed account of her work, see Moore and Vaughan, *Cutting Down Trees*.

30 *Murder at Government House* (New York: Penguin, 1937). Brandeis may be an amalgam of Richards and Lorna Gore-Browne, who came from a prominent Jewish family in Britain. Other models probably contributed to Huxley's portrayal of this character, plus a good measure of the crime novelist's imagination.

31 Huxley, *Murder at Government House*, 145–47.

32 Huxley, *Murder at Government House*, 65. She concludes that it was not involved, and in the end a white settler turns out to be the culprit.

33 Gluckman advised them to turn away these queries by saying, "Sorry, I

can't help you. All these Africans look the same to me." (J. A. Barnes, personal communication with author.)

34 Interview with author, fieldnotes (18 July 1992) held by author.

35 P. B. Mushindo to Audrey Richards, 15 May 1969, Institute for African Studies, University of Zambia (IAS/UNZA), "RLI Manuscripts file." Mushindo referred to an anthropologist who visited in 1969. Richards had done her fieldwork in the mid-1930s and returned briefly in 1957. Mushindo's use of "he or she" was not unusual. Correspondence, research reports, and field notes of RLI anthropologists and their assistants contain frequent use of the construction "he or she," indicating an early attention to issues of gender. Mushindo later wrote *A Short History of the Bemba* (Lusaka: National Education Company of Zambia for the Institute of African Studies, University of Zambia, 1977).

36 See chapter 7 for a more detailed discussion of research assistants' motivations.

37 See George W. Stocking Jr., "The Ethnographer's Magic: Fieldwork in British Anthropology from Tylor to Malinowski," in Stocking, ed., *Observers Observed: Essays on Ethnographic Fieldwork* (Madison: University of Wisconsin Press, 1983), 100, 70–120, where Stocking discusses this contention of M. Wax that social parity is essential for good fieldwork (in "Tenting with Malinowski," *American Sociological Review* 47 [1972]: 1–13) in relation to Malinowski's fieldwork style.

38 *Cutting Down Trees*, 1. The Lozi treated Gluckman as an *induna*, which acknowledged both his age and seniority (in European society), as well as conforming with their tendency to treat all Europeans as chiefs — as demanded of them by most administrators and settlers. (Many of my interviewees commented on the difference in Gluckman's status in Barotseland and Zululand; in the latter he fitted in as a young man and was generally not treated as a chief.)

39 Elizabeth Colson, interview by author, fieldnotes (7 Septemper 1990) held by author. See *The Makah Indians: A Study of an Indian Tribe in Modern American Society* (Minneapolis: University of Minnesota Press, 1953).

40 Gluckman to Firth, 18 December 1944, PRO, CO 927/8/6.

41 RLI administrative secretary to Bush, Secretary for Native Affairs (n.d. but near 18 September 1950), Rhodes House, Oxford, "Mitchell Papers."

42 Gluckman to the Chief Secretary, Northern Rhodesia; National Ar-

chives of Zambia, Lusaka, SEC 1/127, vol. II. Gluckman had met the agricultural officer, John Hart, during the reconnaissance survey. Hart met Colson on her arrival in the field and took her to Chief Chepa's area. (Colson, interview with author, fieldnotes [28 March 1992] held by author.)

43 Rhodes House, Oxford, JCM 5/1, "Mitchell Papers."

44 Interview, with author, fieldnotes (28 March 1992) held by author.

45 Colson, interview with author, fieldnotes (28 March 1992) held by author.

46 Colson, interview with author, fieldnotes (18 July 1992) held by author. *Dona* derives from the Portuguese *doña*, meaning "lady."

47 Colson, *Marriage and Family among the Plateau Tonga of Northern Rhodesia* (Manchester: Manchester University Press, 1958), 266.

48 Mainza Chona, interview with author interview, fieldnotes (13 August 1992) held by author. The Tonga were, of course, aware that Colson was sexually female, but gender *roles* in any culture can be ambiguous even where physical sex is not.

49 Colson, interview with author, fieldnotes (28 March 1992) held by author.

50 Kaciente Chifumpu, interview with Lisa Cliggett, 29 August 1995, transcript held by Cliggett.

51 Mark Chona, interview with author, fieldnotes (13 August 1992) held by author.

52 Board of Trustees Minutes, 16 November 1946, "Mitchell Papers," Rhodes House, Oxford, JCM 3/3.

53 Board of Trustees minutes, 2 December 1946, "Mitchell Papers," Rhodes House, Oxford, JCM 3/3.

54 Board of Trustees minutes, 10 June 1947, "Mitchell Papers," Rhodes House, Oxford, JCM 3/3; and PRO, CO 927/64/2.

55 Richards declined because of the lack of scientific representation on the RLI's board of trustees (Richard Brown, "Anthropology and Colonial Rule: Godfrey Wilson and the Rhodes-Livingstone Institute, Northern Rhodesia," in *Anthropology and the Colonial Encounter*, ed. Talal Asad [New York: Humanities Press, 1973], 196; 173–97) and because she wanted to remain in Britain during the war (Audrey Richards, "The Rhodes-Livingstone Institute, 1933–38," *African Social Research* 24 [1977]: 277, 275–78).

56 Minute by Wilson, undated, 1947, PRO, CO 927/64/2; Richards to Wilson, 14 January 1948, PRO, CO 927/64/3.

57 Richards to Wilson, 14 January 1948, PRO, CO 927/64/3.

58 Ann Laura Stoler "Rethinking Colonial Categories: European Communities and the Boundaries of Rule," in *Colonialism and Culture*, ed. Nicholas B. Dirks (Ann Arbor: University of Michigan Press, 1992), 339–40, 319–52.

59 See David N. Livingstone, "Human Acclimatization: Perspectives on a Contested Field of Inquiry in Science, Medicine, and Geography," *History of Science* 25 (1987): 359–94.

60 Barnes, personal communication with author.

61 Lukhero, interview with author, fieldnotes (30 May 1991) held by author.

62 I. G. Cunnison, *The Luapula Peoples of Northern Rhodesia: Custom and History in Tribal Politics* (Manchester: Manchester University Press, 1959).

63 "Lunda, Obs, 16–11–48, White population Katabulwe." (Ian Cunnison's field notes, IAS/UNZA, "RLI Field Notes.") Cunnison took the entire Luapula River valley as his fieldsite, studying both the Northern Rhodesian and Belgian Congo sides of the river. Katabulwe was on the Belgian side.

64 See Ann L. Stoler's "Making Empire Respectable: the Politics of Race and Sexual Morality in Twentieth-century Colonial Cultures," *American Ethnologist* 16, no. 4 (1989): 634–60.

65 Cunnison's field notes, "African traders." IAS/UNZA, "RLI Field Notes."

66 Cunnison's field notes, IAS/UNZA, "RLI Field Notes."

67 Cunnison, interview with author, fieldnotes (3 August 1993) held by author.

68 "First Annexure to the Research Plan, December 1944, by the Director," 2. (Included in Firth's draft for CSSRC of RLI plan of research, 9 March 1945, PRO, CO 927/8/7.)

69 Barnes to Mitchell, 24 November 1946, "Mitchell Papers," Rhodes House Library, Oxford, JCM 4/1. Polish women refugees in Lusaka were considered prostitutes by British-descent Europeans, who, nevertheless, employed many of them as nursemaids. See Karen Tranberg Hansen, *Distant Companions: Servants and Employers in Zambia, 1900–1985* (Ithaca, N.Y.: Cornell University Press, 1989).

70 Stoler, "Rethinking Colonial Categories," 339.

71 Barnes to Mitchell, 24 November 1946, "Mitchell Papers," Rhodes House, Oxford, JCM 4/1.

72 The hierarchy was expressed consciously, as well as unconsciously as in a group of photos in the South African magazine *Libertas*, arranged with a British official and an Afrikaner farmer at the top, an educated Zulu and a white Portuguese below them, and a Swazi and a Basuto in native dress below them. ("The Post-War Africa," *Libertas* 5, no. 3, [February 1945]: 21, 18–21.)

73 *The Spirit and the Drum: A Memoir of Africa* (Tucson: University of Arizona Press, 1987), 54.

74 Interview with author, fieldnotes (20 September 1993) held by author.

75 No full-scale study of whites was carried out by any RLI researchers, though many of them did detailed research on administrators and their role in rural and urban areas and included this in their published work. See A. L. Epstein, *Politics in an Urban African Community* (Manchester: Manchester University Press, 1958). J. F. Holleman, earlier attached to the RLI, did considerable work on white administrators later in his career when working for the Rhodesian government. See his *Chief, Council and Commissioner: Some Problems of Government in Rhodesia* (London: Oxford University Press, 1968). He and Simon Biesheuvel, a South African industrial psychologist, also did a significant study of white miners on the Copperbelt under the auspices of the National Institute for Personnel Research and the Institute for Social Research of the University of Natal — *White Mine Workers in Northern Rhodesia, 1959–60* (Leiden: Afrika-Studiecentrum, 1973).

76 11 March 1949, PRO, CO 927/64/4.

77 Minute, 15 March 1949, PRO, CO 927/64/4.

78 18 March 1949, PRO, CO 927/64/4.

79 Minute to Gibbins from Wilson, 11 August 1948, PRO, CO 927/64/3.

80 Report from Gluckman to the CSSRC, PRO, CO 927/64/2.

81 See correspondence and minutes in PRO, CO 927/64/2, and PRO, CO 927/64/3.

82 Minute to Gibbins from Wilson, 11 August 1948, PRO, CO 927/64/3. See also the minutes in PRO, CO 927/64/4.

83 Colson, "From Livingstone to Lusaka," 298.

84 Letter to Audrey Richards, 22 July 1949, PRO, CO 927/64/4.

85 Colson to Wilson, 10 March and 23 March 1948; and notes of a discussion, 17 July 1948. (PRO, CO 927/64/3.)

86 PRO, CO 927/64/2.

87 "We are getting far less, when ready to start work, than Makerere

which is still all on paper," Gluckman exclaimed in a letter to Carstairs at the Colonial Office, 25 October 1945. (National Archives of Zambia, Lusaka, SEC 1/127, vol. II, 58/1.)

88 PRO, CO 927/64/3.

89 Minute, 11 August 1948, PRO, CO 927/64/3. A. G. H. Gardener-Brown to Colson, 6 November 1948, National Archives of Zambia, Lusaka, SEC 1/128. On the research side, Firth believed the "transfer of the Institute nearer to the Copper Belt would present practical advantages." (Confidential draft of minutes of the second meeting 25 October 1949, PRO, CO 927/63/3)

90 Minute, 11 December 1948; telegram to Governor of Northern Rhodesia from Secretary of State for the Colonies, 16 December 1948. (PRO, CO 927/64/3.)

91 Extract from "East Africa and Rhodesia," 8 September 1949, No. 1301: "University Site Fixed"; telegram from Gov. Rennie to Lambert, Secretary of State for the Colonies 15 September 1949; letter from Rennie to Lambert 14 September 1949. (PRO, CO 927/64/4) During much of this debate, the CSSRC favored the Salisbury location while the RLI Board of Trustees favored Lusaka, though both wavered at times. (PRO, CO 927/64/4.)

92 Letter from Colson enclosed in letter from Governor Rennie to Lambert, 14 September 1949, PRO, CO 927/64/4.

93 Colson, "From Livingstone to Lusaka," 304–05.

94 "Malinowski's Sociological Theories," *Rhodes-Livingstone Papers* 16 (1949): 27–28.

95 Letter of 28 August 1949, "Mitchell Papers," Rhodes House, Oxford, JCM 5/1.

6. Atop the Central African Volcano

1 Ulf Hannerz, *Exploring the City* (New York: Columbia University Press, 1980). See also Roger Sanjek's "Urban Anthropology in the 1980s: A World View," *Annual Review of Anthropology* 19 (1990): 151–86.

2 Richard Werbner's account of their accomplishments in the area of theory, "The Manchester School in South-Central Africa," *Annual Review of Anthropology* 13 (1984):157–85.

3 *Tribal Cohesion in a Money Economy: A Study of the Mambwe People of Northern Rhodesia* (Manchester: Manchester University Press, 1958).

4 *The Politics of Kinship: A Study in Social Manipulation among the Lakeside Tonga of Nyasaland* (Manchester: Manchester University Press, 1964).

5 *Schism and Continuity in an African Society: A Study of Ndembu Village Life* (Manchester: Manchester University Press, 1957).

6 *Copper Town: Changing Africa, the Human Situation on the Rhodesian Copperbelt* (New York: Harper and Row, 1962). Roger Sanjek, in "Anthropology's Hidden Colonialism: Assistants and their Ethnographers," *Anthropology Today* 9, no. 2 (April 1993): 13–18, mentions Phiri.

7 Karen Tranberg Hansen, "After Copper Town: The Past in the Present in Urban Zambia," *Journal of Anthropological Research* 47 (1991): 441–56.

8 L. H. Gann, "Ex Africa: An Africanist's Intellectual Autobiography," *Journal of Modern African Studies* 31, no. 3 (1993): 482, 477–98. Gann falls into the category of colonialist historian, whose work has been seen by subsequent Africanists as showing only the positive side of colonial rule while neglecting the African perspective. Although this evaluation is justified, Gann nevertheless pioneered the use of local sources rather than simply relying on British archival sources and did more detailed work on the nature and diversity of white colonial society than subsequent historians have done until quite recently. See his *The Birth of a Plural Society: The Development of Northern Rhodesia under the British South Africa Company, 1894–1914* (Manchester: Manchester University Press, 1958) and *A History of Northern Rhodesia: Early Days to 1953* (London: Chatto and Windus, 1964).

9 RLI Circular Newsletter No. 7, July 1955.

10 Saul Dubow, *Racial Segregation and the Origins of Apartheid in South Africa, 1919–36* (Oxford: St. Antony's College/Macmillan, 1989), 56. This policy also conveniently moved the social costs of labor to the rural areas, to which sick, aged, or redundant workers returned.

11 Dubow, *Racial Segregation*, 16–17.

12 Dubow, *Racial Segregation*, 5, 34.

13 Saul Dubow, "Black Hamlet: A Case of 'Psychic Vivisection'," in *The Societies of Southern Africa in the 19th and 20th Centuries*, vol. 19

(London: University of London, Institute of Commonwealth Studies, 1993), 94, 80–105.

14 Dubow, "Black Hamlet," 80.

15 "Rooiyard: A Sociological Survey of an Urban Native Slum Yard," *Rhodes-Livingstone Papers* 13, 1948.

16 Henrika Kuklick *The Savage Within: The Social History of British Anthropology, 1885–1945* (Cambridge: Cambridge University Press, 1991), 140.

17 Godfrey Wilson, "The Economics of Detribalization in Northern Rhodesia," parts I and II, *Rhodes-Livingstone Papers* 5 and 6 (1941) and (1942).

18 *The Two Nations: Aspects of the Development of Race Relations in the Rhodesias and Nyasaland*, Richard Gray, Institute of Race Relations (London: Oxford University Press, 1960), 214. Batson used a team of surveyors from the University of Cape Town. His antecedents and career at the University of Cape Town are discussed in Howard Phillips' *The University of Cape Town, 1918–1948: The Formative Years* (Cape Town: University of Cape Town Press, 1993), 278–80. Mitchell had met Batson and read his published work during the RLI team's course work in Cape Town. (Mitchell, interview with author, fieldnotes [24 November 1992] held by author.)

19 See Michael O'Shea's *Missionaries and Miners* for a general history of the Catholic Church missions and the beginnings of their work on the Copperbelt. (Ndola: Mission Press, 1986.)

20 Kuklick, *Savage Within*, 101–2.

21 Jane L. Parpart, *Labor and Capital on the African Copperbelt* (Philadelphia, Pa.: Temple University Press, 1983), 65.

22 Gray, *The Two Nations*, discusses Ibbotson's survey (210) and Moore's (215).

23 Parpart, *Labor and Capital*, 61. She argues that workers' growing class consciousness had to do with the lack of importance of ethnic identity or status for determining housing and employment on the mines.

24 Johannes Louw, interview with author, fieldnotes (20 April 1993) held by author.

25 See Kuklick, *Savage Within*, 174–77.

26 Johannes Louw, "This is Thy Work: A Contextual History of Applied Psychology and Labour in South Africa" (Ph.D. diss., University of Amsterdam, 1986), 140–41.

27 Louw, "This is Thy Work."

28 J. F. Holleman and Simon Biesheuvel, *White Mine Workers in Northern Rhodesia, 1959–60* (Leiden: Afrika-Studiecentrum, 1973). On the Shona, see J. F. Holleman, "The Pattern of Hera Kinship," *Rhodes-Livingstone Papers* 17 (1949); and *Shona Customary Law* (Cape Town: Oxford University Press, 1952).

29 Studies were also done of Livingstone and Lusaka, so that all the Northern Rhodesian line-of-rail towns were covered. Later Salisbury, Southern Rhodesia; Blantyre, Nyasaland; and a few other towns were covered by the poverty datum line studies.

30 See George Chauncey Jr., "The Locus of Reproduction: Women's Labour in the Zambian Copperbelt, 1927–1953," *Journal of Southern African Studies* 7, no. 2 (1991): 135–64. See Karen Tranberg Hansen, *Distant Companions: Servants and Employers in Zambia, 1900–1985* (Ithaca, N.Y.: Cornell University Press, 1989) on the place of domestic workers in relation to other workers.

31 See A. L. Epstein's *Ethos and Identity: Three Studies in Ethnicity* (London: Tavistock Publications, 1978), especially "Military Ethos and Ethnic Ranking on the Copperbelt," 113–38.

32 See Parpart, *Labor and Capital*, 39, for the use of Nyasaland Africans as clerks.

33 See Megan Vaughan and Henrietta Moore, *Cutting Down Trees: Gender, Nutrition and Agricultural Change in the Northern Province of Zambia, 1890–1990* (London: James Currey, 1994), 49.

34 This observation arose unsolicited from the numerous informal interviews I conducted with Copperbelt residents and retired miners in Luanshya and Ndola in 1991 and 1992.

35 "Better working and living conditions . . . drew Northern Rhodesians to Union Miniere, which employed some 10,500 Northern Rhodesians in 1929. Union Miniere's shift to stabilized labor in 1926 had been accompanied by a dramatic upgrading of living conditions for their workers. By the end of the decade African workers in Elisabethville enjoyed the best food and housing in central Africa." (Parpart, *Labor and Capital*, 32.)

36 Parpart, *Labor and Capital*, 32.

37 The Zambian government would also try to convince the unemployed to leave the cities much later, in the 1980s.

38 Helmuth Heisler, *Urbanisation and the Government of Migration: The*

Interrelation of Urban and Rural Life in Zambia (London: C. Hurst & Co., 1974), 104 ff.

39 See William Cronon's *Nature's Metropolis: Chicago and the Great West* (New York: Norton, 1991) for a discussion of boosterism in the growth of American cities on the midwestern frontier. In the cases discussed by Cronon, however, boosters expected the cities they promoted to be permanent.

40 "The Copperbelt of Northern Rhodesia," Zambia Consolidated Copper Mines Archives, Ndola, Zambia.

41 See Peter Fraenkel, *Wayaleshi* (London: Weidenfeld and Nicolson, 1959), for descriptions of white society on the Copperbelt. In an interview, J. F. Holleman described this society on the eve of independence as "a cockeyed society," where miners with an average of seven years education could earn "as much money as a South African professor and [have] everything handed to them — low cost housing, *free* health care. Maybe [this was] *the* most affluent society on the face of the earth." (interview with author, fieldnotes [6 November 1993] held by author).

42 For an analysis of the economic and political reasons underlying the drive for federation and the unequal economic benefits that resulted — Northern Rhodesian copper profits and Nyasaland labor reserves enabling Southern Rhodesian industrial development — see Prosser Gifford, "Misconceived Dominion: The Creation and Disintegration of Federation in British Central Africa," in Gifford and Roger Louis, eds., *The Transfer of Power in Africa: Decolonization, 1940–60* (New Haven, Conn.: Yale Univeristy Press, 1982), 387–416.

43 See M. W. Swanson, "The Sanitation Syndrome: Bubonic Plague and Urban Native Policy in the Cape Colony, 1900–1909," *Journal of African History* 18, no. 3 (1977): 387–410; Philip Curtin, "Medical Knowledge and Urban Planning in Tropical Africa," *American Historical Review* 90, no. 3 (1985): 594–613; and Susan Parnell, "Creating Racial Privilege: The Origins of South African Public Health and Town Planning Legislation," *Journal of Southern African Studies* 19, no. 3 (1993): 471–88. My own current research on the health services in the Copperbelt towns indicates that similar concerns motivated public health interventions and the development of social services for Africans.

44 Dubow, *Racial Segregation*, 123.

45 Brown speculates about the mines' support for the RLI as follows: "The big capitalist interests of Northern Rhodesia were, it is clear, doubtful

of the value of independently conducted social research and yet were willing, after an initial show of reluctance, to contribute to it; and this remained the pattern throughout the colonial period. The reason for this perhaps lies in their wish to retain good relations with the political authorities in London and Lusaka. In paying for research they were not hiring handmaidens, but were paying a form of hidden taxation by falling in with the expressed wishes of the colonial secretary and the governor of the territory in which they operated. In this way, they may well have hoped to help prolong the extremely favourable conditions under which the BSA Co. and the copper companies existed in Northern Rhodesia." ("Anthropology and Colonial Rule: Godfrey Wilson and the Rhodes-Livingstone Institute, Northern Rhodesia," in *Anthropology and the Colonial Encounter*, ed. Talal Asad (New York: Humanities Press, 1973), 184–85, 173–97.) Brown also mentions the growing public criticism of the mine royalties and Young's secret inquiries into their legality.

46 For a history of labor relations on the Copperbelt see Elena Berger, *Labour, Race and Colonial Rule: The Copperbelt from 1924 to Independence* (Oxford: Clarendon Press, 1974).

47 "Sir Roy Welensky, Obituary," *The Times*, 6 December 1991.

48 Robin Short, *African Sunset* (London: Johnson, 1973), 119–20.

49 A. L. Epstein, *Politics in an Urban African Community* (Manchester: Manchester University Press, 1958), 24.

50 Bob Hitchcock, *Bwana Go Home*, (London: Hale, 1974), 82. "Munt" was a derogatory term that whites used for Africans, derived from *umuntu*, the Bantu term for "person."

51 Heissler, *Urbanisation*, 9.

52 Heissler, *Urbanisation*, 1. Although these administrators may have preferred precontact technologies in their vision of rural development, the technical officers who directed agricultural development schemes often recommended modern Western agricultural practices and technologies for "improving farmers" — hybrid varieties, fertilizer, ploughs (though not usually tractors), and the practice of contouring made popular in the West during the Dustbowl period.

53 Frederick Cooper, *On the African Waterfront: Urban Disorder and the Transformation of Work in Colonial Mombasa* (New Haven, Conn.: Yale University Press, 1987), 257.

54 Frederick Cooper, *Decolonization and African Society* (Cambridge: Cambridge University Press, 1996).

55 Parpart, *Labor and Capital*, 35. The nature of the ore body at Roan also determined need for a skilled, and thus a more stabilized, work-force, according to Parpart, though the South African-owned company, Rhokana, whenever possible tried to follow the migrant labor tradition familiar to its managers from the Rand (36–37).

56 Parpart, *Labor and Capital*, 44.

57 Parpart, *Labor and Capital*, 39, 45.

58 Parpart, *Labor and Capital*, 40–43.

59 Cooper, *On the African Waterfront*, 250.

60 Cooper, *On the African Waterfront*, 255.

61 Audrey Richards, "The Rhodes-Livingstone Institute: An Experiment in Research, 1933–38," *African Social Research* 24 (1977): 275, 275–78. Brown, "Anthropology and Colonial Rule," argues that the riots "did little immediately to forward Young's plans," despite the Governor's revival of his institute scheme in his review of the Copperbelt problem. "What made the difference was the arrival at the colonial office of W. Ormsby-Gore (later Lord Harlech), who made it clear that he approved of Young's scheme and wished the appeal for funds to go ahead even though the permanent officials still counselled delay until the publication of Hailey's survey" (180).

62 Parpart, *Labor and Capital*, 55.

63 Chauncey, "The Locus of Reproduction."

64 "Mourning Ceremony of Chief Kasembe. Recorded by I. Kalima," in Ian Cunnison's private papers. Kalima was allowed to observe the ceremony only after he convinced Tuba and Musumbulwa that Mitchell was the senior officer over Cunnison and, therefore, presumably had a good reason to want to know about an urban ceremony rather than only about the "pure" rural one.

65 See Martin Chanock, *Law, Custom and Social Order: The Colonial Experience in Malaŵi and Zambia* (Cambridge: Cambridge University Press, 1985).

66 Cooper, *Decolonization and African Society*, 18–19.

67 Governor Rennie used this term when trying to convince the CSSRC to fund Colson's research plan in 1948. (Minute from Gibbins to Wilson, CSSRC, 8 November 1948, PRO, CO 927/64/3.)

68 Board of Trustees, Minutes of a Meeting held 14 December 1944, PRO, CO 927/8/6.

69 Topics for the CSSRC Meeting held 23 August 1946, PRO, CO 927/8/7.

70 Colson, "From Livingstone to Lusaka, 1948–51," *African Social Re-*

search 24 (1977): 294, 297–308. Both Wilson's and Gluckman's political problems may have had the character of "archetypal" experiences
for later RLI anthropologists (discussed in chapter 3). See George W.
Stocking Jr., "Philanthropoids and Vanishing Cultures," in Stocking,
ed., *Objects and Others: Essays on Museums and Material Culture*
(Madison: University of Wisconsin Press, 1985), 112–45, for a discussion of such a case in 1931, when Malinowski and Oldham failed to
support a young anthropologist, Paul Kirchoff, against accusations by
the Colonial Office that he was a communist agitator (136–37). In the
1950s Welensky himself told Gluckman he would not be permitted to
return to Northern Rhodesia. (Elizabeth Colson, personal communication with author.)

71 "The Director reported that he had been consulted by Mr. Rheinalt-
Jones, Adviser to the Anglo-American Corporation on African Welfare, about the Institute's finances. Mr. Jones had said he would suggest
that the Corporation give the Institute a capital gift of 5,000 and 1,000
a year for five years, and also 5,000 for four years for a sociological and
sociogeographic study of the Copperbelt." (Board of Trustees Minutes
for the Meeting on 25 August 1947, PRO, CO 927/64/2.)

72 See his "Juridical Techniques and the Judicial Process: A Study in African Customary Law," *Rhodes-Livingstone Papers* 23, 1954.

73 J. A. Barnes, personal communication with author.

74 Mitchell, interview with author, fieldnotes (24 November 1992) held
by author.

75 "The Kalela Dance," *Rhodes-Livingstone Papers* 27, 1956.

76 Mitchell, interview with author, fieldnotes (27 November 1990).

77 Mitchell to Colson, 29 August 1950 and her response, 1 September
1950, "Mitchell Papers," Rhodes House, Oxford, JCM 1/2.

78 Mitchell to the RLI administrative secretary, 19 October 1950, "Mitchell Papers," Rhodes House, Oxford, JCM 1/2; and administrative secretary to Mitchell, 2 May 1951 (JCM 1/3).

79 Mitchell, interview with author, fieldnotes (24 November 1992) held
by author; Mitchell, "The Kalela Dance," vii.

80 Colson, personal communication with author. See J. L. Moreno, *Who
Shall Survive? Foundations of Sociometry, Group Psychotherapy and
Sociodrama* (Washington, D.C.: Nervous and Mental Disease Publica-
tions Company, 1934), and George Lundberg, *Social Research*, 2d ed.
(New York: Greenwood, 1968). Chicago School precedents are dis-
cussed at length by Hannerz, in *Exploring the City*.

81 Mitchell, interview with author, fieldnotes (24 November 1992) held by author.

82 Mitchell to Colson, 28 May 1951, "Mitchell Papers," Rhodes House Oxford, JCM 1/3.

83 Mitchell, interview with author, fieldnotes (24 November 1992) held by author.

84 Mitchell to administrative secretary, 5 June 1951, "Mitchell Papers," Rhodes House, Oxford, JCM 1/3.

85 The research assistants' work and careers are discussed in greater detail in chapter 7.

86 Letter to Barnes, 17 December 1950, "Mitchell Papers," Rhodes House, Oxford, JCM 4/1.

87 Letter to Barnes, 17 December 1950, "Mitchell Papers," Rhodes House, Oxford, JCM 4/1.

88 Mitchell, interview with author, fieldnotes (24 November 1992) held by author.

89 See chapter 4 on the assistants' work.

90 Mitchell to Moss, the director of research at the Social Survey Central Office of Information in London, 26 February 1953, Institute for African Studies, University of Zambia (IAS/UNZA) "RLI Management Files."

91 Mitchell, interview with author, fieldnotes (24 November 1992) held by author. Much of the data remains unanalyzed to this day.

92 Barnes to Mitchell, 6 August 1951, reporting on a letter from Lukhero, "Mitchell Papers," Rhodes House, Oxford, JCM 4/1.

93 Epstein had already acquired a degree in law from Queen's University, Belfast. After service in the Navy during the war, he saw an advertisement for a CSSRC research job requiring experience in law. This led to a scholarship for a preparatory year at the LSE where Arthur Phillips, crown counsel for Kenya, supervised him in law and Audrey Richards in anthropology. (Epstein, interview with author, fieldnotes [1 December 1990] held by author.

94 Epstein, interview with author, fieldnotes (1 December 1990) held by author. He had been exposed to the work of Morris Ginsberg while working as a military camp librarian in Ceylon, though Ginsberg's sociology would have given few clues to organizing empirical work.

95 Epstein, interview with author, fieldnotes (1 December 1990) held by author. This group took on a political character very quickly and while Epstein was away split up over the question of whether Simon Zukas

should become its secretary. (Epstein to Mitchell, 8 August 1951, "Mitchell Papers," Rhodes House, Oxford, JCM 23/4.)

96 Hortense Powdermaker also shared Mitchell's house with Epstein during her year-long study of mass communications and attitudes on the Copperbelt. See her *Coppertown: Changing Africa* (New York: Harper and Row, 1962) and her account of her fieldwork, *Stranger and Friend: The Way of an Anthropologist* (New York: Norton, 1966).

97 Epstein, interview with author, November 1990. See Fraenkel, *Wayaleshi*, for a description of the soap opera. Siteke Mwale, a friend of Epstein and member of the Drama Club, described the anthropologist as being interested in the plays because of the "conflict of cultures, the effects of Westernization and the political aspects of the African response" that they revealed. (Interview with author, fieldnotes [16 April 1992] held by author.)

98 Epstein, interview with author, fieldnotes (1 December 1990) held by author. Epstein also did quantitative work where circumstances made it possible to gather statistics despite the ban on the survey in the mine areas. See, for example, his paper with Mitchell, "Power and Prestige among Africans in Northern Rhodesia: An Experiment," *Proceedings and Transactions of the Rhodesia Scientific Association* 45 (1957): 13–26; and other studies mentioned in Epstein, *Politics in an Urban African Community*.

99 RLI Circular Newsletters no. 7, August 1953 and no. 6, April 1955, Rhodes House, Oxford, uncatalogued Mitchell Papers. Her other assistants who also joined the team were Hosiah Ng'wane and P. J. Mwamba. They joined it in April 1955, making it large enough to divide into Bemba-speaking and Nyanja-speaking teams, the first, under Senior Assistant Katilungu, going to Watson's fieldsite to do a survey of the Lungu area, while the other, under Senior Assistant Tikili, went to Fort Jameson in Eastern Province to do a survey of the town.

100 RLI Circular Newsletter no. 6, July 1953, Rhodes House, Oxford, uncatalogued Mitchell Papers.

101 Ninth Conference of Research Officers, March 1955 (RLI internal report, included with the RLI Circular Newsletters), Rhodes House, Oxford, uncatalogued Mitchell Papers.

102 Mitchell to Colson, n. d., but near 20 March 1951, "Mitchell Papers,"

Rhodes House, Oxford, JCM 1/3. Epstein had also been asked to lecture informally on sociology by some Africans at Ndola, including the headmaster of Kabushi, who offered the use of a classroom at the school for one of the sessions. (Epstein, interview with author, fieldnotes [1 December 1990].)

103 Increasing unemployment due to an economic downturn in the mid-1950s helped to fuel stronger urban protest and provide a field for renewed political activity. See Cherry Gertzel and Morris Szeftel, "Politics in an African Urban Setting: The Role of the Copperbelt in the Transition to the One-Party State, 1964–73," in Gertzel, Baylies, and Szeftel, eds., *The Dynamics of the One Party State in Zambia* (Manchester: Manchester University Press, 1984), 122.

104 The phrase heading this section, "Anthropology and the Struggle for the City," is borrowed from Frederick Cooper, ed., *The Struggle for the City: Migrant Labor, Capital, and the State in Urban Africa* (Beverly Hills, Calif.: Sage Publications, 1983).

105 Parpart, *Labor and Capital*, 39.

106 Monica Wilson, "The First Three Years, 1938–41," *African Social Research* 24 (1977): 279–84, 279.

107 Epstein, interview with author, fieldnotes (1 December 1990) held by author.

108 Epstein, interview with author, fieldnotes (1 December 1990) held by author. Epstein's behavior may have led to Kenneth Kaunda's positive assessment of anthropologists as people who helpfully acted as informants for Congress. (Brown, "Anthropology and Colonial Rule," 194.) At the time of Epstein's research, Kaunda was a member of the Northern Rhodesian ANC, though he would later split the party to create UNIP and become Zambia's first president.

109 Mitchell to administrative secretary, 23 August 1951, "Mitchell Papers," Rhodes House, Oxford, JCM 1/3.

110 "Circular No. 4, To Research Officers," May 1953, "Mitchell Papers," Rhodes House, Oxford, JCM 2/2.

111 Simon Katilungu "Report on Work during Period 23rd March to 17th April 1953," Broken Hill, 18 April 1953, "Mitchell Papers," Rhodes House, Oxford, JCM 24/3.

112 Simon Zukas, interview with author, fieldnotes (25 October 1992) held by author. The government imprisoned him in Livingstone rather than Ndola for fear local Africans would rise up in protest. (Siteke

Mwale, interview with author, fieldnotes [16 April 1992] held by author.)

113 "Confidential Circular No. 3, To Research Officers," April 1953, "Mitchell Papers," Rhodes House, Oxford, JCM 2/1.

114 Gertzel, et al., eds., *The Dynamics of the One Party State,* 123.

115 Gertzel, et al., *The Dynamics of the One Party State,* 125. Michael Burawoy, in *The Colour of Class on the Zambian Copper Mines: From African Advancement to Zambianization* (Manchester: Manchester University Press, 1972), explores the problematic relationship between mine labor's aspirations and national politicians' goals in the period immediately after independence.

116 Zukas, interview with author, fieldnotes (25 October 1992) held by author.

117 See James Ferguson "Mobile Workers, Modernist Narratives: A Critique of the Historiography of Transition on the Zambian Copperbelt. Part One," *Journal of Southern African Studies (JSAS)* 16, no. 3 (1990), and "Part Two," *JSAS* 16, no. 4 (1990); see also Hugh Macmillan's response, "The Historiography of Transition on the Zambian Copperbelt—Another View," *JSAS* 19, no. 4 (1993): 681–712. Ferguson's recent book, *Expectations of Modernity: Myths and Meanings of Urban Life on the Zambian Copperbelt* (Berkeley: University of California Press, 1999), is not likely to be the last word on the subject.

7. Africanizing Anthropology

1 I interviewed or corresponded with some of the researchers and affiliates from this period (Peter Rigby, David Bettison, Raymond Apthorpe) and a number of the students who did vacation work for the RLI (David Phiri, Edward Shamwana, Jacob Mwanza, Lyson Tembo, Peter Siwo). The names of others are drawn from articles written by Fosbrooke and White respectively, "From Lusaka to Salisbury, 1956–60" and "Interregna, 1955–56 and 1960–62," *African Social Research* 24 (1977): 319–26, 327–30. I also interviewed some members of the urban survey team and a number of the rural assistants.

2 N. S. Carey Jones, Assistant Auditor, Northern Rhodesia Government, "Report on the Accounts of the Rhodes-Livingstone Institute, Livingstone," 14 August 1942, National Archives of Zambia, Lu-

saka, RC 1385 (61/2). The practice was officially ended at this Board of Trustees meeting.

3 Many of the RLI studies, both rural and urban, took account of the development of new organizational forms, including the political. Two of the most pertinent studies for this chapter are Epstein's *Politics in an Urban African Community* (Manchester: Manchester University Press, 1958), and Peter Harries-Jones's *Freedom and Labour: Mobilization and Political Control on the Zambian Copperbelt* (Oxford: Blackwell, 1975), based on work done in the run-up to independence in 1964. Religious innovation and its relationship to class and politics also found expression in a number of later Manchester School studies, notably George Bond's *The Politics of Change in a Zambian Community* (Chicago: Chicago University Press, 1976) and Norman Long's *Social Change and the Individual: A Study of the Social and Religious Responses to Innovation in a Zambian Rural Community* (Manchester: Manchester University Press, 1968).

4 The factors that have prevented the social sciences and humanities in African universities from developing a uniquely African perspective have been cogently discussed by Mubanga Kashoki in "Indigenous Scholarship in African Universities: The Human Factor," in Hussein Fahim, ed., *Indigenous Anthropology in Non-Western Countries* (Durham, N.C.: Carolina Academic Press, 1982). Their Eurocentric elements may have been one of the reasons these academic fields did not draw African scholars after independence, as has been repeatedly stated in the critical literature on colonial anthropology. This argument, however, could be as easily applied to the fields that proved to be popular to scholars in developing countries — for example, economics, political science, engineering, medicine, and the agricultural sciences. As Kashoki points out, the career structures of African universities, the focus on topics relevant to development rather than to pushing the boundaries of knowledge, the denigration of African indigenous knowledge, emphasis on teaching and lack of funding for research, and the demands of new governments for educated people to fill administrative posts have been the most important factors in stifling new African scholarly perspectives. My own research suggests that the RLI's assistants did not pursue sociology/anthropology as an academic career for two main reasons. The older research assistants and those involved first in rural research for individual anthropologists had families to support and were unable to go back to finish secondary school

or start university education by the time they had some experience of anthropological work. They were also in great demand for nonacademic jobs in the mines and government both before and after independence. The Munali School students who did vacation work for the RLI, for the most part, went on to get degrees in the fields that were seen as more useful to developing countries. And few of them who aspired to academic careers remained in universities, being instead drawn into posts in the civil service, industry, and politics.

5   Former research assistants often mentioned this factor in my interviews with them.

6   Henry Fosbrooke, "From Lusaka to Salisbury," 321.

7   The role of research assistants in anthropology is only beginning to be explored by scholars. See Sanjek, "Anthropology's Hidden Colonialism: Assistants and their Ethnographers," *Anthropology Today* 9, no. 2 (1993): 13–18.

8   Prins translates *Makapweka* as "the recklessly generous giver." (*The Hidden Hippopotamus: Reappraisal in African History, The Early Colonial Experience in Western Zambia* [Cambridge: Cambridge University Press, 1980], 247.) During the main period of my own research in Zambia (1991–1992) and in subsequent visits in 1995 and 1996, I asked a wide variety of Lozi speakers both in Lusaka and in Western Province to translate this term for me, without initially telling them why I was interested. Some in Western Province immediately recognized it as Gluckman's nickname, but many more there and in Lusaka did not. None translated it in a way that would suggest a pejorative connotation or a sense that the person referred to was reckless. It may, nevertheless, have been subtly critical. The most common interpretations included "some one who gives more than expected" or "everything you could want," or simply "Father Christmas." A siLozi-language radio program after independence that featured generous prizes also used the name, according to one informant. Near Katongo, the site of Gluckman's camp, people recognized both "Dr Gluckman" and "Makapweka" as Gluckman's names and said that they had been the first to give him the nickname. The local residents called me "mwana wa Gluckman" when I arrived for my first visit to Katongo. This means "child of Gluckman" and referred to my interest in what he had done there, not to an actual relationship they believed I had to him, since the local *induna*, Nawala, had explained that I was a historian and not a relative of Gluckman's.

As I was leaving the first time, the *induna* told me that I should pay a small amount of money to each of the people who talked with me, and after I did so, they thanked me and called me "mwana wa Makapweka." I do not speak siLozi and have not been able to make a more thorough investigation than this.

9 Terence Ranger, personal communication with author.

10 Jacob Mwanza, interview with author, fieldnotes (10 March 1992) held by author. RLI anthropologists recognized their dependence on assistants, particularly in the early stages of fieldwork when the research assistant might be necessary to "redeem" the researcher's work. (Barnes to Mitchell, 20 December 1951, "Mitchell Papers," Rhodes House, Oxford, JCM 4/1.)

11 Even earlier, European explorers relied on the cultural, linguistic, and geographical guidance of African assistants. A number of such Africans worked for more than one European explorer, shaping their travels and perhaps also their perceptions of Africa. See Donald Simpson's *Dark Companions: The African Contribution to the European Exploration of East Africa* (London: Elek, 1975).

12 See chapter 1. Also see James Clifford's discussion of Turner and Muchona, in "On Ethnographic Authority" (Gifford, ed., *The Predicament of Culture: Twentieth-Century Ethnography, Literature, and Art* [Cambridge: Harvard University Press, 1988], 49, 21–54): "a long list of distinguished anthropologists have described the indigenous 'ethnographers' with whom they shared, to some degree, a distanced, analytic, even ironic view of custom. These individuals became valued informants because they understood, often with real subtlety, what an *ethnographic* attitude toward culture entailed."

13 Jacques Chileya Chiwale, a Lunda, was born in Ngoma village in Luapula Province. He worked as a typist in the Katanga mines and later for the chief's court in his home area. He was employed very briefly by the RLI anthropologist Ian Cunnison, in Luapula, did typing for Epstein during the course of the urban study, and helped him gain access to Congress through his work for its committee at Ndola. He also worked for Ann Tweedie. He later joined the urban survey team during Fosbrooke's tenure as director. After independence he got a diploma in Social Science and Social Administration from the University of Ghana, Legon-Accra, and worked for the Zambian government. His publication for the RLI was, "Kasaka: A Case-Study in Succession and

Dynamics of a Bemba Village," with Peter Harries-Jones, *Rhodes-Livingstone Journal: Human Problems in British Central Africa* 33 (1963): 1–67. In the 1980s he became involved in writing Lunda history and promoting the Mutomboko traditional ceremony as an annual event.

14 Jacques Chiwale, interview with author, fieldnotes (26 July 1992). He did not specify what it was he understood to be in the back of Cunnison's mind, though one could presume it was an interest in culture that they shared.

15 See Robert Papstein's account of the Luvale History Project and the activities of James Chinjavata, a research assistant of C. M. N. White, a colonial administrator who was twice acting director of the RLI. ("From Ethnic Identity to Tribalism: The Upper Zambezi Region of Zambia, 1830–1981," in Leroy Vail, ed., *The Creation of Tribalism in Southern Africa* [London: James Currey, 1989], 372–94.

16 Kalimosho attended Mombo Primary School and Mabumbu Primary School (run by the Paris Evangelical Mission) in Barotseland, through Standard Three, and completed Standard Six in Livingstone. He worked in Livingstone as a tax collector for the administration from 1943, and Gluckman recruited him there in 1947 to do some work translating texts. During and immediately after Gluckman's last tour of fieldwork in Barotseland, Kalimosho also collected artifacts for him, going from Livingstone to Barotseland to find particular artifacts. During my interviews with him he showed me a letter he had received from Gluckman explaining why he could not return to visit him in 1958. A photo of some members of Kalimosho's family can also be found in Gluckman's photographic collections at the Royal Anthropological Institute. Gluckman lists him among those who voluntarily assisted him in his work, in the first edition of *The Judicial Process among the Barotse of Northern Rhodesia* (Manchester: Manchester University Press, 1955), xxiii.

17 Kalimosho, interview with author, fieldnotes (14 September 1992) held by author.

18 Kalimosho, interview with author, fieldnotes (14 September 1992) held by author.

19 Prins, *The Hidden Hippopotamus*, 192.

20 Barrie Reynolds, *Magic, Divination and Witchcraft among the Barotse of Northern Rhodesia*, (London: Chatto and Windus, 1963). I also

interviewed James O. Lemon, the district commissioner at Kalabo, the district *boma* in Barotseland where the first cases occurred.

21 *Judicial Process*, third ed. (1973), 427.

22 He also later criticized Reynolds's account as biased in favor of the administration's version of events. (*Judicial Process*, third ed., 424–25.)

23 *Judicial Process*, third ed., xxxiii.

24 "I have inserted my Barotse name, 'Makapweka', under my name on the title-page, since young Barotse I have met know me by that name, a name misappropriated by a British District Officer who was unconsciously instrumental in stirring up an outbreak of accusations of witchcraft in Barotseland in 1957 . . ." (xxxiii).

25 A growing literature deals with the meaning of witchfinding and witch-cleansing movements in Zambia and other parts of Africa. See, especially, the work of Mark Auslander, who discusses the relevant literature and provides a perceptive analysis of a recent movement in the Ngoni area and its historical and cultural context. ("Fertilizer has Brought Poison: Crises of Reproduction in Ngoni Society and History," [Ph.D. diss., University of Chicago, 1997].)

26 This was Tor Skudall from the University of Bergen, who kindly allowed me to look at his fieldnotes.

27 Kaciente Chifumpu, interview with Lisa Cliggett, transcript (29 August 1995) held by Cliggett.

28 See chapter 4 and the epilogue.

29 Colson, personal communication with author.

30 Mitchell to Colson, 28 February 1949, "Mitchell Papers," Rhodes House, Oxford, JCM 1/1.

31 Letter from the administrative secretary to all research officers, 14 May 1947, "Mitchell Papers," Rhodes House, Oxford, JCM 1/1.

32 This is part of Colson's research plan submitted to the CSSRC, 26 November 1948. (PRO, CO 927/64/3.)

33 Colson to CSSRC, 26 November 1948. (PRO, CO 927/64/3.)

34 Most former assistants whom I interviewed specifically mentioned Godfrey Wilson and Max Gluckman as critics of colonial policy.

35 Charles Ambler, "Alcohol, Racial Segregation and Popular Politics in Northern Rhodesia," *Journal of African History* 31 (1990): 299, 302, 295–313.

36 Epstein mentions that Lawrence Katilungu and other union leaders

carried on an important discussion of union matters at his home in Luanshya because they were able to get a "proper" drink there. (*Scenes from African Urban Life* [Edinburgh: Edinburgh University Press, 1992], 8.) As he recalled, they laced his drink while he was out of the room, and after they had departed he had to type up his notes while very drunk. (Epstein, personal communication with author.)

37 Merran Fraenkel, interview with author, fieldnotes (18 April 1995) held by author.

38 Simon Katilungu, interview with author, fieldnotes (28 September 1992) held by author.

39 Peter Harries-Jones, *Freedom and Labour: Mobilization and Political Control on the Zambian Copperbelt* (Oxford: Oxford University Press, 1975), 120.

40 Sykes Ndilila came from the Lala area of Northern Rhodesia, near to the Copperbelt. He was an early member of the Federation of African Societies, formed in 1946, which in 1948 became the Northern Rhodesia African Congress (ANC), the first major nationalist political party. Technically, he could not be a member of an African nationalist party while working for the RLI, but I have not been able to discover what his political activities may have been during the early 1950s when he worked for Mitchell. He may have been a member of the United National Independence Party (UNIP) by 1960 — the nationalist party that would come into power after independence — but he was back in the ANC as publicity secretary for Central Province in 1962. See David C. Mulford's *Zambia: The Politics of Independence, 1957–1964* (Oxford: Oxford University Press, 1967), 15–16, 134, and 295–96.

41 J. Clyde Mitchell, interview with author, fieldnotes (24 November 1992) held by author.

42 Davidson Silumesii Sianga grew up in a prosperous family in Barotseland, attended a Paris Evangelical elementary school, and held a number of engineering and clerical positions in Livingstone, N.R.; in Francistown, Bechuanaland; and in Bulawayo, Southern Rhodesia. While in Livingstone on his way home, he heard that the RLI was about to send the anthropologist Max Gluckman to Barotseland and that he needed an interpreter. Sianga applied for the job despite the low pay, because he was "so struck by the idea" that someone would make a study of his homeland. He continued working for the RLI from 1939 until 1954, seconded occasionally to government agriculture department surveys. (From his autobiography, "A Brief Outline History of my

Life," Institute for African Studies, University of Zambia [IAS/UNZA], "RLI Manuscripts File.")

43 Mitchell to Colson, 29 August 1950 and her response, 1 September 1950, "Mitchell Papers," Rhodes House, Oxford, JCM 1/3. Sianga participated in a later rural field training session for Victor Turner in Lambaland and then briefly worked for A. L. Epstein, who later became a RLI researcher, on his urban courts study. (19 October 1950, and 2 May 1951, "Mitchell Papers," Rhodes House, Oxford, JCM 1/3.)

44 Mitchell, interview with author, fieldnotes (24 November 1992) held by author. This attitude toward assistants contrasts with that of some anthropologists and sociologists today who seek assistants for interview work who are as close as possible to being tabulae rasae: "He [the research assistant] was in need of work, was well educated, was from Banaras, and was without ideas, opinions, or knowledge that could make him difficult to guide." (Nita Kumar, *Friends, Brothers, and Informants: Fieldwork Memoirs of Banaras* [Berkeley: University of California Press, 1992], 141.)

45 Mitchell, interview with author, fieldnotes (24 November 1992) held by author.

46 "For the last six months or so the Africans have been running the survey almost entirely on their own." (Mitchell to Barnes, 22 November 1952, "Mitchell Papers," Rhodes House, Oxford, JCM 4/1) Things did not always run smoothly, with Mitchell at one point complaining that the assistants didn't have the necessary "scientific ideology behind them." (Mitchell to McCulloch, 13 April 1953, "Mitchell Papers," Rhodes House, Oxford, JCM 2/1.)

47 Mitchell, interview with author, fieldnotes (24 November 1992) held by author.

48 Ndilila to Mitchell, 22 February 1952, "Mitchell Papers," Rhodes House, Oxford, JCM 9/1.

49 Ndilila to Mitchell, 28 February 1952, "Mitchell Papers," Rhodes House, Oxford, JCM 9/1. Another assistant proudly reported his method of getting around an uncooperative personnel manager. (Lukhero to Mitchell, 14 November 1952, "Mitchell Papers," Rhodes House, Oxford, JCM 24/1.) See also Katilungu's report on the "red tape" he had to go through to get a survey started in Broken Hill. (7 August 1953, "Mitchell Papers," Rhodes House, Oxford, JCM 24/3.)

50 Ndilila to Mitchell, 1 November 1951, "Mitchell Papers," Rhodes

House, Oxford, JCM 23/4. This training session was given by the survey team to potential government social workers, but some of the trainees became RLI team members later. Mitchell also tried to hire a woman from South Africa as senior research assistant for the team, but her parents wouldn't allow her to go to Northern Rhodesia. (8 March 1951, "Mitchell Papers," Rhodes House, Oxford, JCM 4/3.)

51 Possenta Akapelwa, interview with author, fieldnotes (22 October 1992) held by author. And see Harries-Jones's chapter containing Foster Mubanga's account of her political activities in the years before independence. (*Freedom and Labour: Mobilization and Political Control on the Zambian Copperbelt* [Oxford: Oxford University Press, 1975].)

52 Godfrey Shoko Mukonoweshuro was born in Southern Rhodesia near Fort Victoria (now Masvingo), the son of a minister. He attended Alheit Mission School and Adams College, received a B.A. from the University of South Africa, and studied at Ft. Hare in Anthropology and History under Z. K. Matthews. At the time he applied to work at the RLI he was doing a diploma in Education under O. F. Raum and had some research experience. ("Annexure III: Application — Godfrey Mukonoweshuro," "Mitchell Papers," Rhodes House, Oxford, JCM 3/4.)

53 Simon Katilungu was born in the Bemba region of Zambia in Kasama District, the son of a village headman. He began his education at the age of thirteen at Malole Mission School, then at the Kasama Government School, and Munali Secondary School in Lusaka. After working as a welfare assistant for the Rhokana mining company and as a government clerk in the labor department, he got a diploma in social work at Johannesburg's Jan Hofmeyer School. After he worked for the RLI from 1952 to 1959, he was employed briefly at the American library in Lusaka, and then took a number of positions in UNIP. (Interview with author, fieldnotes [28 September 1992] held by author.)

54 Katilungu, interview with author, fieldnotes (28 September 1992) held by author; "Annexure III: Application." The junior assistants usually had a Standard VIII education. (Mitchell to Ngoobo, 27 June 1953, "Mitchell Papers," Rhodes House, Oxford, JCM 2/2.)

55 See 8 June 1953, Mitchell to Simon Katilungu ("Mitchell Papers," Rhodes House, Oxford, JCM 2/2), on the possibility of publishing assistants' papers in the RLI journal; and ibid., 22 May 1953 on the RLI sponsoring Lee Setumo's research. Directors of the Institute had also hoped to employ an African as research officer, in equal status with the

other RLI anthropologists. (Colson, interview with author, fieldnotes [6 September 1990] held by author.)

56 Mentioned in a letter from an assistant to Mitchell were possible re- search topics he would like to do, dealing with race, class, and eth- nicity: "(i) Colour-bar in every walk of life; (ii) Social bars among different classes of people; (iii) Tribalism at work and parties." (11 July 1952, "Mitchell Papers," Rhodes House, Oxford, JCM 25/4.)

57 D. Chansa, mentioned in Mitchell, "The Kalela Dance," *Rhodes- Livingstone Papers* 27 (1956), 18.

58 Mitchell, "The Kalela Dance," 22–28. Secondary school students in this period would have been aware of issues of ethnicity, and RLI an- thropologists would have known that. Elizabeth Colson, the RLI's third director, noticed in the 1940s "the simultaneous emergence among secondary school students of national and tribal consciousness" (cited in "Return to the Malungwana Drift—Max Gluckman, the Zulu Na- tion and the Common Society," *African Affairs* 94, no. 374, [1995]: 39–65, 12, and drawn from Elizabeth Colson, "Contemporary Tribes and the Development of Nationalism," in June Helm, ed., *Essays on the Problem of Tribe* [Seattle: American Ethnological Society, 1968], 204).

59 Mitchell, "The Kalela Dance," 23.

60 7 April and 30 May 1952, "Mitchell Papers," Rhodes House, Oxford, JCM 9/1. In June he reports he is ignoring the "old tribal feeling" of the team and that they are being cooperative. (13 June 1952, "Mitchell Papers," Rhodes House, Oxford, JCM 9/1.) Team members divided themselves along linguistic lines where appropriate for interviewing, and this may have led to their joint use of typewriters. (Mitchell, per- sonal communication with author.) Assistants were also approached by fellow tribesmen wanting work at the RLI, to intercede for them with the director. (Lukhero to Mitchell, 14 November 1952, "Mitchell Papers," Rhodes House, Oxford, JCM 24/1.)

61 These factors were pointed out by Mitchell himself in a personal com- munication to me. Katilungu concurred that ethnicity did not figure much in the assistants' relations with each other. Most of them focused more on the "politics of protest" going on in the country at that time. "Ethnicism" was an "innocent word" compared to the meanings it is given today, he told me after reading the original draft of this chapter, in which I gave much more emphasis to ethnicity. (Katilungu, personal communication with author.)

62 10 March 1952 and 14 March 1952, "Mitchell Papers," Rhodes House, Oxford, JCM 9/1. Mukonoweshuro was at the time the senior research assistant leading the team.

63 7 April 1952, "Mitchell Papers," Rhodes House, Oxford, JCM 9/1.

64 Ndilila to Mitchell, 14 March 1952, "Mitchell Papers," Rhodes House, Oxford, JCM 9/1, and Mukonoweshuro to Mitchell, 7 April 1952, ibid.

65 This was relative to other ethnic groups who had greater access to a secondary education, especially those from eastern and western Northern Rhodesia, closer to Nyasaland's Livingstonia Mission and to the secondary schools in Southern Rhodesia. Ndilila had a Standard VI certificate. (Ndilila to Mitchell, 10 March 1952, "Mitchell Papers," Rhodes House, Oxford, JCM 9/1.)

66 The tribal representative (TR) system had been established by the mining compound managers to deal with minor domestic problems and to bring miners' complaints to the attention of management. At the time of the trial, white managers were trying to increase the authority of the TRS as a counterbalance to the union's growing power. Puta was the chairman of the Nchanga union branch and later vice-general president. (Epstein, *Politics in an Urban African Community*, 98–99.)

67 S. C. Katilungu, "A Study of Relations between Northern Rhodesia African Mine Workers Trade Union, and Mine Compounds Tribal Representatives and Copperbelt Mine Managers," 11. (Manuscript, "Mitchell Papers," Rhodes House, Oxford, JCM 25/2.)

68 Katilungu, "A Study of Relations," 2.

69 Lengwe worked for Epstein on the sociological study of Ndola, as well as on the urban survey team. He had been deemed unfit to do social work for the Chingola Management Board because of a probation officer's report that described him as "politically minded," "anti-European," and having a "personality very difficult to be judged." (Lengwe to the probation officer, 28 April 1953, "Mitchell Papers," Rhodes House, Oxford, JCM 2/2.)

70 "Athletic Meeting Held at Hodgson Training Centre," 24 May 1955, "Mitchell Papers," Rhodes House, Oxford, JCM 9/2.

71 *Facing Mount Kenya* was first published in 1938, after Kenyatta had attended Bronislaw Malinowski's seminars at the London School of Economics. The book itself and other academic productions by Kenyans have been further "reworked" — "remade into usable works in everyday life" — by local communities in Kenya. See David William

Cohen and E. S. Atieno Odhiambo, *Siaya: The Historical Anthropology of an African Landscape* (London: James Currey, 1989), 39–40.

72 Partly because of the multitude of ethnicities in Zambia, nationhood had to be constructed on broader models of African identity than any single ethnicity could provide. Therefore the assistants' knowledge of local ethnicities would not become useful until after independence, when regionally based ethnic groups began to compete for the attention of the state.

73 See the reference below to the use of RLI data by union negotiators.

74 Robin Short, *African Sunset* (London: Johnson, 1973), 122.

75 Letter from Colson to Mitchell, 2 December 1950, "Mitchell Papers," Rhodes House, Oxford, JCM 1/3.

76 Chiwale, interview with author, fieldnotes (6 October 1992) held by author.

77 None of the assistants was a union member at the time of employment by the RLI, though several had been, previous to their joining the survey team. Most were members of political parties, either overtly or covertly, at the time of their RLI work.

78 M. B. Lukhero was born in Feni village, near Ft. Jameson (now Chipata) in Eastern Province. He worked for Marwick briefly and then for a lengthy period with Barnes in his research on the Ngoni. He joined the urban survey team after a short time as a government clerk in Ft. Jameson. When Mitchell moved to UCRN, Lukhero also went to Salisbury to work for him there. See chapter 1 for further details.

79 "Weekly Work Report for October 1–9 1952, Mufulira Team," "Mitchell Papers," Rhodes House, Oxford, JCM 24/1. *Boma* was the term used to refer to the colonial government generally, as well as to its district and provincial headquarters.

80 See Lukhero to Mitchell, 26 August 1952, "Mitchell Papers," Rhodes House, Oxford, JCM 24/1.

81 Chiwale, interview with author, fieldnotes (6 October 1992) held by author.

82 Katilungu, interview with author, fieldnotes (28 September 1992) held by author.

83 Mukonoweshuro to Mitchell, 29 March, 7 April, and 29 May 1952, "Mitchell Papers," Rhodes House, Oxford, JCM 9/1.

84 Lukhero to Mitchell, 26 August 1952, "Mitchell Papers," Rhodes House, Oxford, JCM 24/1.

85 19 April 1955, "Mitchell Papers," Rhodes House, Oxford, JCM 9/2.

86 Lukhero to Mitchell, 21 November 1952, "Mitchell Papers," Rhodes House, Oxford, JCM 24/1. This was not an entirely unfounded assumption. During his directorship, Mitchell frequently used his data to argue with the mines that working and housing conditions needed improvement. (Personal communication with author.)

87 Epstein, interview with author, fieldnotes (10 November 1994) held by author. A. A. Nyirenda came from Nyasaland and worked both for Epstein and for the survey team.

88 Simon Katilungu, "Report on Work during Period 23rd March to 17th April 1953, Broken Hill, 18th April 1953," "Mitchell Papers," Rhodes House, Oxford, JCM 24/3.

89 Offering him the job would have been impossible because of government's awareness of his "Bolshy" tendencies. Fox-Pitt to Colson, 21 September 1950, "Mitchell Papers," Rhodes House, Oxford, JCM 1/3.

90 For example, the 4 September 1952 letter from Mitchell to Nkumbula, asking him to smooth the way for the survey in Mufulira where team members had been accused of being members of the Capricorn Africa Society. ("Mitchell Papers," Rhodes House, Oxford, JCM 24/1.)

91 Epstein to Mitchell, 10 February 1956, "Mitchell Papers," Rhodes House, Oxford, JCM 1/4.

92 Mitchell to McCulloch, 6 June 1953, "Mitchell Papers," Rhodes House, Oxford, JCM 2/2.

93 Interview with author, fieldnotes (6 October 1992) held by author.

94 29 July 1953, "Mitchell Papers," Rhodes House, Oxford, JCM 25/2.

95 30 April 1956, "Mitchell Papers," Rhodes House, Oxford, JCM 1/4.

96 Lukhero, interview with author, fieldnotes (30 May 1991) held by author.

97 Mulford, *Zambia*, 199–206.

98 Edward Mbewe, who worked both as a research assistant and was in charge of statistical analysis using the RLI's Powers-Samas machine, delivered this address. ("Mitchell Papers," Rhodes House, Oxford, JCM 1/3.

99 Nyirenda married soon after and took a job in the Nyasaland Railways. (Epstein, personal communication with author.)

100 According to Epstein, Prudence Smith of the BBC, while in Lusaka arranging for a series of BBC talks, was told by someone at the Secretariat that "they'd had enough of those long-haired Fabian intellec-

tuals" at the RLI. None of the researchers at the time had long hair, Epstein told me, and Max Gluckman was "bald as a coot." Neither was he a Fabian. (Interview with author, fieldnotes [11 November 1994] held by author.)

101 Fosbrooke, interview with author, fieldnotes (18 February 1992) held by author. See also Fosbrooke, "From Lusaka to Salisbury, 1956–60."

102 "RLI, Dons and Subs, 1 January 1955," 5. Minutes of the RLI Board of Trustees, 9 December 1954, ZCCM Archives, Ndola, Zambia, 13.5.10A.

103 While at UCRN, he succeeded in this with one of his research assistants, Gordon Chavunduka, who got a Ph.D., became a lecturer, and did ground-breaking research in medical sociology. He later became the vice chancellor of the University of Zimbabwe and head of the Zimbabwe National Traditional Healers Association. See also a letter from Mitchell to Epstein about Mitchell's intention to encourage African publication, (1 August 1951, "Mitchell Papers," Rhodes House, Oxford, JCM 1/4) and other letters about specific assistants whom he hoped to encourage (7 May 1953 and 22 May 1953, "Mitchell Papers," Rhodes House, Oxford, JCM 2/2).

104 The research assistants mention the high quality of the housing in their farewell address to Mitchell (n.d., "Mitchell Papers," Rhodes House, Oxford, JCM 1/3).

105 The director may also have had chickens wandering about. (McCulloch to Mitchell, 30 June 1953, "Mitchell Papers," Rhodes House, Oxford, JCM 2/2; McCulloch to Mitchell, 31 March 1953, IAS/UNZA, "RLI Management Files.")

106 Peter Rigby, interview with author, fieldnotes (2 March 1993) held by author.

107 Katilungu, interview with author, fieldnotes (28 September 1992) held by author.

108 See RLI management file "Flywell Banda's Cock" for details of the court case brought by the clerk against Fosbrooke. (Uncatalogued papers in Manuscripts Cabinet, Institute for African Studies, UNZA.)

109 Katilungu, interview with author, fieldnotes (28 September 1992) held by author. The point Katilungu made is also summed up by Epstein's characterization of the differences between colonial administrators and anthropologists in the rural areas: "However the anthro-

pologist might enjoy the prestige that attached to a white skin, the anthropologist was plainly distinguished from the District Officer by his lack of power. Most anthropologists, I suspect, kept a sharp watch on their tempers, careful not to express anger because they were so dependent on the goodwill of their people. A DO had less compunction in giving vent to his frustration." (Personal communication with author.)

110 Katilungu, interview with author, fieldnotes (28 September 1992) held by author.

111 Katilungu, for example, immediately got two job offers when he resigned in 1959. He decided to work for "the Yankee boys" at the American library in Lusaka. He stayed there only briefly because of the American diplomatic community's prohibition against political activity on the part of employees. He then became divisional secretary for UNIP in Central Province; personal private secretary to Kenneth Kaunda, the future president of Zambia; and party educational secretary. After independence, he held various posts including High Commissioner to Britain and chair of Zambia Airways. ("Profile: Recently Appointed Chairman of Zambia Airways, Simon Katilungu," from the RST Group magazine, *Horizon* 12, no. 8 [August 1969]: 10–13.)

8. The Culture of Fieldwork

1 Peter Siwo, interview with author, fieldnotes (29 January 1992) held by author.

2 Alastair Heron, interview with author, fieldnotes (5 August 1993) held by author. Also see Alastair Heron's, "The Years of Transition, 1963–67," *African Social Research* 24 (1978): 331–34. Robert Serpell, interview with author, fieldnotes (3 May 1990) held by author. See also Robert Serpell's "Setting Research Priorities for a University Research Institute in Southern Africa," in Michael Malefetsane Sefali, ed., *Southern Africa: Research for Development* (Roma, Lesotho: Institute of Southern African Studies, 1988), 251–67.

3 See P. O. Nsugbe's "Brief but Black Authority, 1968–70," *African Social Research* 24 (1977): 335–40.

4 See Juliano M. Kabamba's "The Institute for African Studies in Retrospective: A Review, 1983–1986," *IAS Research Report* (Lusaka: Institute for African Studies, 1989).

5 Magubane, "Pluralism and Conflict Situations in Africa: A New Look," *African Social Research* 7 (1969): 529–54; and "A Critical Look at the Indices Used in the Study of Social Change in Colonial Africa," *Current Anthropology* 12 (1971): 419–45.

6 Kashoki to Moyo, 6 March 1984 (copy given by Kashoki to the author). Moyo had confused Wilson with William Watson, who served in the British airforce during the war.

7 "The Institute for African Studies in the University of Zambia and the Future of Social Science Research into the 21st Century," address to the conference on the 50th Anniversary of the Institute for African Studies, 19 June 1989, (unpublished manuscript), 7. Kashoki was Vice-Chancellor of Copperbelt University in Kitwe, Zambia, at the time.

8 For an analysis of this problem in the area of women's studies in Zambia, see Karen Tranberg Hansen and Leslie Ashbaugh, "Women on the Front Line: Development Issues in Southern Africa," *Women and International Development Journal* 2 (1991): 205–40.

9 For the Israeli school, see Raymond Firth's "Max Gluckman, 1911–1975," *Proceedings of the British Academy* 61 (1975): 478–96; E. Marx, "Anthropological Studies in a Centralized State: Max Gluckman and the Israel Bernstein Research Project," *Jewish Journal of Sociology* 17 (1975): 131–50; and T. van Teeffelen, "The Manchester School in Africa and Israel: A Critique," in S. Diamond, ed., *Anthropology: Ancestors and Heirs* (The Hague: Mouton, 1980), 347–75. For Uberoi's approach, see *Politics of the Kula Ring: Science and Culture* (Manchester: Manchester University Press, 1978); and *The Other Mind of Europe: Goethe as Scientist* (Oxford: Oxford University Press, 1984). For the shop-floor ethnographies, see Sheila Cunnison, "The Manchester Factory Studies, the Social Context, Bureaucratic Organisation, Sexual Divisions and their Influence on Patterns of Accommodation between Workers and Management," in Frankenberg, ed., *Custom and Conflict*; Isabel Emmett and D. H. J. Morgan, "Max Gluckman and the Manchester Shop-Floor Ethnographies," in Frankenberg, ed., *Custom and Conflict*; Bruce Kapferer, *Strategy and Transaction in an African Factory* (Manchester: Manchester University Press, 1972); and Michael Burawoy, *The Colour of Class on the Zambian Copper Mines: From African Advancement to Zambianization* (Manchester: Manchester University Press, 1972).

10 Scarlett Epstein received a Ph.D. at Manchester in 1958, based on fieldwork in India. She met and married Bill Epstein in Manchester, and

they went on to do fieldwork in New Guinea. Her work in applied anthropology included a fellowship at the Institute of Development Studies at Sussex and a Research Professorship in the School of African and Asian Studies there. She directed the Cross-Cultural Study of Population Growth and Rural Poverty from 1973 to 1977, one of the more famous products of which was the film *Maragoli*. Her publications include *Economic Development and Social Change in South India* (Manchester: Manchester University Press, 1962) and, more recently, *Women, Work and Family* (London: Croom Helm, 1986). (Interview with author, fieldnotes [3 March 1995] held by author.) Norman Long got a Ph.D. from Manchester in 1967, based on fieldwork in Zambia (1962–64) and, among other posts, held a lectureship in Sociology at the University of Zambia in 1967–68. His work in applied anthropology has primarily taken place from a base at the Agricultural University of Wageningen, The Netherlands, where he is the Professor of Development Sociology. His publications include *Social Change and the Individual* (Manchester: Manchester University Press, 1968); *An Introduction to the Sociology of Rural Development* (London: Tavistock, 1977); and, with coeditor Ann Long, *Battlefields of Knowledge: The Interlocking of Theory and Practice in Social Research and Development* (London: Routledge, 1992). (Interview with author, fieldnotes [11 April 1995] held by author.) For a consideration of the RLI's legacy to rural sociology, see Jan Kees van Donge's "Understanding Rural Zambia Today: The Relevance of the Rhodes-Livingstone Institute," *Africa* 55, no. 1 (1985): 60–75.

11 See Thayer Scudder and Elizabeth Colson, "Long-Term Field Research in Gwembe Valley, Zambia," in G. Foster, T. Scudder, E. Colson, and R. Kemper, eds., *Long-Term Field Research in Social Anthropology*, (New York: Academic Press, 1979), 227–54; Elizabeth Colson, "Overview," *Annual Review of Anthropology* 18 (1989): 1–16; and S. Clark, E. Colson, J. Lee, and T. Scudder, "Ten Thousand Tonga: A Longitudinal Anthropological Study from Southern Zambia, 1956–1991," *Population Studies*, 1995.

12 Matshakaza B. Lukhero, *Ngoni Nc'wala Ceremony* (Lusaka, Zambia: NECZAM, 1993); Chileya J. Chiwale and Munona Chinyanta, *Mutomboko Ceremony and the Lunda-Kazembe Dynasty* (Lusaka, Zambia: Kenneth Kaunda Foundation, 1989).

13 John Hudson: interview with author, fieldnotes (3 November 1992) held by author.

14 Jacob Mwanza, for example, thought anthropology was irrelevant. (Interview with author, fieldnotes [10 March 1992] held by author.) Edward Shamwana also believed the RLI work had no influence on his subsequent career. (Interview with author, fieldnotes [7 October 1992] held by author.) Lyson Tembo, on the other hand, felt its influence was important (interview with author, fieldnotes [28 October 1992] held by author), and David Phiri pursued an undergraduate degree in anthropology (interview with author, fieldnotes [28 April 1992] held by author). All four had done vacation work for the RLI while studying at Munali.

15 I interviewed a large number of informants, both in groups and individually, in some, though not all, of the former RLI fieldsites. The sites included Luanshya, one of the Copperbelt towns. I also visited the rural sites of Gluckman, Colson, Watson, Barnes, and Cunnison for varying periods of time, from a few days to a few weeks. I also interviewed friends, informants, and former assistants whom I located in Lusaka and other cities. In some cases I was allowed to see the fieldnotes of subsequent anthropologists who picked up local stories about the former RLI researchers, in the Gwembe and the Lozi sites, in particular.

16 RLI Uncatalogued file: Printing of Publications #78b: 19 August 1949: Colson to Mrs. Hope Hay. (IAS/UNZA, Lusaka, Zambia)

17 *The Judicial Process among the Barotse of Northern Rhodesia*, 2d ed. (Manchester: Manchester University Press, 1967), xxxiii.

18 J. A. Barnes has previously discussed the variety of uses and definitions for the concept in "Network Analysis: Orienting Notion, Rigorous Technique or Substantive Field of Study?" in Paul W. Holland and Samuel Leinhardt, eds., *Perspectives on Social Network Research* (New York: Academic Press, 1979), 403–23.

19 Richard Werbner, "The Manchester School in South-Central Africa," *Annual Review of Anthropology* 13 (1984): 157, 157–85.

20 For a list of many of the places where Manchester School anthropologists and sociologists subsequently held chairs or professorships, see Ronald Frankenberg, "A Social Anthropology for Britain?" in Frankenberg, ed., *Custom and Conflict in British Society* (Manchester: Manchester University Press, 1982), 1–35; 1.

21 A. L. Epstein, *Urbanization and Kinship: The Domestic Domain on the Copperbelt of Zambia, 1950–1956* (London: Academic Press, 1981); J. Clyde Mitchell, *Cities, Society, and Social Perception: A Central African Perspective* (Oxford: Oxford University Press, 1987).

22 Harold Perkin, *The Rise of Professional Society: England since 1880*, (London: Routledge, 1989), 9–17.

23 Missionary-ethnographers can be included in this group, though they usually did not have as much power to control or thwart social anthropologists in the field relative to administrators, who drew on the colonial government's power.

24 J. A. Barnes, personal communication with author. Also see his article, "Kinship Studies: Some Impressions of the Current State of Play," *Man* n.s. 15: 293–303, reprinted in Barnes, *Models and Interpretations*, 169–70.

25 J. A. Barnes, personal communication with author. See Stocking for details of its founding. (George W. Stocking Jr., *After Tylor: British Social Anthropology, 1888–1951* [London: Athlone Press, 1995], 427–28.

26 J. A. Barnes, personal communication with author.

27 Fosbrooke explained J. Matthews' behavior at the conference as the result of a brain tumor ("From Lusaka to Salisbury, 1956–60" *African Social Research* 24 [1977]: 321, 319–26), and he encouraged the RLI Board of Trustees to remove Rigby from his post unless he complied with peacetime military service requirements. (Minutes of the 19th meeting of the Standing Committee, 23 March 1960, National Archives of Zambia, Lusaka, SEC 5/446.) Rigby went on to do work in Tanzania and developed an amicable relationship with Fosbrooke there. (Rigby, interview with author, fieldnotes [2 March 1993] held by author.) See also Rigby, *Persistent Pastoralists: Nomadic Societies in Transition* (London: Zed Books, 1985), and *African Images: Racism and the End of Anthropology* (Oxford: Berg, 1996).

28 "The Anthropology of Incommensurability," in his *Galileo: Courtier: The Practice of Science in the Culture of Absolutism* (Chicago: University of Chicago Press, 1993), 211–44.

29 J. A. Barnes, personal communication with author.

30 "Quarterly Newsletter No. 3," Rhodes House Library, Oxford, "uncatalogued Mitchell Papers."

31 For the sensitivity of Balandier's research to urban and labor issues, see Frederick Cooper, *Decolonization and African Society: The Labor Question in French and British Africa* (Cambridge: Cambridge University Press, 1996), 371–73.

32 Mitchell, personal communication with author. *Kabadula* was one of the African words for the style of baggy shorts worn by administrators. Some male anthropologists at the RLI wore a similar style of shorts.

33 In his reactions to an earlier version of this argument, Simon Katilungu
    suggested that I title this section "Partnership in Human Field" and
    emphasized that he did not mean the kind of partnership used in rhet-
    oric promoting the federation. (Katilungu, personal communication
    with author.)

34 Ralph Grillo and Alan Rew, eds., *Social Anthropology and Develop-
    ment Policy*, ASA Monographs 23 (London: Tavistock Publications,
    1985), 21–24.

35 See Lynette Schumaker, "Landscaping Race," in Peter Pels and Oscar
    Salemink, eds., *Colonial Subjects: Essays in the Practical History of
    Anthropology* (Ann Arbor: University of Michigan Press, 1998).

36 Whether or not anthropology is a subversive activity is a question that
    has interested anthropologists mainly since the 1960s, particularly
    those with neo-Marxist and New Left perspectives. See Dell Hymes,
    ed., *Reinventing Anthropology* (New York: Pantheon Books, 1972).

37 Ever since the move from gentlemanly armchair anthropology to the
    field, anthropology has always attracted more of the socially marginal
    than other disciplines. The RLI researchers were not the first South
    African, female, Celtic, or Jewish anthropologists.

38 Max Gluckman, "History of the Manchester 'School' of Social Anthro-
    pology and Sociology," undated manuscript, Department of Social An-
    thropology, University of Manchester. Also cited in Werbner, "Man-
    chester School."

39 Gluckman, "History of the Manchester 'School.' "

40 Gluckman, "History of the Manchester 'School,' " 4.

41 Gluckman, "History of the Manchester 'School,' " 8.

42 George W. Stocking Jr., "The Ethnographer's Magic: Fieldwork in Brit-
    ish Anthropology from Tylor to Malinowski," in Stocking, ed., *Ob-
    servers Observed: Essays on Ethnographic Fieldwork* (Madison: Uni-
    versity of Wisconsin Press, 1983); Anna Grimshaw and Keith Hart,
    Anthropology and the Crisis of the Intellectuals, Prickly Pear Pamphlet
    No. 1 (Cambridge: Prickly Pear Press, 1993).

43 Because of this wide-ranging style of data collection, Mitchell and
    Barnes could answer questions based on their Lamba survey fieldnotes
    that they had not anticipated during the fieldwork. (Mitchell, interview
    with author, fieldnotes (27 November 1990) held by author.) A re-
    analysis of Malinowski's work led to the publication of a book by one
    of Gluckman's students, J. Singh Uberoi, *The Politics of the Kula Ring:
    An Analysis of the Findings of Bronislaw Malinowski* (Manchester:

Manchester University Press, 1962). (Epstein, interview with author, fieldnotes [1 December 1990] held by author.)

44 Mitchell points to this as an important difference between his own work and Gluckman's equilibrium approach. (Interview with author, fieldnotes [24 November 1992] held by author.)

45 Epstein, interview with author, fieldnotes (1 December 1990) held by author.

46 Epstein, interview with author, fieldnotes (1 December 1990) held by author.

47 See Susan Leigh Star and James R. Griesemer, "Institutional Ecology, 'Translations,' and Boundary Objects: Amateurs and Professionals in Berkeley's Museum of Vertebrate Zoology, 1907–39," *Social Studies of Science* 19 (1989): 387–420, and James R. Griesemer, "Modeling in the Museum: On the Role of Remnant Models in the Work of Joseph Grinnell," *Biology and Philosophy* 5 (1990): 3–36.

48 See, in particular, the lengthy discussion in the "RLI Quarterly Newsletter No. 4, October 1954," Rhodes House Library, Oxford, "uncatalogued Mitchell Papers."

49 Again, see Star and Griesemer, "Institutional Ecology, 'Translations,' and Boundary Objects."

50 Lisa Cliggett, personal communication with author.

51 See J. A. Barnes, "Editorial Note," in M. B. Lukhero, "Chieftainship, Tradition and Change in Ngoni Society," *Cambridge Anthropology* 21, no. 2 (1999/2000): 17–40; 19–20. See also, J. A. Barnes, "Obituary: Matshakaza Blackson Lukhero, *Anthropology Today* 12, no. 3 (1996): 24.

Epilogue

1 Kaciente Chifumpu, interview with Lisa Cliggett, transcript (29 August 1995) held by Cliggett. Colson has pointed out that she did not visit Gwembe villages in 1978 because of the Rhodesian war, but she did see Gwembe Tonga people in Lusaka and in the Plateau villages. (Personal communication with author.)

2 Barnes, interview with author, fieldnotes (12 August 1993) held by author.

BIBLIOGRAPHY

Archives and Collections

Barnes Papers, Cambridge, Box 1 (or 201), "RLI Central Office, 1944–1948"
Barnes Papers, Cambridge, Box 2, "RLI Central Office, 1949–1951"
Barnes Papers, Cambridge, Box 5, "Official Letters"
Ian Cunnison's private papers

National Archives of Zambia, Lusaka, SEC 1/127
National Archives of Zambia, Lusaka, SEC 1/130
National Archives of Zambia, Lusaka, SEC 1/131
National Archives of Zambia, Lusaka, RC/1384
National Archives of Zambia, Lusaka, B1/4/MISC/6/3
National Archives of Zambia, Lusaka, RC 1385 (61/2)

PRO, CO 927/8/6
PRO, CO 927/8/7
PRO, CO 927/41/6
PRO, CO 927/64/2
PRO, CO 927/64/3
PRO, CO 927/64/4

Rhodes House, Oxford, uncatalogued Mitchell Papers
Rhodes House, Oxford, JCM 1/1
Rhodes House, Oxford, JCM 1/2
Rhodes House, Oxford, JCM 1/3
Rhodes House, Oxford, JCM 1/4
Rhodes House, Oxford, JCM 2/1
Rhodes House, Oxford, JCM 2/2
Rhodes House, Oxford, JCM 3/3
Rhodes House, Oxford, JCM 3/4

Rhodes House, Oxford, JCM 4/1
Rhodes House, Oxford, JCM 4/3
Rhodes House, Oxford, JCM 5/1
Rhodes House, Oxford, JCM 9/1
Rhodes House, Oxford, JCM 9/2
Rhodes House, Oxford, JCM 23/4
Rhodes House, Oxford, JCM 24/1
Rhodes House, Oxford, JCM 24/3
Rhodes House, Oxford, JCM 25/2
Rhodes House, Oxford, JCM 25/4

RLI Files, Institute for African Studies, University of Zambia (IAS/UNZA)

Wilson Papers, University of Cape Town, Social Anthropology Department

Zambia Consolidated Copper Mines Archives (ZCCM), Ndola, Zambia, 13.5.10A
ZCCM Archives, Ndola, Zambia, 14.2.3B

Interviews

Akapelwa P., interview with author, fieldnotes (22 October 1992) held by author
Barnes J. A., interview with author, fieldnotes (12 August 1993) held by author
Blunden J., interview with author, fieldnotes (15 November 1993) held by author
Chifumpu K., interview with Lisa Cliggett, transcript (29 August 1995) held by Cliggett
Chimuka A. S., interview with author, fieldnotes (14 September 1992) held by author
Chiwale J. C., interview with author, fieldnotes (24 January 1992) held by author
Chiwale J. C., interview with author, fieldnotes (26 July 1992) held by author
Chiwale J. C., interview with author, fieldnotes (6 October 1992) held by author
Chona M., interview with author, fieldnotes (13 August 1992) held by author

Colson E., interview with author, fieldnotes (6 September 1990) held by author

Colson E., interview with author, fieldnotes (7 Septemper 1990) held by author

Colson E., interview with author, fieldnotes (28 March 1992) held by author

Colson E., interview with author, fieldnotes (18 July 1992) held by author

Cunnison I., interview with author, fieldnotes (3 August 1993) held by author

Epstein A. L., interview with author, fieldnotes (1 December 1990) held by author

Epstein A. L., interview with author, fieldnotes (10 November 1994) held by author

Epstein A. L., interview with author, fieldnotes (11 November 1994) held by author

Epstein S., interview with author, fieldnotes (3 March 1995) held by author

Fosbrooke H., interview with author, fieldnotes (18 February 1992) held by author

Fraenkel M., interview with author, fieldnotes (18 April 1995) held by author

Heron A., interview with author, fieldnotes (5 August 1993) held by author

Holleman J. F., interview with author, fieldnotes (5 November 1993) held by author

Holleman J. F., interview with author, fieldnotes (6 November 1993) held by author

Holleman J. F., interview with author, fieldnotes (7 November 1993) held by author

Hudson J., interview with author, fieldnotes (3 November 1992) held by author

Kalimosho D., interview with author, fieldnotes (14 September 1992) held by author

Katilungu S., interview with author, fieldnotes (28 September 1992) held by author

Long N., interview with author, fieldnotes (11 April 1995) held by author

Louw J., interview with author, fieldnotes (20 April 1993) held by author

Lukhero M. B., interview with author, fieldnotes (30 May 1991) held by author

Lukhero M. B., interview with author, fieldnotes (27 February 1992) held by author

Lukhero M. B., interview with author, fieldnotes (29 May 1992) held by author

Marwick M., interview with author, fieldnotes (25 November 1992) held by author

Mitchell J. C., interview with author, fieldnotes (31 October 1990) held by author

Mitchell J. C., interview with author, fieldnotes (19 November 1990) held by author

Mitchell J. C., interview with author, fieldnotes (27 November 1990) held by author

Mitchell J. C., interview with author, fieldnotes (11 December 1990) held by author

Mitchell J. C., interview with author, fieldnotes (24 November 1992) held by author

Mitchell J. C., interview with author, fieldnotes (29 September 1993) held by author

Mitchell J. C., interview with author, fieldnotes (10 August 1994) held by author

Mtonga M., interview with author, fieldnotes (11 July 1991) held by author

Mwale S., interview with author, fieldnotes (16 April 1992) held by author

Mwanza J., interview with author, fieldnotes (10 March 1992) held by author

Phiri D., interview with author, fieldnotes (28 April 1992) held by author

Rigby P., interview with author, fieldnotes (2 March 1993) held by author

Serpell R., interview with author, fieldnotes (3 May 1990) held by author

Shamwana E., interview with author, fieldnotes (7 October 1992) held by author

Simons H. J., interview with author, fieldnotes (7 May 1992) held by author

Siwo P., interview with author, fieldnotes (29 January 1992) held by author

Tembo L., interview with author, fieldnotes (28 October 1992) held by author

Phillips H., interview with author, fieldnotes (14 May 1993) held by author van Velsen R., interview with author, fieldnotes (20 September 1993) held by author

Wilson F., interview with author, fieldnotes (6 May 1992) held by author

Zukas S., interview with author, fieldnotes (25 October 1992) held by author

Books, Articles, Theses

Allan W., Gluckman M., Peters D. U. and Trapnell C. G., "Land Holding and Land Usage among the Plateau Tonga of the Mazabuka District: A Reconnaissance Survey," *Rhodes-Livingstone Papers* 14 (1948).

Allan W., "Studies in African Land Usage," *Rhodes-Livingstone Papers* 14 (1949).

———, *The African Husbandman* (London: Oliver & Boyd, 1965).

Ambler C., "Alcohol, Racial Segregation and Popular Politics in Northern Rhodesia," *Journal of African History* 31 (1990): 295–313.

Anderson D. M., "Depression, Dust Bowl, Demography and Drought: The Colonial State and Soil Conservation in East Africa during the 1930s," *African Affairs* 83, no. 332 (1984): 321–43.

Anderson D. M. and Grove R. eds., *Conservation in Africa: People, Policies and Practice* (Cambridge: Cambridge University Press, 1987).

Anderson D. M., "Cow Power: Livestock and the Pastoralist in Africa," *African Affairs* 92, no. 366 (1993): 121–34.

Anthony K. R. M. and Uchendu V. C., "Agricultural Change in Mazabuka District, Zambia," *Food Research Institute Studies* 9 (1970): 215–67.

Appadurai A., "The Production of Locality," in Richard Fardon, ed., *Counterworks: Managing the Diversity of Knowledge* (London: Routledge, 1995), 207.

Asad T., ed., *Anthropology and the Colonial Encounter* (New York: Humanities Press, 1973).

Auslander M., "Fertilizer Has Brought Poison: Crises of Reproduction in Ngoni Society and History," (Ph.D. Dissertation, University of Chicago, 1997).

Balstad Miller R., "Science and Society in the Early Career of H. F. Verwoerd," *Journal of Southern African Studies* 19, no. 4 (1993): 634–61.

Barkan E., *The Retreat of Scientific Racism* (Cambridge: Cambridge University Press, 1992).

Barnes J. A., "The Collection of Genealogies," *Rhodes-Livingstone Journal* 5 (1947): 48–55.

——, "History in a Changing Society," *Rhodes-Livingstone Journal* 11 (1951): 1–9.

——, "Obituary: Matshakaza Blackson Lukhero" *Anthropology Today* 12, no. 3 (1996): 24.

——, "Editorial Note," in M. B. Lukhero, "Chieftainship, Tradition and Change in Ngoni Society," *Cambridge Anthropology* 21 (2) (1999/2000): 17–40; 19–20.

Barnes J. A., Mitchell J. C. and Gluckman M., "The Village Headman in British Central Africa," *Africa* 19 (1949): 89–106.

Barnes J. A. and Mitchell J. C., "The Lamba Village: A Report of a Social Survey," *Communication (New Series)* 24 (Cape Town: School of African Studies, University of Cape Town, 1950).

Behar R. and Gordon D. A. eds., *Women Writing Culture* (Berkeley: University of California Press, 1995).

Beinart W., "Introduction," in David M. Anderson and Richard Grove, eds., *Conservation in Africa: People, Policies and Practice* (Cambridge: Cambridge University Press, 1987), 15–19.

Beinart W. and Bundy C., *Hidden Struggles in Rural South Africa* (London: James Currey, 1987).

Berger E., *Labour, Race and Colonial Rule: The Copperbelt from 1924 to Independence* (Oxford: Clarendon Press, 1974).

Biagioli M., "The Anthropology of Incommensurability," in Biagioli, *Galileo: Courtier: The Practice of Science in the Culture of Absolutism* (Chicago: University of Chicago Press, 1993), 211–44.

Bond G., *The Politics of Change in a Zambian Community* (Chicago: Chicago University Press, 1976).

Brockway F., *The Colonial Revolution* (London: Hart-Davis, MacGibbon, 1973).

Brown R., "Anthropology and Colonial Rule: Godfrey Wilson and the Rhodes-Livingstone Institute, Northern Rhodesia," in Talal Asad, ed., *Anthropology and the Colonial Encounter* (New York: Humanities Press, 1973) 173–98.

——, "Passages in the Life of a White Anthropologist: Max Gluckman in Northern Rhodesia," *Journal of African History* 20 (1979): 525–41.

Burawoy M., *The Colour of Class on the Zambian Copper Mines: From African Advancement to Zambianization* (Manchester: Manchester University Press, 1972).

Burrows H. R., Kerr A. and Matthews Z. K., eds., *A Short Pictorial History of the University College of Fort Hare, 1916–1959* (Lovedale, South Africa: Lovedale Press, 1961).

Butler J., Elphick R. and Welsh D., eds., *Democratic Liberalism in South Africa: Its History and Prospect* (Cape Town: David Philip, 1987).

Cain J., "Intimate Working: Collaborations between Husband and Wife in the Early Scientific Careers of Anne Roe and George Gaylord Simpson," n.d., manuscript, University College London.

Callaway H., *Gender, Culture and Empire: European Women in Colonial Nigeria* (Oxford: Macmillan Press, 1987).

——, "Ethnography and Experience: Gender Implications in Fieldwork and Texts," in Judith Okely and Helen Callaway, eds., *Anthropology and Autobiography* (London: Routledge, 1995).

Carstens P., Klinghardt G. and West M., eds., *Trails in the Thirstland: The Anthropological Field Diaries of Winifred Hoernlé* (Centre for African Studies Communications No. 14, University of Cape Town, 1987).

Cesara M., *Reflections of a Woman Anthropologist: No Hiding Place* (London: Academic Press, 1982).

Chabal P., *Power in Africa: An Essay in Political Interpretation* (London: Macmillan, 1994).

Chanock M., *Law, Custom and Social Order: The Colonial Experience in Malaŵi and Zambia* (Cambridge: Cambridge University Press, 1985).

Chauncey Jr., G., "The Locus of Reproduction: Women's Labour in the Zambian Copperbelt, 1927–1953," *Journal of Southern African Studies* 7, no. 2 (1991): 135–64.

Chiwale C. J. and Chinyanta M., *Mutomboko Ceremony and the Lunda-Kazembe Dynasty* (Lusaka, Zambia: Kenneth Kaunda Foundation, 1989).

Chiwale C. J. and Harries-Jones P., "Kasaka: A Case-Study in Succession and Dynamics of a Bemba Village," *Rhodes-Livingstone Journal* 33 (1963): 1–67.

Clammer J., *The New Economic Anthropology* (New York: St. Martin's Press, 1978).

Clark J. D., "Digging On: A Personal Record and Appraisal of Archaeological Research in Africa and Elsewhere," *Annual Review of Anthropology* 23 (1994): 1–23.

Clark S., Colson E., Lee J. and Scudder T., "Ten Thousand Tonga: A Longitudinal Anthropological Study from Southern Zambia, 1956–1991," *Population Studies*, 1995.

Clifford J., "On Ethnographic Authority," in P. Gifford, ed., *The Predicament of Culture: Twentieth-Century Ethnography, Literature, and Art* (Cambridge: Harvard University Press, 1988), 21–54.

Cohen D. W. and Atieno Odhiambo E. S., *Siaya: The Historical Anthropology of an African Landscape* (London: James Currey, 1989).

Colson E., *The Makah Indians: A Study of an Indian Tribe in Modern American Society* (Minneapolis: University of Minnesota Press, 1953).

———, *Marriage and Family among the Plateau Tonga of Northern Rhodesia* (Manchester: Manchester University Press, 1958).

———, "Competence and Incompetence in the Context of Independence," *Current Anthropology* 8 (1967): 92–100, 108–9.

———, "Contemporary Tribes and the Development of Nationalism," in J. Helm, ed., *Essays on the Problem of Tribe* (Seattle: University of Washington Press, 1968).

———, *Tradition and Contract: The Problem of Order* (Chicago: Aldine, 1974).

———, "The Institute under Max Gluckman, 1942–47," *African Social Research* 24 (1977): 285–95.

———, "From Livingstone to Lusaka, 1948–51," *African Social Research* 24 (1977): 297–308.

———, "Overview," *Annual Review of Anthropology* 18 (1989): 1–16.

Colson E. and Gluckman M., eds., *Seven Tribes of British Central Africa* (London: Published on behalf of the Rhodes-Livingstone Institute, Northern Rhodesia by Oxford University Press, 1951).

Comaroff J. L., "Dialectical Systems, History and Anthropology: Units of Study and Questions of Theory," *Journal of Southern African Studies* 8, no. 1 (1981): 143–72.

Comaroff J. and Comaroff J., *Ethnography and the Historical Imagination* (Boulder, Colo.: Westview Press, 1992).

Cooper F., ed., *The Struggle for the City: Migrant Labor, Capital, and the State in Urban Africa* (Beverly Hills, Calif.: Sage Publications, 1983).

———, *On the African Waterfront: Urban Disorder and the Transformation of Work in Colonial Mombasa* (New Haven, Conn.: Yale University Press, 1987).

———, *Decolonization and African Society: The Labor Question in French and British Africa* (Cambridge: Cambridge University Press, 1996).

Cornwall A. and Lindisfarne N., eds., *Dislocating Masculinity: Comparative Ethnographies* (London: Routledge, 1996).

Crehan K., *The Fractured Community: Landscapes of Power and Gender in Rural Zambia* (Berkeley: University of California Press, 1997).

Cronon W., *Nature's Metropolis: Chicago and the Great West* (New York: Norton, 1991).

Cunnison I. G., "History on the Luapula," *Rhodes-Livingstone Papers* 21 (1951).

———, *The Luapula Peoples of Northern Rhodesia: Custom and History in Tribal Politics* (Manchester: Manchester University Press, 1959).

Cunnison S., "The Manchester Factory Studies, the Social Context, Bureaucratic Organisation, Sexual Divisions and their Influence on Patterns of Accommodation between Workers and Management," in Frankenberg R., ed., *Custom and Conflict in British Society* (Manchester: Manchester University Press, 1982), 94–139.

Curtin P., "Medical Knowledge and Urban Planning in Tropical Africa," *American Historical Review* 90, no. 3 (1985): 594–613.

Dirks N., ed., *Colonialism and Culture* (Ann Arbor: University of Michigan Press, 1992).

Dubow S., *Racial Segregation and the Origins of Apartheid in South Africa, 1919–36* (Oxford: St. Antony's College/Macmillan, 1989).

———, "Wulf Sachs Black Hamlet — A Case of 'Psychic Vivisection'," *African Affairs*, no. 369 (1993): 519–56.

———, "Black Hamlet: A Case of 'Psychic Vivisection'," in *The Societies of Southern Africa in the 19th and 20th Centuries*, vol. 19 (London: University of London, Institute of Commonwealth Studies, 1993).

———, *Scientific Racism in Modern South Africa* (Cambridge: Cambridge University Press, 1995).

Elphick R., "Mission Christianity and Interwar Liberalism," in Butler J., Elphick R. and Welsh D., eds., *Democratic Liberalism in South Africa: Its History and Prospect* (Cape Town: David Philip, 1987), 64–80.

Emmett I. and Morgan D. H. J., "Max Gluckman and the Manchester Shop-Floor Ethnographies," in Frankenberg R., ed., *Custom and Conflict in British Society* (Manchester: Manchester University Press, 1982), 140–65.

Epstein A. L.,"Juridical Techniques and the Judicial Process: A Study in African Customary Law, *Rhodes-Livingstone Papers* 23 (1954).

Epstein A. L., *Politics in an Urban African Community* (Manchester: Manchester University Press, 1958).

———, *Ethos and Identity: Three Studies in Ethnicity* (London: Tavistock Publications, 1978).

——, *Urbanization and Kinship: The Domestic Domain on the Copperbelt of Zambia, 1950–1956* (London: Academic Press, 1981).

——, *Scenes from African Urban Life* (Edinburgh: Edinburgh University Press, 1992).

Epstein A. L. and Mitchell J. C., "Power and Prestige among Africans in Northern Rhodesia: An Experiment," *Proceedings and Transactions of the Rhodesia Scientific Association* 45 (1957): 13–26.

Epstein S., *Economic Development and Social Change in South India* (Manchester: Manchester University Press, 1962).

——, *Women, Work and Family* (London: Croom Helm, 1986).

Fardon R., ed., *Localizing Strategies: Regional Traditions of Ethnographic Writing* (Smithsonian Institute: Scottish Academic Press, 1990).

——, *Counterworks: Managing the Diversity of Knowledge* (London: Routledge, 1995).

Feierman S., *Peasant Intellectuals* (Madison: University of Wisconsin Press, 1990).

Ferguson J., "Mobile Workers, Modernist Narratives: A Critique of the Historiography of Transition on the Zambian Copperbelt. Part Two," *Journal of Southern African Studies* 16, no. 4 (1990).

——, *Expectations of Modernity: Myths and Meanings of Urban Life on the Zambian Copperbelt* (London: University of California Press, 1999) 32–33.

Firth R., "Max Gluckman, 1911–1975," *Proceedings of the British Academy* 61 (1975): 478–96.

Fleck L., *The Genesis and Development of a Scientific Fact* (Chicago: University of Chicago Press, 1979).

Fortes M., and Patterson S., eds., *Studies in African Social Anthropology* (London: Macmillan, 1975).

Fosbrooke H., "From Lusaka to Salisbury, 1956–1960," *African Social Research* 24 (1977): 319–26.

Fox Keller E., *A Feeling for the Organism: The Life and Work of Barbara McClintock* (San Francisco: W. H. Freeman, 1983).

Frankenberg R., "Economic Anthropology or Political Economy? (I): the Barotse Social Formation — A Case Study," in Clammer J., ed., *The New Economic Anthropology* (New York: St. Martin's Press, 1978).

——, "A Social Anthropology for Britain?" in Frankenberg R., ed., *Custom and Conflict in British Society* (Manchester: Manchester University Press, 1982), 1–35.

——, ed., *Custom and Conflict in British Society* (Manchester: Manchester University Press, 1982).

Füredi F., *Colonial Wars and the Politics of Third World Nationalism* (London: I. B. Tauris, 1994).

——, *The Silent War: Imperialism and the Changing Perception of Race* (London: Pluto Press, 1998).

Gann L. H., *The Birth of a Plural Society: The Development of Northern Rhodesia under the British South Africa Company, 1894–1914* (Manchester: Manchester University Press, 1958).

——, *A History of Northern Rhodesia: Early Days to 1953* (London: Chatto and Windus, 1964).

——, "Ex Africa: an Africanist's Intellectual Autobiography," *Journal of Modern African Studies* 31, no. 3 (1993): 477–98.

Gertzel C. and Szeftel M., "Politics in an African Urban Setting: The Role of the Copperbelt in the Transition to the One-Party State, 1964–73," in Gertzel C., Baylies C. and Szeftel M., eds., *The Dynamics of the One Party State in Zambia* (Manchester: Manchester University Press, 1984).

Gertzel C., Baylies C. and Szeftel M., eds., *The Dynamics of the One Party State in Zambia* (Manchester: Manchester University Press, 1984).

Gifford P., "Misconceived Dominion: The Creation and Disintegration of Federation in British Central Africa," in Gifford and W. R. Louis, eds., *The Transfer of Power in Africa: Decolonization, 1940–1960* (New Haven, Conn.: Yale Univeristy Press, 1982), 387–416.

——, ed., *The Predicament of Culture: Twentieth-Century Ethnography, Literature, and Art* (Cambridge: Harvard University Press, 1988).

Gifford P. and Louis W. R., eds., *The Transfer of Power in Africa: Decolonization, 1940–1960* (New Haven, Conn.: Yale University Press, 1982).

——, eds., *Decolonization and African Independence: The Transfers of Power, 1960–1980* (New Haven, Conn.: Yale University Press, 1988).

Gluckman M., "Analysis of a Social Situation in Modern Zululand," *Bantu Studies (African Studies)* 1940 and 1942 (republished in *Rhodes-Livingstone Papers* 28 in 1958, with a foreword by J. Clyde Mitchell).

——, "Economy of the Central Barotse Plain," *Rhodes-Livingstone Papers* 7 (1942).

——, "Essays on Lozi Land and Royal Property," *Rhodes-Livingstone Papers* 10 (1944).

——, "Seven-Year Research Plan of the Rhodes-Livingstone Institute of

Social Studies in Central Africa," *Rhodes-Livingstone Journal* 4 (1945): 1–33.

——, "The Use of Sociological Research in Museum Display," *Rhodes-Livingstone Journal* 4 (1945): 66–73.

——, "Human Laboratory across the Zambesi," *Libertas* 6, no. 4 (1946): 38–49.

——, "Land Holding & Land Usage among the Plateau Tonga of Mazabuka District: A Reconnaissance Survey, 1945," *Rhodes-Livingstone Papers* 14 (1948).

——, "Malinowski's Sociological Theories," *Rhodes-Livingstone Papers* 16 (1949): 27–28.

——, "Social Anthropology in Central Africa" *Rhodes-Livingstone Journal* 20 (1956): 17.

——, *The Judicial Process among the Barotse of Northern Rhodesia*, 2d ed. (Manchester: Manchester University Press, 1967).

——, "Anthropology and Apartheid," in Fortes M. and Patterson S.. eds., *Studies in African Social Anthropology* (London: Macmillan, 1975), 21–40.

Gordon R., "Apartheid's Anthropologists: The Genealogy of Afrikaner Anthropology," *American Ethnologist* 15, no. 3 (1988): 536–37.

——, "Early Social Anthropology in South Africa," *African Studies* 49, no.1 (1990): 15–48.

Gray R., Institute of Race Relations, *The Two Nations: Aspects of the Development of Race Relations in the Rhodesias and Nyasaland* (London: Oxford University Press, 1960).

Griesemer J. R., "Modeling in the Museum: On the Role of Remnant Models in the Work of Joseph Grinnell," *Biology and Philosophy* 5 (1990): 3–36.

Grillo R. and Rew A., eds., *Social Anthropology and Development Policy*, ASA Monographs 23 (London: Tavistock Publications, 1985).

Grimshaw A. and Hart K., *Anthropology and the Crisis of the Intellectuals*, Prickly Pear Pamphlet No. 1 (Cambridge: Prickly Pear Press, 1993).

Hailey M. (Lord), *African Survey* (London: Oxford University Press, 1938).

Hammond-Tooke W. D., *Imperfect Interpreters: South Africa's Anthropologists, 1920–1990* (Johannesburg: Witwatersrand University Press, 1997).

Hansen K. T., *Distant Companions: Servants and Employers in Zambia, 1900–1985* (Ithaca, N.Y.: Cornell University Press, 1989).

——, "After Copper Town: The Past in the Present in Urban Zambia," *Journal of Anthropological Research* 47 (1991): 441–56.

Hansen K. T. and Ashbaugh L., "Women on the Front Line: Development Issues in Southern Africa," *Women and International Development Journal* 2 (1991): 205–40.

Hannerz U., *Exploring the City* (New York: Columbia University Press, 1980).

Harries-Jones P., *Freedom and Labour: Mobilization and Political Control on the Zambian Copperbelt* (Oxford: Oxford University Press, 1975).

Harwood J., *Styles of Scientific Thought: The German Genetics Community, 1900–33* (London: University of Chicago Press, 1993).

Heisler H., *Urbanisation and the Government of Migration: The Interrelation of Urban and Rural Life in Zambia* (London: C. Hurst, 1974).

Hellman E., "Rooiyard: A Sociological Survey of an Urban Native Slum Yard," *Rhodes-Livingstone Papers* 13, 1948.

Helm J., ed., *Essays on the Problem of Tribe* (Seattle: University of Washington Press, 1968).

Henkel R., *Christian Missions in Africa: Zambia* (Berlin: Dietrich Reimer Verlag, 1989).

Herkovits M., "The Cattle Complex of East Africa," *American Anthropologist* 28 (1926): 361–88.

——, "The Culture Areas of Africa," *Africa* 3, no. 1 (1930): 59–77.

Heron A., "The Years of Transition, 1963–67," *African Social Research* 24 (1978): 331–34.

Hobhouse L. T., Wheeler G. C. and Ginsburg M., *The Material Culture and Social Institutions of the Simpler Peoples: An Essay on Correlation* (London: Chapman & Hall, 1915).

Hobsbawm E. and Ranger T., *The Invention of Tradition* (Cambridge: Cambridge University Press, 1983).

Holleman J. F., "The Pattern of Hera Kinship," *Rhodes-Livingstone Papers* 17 (1949).

——, *Shona Customary Law* (Cape Town: Oxford University Press, 1952).

——, "Accommodating the Spirit among Some North-Eastern Shona Tribes," *Rhodes-Livingstone Papers* 22 (1953).

——, *Chief, Council, and Commissioner: Some Problems of Government in Rhodesia* (London: Oxford University Press, 1968).

Holleman J. F. and Biesheuvel S., *White Mine Workers in Northern Rhodesia, 1959–60* (Leiden: Afrika-Studiecentrum, 1973).

Hugo P., ed., *Truth Be in the Field: Social Science Research in Southern Africa* (Pretoria: University of South Africa Press, 1990).

Husbands W., "Nature, Society, and the Origin of Tourism at Victoria Falls (Zambia)," unpublished paper, 1994.

Hutchinson S., *Nuer Dilemmas* (Berkeley: University of California Press, 1996).

Huxley E., *Murder at Government House* (New York: Penguin, 1937).

Hymes D., ed., *Reinventing Anthropology* (New York: Pantheon Books, 1972).

Innes D., "Sir Alfred Chester Beatty," *Horizon* 11, no. 3 (1968): 18–21.

Innes D., *Anglo: Anglo American and the Rise of Modern South Africa* (Johannesburg: Ravan Press, 1984).

Jardine N., Secord A. and Spary E. C., eds., *Cultures of Natural History* (Cambridge: Cambridge University Press, 1996).

Jules-Rosette B., "Decentering Ethnography: Victor Turner's Vision of Anthropology," *Journal of Religion in Africa* 24, no. 2 (1994): 160–81.

Kabamba J. M., "The Institute for African Studies in Retrospective: A Review, 1983–1986," *IAS Research Report* (Lusaka: Institute for African Studies, 1989).

Kapferer B., *Strategy and Transaction in an African Factory* (Manchester: Manchester University Press, 1972).

Karp I., *Museums and Their Communities* (Washington: Smithsonian Institution Press, 1992).

Karp I. and Lavine S., eds., *Exhibiting Cultures* (Washington: Smithsonian Institution Press, 1991).

Kashoki, M., "Indigenous Scholarship in African Universities: The Human Factor," in Fahim H., ed., *Indigenous Anthropology in Non-Western Countries* (Durham: Carolina Academic Press, 1982).

——, "The Institute for African Studies in the University of Zambia and the Future of Social Science Research into the 21st Century," address to the conference on the 50th Anniversary of the Institute for African Studies, 19 June 1989 (manuscript).

de Kock L., "English and the Colonisation of Form," *Journal of Literary Studies* 8, nos. 1–2 (1992): 32–54.

——, " 'Drinking at the English Fountains': Missionary Discourse and the Case of Lovedale," *Missionalia* 20, no.2 (August 1992): 116–38.

Kuhn T., *The Structure of Scientific Revolutions* (Chicago: University of Chicago Press, 1962).

Kuklick H., "Professional Status and the Social Order," manuscript, n.d.

——, "The Sociology of Knowledge: Retrospect and Prospect," *Annual Reviews in Sociology* 9 (1983): 287–310.

——, *The Savage Within: The Social History of British Anthropology, 1885–1945* (Cambridge: Cambridge University Press, 1991).

——, "Contested Monuments — The Politics of Archaeology in Southern Africa," in George W. Stocking Jr., *Colonial Situations — Essays on the Contextualization of Ethnographic Knowledge* (Madison: University of Wisconsin Press, 1991), 135–69.

——, "Speaking with the Dead," *Isis* 89 (1998): 103–11.

Kuklick H. and Kohler R., "Science in the Field," *Osiris* 11 (1996): 237–58.

Kumar N., *Friends, Brothers, and Informants: Fieldwork Memoirs of Banaras* (Berkeley: University of California Press, 1992).

Kuper A., *Anthropology and Anthropologists: The Modern British School* (London: Routledge, 1983).

Latour B., *Science in Action: How to Follow Scientists and Engineers Through Society* (Cambridge: Harvard University Press, 1987).

Latour B. and Woolgar S., *Laboratory Life: The Construction of Scientific Facts*, 2d ed. (Princeton, N.J.: Princeton University Press, 1986).

Leigh Star S. and Griesemer J. R., "Institutional Ecology, 'Translations,' and Boundary Objects: Amateurs and Professionals in Berkeley's Museum of Vertebrate Zoology, 1907–39," *Social Studies of Science* 19 (1989): 387–420.

Liswaniso M., "The Livingstone Museum — Storehouse of Zambian Culture," *Horizon* 11, no. 11 (1968): 13–17.

Livingstone D. N., "Human Acclimatization: Perspectives on a Contested Field of Inquiry in Science, Medicine, and Geography, *History of Science* 25 (1987): 359–94.

Long N., *Social Change and the Individual: A Study of the Social and Religious Responses to Innovation in a Zambian Rural Community* (Manchester: Manchester University Press, 1968).

——, *An Introduction to the Sociology of Rural Development* (London: Tavistock, 1977).

Long N. and Long A., eds., *Battlefields of Knowledge: The Interlocking of Theory and Practice in Social Research and Development* (London: Routledge, 1992).

Louis W. R. and Robinson R., *The Transfer of Power in Africa: Decolonization, 1940–1960* (New Haven, Conn.: Yale University Press, 1982),.

———, "The United States and the Liquidation of the British Empire in Tropical Africa, 1941–1951," in Louis and Robinson, *The Transfer of Power in Africa: Decolonization, 1940–1960* (New Haven, Conn.: Yale University Press, 1982), 31–56.

Louw J., "This is Thy Work: A Contextual History of Applied Psychology and Labour in South Africa," Ph.D. diss., University of Amsterdam, 1986.

Low A., "The End of the British Empire in Africa," in P. Gifford and W. Roger Louis, eds., *Decolonization and African Independence: The Transfers of Power, 1960–1980* (New Haven, Conn.: Yale University Press, 1988), 33–72.

Lukhero M. B., *Ngoni Nc'wala Ceremony* (Lusaka, Zambia: NECZAM, 1993).

———, "Chieftainship, Tradition and Change in Ngoni Society," *Cambridge Anthropology* 21, no. 2 (1999/2000): 17–40; 19–20.

MacMillan H., " 'Paralyzed Conservatives': W. M. Macmillan, the Social Scientists and 'The Common Society,' " in MacMillan H. and Marks S., eds., *Africa and Empire: W. M. Macmillan, Historian and Social Critic* (Aldershot, Eng.: Temple Smith, 1989), 72–90.

———, "Return to the Malungwana Drift — Max Gluckman, the Zulu Nation and the Common Society," paper presented at the conference "Ethnicity, Society and Conflict in Natal," University of Natal, Pietermaritzburg, 14–16 September 1992.

———, "The Historiography of Transition on the Zambian Copperbelt — Another View," *Journal of Southern African Studies* 19, no. 4 (1993): 681–712.

———, "Return to the Malungwana Drift — Max Gluckman, the Zulu Nation and the Common Society," *African Affairs* 94, no. 374 (1995): 39–65.

MacMillan H. and Marks S., eds., *Africa and Empire: W. M. Macmillan, Historian and Social Critic* (Aldershot, Eng.: Temple Smith, 1989).

Magubane B., "Pluralism and Conflict Situations in Africa: A New Look," *African Social Research* 7 (1969): 529–54.

——, "A Critical Look at the Indices Used in the Study of Social Change in Colonial Africa," *Current Anthropology* 12 (1971): 419–45.

Mair L., *Methods of Study of Culture Contact in Africa*, Memorandum 15 of the International African Institute (London: International African Institute, 1946).

——, ed., *Materials for the Study of Culture Contact* (London, 1938).

Malinowski B., *The Dynamics of Culture Contact* (New Haven: Yale University Press, 1938), republished in Mair L., *Methods of Study of Culture Contact in Africa*, Memorandum 15 of the International African Institute (London: International African Institute, 1946).

Marwick A., *A History of the Modern British Isles, 1914–1999* (Oxford: Blackwell Publishers, 2000).

Marwick M., *Sorcery in Its Social Setting: A Study of the Northern Rhodesia Ceŵa* (Manchester: Manchester University Press, 1965).

Marx E., "Anthropological Studies in a Centralized State: Max Gluckman and the Israel Bernstein Research Project," *Jewish Journal of Sociology* 17 (1975), 131–50.

Masefield G. B., *A History of the Colonial Agricultural Service* (Oxford: Clarendon Press, 1972).

Mitchell J. C., "The Collection and Treatment of Family Budgets in Primitive Communities as a Field Problem," *Rhodes-Livingstone Journal* 8 (1949): 50–56.

——, *The Yao Village: A Study in the Social Structure of a Nyasaland Tribe* (Manchester: Manchester University Press, 1956).

——, "The Kalela Dance," *Rhodes-Livingstone Papers* 27 (1956).

——, "The Shadow of Federation, 1952–55," *African Social Research* 24 (1977): 309–18.

——, *Cities, Society, and Social Perception: A Central African Perspective* (Oxford: Oxford University Press, 1987).

Moore R. J. B, *These African Copper Miners* (London: Livingstone Press, 1948).

Moore S. F., *Anthropology and Africa* (Charlottesville: University Press of Virginia, 1994).

Moreno J. L., *Who Shall Survive? Foundations of Sociometry, Group Psychotherapy and Sociodrama* (Washington, D.C.: Nervous and Mental Disease Publications Company, 1934).

Morgan K., *Labour in Power, 1945–1951* (Oxford: Oxford University Press, 1984).

Mulford D. C., *Zambia: The Politics of Independence, 1957–1964* (Oxford: Oxford University Press, 1967).

Mulkay M., *Science and the Sociology of Knowledge* (London: Allen and Unwin, 1979).

Murray B. K., *Wits: The "Open" Years* (Johannesburg: Witwatersrand University Press, 1997).

Mushindo P., *A Short History of the Bemba* (Lusaka: National Education Company of Zambia for the Institute of African Studies, University of Zambia, 1977).

Nsugbe P. O., "Brief but Black Authority, 1968–70," *African Social Research* 24 (1977): 335–40.

Okely J. and Callaway H., eds., *Anthropology and Autobiography* (London: Routledge, 1995).

Oliver R., *The Missionary Factor in East Africa* (London: Longmans, Green, 1952).

O'Shea M., *Missionaries and Miners* (Ndola: Mission Press, 1986.).

Papstein R., "From Ethnic Identity to Tribalism: The Upper Zambezi Region of Zambia, 1830–1981," in L. Vail, ed., *The Creation of Tribalism in Southern Africa* (London: James Currey, 1989), 372–94.

Parnell S., "Creating Racial Privilege: The Origins of South African Public Health and Town Planning Legislation," *Journal of Southern African Studies* 19, no. 3 (1993): 471–88.

Parpart J. L., *Labor and Capital on the African Copperbelt* (Philadelphia: Temple University Press, 1983).

Pels P., "The Anthropology of Colonialism," *Annual Review of Anthropology* 26 (1997): 163–234.

Pels P. and Salemink O., "Introduction: Five Theses on Ethnography as Colonial Practice," *History and Anthropology* 8, nos. 1–4 (1994): 1–34.

Pels P. and Salemink O., eds., *Colonial Subjects: Essays in the Practical History of Anthropology* (Ann Arbor: University of Michigan Press, 1998).

Perkin H., *The Rise of Professional Society: England Since 1880* (London: Routledge, 1989).

Peters D. U., "Land Usage in Serenje District," *Rhodes-Livingstone Papers* 19 (1950).

Phillips H., *The University of Cape Town, 1918–1948: The Formative Years* (Cape Town: University of Cape Town Press, 1993).

Poovey M., *A History of the Modern Fact: Problems of Knowledge in the*

Sciences of Wealth and Society (Chicago: University of Chicago Press, 1998).

Powdermaker H., *Coppertown: Changing Africa* (New York: Harper & Row, 1962).

——, *Stranger and Friend: The Way of an Anthropologist* (New York: W. W. Norton, 1966).

Prins G., *The Hidden Hippopotamus: Reappraisal in African History, The Early Colonial Experience in Western Zambia* (Cambridge: Cambridge University Press, 1980).

Ranger T. and Vaughan O., eds., *Legitimacy and the State in Twentieth-Century Africa* (London: Macmillan, 1993).

Ranger T., "The Invention of Tradition Revisited," in Ranger and Olufemi Vaughan, eds., *Legitimacy and the State in Twentieth-Century Africa* (London: Macmillan, 1993), 62–111.

Read M., "Tradition and Prestige Among the Ngoni," *Africa* 9 (1936): 453–84.

——, "The Moral Code of the Ngoni and Their Former Military State," *Africa* 11 (1938): 1–24.

——, "Native Standards of Living and African Culture Change," *Africa* 11, Supplement (1938).

——, "Migrant Labour in Africa and its Effect on Tribal Life," *International Labour Review* 45 (1942): 605–31.

Reynolds B., *Magic, Divination and Witchcraft among the Barotse of Northern Rhodesia* (London: Chatto & Windus, 1963).

Richards A., *Land, Labour and Diet: An Economic Study of the Bemba Tribe* (London: Oxford University Press, 1939).

——, "Malinowski," *New Society* 41 (1963): 16–17.

——, "The Rhodes-Livingstone Institute: An Experiment in Research, 1933–38," *African Social Research* 24 (1977): 275–78.

Rigby P., *Persistent Pastoralists: Nomadic Societies in Transition* (London: Zed Books, 1985).

——, *African Images: Racism and the End of Anthropology* (Oxford: Berg, 1996).

Roper M. and Tosh J., eds., *Manful Assertions: Masculinities in Britain Since 1800* (London: Routledge, 1991).

Roper M. and Tosh J., "Introduction: Historians and the Politics of Masculinity," in Roper and Tosh, eds., *Manful Assertions: Masculinities in Britain Since 1800* (London: Routledge, 1991), 1–24.

Rosaldo M. and Lamphere L., eds., *Woman, Culture, and Society* (Stanford: Stanford University Press, 1974).

Rotberg R. I., *Christian Missionaries and the Creation of Northern Rhodesia, 1880–1924* (Princeton: Princeton University Press, 1965).

———, *Black Heart: Gore-Browne and the Politics of Multiracial Zambia* (Berkeley: University of California Press, 1977).

Rudwick M. J. S., "The Emergence of a Visual Language for Geological Science, 1760–1830," *History of Science* 14 (1976): 149–95.

Sanjek R., "Urban Anthropology in the 1980s: A World View," *Annual Review of Anthropology* 19 (1990): 151–86.

———, "Anthropology's Hidden Colonialism: Assistants and their Ethnographers," *Anthropology Today* 9, no. 2 (April 1993): 13–18.

———, ed., *Fieldnotes: The Makings of Anthropology* (Ithaca, N.Y.: Cornell University Press, 1990).

Saunders C., *The Making of the South African Past: Major Historians on Race and Class* (Cape Town: David Philip, 1988).

Schumaker L., "A Tent with A View: Colonial Officers, Anthropologists, and the Making of the Field in Northern Rhodesia, 1937–1960," in Kuklick H. and Kohler R., eds., "Science in the Field," *Osiris* 11 (1996): 237–58.

———, "Landscaping Race," in P. Pels and O. Salemink, eds., *Colonial Subjects: Essays in the Practical History of Anthropology* (Ann Arbor: University of Michigan Press, 1998).

Schuster J. A., "Methodologies as Mythic Structures: A Preface to the Future Historiography of Method," *Metascience*, nos. 1–2 (1984): 15–36.

Schuster J. A. and Yeo R. R., eds., *The Politics and Rhetoric of Scientific Method* (Dordrecht: D. Reidel, 1986).

Scudder T. and Colson E., "Long-Term Field Research in Gwembe Valley, Zambia," in Foster G., Scudder T., Colson E. and Kemper R., eds., *Long-Term Field Research in Social Anthropology* (New York: Academic Press, 1979), 227–54.

Searle G. R., *The Quest for National Efficiency* (Berkeley: University of California Press, 1971).

Serpell R., "Setting Research Priorities for a University Research Institute in Southern Africa," in Michael Malefetsane Sefali, ed., *Southern Africa: Research for Development* (Roma, Lesotho: Institute of Southern African Studies, 1988), 251–67.

Short R., *African Sunset* (London: Johnson, 1973).

Siegel B., "The 'Wild' and 'Lazy' Lamba: Ethnic Stereotypes on the Central African Copperbelt," in Vail L., ed., *The Creation of Tribalism in Southern Africa* (London: James Currey, 1989), 372–94.

Simpson D., *Dark Companions: The African Contribution to the European Exploration of East Africa* (London: Elek, 1975).

Shapin S., "The House of Experiment in Seventeenth-Century England," *Isis* 79 (1988): 373–404.

——, *A Social History of Truth: Civility and Science in Seventeenth-Century England* (Chicago: University of Chicago Press, 1994).

Simons H. J. and Simons R., *Class and Colour in South Africa, 1850–1950* (London: International Defence and Aid Fund for Southern Africa, 1983).

"Sir Roy Welensky, Obituary," *The Times*, 6 December 1991.

Smith E. and Dale A., *The Ila-Speaking Peoples of Northern Rhodesia*, 2 vols. (London: Macmillan, 1920).

Smith M. R., *Harpers Ferry Armory and the New Technology* (Ithaca, N.Y.: Cornell University Press, 1977).

Sonnabend H. and Sofer C., *South Africa's Stepchildren* (Johannesburg: South African Institute of Race Relations, 1947–48).

Soojung-Kim Pang A., "Spheres of Interest: Imperialism, Culture, and Practice in British Solar Eclipse Expeditions, 1860–1914," Ph.D. diss., University of Pennsylvania, 1991.

Stepan N. L., "Race and Gender: The Role of Analogy in Science," *Isis* 77 (1986): 261–77.

Stocking Jr. G. W., "Tenting with Malinowski," *American Sociological Review* 47 (1972):1–13.

——, "The Ethnographer's Magic: Fieldwork in British Anthropology from Tylor to Malinowski," in Stocking, ed., *Observers Observed: Essays on Ethnographic Fieldwork* (Madison: University of Wisconsin Press, 1983), 70–120.

——, "Philanthropoids and Vanishing Cultures," in Stocking, ed., *Objects and Others* (Madison: University of Wisconsin Press, 1985), 112–45.

——, "Paradigmatic Traditions in the History of Anthropology," in Stocking, *The Ethnographer's Magic and Other Essays in the History of Anthropology* (Madison: University of Wisconsin Press, 1992), 342–61.

——, *After Tylor: British Social Anthropology, 1888–1951* (London: Athlone Press, 1995).

——, ed., *Observers Observed: Essays on Ethnographic Fieldwork* (Madison: University of Wisconsin Press, 1983).

——, ed., *Objects and Others* (Madison: University of Wisconsin Press, 1985).

——, ed., *Colonial Situations: Essays on the Contextualization of Ethnographic Knowledge* (History of Anthropology 7, Madison: University of Wisconsin Press, 1991).

Stoler A. L., "Making Empire Respectable: The Politics of Race and Sexual Morality in 20th-century Colonial Cultures," *American Ethnologist* 16, no. 4 (1989): 634–60.

——, "Rethinking Colonial Categories: European Communities and the Boundaries of Rule," in *Colonialism and Culture*, ed. Nicholas B. Dirks (Ann Arbor: University of Michigan Press, 1992), 319–52.

——, *Race and the Education of Desire: Foucault's "History of Sexuality" and the Colonial Order of Things* (London: Duke University Press, 1995).

Swanson M. W., "The Sanitation Syndrome: Bubonic Plague and Urban Native Policy in the Cape Colony, 1900–1909," *Journal of African History* 18, no. 3 (1977): 387–410.

Swartz M. J., "Inter-hierarchical Roles: Professional and Party Ethics in Tribal Areas in South and Central Africa," in Swartz, ed., *Local-Level Politics: Social and Cultural Perspectives* (Chicago: Aldine, 1968).

Tawney R. H., *The Acquisitive Society* (London: Bell, 1921).

Thomas N., *Colonialism's Culture: Anthropology, Travel, and Government* (London: Polity Press, 1994).

Thompson L., *A History of South Africa* (New Haven, Conn.: Yale University Press, 1990).

Toulmin S., *Human Understanding* (Oxford: Clarendon Press, 1972).

Trapnell C. G. and Clothier J. N., *The Soils, Vegetation and Agricultural Systems of North-Western Rhodesia* (Lusaka: Government Printer, 1957).

Traweek S., *Beamtimes and Lifetimes: The World of High Energy Physicists* (Cambridge: Harvard University Press, 1988).

Turner E., *The Spirit and the Drum: A Memoir of Africa* (Tucson: University of Arizona Press, 1987).

——, "Changes in the Status of Senior Women Anthropologists After Feminist Revisions," paper for the Association for Feminist Anthropology, panel titled "Through a Gendered Looking Glass: Women Doing

Ethnography Before and After 1974," American Anthropological Association Meetings, 1995.

Turner V., *Schism and Continuity in an African Society: A Study of Ndembu Village Life* (Manchester: Manchester University Press, 1957).

———, *The Forest of Symbols: Aspects of Ndembu Ritual* (Ithaca, N.Y.: Cornell University Press, 1967).

Tweedie A., "Change and Continuity in Bemba Society," D.Phil., thesis, University of Oxford, 1966.

Uberoi J. S., *The Politics of the Kula Ring: An Analysis of the Findings of Bronislaw Malinowski* (Manchester: Manchester University Press, 1962).

———, *The Other Mind of Europe: Goethe as Scientist* (Oxford: Oxford University Press, 1984).

Vail L., ed., *The Creation of Tribalism in Southern Africa* (London: James Currey, 1989).

van Donge J. K., "Understanding Rural Zambia Today: The Relevance of the Rhodes-Livingstone Institute," *Africa* 55, no. 1 (1985): 60–75.

Vansina J., *Paths in the Rainforests: Toward a History of Political Tradition in Equatorial Africa* (London: James Currey, 1990).

van Teeffelen T., "The Manchester School in Africa and Israel: A Critique," in S. Diamond, ed., *Anthropology: Ancestors and Heirs* (The Hague: Mouton, 1980), 347–75.

van Velsen, *The Politics of Kinship: A Study in Social Manipulation among the Lakeside Tonga of Nyasaland* (Manchester: Manchester University Press, 1964).

Vaughan M., "Colonial Discourse Theory and African History, Or has Postmodernism Passed Us By?" *Social Dynamics* 20, no. 2 (1994): 1–23.

Vaughan M. and Moore H. L., *Cutting Down Trees: Gender, Nutrition and Agricultural Change in the Northern Province of Zambia, 1890–1990* (London: James Currey, 1994).

Vincent J., *Anthropology and Politics* (Tucson: University of Arizona Press, 1990).

Watson W., *Tribal Cohesion in a Money Economy: A Study of the Mambwe People of Northern Rhodesia* (Manchester: Manchester University Press, 1958).

Weiler P., *British Labour and the Cold War* (Stanford, Calif.: Stanford University Press, 1988).

Welsh D., "Social Research in a Divided Society: The Case of South Africa," *Social Dynamics*, no. 1(1975): 19–30.

Werbner R., "The Manchester School in South-Central Africa," *Annual Review of Anthropology* 13 (1984): 157–85

White C. M. N., "Interregna, 1955–56 and 1960–62," *African Social Research* 24 (1977): 327–30.

Whitehead F., "The Government Social Survey," in Martin Bulmer, ed., *Essays on the History of British Sociological Research* (Cambridge: Cambridge University Press, 1985), 83–100.

Whitehead T. L. and Price L., "Summary: Sex and the Fieldwork Experience," in Whitehead and Mary Ellen Conaway, *Self, Sex, and Gender in Cross-Cultural Fieldwork* (Urbana: University of Illinois Press, 1986), 289–304.

Wilson G., "The Economics of Detribalization in Northern Rhodesia," Parts I and II, *Rhodes-Livingstone Papers* 5 and 6 (1941) and (1942).

Wilson G. and Wilson M., *The Analysis of Social Change: Based on Observations in Central Africa* (London: Cambridge University Press, 1968).

Wilson M., *Reaction to Conquest: Effects of Contact with Europeans on the Pondo of South Africa* (London: Oxford University Press, 1936).

——, "Development in Anthropology," *Race Relations Journal* 22, no. 4 (1955): 6–11.

——, "Lovedale: Instrument of Peace," in *Outlook on a Century: South Africa 1870–1970*, ed. Francis Wilson and Dominique Perrot (Lovedale, South Africa: Lovedale Press, 1973).

Wilson M., ". . . So Truth Be in the Field . . .": *Social Science Research in Southern Africa* (Johannesburg: South African Institute of Race Relations, 1975).

——, "The First Three Years, 1938–41," *African Social Research* 24 (1977): 279–84.

Wilson M. and Mafeje A., *Langa: A Study of Social Groups in an African Township* (Cape Town: Oxford University Press, 1963).

Wright M., "Technology, Marriage and Women's Work in the History of Maize-Growers in Mazabuka, Zambia: A Reconnaissance," *Journal of Southern African Studies* 10, no. 1 (1983): 71–85.

Wylie K. C. and Hickey D., *An Enchanting Darkness: The American Vision of Africa in the Twentieth Century* (East Lansing: Michigan State University, 1993).

INDEX

Abercorn (Mbala), 188
Aborigines Protection Society, 27,
    270n. 16
Acculturation, 79, 83
Administrator(s), 14, 16, 18, 50–
    51, 88, 123, 137, 140–41, 149,
    160, 167, 187, 190, 193, 214–
    15, 332n. 109; administrator-
    ethnographers, 58, 99, 102, 228,
    230, 240–46; Africans' attitudes
    toward, 127–28, 164–65, 200–
    203, 207, 220; attitudes to an-
    thropology, 64–68, 109, 112,
    122, 130, 134, 143, 223–34; in-
    fluence on anthropology, 7, 45–
    49, 70–71, 85, 91–93, 176,
    195–98, 200–203, 224–25,
    257–58; relationships with an-
    thropologists, 18, 39–42, 60, 76,
    99, 101, 230, 241–48, 281n. 84;
    in towns, 162, 164–65. *See also*
    Technical officers
African Marriage Survey, 107
African National Congress (ANC).
    See Northern Rhodesian African
    National Congress (ANC)
African nationalism, 186, 188–89,
    208, 213, 215, 218, 220–21,
    223–24, 230, 244
African Salaried Staff Association,
    216

African Survey, 85
Africanization, 17, 197; definition,
    16, 268n. 30
Afrikaans, 44, 46–47, 137
Afrikaners, 44–46, 76, 142–43,
    149
Aginsky, Bert, 133
Aginsky, Ethel, 133
Agriculturists. *See* Technical
    officers
Akapelwa, Possenta, 211
Allan, William, 39, 40, 69, 76, 86,
    233, 244
Amalgamation, 26, 164. *See also*
    British Central African
    Federation
American Metal Company, 31. *See
    also* Mines
"Analysis of a Social Situation in
    Modern Zululand" (Gluckman),
    42–49, 56, 78–79, 138, 153,
    156, 174, 179, 213, 274n. 9,
    286n. 14
Anglo-American Corporation, 31,
    34, 58, 173, 176. *See also* Mines
Anglo-Boer War, 44
Anthropologization, 15–17; defini-
    tion, 15
Anthropology: applied, 66, 111,
    113, 119, 228, 232; of colonial-
    ism, 7, 122; development, 232,

Anthropology: (*continued*)
248, 334n. 10; diffusionist, 68,
89, 102, 256; ethnomusicological, 232; evolutionary, 67, 102,
256; functionalist, 23–24, 29,
50, 241, 269n. 1; legal, 232;
Marxist, 58; physical, 89; professional strategies of, 240–41,
297n. 138; quantitative, 214; social, 4, 19, 23, 29, 33, 41, 54–55,
59, 66–68, 84, 88, 90, 101–2,
112–115, 118, 132, 150–51,
173, 226, 230, 232, 236, 243,
245, 247, 252, 255–56;
structural-functionalist, 45, 89,
90, 102, 113, 115; teamwork in,
22, 75, 87, 98, 113, 239, 253; urban, 20, 29, 34, 65, 72, 83, 87,
89, 116, 118, 145–48, 152–53,
155–57, 159, 171–74, 177, 179–
82, 190, 195, 205, 208, 229,
232. *See also* Ethnographers, indigenous; Ethnography; Functionalism; Fieldwork; Sociology
Anti-Semitism, 64. *See also* Jews
Apartheid, 34, 44–46, 74, 90, 91,
149, 251, 287n. 26. *See also*
Color bar; Race; Segregation
Apthorpe, Raymond, 190
Archeology, 32, 52, 54, 101, 102
Archers, The, 25
Argyle, John, 190
Association of Social Anthropolo-
gists, 241
Australia, 110
Australian National University, 74
Ayer, Frank, 63

Balandier, Georges, 246
Banda, Hastings Kamuzu, 222
Banda, P. P., 191
Banda, Rhupia, 191

Barnes, Frances, 3, 130
Barnes, John A., 1–3, 73–76, 80–
88, 91–93, 98, 100, 104–6, 110,
116–19, 127, 138, 141–42, 173,
175, 179–80, 241, 258, 263n. 1,
284n. 1, 289n. 42, 292n. 82,
301n. 23
Barotse, 39, 202, 234. *See also* Lozi
Barotseland (protectorate), 39, 40,
49–50, 53, 64–65, 71, 81, 97,
103–4, 118, 193, 199–200, 202
Barotse Native Authority: reform
of, 281n. 85
Batson, Edward, 157, 175, 309n.
18
BBC (radio), 25, 55, 286n. 16
Beatty, A. Chester, 31, 271n. 28
Belgian Congo, 29, 35, 82, 133,
139–40, 159, 162
Bemba, 81, 86, 117, 131–32, 153,
161, 182, 209, 212
Bettison, David, 157–59, 190
Bheshu, 43–45, 275n. 20
Biagioli, Mario, 244
Biesheuvel, Simon, 88, 160, 228
Bisa, 212
Bohannan, James (Jim), 110, 115
Bohannan, Laura, 110, 115
Boosterism, definition of, 162–63
Booth, Charles, 25, 157
Boundary objects, 257–58
Bowley, A. L., 157
Brandeis, Olivia, 129–30, 302n. 30
Britain, 24, 26, 27, 74, 86, 102,
110, 118, 146, 150, 164, 166,
178, 250
British Central African Federation,
4, 21, 26, 39, 77, 147–49, 164,
168, 171–72, 182–83, 190, 208,
218, 223–24, 228, 243, 288n.
33, 311n. 42. *See also* Amalga-
mation

British South Africa Company (BSAC), 53, 58, 96, 140, 164. *See also* Mines

Broken Hill (Kabwe), 39–40, 55–56, 60–61, 64, 147, 158, 162, 167, 172, 175, 181, 222

Broken Hill Development Company, 61. *See also* Mines

Brown, Richard, 31, 40, 54, 57, 63, 65

Bulawayo, 119

Bushmen, 32

Callaway, Helen, 122

Cambridge Expedition to the Torres Straits, 157

Capricorn Africa Society, 187, 216

Carnegie Commission, 30

Carnegie Corporation, 29

"Carrying capacity," 69

Cary-Jones, Hugh, 39

Case-study method, 107, 153, 180, 252, 299n. 151

Cattle complex, 28, 270n. 19

Census form, 106, 175, 188, 208

Central Africa, 19, 34–35, 76–77, 85, 115, 120, 124, 128, 146–47, 149–50, 154–55, 158, 183, 192, 194, 196, 206, 233, 236–37, 245, 250–53, 257–58

Central African Post, 143–44

Chabal, Patrick, 16

Cha Cha Cha campaign, 29, 186, 223

Chapoloko, James, 220

Chavunduka, Gordon, 331n. 103

Chewâ, 1

Chibaro (labor system), 53

Chicago School (of sociology), 29, 175

Chitemene (farming system), 87

Chiwale, Jacques Chileya, 197, 221, 233, 321n. 13

Christians, 43, 200–201, 204

Christian sociology, 59, 158

Citupa, definition of, 167

Clack, G., 190

Clark, Betty, 39

Clark, Desmond, 1, 32, 39–40, 63–64, 76, 102–3

Class, 18, 25, 35, 109–10, 137–40, 142, 168, 182, 191, 211, 240, 250, 309n. 23

Clay, Gervas, 68

Clifford, James, 12

Close, Ann, 118

Cohen, Andrew, 26, 75, 85, 143–44. *See also* Colonial Office

Cold War, 27, 30, 73, 215, 243. *See also* MacCarthyism

Colonial Development and Welfare Fund (CDWF), 31, 99, 119, 144, 171, 182

Colonial Office: 21, 27, 30, 31, 55, 60, 85, 111–12, 128, 130, 136, 143–44, 165, 167. *See also* Cohen, Andrew; Creech Jones, Arthur (colonial secretary)

Colonial Social Science Research Council (CSSRC), 1, 27, 32, 110–12, 136, 141, 143, 145–47, 151, 172–73

Color bar, 12, 20, 61, 77, 148, 206–7, 222, 224. *See also* Apartheid; Race; Segregation

Coloreds, 139, 142, 161

Colson, Elizabeth, 19, 70, 75–76, 82, 85–88, 93–97, 104–7, 110–11, 117–24, 130–36, 155, 175, 183, 190, 203–4, 230–36, 241, 258, 260, 300n. 7; as director, 119, 143–45, 148, 150, 173, 206; as *Kamwale,* 134, 260

Communism, 27, 64, 215. *See also* Communists

Communists, 64, 71, 188, 273n. 4, 275n. 20; Party, 74. *See also* Communism

Cooper, Frederick, 170

Copperbelt, 36, 53–63, 70–78, 83, 86, 101, 118, 145–50, 158–66, 168–69, 171–74, 182, 189, 204, 212, 218–19, 255; survey of, 19–20, 61, 66, 118, 146, 157, 170, 173–77, 180, 186, 188, 195, 208–10, 216, 218. *See also* Mines

Coproduction of knowledge: cultural, 3; scientific, 227

Creech Jones, Arthur (colonial secretary), 26, 144. *See also* Colonial Office

Culture brokers, 11–14, 192–94, 196, 201, 233, 249. *See also* Ethnographers, indigenous; Research assistant(s)

Culture contact, 44–45, 56, 78, 156, 240. *See also* Malinowski, Bronislaw

Cunnison, Ian, 82, 108, 110, 113, 117–19, 139, 141, 169, 197

Dale, A., 85

David Livingstone Memorial Museum, 54

Deane, Phyllis, 75–76, 85, 98, 100, 104–7, 157

Deregowski, Jan, 228

Detribalization, 57, 83, 156, 167

Development, 21, 26, 119; African, 165; agricultural, 58–59; colonial, 112; planning of, 14, 25, 28, 171, 231; planning movement, 19; rural, 231; schemes, 190, 249; uneven, 57–58; Zam-bian, 231. *See also* Underdevelopment

Dialectics, 72, 73, 115–16

Discourse theory, colonial, 8–9, 266n. 16

Durkheim, Emile, 90, 115

Dutch Reformed Church, 44

East Africa, 35, 64, 182

Ecologists, 69, 86. *See also* Technical officers

Elizabethville, 141

Elliot, Marjorie, 117–18

Epstein, A. L. (Bill), 27, 61, 78, 83, 110, 117–18, 153–54, 164, 172–77, 180–90, 208, 220, 222–29, 236, 252–55, 315nn. 93, 94, 95, 316nn. 97, 98, 317n. 108

Epstein, Scarlett, 232, 333n. 10

Equilibrium, 56–57, 116, 254; model of society, 115

Ethnicity, 78, 83, 139, 142, 156, 159–61, 173–74, 191, 194–97, 200–201, 204, 209–13, 233, 244, 249, 299n. 149, 309n. 23, 327n. 58, 329n. 72. *See also* Tribe(s)

Ethnographers, indigenous, 1–2, 11–14, 259, 267n. 24, 321n. 12. *See also* Anthropology; Ethnography

Ethnograhic map, 79

Ethnography, 85, 201; historical, 1, 3, 10, 266n. 20. *See also* Anthropology

Ethnolinguistics, 47

Ethnology, German, 47

Ethnos, 44

Evans-Pritchard, E. E., 52, 85, 110, 115, 118, 291n. 71, 302n. 28

Facts, 72, 283n. 100; social, 50

Fascism, 27, 64

Federal Party, 187, 216–17

Federation of Rhodesia and Nyasaland. *See* British Central African Federation

Field generation, 18, 23, 37, 39, 75, 117, 155, 186

Field science, 6, 17, 66

Fieldwork, 1, 4–6, 11, 17–18, 21, 25, 56–66, 76–78, 89, 93; conditions of, 6, 98–99, 293n. 95; ethos of, 65, 9–10, 71, 247; relationships within, 2, 6, 12, 16, 37, 39–42, 239, 249; rules for, 86, 92–97, 291n. 71, 293n. 85; styles of, 2, 46–48, 50, 69, 72–74, 114–15, 123, 246. *See also* Anthropology; Ethnography; Style(s); Work culture

Firth, Raymond, 41, 85, 110

Forde, Darryl, 110

Fort Hare (South African Native College), 35, 55, 212

Fortes, Meyer, 106, 110, 115

Fosbrooke, Henry, 146, 154, 190–91, 211, 223–26, 228, 232, 244, 336n. 27

Fox Keller, Evelyn, 124

Fox-Pitt, Thomas, 39, 71, 122–23, 283n. 99

Frankenberg, Ronald, 228

Fulbright Act, 30

Functionalism, 4, 19, 44–46, 85; paradigm, 84–85, 113, 247. *See also* Anthropology

Gann, Lewis, 117, 145, 153, 308n. 8

Gender, 18–89, 119–21, 123–27, 134–37, 191, 210–14, 300nn. 7, 8, 10, 301n. 23, 303n. 35, 304n. 48

Genealogical method, 22, 36, 86–87, 157, 242, 289n. 42

Gifford, Edward, 106

Ginsburg, Morris, 110, 315n. 94

Gluckman, Emanuel, 77

Gluckman, Mary, 39, 291n. 71

Gluckman, Max, 34, 56, 78, 115–18, 151–59, 173–74, 179, 198, 202–3, 226–32, 234–35, 240, 246–48, 251–58, 270n. 19, 281n. 84, 284nn. 1, 5, 296n. 127, 302n. 28; as *Makapweka*, 202, 320n. 8, 323n. 24; in Manchester, 4, 27, 112, 149, 172, 236, 245, 296n. 128; in Northern Rhodesia (Zambia), 19, 33, 48–55, 64–76, 78–85, 86–89, 92–99, 101–14, 123–29, 133–36, 141–46, 171–72, 180, 186, 193, 199–201, 204–8, 213, 237, 242–44, 256, 295n. 107, 301n. 22, 303n. 38, 314n. 70; at Oxford, 110, 144, 146; at Wits, 90; in Zululand, 39–46, 77, 93, 114, 138, 275nn. 18, 20

Gore-Browne, Lorna, 128, 129

Griaule, Marcel, 246

Groundnuts Scheme, 26

Hailey, M. (lord), 85

Handmaidens of colonialism, 7, 230

Hannerz, Ulf, 153

Hansen, Karen, 153

Harvard University, 90, 132

Heissler, Helmut, 165

Hellman, Ellen, 88, 90–91, 156

Hera, 80, 82, 118

Heron, Alastair, 228–29

Herskovits, Melville, 28, 270n. 19

Hertzog, J. B. M. (general), 155
Hibbert, J. G., 143
Hoernlé, R. F. A., 89, 286n. 18
Hoernlé, Winifred, 88, 90, 240
Holland, 44
Holleman, J. F. (Hans), 42–48, 65, 75–82, 83, 87, 92, 104, 108, 114–19, 160, 201, 228, 242, 274n. 8, 287n. 26, 298n. 140
Hollerith Machine, 176, 178
Hrdlicka, Ales, 32
Hughes, A. J. B., 108, 117–19
Huxley, Elspeth, 129–30, 302n. 30
Hyam, Bubbles, 108, 175

Ibbotson, Percy, 158
Ila, 85, 204
Incommensurability, 241, 245, 298n. 146
Indians, 138–40, 142
Induna(s), 200–201, 295n. 107, 303n. 38; definition of, 103
Industrial and Commercial Workers Union (ICU), 77, 284n. 3
Institute for Social Anthropology (Oxford), 118
Intellectuals, 193; definition of, 14, 268n. 29
Intercalary roles. *See* Interhierarchical roles
Interhierarchical roles, 86, 115, 251–52, 281n. 84, 287n. 26
International African Institute (IAI), 29, 56, 107, 119
International Institute of African Languages and Cultures, 30
International Missionary Council, 60
Israeli School (of sociology/social anthropology), 232

Jeffries, M. D. W., 88, 291n. 65
Jews, 43, 77, 188; as traders, 139–41. *See also* Anti-Semitism
Johannesburg, 53, 91, 93, 104, 156
Jules-Rosette, Bennetta, 13

Kadalie, Clements, 77
Kafunya, Albert, 76
"Kalela Dance, The" (Mitchell), 153, 173–74, 208, 211
Kalima, Ivor, 169, 313n. 64
Kamwale. See Colson, Elizabeth
Kariba Dam: resettlement study of, 146, 155, 190, 203, 232
Kashoki, Mubanga, 229–31, 319n. 4
Katanga mines, 53, 162. *See also* Mines
Katilungu, Lawrence, 181, 220
Katilungu, Simon, 185, 210–13, 218, 220–6, 326n. 53, 327n. 61, 331n. 109, 332n. 111
Katongo Camp, 103, 199, 295n. 106
Kay, George, 157, 190
Kenya, 204
Kenyatta, Jomo, 214, 328n. 71
Kinship, 80, 86, 115, 241
Kitwe, 147, 182, 210
Kluckhohn, Clyde, 106, 132
Konkola, Dixon, 221–22
Krige, Eileen, 91
Kuhn, Thomas, 113, 241
Kuklick, Henrika, 5
Kumpulula, Rajabu, 75
Kunda, 161
Kuper, Adam, 4
Kuper, Hilda, 88, 91

Labor migration, 69, 80–82, 86, 118, 155–56, 159, 162, 194, 246, 308n. 10, 313n. 55

Laboratory, 6, 63; field, 84, 133; human, 29, 34, 76, 79, 256; racial, 19, 32
Labour Party (Britain), 25, 26
Lake Kariba, 203
Lakeside Tonga, 117, 133, 153
Lamba, 70, 86–87, 98, 175, 208; survey, 109, 115, 179–80
Langa, 89
Lengwe, Joachim, 182, 213–14, 328n. 69
Lestrade, G. P., 87–90
Lewanika, Mwendaweli, 39, 118
Lewin, Julius, 88, 91
Libertas, 79, 286n. 17
Livingstone, David, 6, 52–53, 59, 101, 200
Livingstone (town), 19, 32, 39–42, 51–54, 60, 76, 77–83, 100–109, 111, 119, 144–47, 175, 208, 252–53, 277n. 35
Livingstone Mail, 54
Livingstonia Mission School, 35
London, 25, 31, 63, 105, 110, 180
London School of Economics (LSE), 29, 41, 55–56, 110, 153, 180
Long, Norman, 232, 334n. 10
Longton, Janet, 186
Lovedale Mission, 55, 278n. 40; school, 35
Lovedale Press, 33
Lozi, 39, 49–51, 53, 69, 71, 76, 81, 92, 97, 103, 118, 172, 186, 200–204, 212, 235, 258. *See also* Barotse
Luanshya, 61, 63, 150, 153, 169, 173, 176, 181, 186, 188, 208, 220
Luapula River, 82, 113, 133, 139, 141
Luchazi, 199, 201
Lukhero, Matshakaza Blackson, 1–

3, 18, 75–76, 83, 96, 175, 180, 210, 216, 222, 233, 258, 261, 329n. 78
Lunda, 80, 117–18, 169
Lundberg, George, 175
Lusaka, 9, 12, 19, 21, 40, 54, 56, 68, 81, 100–101, 119, 145–50, 173, 181, 185, 195, 207, 237, 243
Luvale, 161, 190, 199, 201

MacCrone, I. D., 88
Macmillan, Hugh, 40, 56
Macmillan, W. M., 33, 78–79
Macro-study, 80, 118
Magubane, Bernard, 229–31
Mahaci, Dyson Dadirayi, 75
Mahlabatini, 42
Maila, David Kalimosho, 76, 198–204, 332n. 16
Mair, Lucy, 98, 106, 119
Makapweka. See Gluckman, Max
Makishi, 200, 293n. 87
Malaŵi, 16. *See also* Nyasaland
Malemia survey, 205
Malinowski, Bronislaw, 29, 41–47, 49, 53, 55–57, 60, 78, 85, 106–7, 115, 128, 132, 156, 214, 240, 286n. 15, 293n. 92, 302n. 28. *See also* Culture contact
Mambwe, 117, 153
Manchester School (of social anthropology), 4, 5, 11, 36–37, 42, 72, 107–8, 150–54, 226, 228, 235, 250–52; "Conflict School," 116
Manchester United (football club), 245
Marwick, Joan, 75, 86, 93, 97, 179
Marwick, Max, 1, 75, 83–86, 92–97, 100, 104, 175, 179, 228, 284n. 1, 291n. 65

Marx, Karl, 115. *See also* Marxism

Marxism, 57, 73–74, 102, 251, 296n. 127, 299n. 150. *See also* Marx, Karl

Mashonaland Province, 80

Material culture, 14, 54, 86, 101–3

Matrilineality, 80–83

Matthews, J., 190

Matthews, Z. K., 56

Maybin, John (governor), 62

Mazabuka District, 40, 87, 118, 145

Mbeni dance associations, 168

Mbewe, Edward, 176, 179, 330n. 98

McCarthyism, 25, 27, 74. *See also* Cold War

McCulloch, Merran, 185–86

Microhistories, 153

Micropolitics, 251

Middleton, John, 110

Miners: African, 27, 34, 56, 91, 166, 168–69, 184, 217; white, 57, 162–63

Mines, 2, 19, 31, 35–36, 41, 50–58, 61, 76, 86, 155, 159, 162–73, 176–78, 181–82, 184–86, 188, 194, 205–8, 213, 216–17, 233, 242, 255, 311n. 45, 314n. 71. *See also* American Metal Company; Anglo-American Corporation; Broken Hill Development Company; British South Africa Company (BSAC); Copperbelt; Katanga mines; Rand mines; Rhodesian Selection Trust; Rhokana Corporation; Roan Antelope Mine

Missionary(ies), 7, 13, 16, 30, 50–60, 82, 85, 91–92, 99, 101, 120, 127–28, 157–60, 196–97, 200, 214, 234, 241, 258; missionary-ethnographers, 58

Mitchell, Edna, 93–94

Mitchell, J. Clyde, 21, 29, 33, 61–66, 72–78, 82–87, 92–97, 104–8, 110–19, 133, 151, 157, 169, 180, 205, 216, 222–23, 229, 236, 241, 243, 252–53, 257, 284n. 1; as director of RLI, 146, 150–54, 173–79, 181–83, 186, 190, 208–9, 211–12, 220–21, 224, 227–28, 244, 253

Moffat (mission family), 59, 117

Moffat, Robert, 117

Monckton Commission, 218

Mongu, 39, 103

Moore, Henrietta, 125

Moore, Leopold, 54

Moore, R. J. B., 158

Moreno, J. L., 175

Movement for Colonial Freedom, 27, 74

Moyo, Steven, 229

Muchona, 13, 15

Mufulira, 219

Mukonoweshuro, Godfrey, 211–12, 326n. 52

Mumbe, Roger, 191

Munali Secondary School, 12, 20, 148, 191, 195, 228, 233, 247

Munro, Donald, 228

Museums, 17, 255–26, 277n. 36, 294n. 103

Mushindo, Paul B., 131, 303n. 35

Mvula, Rafael Almakio, 75

Mwamba, P. J., 316n. 99

Mwanza, Jacob, 191

Mwanza, Lazarus, 191

Nairobi, 93

Nalolo, 234

Nama, 90

Natal University College, 83, 174
National efficiency, 23
National Institute for Personal Research (NIPR), 33
National Institute of Industrial Psychology, 160
Nationalist Party (South Africa), 44, 77, 155
"Native question," 32, 78, 155
Native Welfare Society (Southern Rhodesia), 158
Ndebele, 53, 118, 119
Ndembu, 117, 153
Ndilila, Sykes, 153, 174, 208–9, 212, 324n. 40
Ndola, 147, 180–81, 222
Negrophiles, 60, 165
Network(s), 5, 17–18, 75, 103, 119, 152, 160, 168, 182, 204, 227, 238; communication, 98; concept of, 235; intellectual, 236; political, 215; research, 104, 232, 256; social, 37, 39, 76, 112, 228. *See also* Network analysis
Network analysis, 29, 116, 153, 251, 298n. 146. *See also* Network(s)
New York University Field Laboratory, 133
Ng'wane, Hosiah, 316n. 99
Ngoni, 1–3, 18, 80–83, 96, 127, 130, 203, 258, 286n. 19, 287n. 19
Ngoniland, 96
Nguni, 35, 76
Nigeria, 229
Nkumbula, Harry, 220, 330n. 90
Nongoma, 42, 45–46, 65
North Africa, 64, 246
Northern Rhodesia, 1, 4, 16, 26, 51, 60, 71–73, 77, 83, 88, 127, 133, 149, 195, 201–2, 207, 225, 228; government of, 16, 54, 59, 64, 69, 101, 122, 144–48, 166, 172, 183, 188, 192, 223, 330n. 100; Legislative Council (LegCo), 54, 64; mining in, 30–31, 50, 53–58, 76, 86, 159, 172–73, 178, 194, 216; as research site, 19–20, 27, 29, 32, 34, 49–50, 62, 65, 74–76, 79–80, 85, 91, 98–99, 109, 112–13, 117–20, 128–32, 138–43, 158–60, 167, 226, 247, 251, 256. *See also* Zambia
Northern Rhodesian African National Congress (ANC), 168, 181, 186, 188–89, 215, 220–22
Nsugbe, Philip, 229
Nyakyusa, 56
Nyalugwe, Crispin, 191
Nyasaland, 1, 4, 26, 35–36, 76, 80, 82, 95, 117, 119, 133, 143, 147, 149, 153, 161, 173, 180, 195, 205, 222–23. *See also* Malawi
Nyau secret societies, 95
Nyirenda, Ackson, 185–86, 218, 222–23, 330n. 99

Objectivity, 72, 221
Oldham, J. H., 30, 60
Oxford structuralist school, 110, 118
Oxford University, 19, 33, 42–45, 52, 75, 88, 105, 110–13, 117–18, 136, 144, 150, 205, 252

Papua New Guinea, 74
Participant observation, 43, 45, 48, 98, 102, 124, 180–84, 197, 211, 247–49, 256. *See also* Participant observer
Participant observer, 10, 43. *See also* Participant observation

Patrilineality, 83
Pearsall, Marion, 117, 133
Perkins, Harold, 240
Peters, D. U., 39–40, 76, 83, 86
Phiri, David, 191
Phiri, Frederick, 153
Pickard, T. R., 62, 63
Polygyny, 199; definition of, 106
Pondo, 55, 91
Pondoland, 39, 89, 91, 156
Population studies, 232
Poverty datum line studies, 155, 157–59, 190, 228
Powdermaker, Hortense, 61, 153, 316n. 96
Powers-Samas Machine, 176, 179
Processual analysis, 153
Psychology, 88, 226; cross-cultural, 228; industrial, 159–60, 166; occupational, 160, 228; social, 83, 183, 228
Puta, Robinson, 181, 186, 213

Race, 27, 29, 57, 79, 119–22, 126, 184, 210, 214, 224, 250, 254–25; categories of, 135–43, 306n. 72; definitions, 137; partnership, 171, 247; politics of, 137, 148, 213; relations, 29–33, 88–89. *See also* Apartheid; Color bar; Segregation
Radcliffe College, 132
Radcliffe-Brown, A. R., 34, 45, 67, 85, 89, 90, 115, 240
Rand mines, 31, 53, 81, 159–60, 162, 166, 172. *See also* Mines
Read, Margaret, 1, 18, 80–85, 123, 128, 263n. 1, 286n. 19, 287n. 19, 300n. 12
Reanalysis, 109, 115, 237, 253
Reconnaissance survey (Mazabuka District), 40, 69, 70

Refugee/forced migragion studies, 232
Rennie, Gilbert (governor), 120, 145
Research assistant(s), 73, 75, 169, 174, 229, 235–36, 325n. 44; attitudes to ethnicity of, 211–12, 327nn. 60, 61, 329n. 72; careers of, 1, 83, 194, 223, 226, 232–33, 319n. 4, 326n. 55, 331n. 103, 332n. 111, 335n. 14; class of, 216–27; education of, 35, 58, 148, 194–95, 200, 204, 206, 209, 212, 224, 273, 326n. 55; ethos of, 247; gender of, 211, 326n. 50; goals of, 249; influence on anthropology of, 7, 10–13, 20, 35, 97, 105, 243, 250–58; invisibility of, 12, 267n. 22; perceptions of anthropology, 15, 20, 126–27, 131–32, 135, 198–204, 207, 258, 323n. 34, 337n. 33; political activities of, 186, 204, 208, 214–26, 221, 238, 251, 294n. 96, 329n. 77; professional status of, 209, 211–12, 220–22, 226, 248; publications of, 99, 206, 211, 223–24, 331n. 103; racial concerns of, 212–13, 222, 225; salaries of, 145, 206; social background of, 35–36, 39, 92, 196–97, 204, 209; training of, 97, 181, 205, 209, 211; in survey teams, 22, 152–55, 158, 175–80, 182–95, 204–12, 215–20, 224, 294n. 96, 316n. 99, 325n. 46. *See also* Culture brokers; Ethnographers, indigenous
Research schools, 5, 22, 37, 115, 150
Reynolds, Barrie, 201
Rheinallt Jones, 88, 173, 314n. 71

Rhodes, Cecil, 6, 52–53, 58, 276n. 29

Rhodesian Selection Trust, 31, 63. *See also* Mines

Rhodes-Livingstone Institute (RLI): Board of Trustees of, 111, 118, 136, 145, 172, 176, 206, 223, 304n. 55; conferences of, 107, 109, 117, 145, 154–55, 173, 185, 205–7, 244, 247, 252–23; founding of, 264n. 8; headquarters of, 207, 224–25, 233, 237–38, 248, 252–23, 307nn. 89, 91; influence of, 233; institutional networks of, 228; journal of, 99, 107, 112, 190, 233, 243–44; names of, 52, 229; researchers' careers, 111–12, 150–51, 223, 225–26, 251, 297n. 138, 298n. 142; research program of, 205, 226–29, 231, 236, 239, 251, 257; studies of Europeans, 306n. 75, 308n. 8, 311n. 41; teamwork at, 75, 87, 98, 113, 239, 253; urban surveys, 155, 158, 175, 188, 190–95, 204–12, 215–20, 224, 294n. 96, 310n. 29. *See also* Copperbelt: survey of; Research assistant(s): in survey teams; Seven-Year Plan (RLI): of Colson; of Gluckman

Rhodes-Livingstone Museum, 1, 14, 32, 39, 63, 76, 99, 101–3, 201, 277n. 36

Rhokana Corporation, 31. *See also* Mines

Richards, Audrey, 27, 29, 49, 53–54, 80–86, 101, 106, 110, 123, 128–32, 136, 153, 180, 190, 204, 263n. 1, 302n. 28, 303n. 35, 304n. 55

Richardson, Elsey, 108, 175–77, 182

Rigby, Peter, 190

"RLI way, the," 2, 180, 238, 258

Roan Antelope Mine, 63, 166, 169, 220. *See also* Mines

Robinson, E. G., 85

Rockefeller Foundation, 29, 30

Rowntree, Seebohm, 157

Royal Anthropological Institute (RAI), 49

Saasa, Oliver, 229

Sachs, Wulf, 88, 289n. 51

Saffery, A. L., 168

Salisbury, 119, 147–49, 157, 180

Sampling frame, definition of, 177

Sanjek, Roger, 11

Schapera, Isaac, 33, 78–79, 86–88, 97, 111, 118, 240–41

Schoeman, P. J., 42, 44–48, 83, 114, 287n. 26

Scientific planning movement, 23, 104

Scientific revolutions, 241

Scudder, Thayer, 190, 232, 236, 258

Segregation, 33–34, 77–78, 156, 160, 183, 187, 213, 224–25, 251, 286n. 18. *See also* Apartheid; Color bar; Race

Serpell, Robert, 228–9

Settlers: culture of, 4, 143–44, 214; influene on anthropology, 7, 121–23, 134–39; perceptions of anthropology, 50, 54–55, 60–64, 134–39; political power of, 26, 77, 148–49, 163–65, 182, 189, 207; relations with anthropologists, 4, 18–19, 39–40, 92, 99, 101, 129, 252–53, 294n. 96, 300n. 11

Seven-Year Plan (RLI): of Colson, 117, 119, 145; of Gluckman, 66, 68, 129, 133, 143, 150, 256, 288n. 32. *See also* Rhodes-Livingstone Institute (RLI): research program of

Shamwana, Edward, 191

Shaul, J. H. R., 99, 180

Shipopa, Benjamin, 75, 93, 204, 292n. 76

Shona, 80, 212

Shop-floor ethnographies, 232

Sianga, Davidson, 39, 70, 76, 83, 86, 118, 174–75, 208, 324n. 42

Silverman, Philip, 234

Simons, H. J. (Jack), 56, 89, 290n. 54

Situational analysis, 42, 156, 174, 251

Siwo, Peter, 191

Smith, Edwin, 85

Social anthropology. *See* Anthropology: social

Social geographies, 235

Social psychology. *See* Psychology: social

Socialists, 71, 77, 91

Sociology, 183, 206, 232, 236; definition of, 34; industrial, 232; medical, 232; political, 89; of work, 78; relationship to social anthropology, 67. *See also* Anthropology: social

Sofer, Cyril, 106

Sonnabend, Henry, 88, 105–7

Sophiatown, 91

Sotho, 53

South Africa, 19, 26, 30–35, 39, 40–47, 50, 55, 59, 65, 69, 73, 76–78, 89–90, 98, 116, 137, 149–50, 155–57, 159, 163, 165, 173, 195–96, 205, 242, 246–47, 250

South African Institute for Personnel Research (NIPR), 160

South African Institute of Race Relations (SAIRR), 33, 72–73, 79, 90

Southern Africa, 16, 18, 22, 28–29, 31–32, 35, 41, 50, 52, 58, 76–77, 85, 96, 114, 156–57, 160, 166, 183, 206, 251

Southern Rhodesia, 4, 21, 26, 35, 47–48, 53, 55, 59, 69, 80, 82, 87, 100, 118–19, 147–49, 157–58, 162, 164, 180, 195, 212, 216, 222–24. *See also* Zimbabwe

Soviet Union, 27, 73

Statistics, 152, 166, 175, 206, 209, 214, 316n. 98; statistical analysis, 20, 107, 176, 179, 242

Stephenson, A., 160

Stephenson, Chirupula, 62, 137

Stocking, George W., Jr., 5, 132

Stoler, Ann Laura, 122, 137, 142

Strikes, 91, 101, 158, 167–68, 170–71, 186, 188, 218, 313n. 61

Style(s), 24, 29, 42, 104; of administrators, 109, 245; of clothing, 46–50, 134, 138, 296n. 131, 336n. 32; concept of, 84, 288n. 35; of fieldwork, 45–50, 52, 69, 102, 114, 122; of gender, 123–24, 137; of practice, 238, 246; of the RLI, 18–19, 37, 109, 233, 245–46, 296n. 132; of thought, 238; of the working class, 110, 245. *See also* Fieldwork; Work culture

Sutcliffe, Robert, 190

Suu, Francis, 39, 76, 193

Swazi, 47
Symbolic interaction, 153

Tallensi, 115
Tanganyika, 23, 26, 30, 56, 82, 224
Tawney, R. H., 59, 104, 215
Technical officers, 25, 39, 67–72, 101, 109, 129, 314, 242; agricultural, 65–66, 69, 70–76, 82, 86–87, 133–34, 233, 244, 312n. 52; labor, 73, 165. *See also* Administrator(s); Ecologists; Technical officers
Tembo, Lyson, 191
Thought collectives, 235, 238
Tiv, 115
Tonga, 40, 53, 70, 96–97; Plateau, 69, 80–81, 87, 105, 107, 119, 133–35, 204, 234; Gwembe, 135, 190, 203, 232, 234, 236, 258
Traders, 13, 42, 53, 92, 139, 140
Traditional ceremonies, 17, 194; Kuomboka (Lozi), 50, 51; Mutomboko (Lunda), 321n. 13; Nc'wala (Ngoni), 2
Transactionalism, 153
Trapnell, Colin, 39–40, 69–70, 76, 86–87, 233
Tribe(s), 159–60; concept of, 56, 170; as unit of analysis, 114–15, 156, 278n. 46, 299n. 149. *See also* Ethnicity
Trobriand Islands, 41, 43, 132
Tswana, 35, 76
Turner, Edith, 117, 143, 245
Turner, Victor, 13, 108, 117, 153, 175, 196, 208
Tuskegee Institute, 29
Tweedie, Ann, 127, 302n. 24

Uberoi, J. Singh, 232, 274n. 5
Underdevelopment, 58–59. *See also* Development
Union Miniere, 35, 310n. 35
Union(s), 165, 195, 208, 215, 230, 294n. 96; of African miners, 27, 168, 170, 181, 185–89, 192, 204, 213, 216–27, 219–20; of railway workers, 77, 222; of white miners, 163
United National Independence Party (UNIP), 189, 211, 221, 223
United Nations (UN), 27
United States, 24–25, 27, 29, 61, 74, 110, 166, 250
University College, London, 110
University College of Rhodesia and Nyasaland (UCRN), 112–13, 154, 222–5, 227–8, 253
University of Cambridge, 55, 57, 85, 104
University of Delhi, 232
University of Manchester, 4, 19, 22, 27, 33–38, 41–42, 73–74, 105, 109–10, 149–50, 152, 172–73, 205, 223, 226–27, 232, 236, 245, 252–53
University of Minnesota, 132–33, 136
University of South Africa, 183
University of Stellenbosch, 42, 44, 47, 82, 87
University of the Witwatersrand, 19, 43, 88–91, 156, 290n. 65
University of Zambia, 226, 228
Urban survey team (RLI). *See* Copperbelt: survey of; Research assistant(s): in survey teams; Rhodes-Livingstone Institute (RLT): urban surveys
Utility scheme, 24

Van Velsen, Jaap, 117, 153, 226, 228

Van Velsen, Ruth, 143, 190

Van Warmelo, N. J., 83, 287n. 26

Vaux, H., 51

Victoria Falls, 32, 52, 54, 109; Conference, 26, 148

Vincent, Joan, 5

Volkekunde, 44, 47, 246, 287n. 26, 290n. 56. *See also* Volkekundige(s)

Volkekundige(s), 44–47, 83, 114, 184, 246. *See also* Volkekunde

Watchtower Church (Jehovah's Witnesses), 168, 292n. 78

Watson, William (Bill), 117, 153, 185, 188, 190

Welensky, Roy, 39, 77, 163

Werbner, Richard, 153, 236

West Africa, 29, 182

White, Charles M. N., 154, 190, 225, 228, 322n. 15

Wiese, Carl, 96

Wilson, Francis, 60

Wilson, Godfrey, 19, 30, 33, 39–40, 50, 83, 99, 129, 136, 137, 147, 156–57, 167, 171–75, 181, 185, 229–30, 278n. 47, 281n. 82; as director, 55–66, 72–74, 158, 186, 242, 314n. 70

Wilson, John Dover, 56

Wilson, Monica (Hunter), 30, 33,

39, 55–57, 60, 72, 89, 91, 156, 276n. 33, 278n. 47, 283n. 105

Winterbottom, J. M., 99, 107

Witchcraft, 135, 199–203

Work culture, 75, 84, 207, 231–22, 237, 245, 247–48, 250–54; definition of, 9–10, 238–39, 266n. 18. *See also* Fieldwork; Styles

World Council of Churches, 158

World War One, 23–24, 288n. 33

World War Two, 19, 23, 25, 30, 35, 57, 61, 63, 67, 76, 90, 137–38, 160, 165, 191, 194, 242

Yao, 80, 82, 93–94, 115, 153, 174

Young, Hubert, 32, 54, 60, 84, 101, 163, 167

Zambezi (Zambesi) River, 52–53, 76, 109

Zambia, 1–2, 4, 10, 12, 15–17, 35, 52, 160, 165, 188–89, 191–92, 226, 237. *See also* Northern Rhodesia

Zimbabwe, 16. *See also* Southern Rhodesia

Zukas, Simon, 187, 315n. 95, 317n. 112

Zulu, 41–43, 45–48, 81, 97, 114, 275n. 20

Zululand, 40–46, 65, 77–78, 93, 201

Lyn Schumaker is Wellcome Research Lecturer
at the Wellcome Unit for the History of Medicine,
University of Manchester.

Library of Congress Cataloging-in-Publication Data

Schumaker, Lyn.
Africanizing anthropology : fieldwork, networks, and the
making of cultural knowledge in central Africa / Lyn
Schumaker.
p. cm.
Includes bibliographical references and index.
ISBN 0-8223-2678-7 (cloth : alk. paper) —
ISBN 0-8223-2673-6 (pbk. : alk. paper)
1. Ethnology — Zambia — History. 2. Rhodes-Livingstone
Institute — History. 2. Ethnology — Zambia — Field work.
4. Ethnology — Africa, Southern — History. I. Title.
GN657.R4 S38 2001
305.8'0096894 — dc21   2001028054